LAW AND LITERATURE

LAW AND LITERATURE

JOURNEYS FROM HER TO ETERNITY

MARIA ARISTODEMOU

OXFORD
UNIVERSITY PRESS

OXFORD

UNIVERSITY PRESS

Great Clarendon Street, Oxford OX2 6DP

Oxford University Press is a department of the University of Oxford.
It furthers the University's objective of excellence in research, scholarship,
and education by publishing worldwide in

Oxford New York

Athens Auckland Bangkok Bogotá Buenos Aires Calcutta
Cape Town Chennai Dar es Salaam Delhi Florence Hong Kong Istanbul
Karachi Kuala Lumpur Madrid Melbourne Mexico City Mumbai
Nairobi Paris São Paulo Shanghai Singapore Taipei Tokyo Toronto Warsaw

with associated companies in Berlin Ibadan

Oxford is a registered trade mark of Oxford University Press
in the UK and in certain other countries

Published in the United States
by Oxford University Press Inc., New York

British Library Cataloguing in Publication Data

Data available

Library of Congress Cataloging in Publication Data

Data available

ISBN 0–19–876436–7

1 3 5 7 9 10 8 6 4 2

Typeset in Adobe Minion
by RefineCatch Limited, Bungay, Suffolk
Printed in Great Britain by
Biddles Ltd., Guildford and King's Lynn

I've travelled the world, lain with the devil,
cursed God above, cast down and hidden,
forsaken everything: to bring you my love.
                                    P. J. Harvey

This desire to possess her is a wound,
nagging at me like a shrew.
But I know that to possess her
is therefore not to desire her.
That little girl will just have to go.
Go! Go! From her to eternity.
                    Nick Cave and the Bad Seeds

CONTENTS

1

IN THE BEGINNING . . .
INVENTING REALITY, A
SHORT MURDER MYSTERY

We live in a world ruled by fictions of every kind—mass-merchandising, advertising, politics conducted as a branch of advertising, the pre-empting of any original response to experience by the television screen. We live inside an enormous novel. It is now less and less necessary for the writer to invent the fictional content of his novel. The fiction is already there. The writer's task is to invent the reality.

J. G. Ballard, *Crash*

1 NARRATIVE EVASIONS, FANTASIES,
AND HIERARCHIES

What is the ontological status of law and of literature? Or, conversely, to follow Lacan's suggestion that 'the real is the impossible',[1] the unimaginable, what is the *imaginary* status of law and of literature? While we can agree that, unlike literature, law deals in the material world of life and death, both law and literature are, in the first instance, signs on a page. Both the legal and literary worlds are constructed by and depend for their definition and existence on words; such words create alternative, fictional worlds which can appear to be inevitable.

Any attempt to order the world, by means of symbols and language, in law or in literature, aims to capture, tame, and order a labyrinthine universe whose origins, design, and designer lie beyond our knowledge. Both law and literature are artificial constructs, concepts, or abstractions like time or identity, aiming to create, and, especially in law's case, to impose, order out of chaos: to write on the bodies and very souls of the subjects and fulfil as well as replace their unfulfillable desires. In the process, these attempts become their own labyrinths, confusing as much as enlightening not

---

[1] 'Since the opposite of the possible is certainly the real, we would be led to define the real as the impossible': *The Four Fundamental Concepts of Psychoanalysis* (Paris, 1973; Harmondsworth: Penguin, 1979), trans. Alan Sheridan, at 167.

only those who try to enter but also themselves.[2] While the artist, however, admits, and sometimes draws attention to the contingency and artificiality of her constructions, legal language aims to conceal its artificial origins. While the artist confesses to the fact that his creations are arbitrary, incomplete, hypothetical, and provisional, the lawyer persists in pretending that they are natural, inevitable, and can provide not only all the answers, but also all the right answers. For the yearning to believe in a point of origin, in a universe with a beginning, a middle, and an end, which functions in accordance with clear rules and predictable outcomes is as strong as the impossibility of its discovery.

Ignorance about our past, incomprehension of the present, and fear of the future motivates, whether consciously or unconsciously, our efforts as writers and as readers, in law or in literature, to understand and thereby control our world. All such reading and writing takes place in a state of desire, our desire for the other and for the other's desire, the Lacanian mirror that will confer to us a sense of fullness and help us recapture the lost plenitude of childhood. Stories play a special role in this search; with stories we try to remember the past, cope with the present and imagine the future, making them up to cover what we do not know or cannot accept. The desire for narrative, for a beginning, a middle, and an end, is a desire for self-recognition and confirmation of our fragile sense of identity. Writing and reading, in law or literature, temporarily provide the illusion of anchors in a world devoid of foundations. Truth, unity, and closure, however, come only with the self's dissolution, with the promise of finality held out only by death.

Once upon a time, Aristotle praised narrative and tragedy in particular for its ability to cleanse, and thereby cure, the audience of fear and pity. The desire for narrative as a means of understanding ourselves and our world is central, however, not just to tragedy but to all narrative, including the narratives weaved by law, literature, and law and literature. Theories of the origin and ends of law, theories of justice, freedom, rights, adjudication, and interpretation, all participate in the attempt to order our world, reducing its potential chaos into manageable categories. The seemingly endless attempt to find meaning in our beliefs, words, and actions, reflects our attempt to find a foundation, a transcendental signifier to counteract our fear of the unknown. Ideas, theories, myths have a special role to play in this search: they are the result of the human, (perhaps, as I suggest in my closing chapter, the *male*), craving for order, generality, and origin and aim to reduce the chaotic, heterogeneous, and different to the known, one and identical.

No narrative, however, is ever complete; there are always gaps, silences, ignorances. Narratives give the appearance of resolving the contradictions whose existence gave rise to the need for narrative in the first place. Linear narratives in particular endow the conclusion with a seeming inevitability, appearing to supply new answers when they are reproducing answers that were always already presupposed.[3] Narratives thus

---

[2] I develop this theme further in my closing chapter.

[3] That fantasy is a narrative (and vice versa) see Slavoj Žižek, 'The Seven Veils of Narrative' in Dany Rebus (ed.), *Key Concepts of Lacanian Psychoanalysis* (London: Rebus Press, 1998).

invent rather than reflect our lives, ourselves, and our worlds. Whether in law, in literature, or, as with this book, in law *and* literature, narratives are not neutral: they investigate but also suggest, create, and legislate meanings.

In our culture, furthermore, some narratives have been privileged over others: poetry is distinguished from philosophy, ethics from aesthetics, reason from the emotions, law from literature. In legal education, stories told by judges and legal philosophers are privileged over alternative stories about the origins, function, and desirability of law. Philosophy in particular claimed the right to tell others what to say and do, what is true or false, reasonable and foolish. For Plato the layman's knowledge of society could not be trusted as lay people lack the faculties and leisure to judge between right and wrong. By denying the layman's knowledge, philosophy helped justify hierarchical divisions in the name of the pursuit of truth. While the fictional, the rhetorical, and the literary were said to be concerned with style, philosophy, it was claimed, is an autonomous discipline in pursuit of timeless truths and distinct, if not superior, even to theology. In turn, the philosopher is a 'man' of knowledge, not opinion or faith, and his work not that of an artist but of a law-giver, legislating for human reason.[4]

Attempts to keep philosophy separate from literature and maintain it as a superior discourse are, however, doomed since even philosophy cannot hope to escape language. Philosophy relies for its own definition and existence on differentiating itself from other kinds of language, in particular the fictional, literary, and rhetorical. Although purporting to pronounce irrefutable truths, philosophy can only do so by ignoring the constitutive and metaphorical nature of language. Derrida's critique of foundationalism in philosophy displaces the boundary between philosophy and literature: the language and form chosen by those claiming to write a philosophical treatise is not separable from the philosophical content; conversely, literary texts and literary criticism make as many philosophical assumptions as writing that claims to be purely philosophical. By showing how language distracts and frustrates the philosopher's search for truth and presence, Derrida concludes that philosophy, political theory and, of course, law, function in the same way as literature.[5] Philosophy's dependence on language means that it is no more privileged than other forms of language and can not therefore purport to constitute the foundation for other disciplines. In deconstructive and psychoanalytic readings in particular, this allegedly pure and self-referential language returns to haunt the text's unity, coherence, and independence. With them go law's and reason's imperiousness; philosophers and legislators cannot

---

[4] For a discussion of the intellectual as an 'interpreter' rather than a 'legislator' see Zygmunt Bauman, *Intimations of Postmodernity* (London and New York: Routledge, 1992), at 1–25. I return to this theme in chapter 9.

[5] See, for example, Jacques Derrida, 'Force and Signification' in *Writing and Difference* trans. Alan Bass, (London: Routledge, 1978), at 27: 'Metaphor in general, the passage from one existent to another, or from one signified meaning to another, authorized by the initial *submission* of Being to the existent, the *analogical* displacement of Being, is the essential weight which anchors discourse in metaphysics, irremediably repressing discourse into its metaphysical state.'

escape the rhetorical or the literary: like all writers, they are at the mercy of a language that we neither possess nor control.

It is part of the inspiration of the Law and Literature project that the divisions we make between different ways of reading, writing, and learning and between different disciplines are therefore cultural rather than natural, constructed rather than given. Such divisions, which are created by but also depend on our linguistic practices, are, furthermore, hierarchical, made by those with an interest in presenting their version of the truth as superior to that of other peoples'. The project shares our contemporary disbelief in the ability of any one method, story, theory, or discipline to find out the 'truth', not least because the latter may be nothing more than an illusion masking underlying power struggles over the right to define our world. Nietzsche's return to aesthetic experience as both instructive and valuable, Foucault's critique of the human sciences, and Derrida's attack on foundationalism in philosophy have rewritten the ancient quarrel between poetry and philosophy. Plato started the quarrel and resolved it by expelling poets from his ideal state. This time, however, the quarrel is resolved at philosophy's expense. From Plato onwards generations of philosophers keen to carve out a separate role for philosophy as the arbiter of truth used the same poetic techniques they decried in order to achieve their purpose. In brief, law was always already literature and, as I argue shortly, literature was always already law.

The attempt to keep philosophy and law separate from literature is also, as I suggest in my closing chapter, part of the attempt to exclude woman from the legal labyrinth: Nietzsche's appeal to aesthetics did not prevent him from pronouncing woman as the enemy of truth.[6] Conversely, Wittgenstein was one of generations of male philosophers who saw their project as a struggle to affirm abstract language, reason, and common sense against the temptation and perils of woman's playful, seductive, and deceptive language.[7] It is therefore impossible, as Derrida comments, 'to dissociate the questions of art, style and truth from the question of woman'.[8] The male lawyer's preference for abstract language, reason, and intellectuality is also an attempt to deny the tactile, the bodily, and the sensual: to suppress, supposedly by overcoming, but instead by imitating with words, woman's capacity to procreate with her body. To deny, that is, every subject's 'first home, first body, first love':[9] the mother.

---

[6] See Friedrich Nietzsche, *Beyond Good and Evil: Prelude to a Philosophy of the Future*, trans. R. J. Hollingdale, (London: Penguin, 1973) [1886]), para. 232: woman 'does not *want* truth: what is truth to a woman! From the very first nothing has been more alien, repugnant and inimical to woman than truth—her great art is the lie, her supreme concern is appearance and beauty.'

[7] See discussion by Peter Middleton in *Literature Teaching Politics*, Vol. 6 (1985); quoted and discussed by Janet Todd, *Feminist Literary History* (Oxford: Polity Press, 1988), at 130.

[8] Jacques Derrida, *Spurs: Nietzsche's Styles*, trans. Barbara Harlow (Chicago: Chicago University Press, 1979), at 71.

[9] Luce Irigaray, 'The bodily encounter with the mother' in Margaret Whitford (ed.), *The Irigaray Reader* (Oxford: Blackwell, 1991), at 39.

2 EARLY BEGINNINGS

Studies in Law and Literature to date have rested on two related claims: first the instrumental view that literature can help produce better lawyers by teaching lawyers how to read, speak, and write more effectively; and secondly the humanistic belief that literature can make lawyers better persons by giving lawyers a sense of the complex nature of the human condition as depicted in 'great' books. Literature, it is said, can broaden and enhance the students' 'ethical consciousness' by exposing them to and reminding them of the value judgments implicit in their work, widen the dimensions of a problem, de-mystify law's claims, encourage self and social criticism, give an impetus for change and reform, in short, 'liberate'![10]

Both these claims are problematic; it is not at all certain that the skills fostered by literature could not be acquired by other methods, nor that those versed in the humanities will be 'nicer' than other people. The idealist notion that we can change lawyers, and the world, through literature ignores the fact that as Eagleton puts it, not everyone who has read *King Lear* is a 'good' person.[11] Claims about the 'liberating' or 'humanising' potential of literature cannot be assumed without inquiring into whether morality can be taught at all and, if so, how. Does knowing about morality necessarily make somebody a moral person? Do those who understand the 'moral law' necessarily act in accordance with their knowledge? The view that education can have a transformative power ignores the fact that education is itself part of society and that somebody will be educating the educators. As Terry Eagleton summarises, humanist readings searched, and invariably found, unity and coherence to literary texts, reconciling and resolving dangerous contradictions and differences in favour of order, stability, and a single meaning. That such meanings varied from one critic to the next did not dampen the enthusiasm for the search. The view that each text can illuminate our moral experience by expressing a coherent view of life, however, invites the criticism that humanist critics imposed their *own* coherent understanding of experience on the text.[12] The Socratic view that immorality is due to ignorance of the good must also be balanced against Plato's dictatorial elitism where moral expertise is the prerogative of the philosopher-king as only the wise can acquire knowledge of the good. It is therefore idealistic, and dangerous, to expect, and there is no reason to assume, that lawyers immersed in literature will have better abilities to identify and apply moral and political values than other lawyers.

If literature's claim to teach moral values cannot be assumed, then the claim that literature can offer a critique of the law and offer alternatives for reform must also

---

[10] I address these claims in 'Studies in Law and Literature; Directions and Concerns' *Anglo-American Law Review*, 1993, 157.

[11] Terry Eagleton, *Literary Theory: An Introduction* (Oxford: Basil Blackwell, 1996), at 30.

[12] ibid., especially at 15–46.

be examined: against the view that literature can teach moral values, one must remember that readings of literature are themselves contested and the values to be derived from literature vary from one theorist to the next. Thus whilst F. R. Leavis saw literature as embracing the whole of the human experience, Marxist critics see in texts a perpetuation of middle class ideology, feminists see a prefer-ence for the male over female, gay critics compulsory heterosexuality, post-colonial critics a preference for the European master, Nietzscheans the ressentient indi-vidual, and deconstructionists contradictions. If we are seeking to derive lessons from literature and use literature as a critique of the law, we must also be alive to the critique of literature itself: for literature is itself an ideology and to seek to use it as a 'humanising' or 'softening' effect on lawyers may mean choosing one ideol-ogy over another.

More importantly, such claims risk undermining the innovative nature of the pro-ject which has radical implications for our understanding of the nature of law as well as for the methods of its instruction. The problem stems from critics' readiness to appeal to literature as a form of critique of legal discourse without enquiring into the discourses informing the writing, reading, and interpretation of literature itself. Too often, writers approach literature with a sense of almost religious awe, forgetting that literary texts, like legal texts, are part of a society's ideological practices and that criticism must challenge rather than submit to the ideological messages hidden in all texts, literary or legal. The point is not to forget that literature does not just represent or reflect reality, it also participates in making and shaping it, contributing to our sense of what is natural, common sense, and inevitable. Along with, amongst others, law, government, education, popular entertainment, art is one of the ways in which a society makes and sustains its identity. Literature participates in a culture's existing order of things and, like law, helps to create, and sustain the dominant picture of society.[13] Indeed literature's power to influence behaviour and reproduce the status quo is greater than more blatantly repressive institutions like the police and criminal justice; being perceived as an external oppressive force, law is less persuasive than art and literature, especially when the latter is held out to be autonomous from social institutions and conventions. In short, as Bataille put it, 'Literature is not innocent. It is guilty and should admit itself so'.[14]

Thus classic realism, to take one example, still the dominant form in literature and popular culture, has received special criticism for contributing to our sense of the subject as knowing, responsible, and autonomous. Realist fiction's reliance on an omniscient narrator able to adjudicate the development of the narrative from a beginning to a middle to an end enhanced the Enlightenment's view of man as in full

---

[13]   For Althusser cultural production was part of the ideological state apparatus by which a state obtains and maintains consent to society's dominant values and existing practices: Louis Althusser, 'Ideology and Ideological State Apparatus', in *Lenin and Philosophy* (New York: Monthly Review Press, 1971).

[14]   Georges Bataille, *Literature and Evil* trans. Alastair Hamilton, (London and New York: Marion Boyars, 1973), [1957], at x.

possession of himself and of language as a transparent mediator of reality.[15] For post-colonial critics, however, the novel was implicated in affirming not only bourgeois culture but also empire-building; both the content and the structure of the novel, argues Edward Said, cultivated a system of values that placed the white European author and reader at the centre and both literally and metaphorically 'arrested' colonized groups into the role of the Other.[16] Literature therefore partook of the ideology of imperialism, imparting 'moral' superiority which was just as important as economic, legal, and military superiority for the survival of empire. Law of course performed a complementary function, bolstering western rule by writing not only on the bodies of the colonized but on its souls by claiming to be neutral, universal, and objective. Its wholesale importation into the colonies was significant not just in terms of the coercive role its rules, courts, and penal machinery would exert, but the ideological role of making that same coercion appear natural and inevitable.[17] Literary and legal texts thus coexist and overlap, sustaining and reinforcing each other and raising the question, what view of man, woman, and the world is offered by these texts.

The status of 'literature' attributed to some texts and not others also depends on a combination of historical, economic, legal, and political factors that vary from one culture and from one generation to the next. Texts not written as literature such as legal reports, political, historical, scientific, or philosophical treatises may be analysed for their artistic or poetic merit; conversely much imaginative writing may be denied the status of literature by elitist judgments policing the boundaries of the subject. As Derrida concludes, like law, literature is an institution created by social, legal, and political processes that themselves vary from one culture and historical period to the next.[18]

In short, the law and literature critic participates, no less than any other critic, in her share of hermeneutic violence and the Nietzschean will to power. Both law and literature are social institutions situated in a culture that constitutes them as distinct discourses at the same time as it is constituted by them. By confronting two disciplines that have traditionally been kept apart in this wider context, looking for textual and thematic affinities and contrasts, we can enquire into how legal and literary institutions and discourses help constitute the human subject, before going on to explore whether, and if so how, literature helps to demystify or to reinforce the narratives that help to legitimate the legal order. Underlying this approach is the belief that the way

[15] Ian Watt, *The Rise of the Novel* (London: Chatto & Windus, 1957); argues that realist fiction emerged with the rise of the bourgeoisie in the eighteenth and nineteenth centuries and that the values affirmed by such fiction (for instance individualism, enterprise, and marriage), were the values espoused by bourgeois society.

[16] See especially Edward W. Said, *Orientalism* (New York: Pantheon, 1978) and Edward W. Said, *Culture and Imperialism* (London: Vintage, 1994).

[17] See, for example, Peter Fitzpatrick, *The Mythology of Modern Law* (London and New York: Routledge, 1992).

[18] Jacques Derrida, *Acts of Literature*, (ed.) Derek Attridge (London: Routledge, 1992) especially Derek Attridge's Introduction, 'This Strange Institution Called Literature' and 'The First Session'.

we read and derive meanings from texts and the underlying assumptions and consequences of those readings, is important in social, political, and ethical terms.

For some critics, the view that literature can be studied not for its enjoyment but educative value is, as Poe called it 'didactic heresy' put forward by utilitarians and moralists and ignores the view that 'art is for art's sake', or, in Emerson's slogan, that 'beauty is its own excuse for being'. The fact that literature is an ideological construct enables us to answer the objection that by turning to literature to address legal problems we sully the integrity of art with our political agendas. The answer to such criticisms is that literature is always already political. Conversely, to the criticism that we are turning literature into a philosophic treatise we can reply that rather than converting literature into philosophy we are acknowledging the literary and the aesthetic in philosophy and law.

The crucial role played by rhetoric and the aesthetic in the making, maintenance, and continuation of law has been investigated in recent years by Peter Goodrich. In works such as *Languages of Law*, *Oedipus Lex* and *Law in the Courts of Love*, he has argued for the primacy of the aesthetic in the making of legal judgments and the constitution of the legal subject:

Law is a literature which denies its literary qualities. It is a play of words which asserts an absolute seriousness; it is a genre of rhetoric which represses its moments of invention or of fiction; it is a language which hides its indeterminacy in the justificatory discourse of judgment; it is procedure based on analogy, metaphor and repetition and yet it lays claim to being a cold or disembodied prose, a science without poetry or desire; it is a narrative which assumes the epic proportions of truth; it is, in short, a speech or writing which forgets the violence of the word and the terror or jurisdiction of the text.[19]

Premised on the suggestion that 'rhetoric is the pre-modern form of psychoanalysis' his technique has included analysing the surface of the text, its signs, symptoms, and slips to reveal inexplicit passions and unconscious emotions in the law. His aim is to engage in a 'strip-tease' of the text to unleash the unconscious realm of the law which depends on 'the other of reason', that is imagination or affection. In the same way that for Freud the interpretation of dreams was the royal road to a knowledge of the unconscious activities of the mind, legal language, for Goodrich is not accidental but forms the royal road to the institutional unconscious. 'Legality', he concludes, 'does not belong to the moral but to the aesthetic order. There is a validity to aesthetic judgements, but it is founded upon feeling not upon concepts.'[20] Moreover, legal discourse's attempt to deny its reliance on images and the aesthetic in general is not gender neutral: it is an attempt to deny and repress the presence of 'a feminine genealogy within the ancient constitution, a feminine unconscious to the doctrines of

---

[19] Peter Goodrich, *Law in the Courts of Love: Literature and other minor jurisprudences* (London and New York: Routledge, 1996), at 112. For a concise introduction to Goodrich's work see especially Adam Gearey, '"Mad and Delirious Words": Feminist Theory and Critical Legal Studies in the Work of Peter Goodrich' *Feminist Legal Studies*, vol. 6 (1), (1998) 121–33.

[20] Peter Goodrich, '*Jani anglorum*: signs, symptoms, slips and interpretation in law' in Costas Douzinas, Peter Goodrich and Yifat Hachamovitch (eds.), *Politics, Postmodernity and Critical Legal Studies: The Legality of the Contingent* (London and New York: Routledge, 1994), at 107, and 26–7.

common law'; to undress the legal text is therefore to expose its reliance on images and on woman to secure its foundations and to threaten its alleged unity and coherence by reminding it that it 'was never one'.[21]

In short, rather than buttressing both law and literature as distinct disciplines, we need an approach that is sensitive both to the *literary qualities of law and to the law-making qualities of literature*. An approach, in other words, that is responsive to the delights as well as dangers of these two indistinct and inter-penetrating, disciplines.

3 LAW, LITERATURE, AND LAW AND LITERATURE AS SITES OF STRUGGLE

The shifting definitions of the ambits of both law and literature suggest that the differences between them are not natural and immutable but cultural, relative, and contingent. Both legal and literary fictions attempt to reduce the world to manageable categories rendering the difference between them a matter of degree rather than of essence. But the effects of any ideology, however pervasive, are never fully successful; literature's relationship to dominant values is, like law's, not monolithic but contradictory and fragmentary. Although culture is one way consent to the status quo is maintained, the possibility remains of entering the gaps and silences of all texts and challenging such consent and such control.[22]

The more modest hope in this book is that literary texts, and above all, our readings of them, will be less reductive of the world's varied meanings than legal texts. Literature contains its own ideology and expresses its own values and prejudices, but it is also more likely than law to challenge received ideologies, values, and prejudices. Eagleton for instance concedes that literature and the aesthetic in general, though born of, and partaking in, the dominant ideology, can nevertheless provide 'an unusually powerful challenge and alternative to the dominant ideological forms, and is in that sense an eminently contradictory phenomenon'.[23] Such is its ambivalent nature that it can resist dominant social practices, and even transcend them. If the institution called literature is, as I suggest, another form of law-making, it is also often quicker and more likely than other forms of legislation to challenge existing laws and dominant values. This is partly because, as Adorno suggested, the discrediting of the aesthetic in capitalist culture with its emphasis on utilitarian benefits, secures for it a relative autonomy.[24] As a result, whilst literature may reflect and

---

[21] Peter Goodrich, *Oedipus Lex: Psychoanalysis, History Law* (Los Angeles and London: University of California Press, 1995), at 146 and 155.

[22] Walter Adamson, *Hegemony and Revolution: A Study of Antonio Gramsci's Political and Cultural Theory* (Berkeley and Los Angeles: University Of California Press, 1980), at 183.

[23] Terry Eagleton, *The Ideology of the Aesthetic* (Oxford: Basil Blackwell, 1990), at 3.

[24] This also means, as Adorno acknowledged, that art is condemned to relative impotence: 'Works are most critical when they first see the light of day; afterwards they become neutralized because, among other things, the social conditions have changed. Neutralization is the social price art pays for its autonomy': Theodor Adorno, *Aesthetic Theory*, trans. C. Lenhardt, (London: Routledge, 1984) at 325.

reinforce existing assumptions, it can also criticize and interrogate given categories and values.

Foucault, for example, acknowledges a limited role for the aesthetic away from the all-encompassing struggle for power. The point, as Simon During suggests, is that although literary *studies* belong to epistemic knowledge, literature itself can escape the assumptions of the human sciences and perform a liberatory role.[25] Derrida also acknowledges the radical potential of literature: as an institution, he says, literature overflows the institution, breaks the rules, and invents new rules: 'it allows one to *say everything, in every way* . . . to break free of the rules, to displace them, and thereby to institute, to invent and even to suspect the traditional difference between nature and institution, nature and conventional law, nature and history'.[26] Fictions therefore do not just replicate culture; like legal texts, they are sites of struggle where cultural meanings and dominant assumptions can be criticized and contested. In that sense, literature and the aesthetic in general, is a contradictory phenomenon and it is by interrogating the contradictions that a more self-conscious and critical approach to both law and culture can be taken.

The law and literature project suggests that an understanding of legal institutions and principles cannot come from within law itself, nor only from its social, economic, and historical contexts. Such an understanding must be accompanied with an understanding of the cultural sphere without which no meaningful social change can occur. Both law and literature are products of the same social, historical, and cultural forces. The fact that literature occurs in a social context, that it is part of our society's culture, and that it is intimately connected with other social institutions, means that through literature one may study aspects of our society, including the legal framework. Furthermore, literature, and popular culture in particular, influence the public's attitudes towards the legal system, the legal profession, and towards law as a system of rules working with and in competition with other normative systems. The project advocates a return to interdisciplinary enquiries, contextuality, and perspectivism in a bid to put legal doctrine back in the cultural context in which it belongs and from which it was divorced by positivist methodologies in legal studies. This approach will help broaden our understanding of law as part of our culture, a culture that it shares with literature; at the same time it hopes to enhance our understanding of ourselves as subjects of language, law, and culture.

By refusing hierarchies between forms of knowledge and belief, such an approach allows alternative ways of seeing and learning in legal education and challenges the insularity of law and legal studies when dealing with issues that are of wider relevance and concern; when dealing, indeed, to borrow Robert Cover's phrase, 'in pain and death'.[27] Bringing together two disciplines that have traditionally been kept apart may help us understand the interests involved in keeping the separation: in particular, as I

[25] Simon During, *Foucault and Literature: Towards a Genealogy of Writing* (London: Routledge, 1992), at 113–18.

[26] Jacques Derrida, *Acts of Literature, supra,* at 36–7.

[27] Robert Cover, 'Violence and the Word' 95 *Yale Law Journal* (1986) 1601.

suggest in my closing chapter, the interest in excluding Ariadne from the legal labyrinth. To recognize that the present definitions and teaching of law contain their own
ideological preferences may help broaden the range of what is considered 'relevant' in
law and in legal education. Where the legal labyrinth appeared inviolable to entry, the
approach suggested by Ariadne in my closing chapter may open new doors into what
is, after all, a constantly moving, changing, and growing edifice.

While judges and legislators are constrained by precedent and financial and political interests, literature enjoys the freedom to take risks, dislocate old laws and structures, and articulate new imaginaries which may in turn become laws. The fact that
these laws reside in the worlds of dreams or possibility rather than in the so-called real
world makes them more, rather than less, important for enabling us to map and
envision new selves and new conditions. Indeed, as I stress later in this chapter, the
'artificiality' of art may be its strength: *to help us recognize our own artificiality*, by
reminding us that what appears to be 'real' or natural is a product of historical and
cultural contingencies, and therefore no less artificial and perhaps more artificial than
the sound of our dreams. Indeed, as I suggest in my reading of Borge's *Ficciones*, the
stuff our dreams are made of is also the stuff that maps our making as human
subjects; and that the refusal to acknowledge our dream is a refusal to acknowledge, in
Lacanian terms, the Real of our desires.

4 WRITING AGAINST: LANGUAGE AS
THE SITE OF STRUGGLE

To interrogate the messages created and inscribed by both legal and literary fictions
we must go back not only to the narratives they tell but to the language they employ to
tell their stories. Language, in law, or in literature, is not a transparent mediator
between experience and reality but provides the terms by which reality is constituted.
It is through language that we come to understand and constitute ourselves as
subjects; language shapes our understanding of ourselves and the world, imposes
straitjackets on our thinking, our ability to express our dreams, and our capacity to
envisage reform.

The emphasis on literature as a reflection of the world, and on the author's intentions in describing such a world assumed that it is possible to separate the author's
views, intentions, or experience from her formulation of them. Such formulations,
however, can only ever take place in language, a language moreover that does not
belong to the author but which moulds and constitutes as much as expresses those
thoughts. Postmodern theorists' denunciation of the illusion of unitary truths can not
be separated from the dismissal of the idea of meaning as being either static or
controllable: the Enlightenment ideal and optimism in ordering the world had relied
on a view of language where signs reflected the real world. Signs, however, do not

mean anything in themselves but derive their meaning from the context in which they are used and over time. A text's meaning depends instead on its relation to other elements, on difference, and is ultimately dependent on what it seeks to exclude. By showing how the privileged term in any text depends for its identity on the supplement, Derrida goes further and shows that every text calls its own premises into question and ultimately contradicts itself.[28] The insight that meaning is not inherent in a sign challenges the view that there is a one to one correspondence between linguistic propositions and reality; instead of a single, physical reality reflected by our language, what we have is a reality constructed by language. The consequence is that texts are not closed entities with a single meaning but are liable to a multitude of interpretations, or perspectives, depending on who reads them and in what circumstances. Distinctions between surface and depth, signifier and signified, subject and object, content and style, sign and meaning no longer appear natural or given; instead, like knowledge and the will to truth, they are part of the will to power.

The view that meaning is fixed was itself based on a view of 'man' as a responsible and autonomous agent with the ability to use language to create and express himself. Once the ability of language to express reality is questioned, however, this view of 'man' also appears as an ideal, a product of historical and cultural circumstances. The unique, stable, authentic individual favoured by modernist theories is also at the mercy of language and thus no more than a myth. For Lacan, the ego is not the central agency of the personality but a false self haunted by the unconscious and conceptualized around linguistic signs. Even human biology and the human body are not timeless essences but concepts that arrive to us through the lens of language and to which we accede on learning to talk.[29] The human subject, as Malcolm Bowie puts it, 'is no longer a substance endowed with qualities, or a fixed shape possessing dimensions . . . it is a series of events within language, a procession of turns, tropes, and inflections'.[30] Our thoughts, speech, and writing are produced within a specific language and a specific discourse. It is through language that the infant comes to (mis)recognize herself as a unified subject and takes her place in the family, law, and society, accepting the subjectivity ascribed to her in the existing symbolic order as 'obvious' and 'natural'.

Feminist, lesbian, gay, and post-colonial critics have further added to the deconstruction of the subject by pointing out that the subject conceived by reason was heterosexual man and refusing to continue to play the role of the other who serves to guarantee that subject's sense of autonomy. As Angela Carter asks of Descartes, 'I think, therefore I am but if I take time off from thinking, what then?'.[31] The inference

---

[28] See especially ' . . . That Dangerous Supplement . . . ' in *Of Grammatology*, trans. Gayatri Chakravorty Spivak (Baltimore and London: Johns Hopkins University Press, 1976) [1967].

[29] See especially 'The Function and Field of Speech and Language in Psychoanalysis' in Jacques Lacan, *Écrits: A Selection*, trans. Alan Sheridan, (London: Tavistock, 1977); I discuss this further in chapters 2 and 4.

[30] Malcolm Bowie, *Lacan* (London: Fontana, 1991), at 76.

[31] Angela Carter, *Heroes and Villains* (London: Heinemann, 1969), at 98.

is that in the same way that language, culture, and reason have a history the nature of man, and woman, is not timeless or universal but provisional and contingent. As Foucault pointed out, our man-based way of looking at the world is relatively recent: 'Man is an invention of recent date. And perhaps one nearing its end'.[32]

Hope and possibility for change stem from the fact that language is not a static phenomenon but a process. Saussure's insight that language is a system of differences without positive terms also means that language has the potential to act as a liberating medium for reform and for our understanding of ourselves. The identity of the human subject, as Kristeva elaborates, is also not static but always in process: human beings can therefore contest dominant meanings and create new meanings from the signs available to them. The semiotic chora, as the repository of repressed and pre-linguistic signifiers, re-emerges to disrupt the symbolic order, enabling us to reconstruct ourselves through language.[33] In this, she is helped by the fact that linguistic signs are not closed but contain contradictions and can therefore be deconstructed and demythologized. Signs, in law as in literature, are polysemic rather than univocal, hybrid rather than pure and thus open to negotiation by individuals and communities who can exploit their cracks and contradictions to create new meanings: 'we are born into language', writes Cixous, 'and I cannot do otherwise than to find myself before words . . . So there is nothing to be done, except to shake them like apple trees, all the time'.[34]

In sum, the dialectical relationship between the construction of human subjectivity and language suggests that it is in language that the ideologies inscribed in language must be challenged and the space where change may take place. Literature, as a public and persuasive use of language can influence and hasten this process by renegotiating meanings and, with them, our understanding of ourselves and our worlds. Literature, as Todorov suggests, exists by words but its dialectical vocation is to say more than language says, to transcend and go beyond verbal divisions: 'Literature is a kind of murderous weapon by which language commits suicide'.[35] The capacity of literary texts to 'murder' language can compete with law's power to adjudicate over people's lives, property, and liberty.

Legal theorists are generally interested in legal language and the legal subject. The creation of human subjectivity, however, is not limited to the legal realm, nor is legal language divorced from a society's use of language in other spheres. Successive critical

---

[32] Michel Foucault, *The Order of Things: An Archaeology of the Human Sciences* trans. Alan Sheridan, (New York: Vintage, 1970), at 387.

[33] Julia Kristeva, *Revolution in Poetic Language*, trans. Margaret Waller, (New York: Columbia University Press, 1984) at 37: 'when the speaking subject is no longer considered a phenomenological transcendental ego nor the Cartesian ego but rather a *subject in process/on trial [sujet en proces]*, as is the case in the practice of the *text*, deep structures or at least transformational rules are disturbed and, with them, the possibility of semantic and/or grammatical categorial interpretation'.

[34] 'Extreme Fidelity' in Susan Sellers (ed.), *The Hélène Cixous Reader* (London and New York: Routledge, 1994), at 132.

[35] Tzvetan Todorov, *The Fantastic: A Structural Approach to a Literary Genre* trans. Richard Howard,(Ithaca, New York: Cornell University Press, 1975), at 156.

theories in law have not achieved the radical changes they hoped to achieve in the form or content of the law. If we are dissatisfied with the opportunities for criticism and reform from within 'Law's Empire', we must turn our attention to the wider realm of language and culture. Language is a key category for understanding how human subjectivity is created and sustained and a major instrument for prompting changes in other areas. As Derrida puts it, 'what the institution cannot tolerate is for anyone to tamper with language . . . Nationalism and universalism can bear revolutionary ideologies that challenge the content as long as they don't challenge the borders of language and all the juridico-political contracts that it guarantees'.[36] Conversely, as George Orwell showed in *1984*, to dictate over the meaning of words is to permit totalitarianism. Lyotard puts it more succinctly: 'To arrest the meaning of words once and for all, that is what Terror wants'.[37]

Two groups that have paid particular attention to language—indeed, as Henry Louis Gates puts it, have been writing as if their life depended on it[38]—are feminist theorists and post-colonial men and women. Like Ariadne in my sequel to this chapter, both groups realized that although laws could be changed overnight, language was a more intransigent and invisible adversary and thus had to be the focus of their struggle. To contest the view that human nature and language are fixed is not to deny those concepts but to *expand* them. Such an expansion may enable us to express hitherto unspoken dreams and possibilities, in law as much as in literature.

5 OTHER THAN REASON: EMOTIONS, AESTHETICS, IMAGINATION, BODY, WOMAN . . .

Before and after Plato poets and image-makers of all kinds performed the task of teaching the citizens the values of Athenian society from familial to city rules and obligations as well as according the city a sense of its own identity, past history, and future hopes. Neither playwrights nor play-goers treated the experience of writing or attending a play as separate from their participation in city matters; in the theatre, as we see in the chapters on *Oedipus* and the *Oresteia*, ethical issues about how to live and govern were routinely examined and debated, if not necessarily resolved. At the same time the 'private' emotions depicted and aroused by dramatists were part of the audience's experience and response to 'public' or political issues. With modernism, however, emotions are dismissed as undifferentiated and unpredictable instincts that

---

[36] 'Living on: Border lines' in Harold Bloom (ed.), *Deconstruction and Criticism* (London: Routledge, 1979), at 94–5.

[37] Quoted in Michel de Certeau, *The Practice of Everyday Life* (Berkeley, Calif. University of California Press, 1984), at 165.

[38] 'Writing Race and the Difference it Makes' in Henry Louis Gates Jr (ed.), *Race, Writing and Difference* (Chicago and London: University of Chicago Press, 1985), at 13.

can not be relied upon to inform matters of legislation or government.[39] The modernist inclination to see literature and art in general as concerned with emotions, play, and aesthetics and law as concerned with reason and ethics also espouses the priority of general rules and principles in contrast to attending to the concrete and the particular. As Martha Nussbaum has argued, literature's commitment to the particular avoids the arrogant as well as dictatorial attempt to attach weight to our actions in a way that the contingency of life does not allow.[40] The male philosopher's distrust of emotions as clouding clarity of judgment and his attempt to expulse them from ethical thinking is again, as I argue in my closing chapter, not divorced from his fear of woman: to attend to the particular and the emotional may lead away from the modernist and masculinist model of justice and rights, towards a model based on connectedness, towards acknowledging, that is, Ariadne's difference and her different voice.[41]

At the hands of philosopher-kings keen to carve out a role for themselves as truth-bearers that was separate from and superior to that of poets and artists, imagination was dismissed as falsehood and indeed blasphemy; for Plato artists, by purporting to simulate reality in effect rivalled the role of, and sinned against, the gods. Richard Kearney's study on the role of the imagination describes how classical and medieval thinkers followed Plato in condemning the imagination as unreliable, unpredictable, and irreverent, suspecting it of threatening the natural order of things by making everything, as Aquinas put it, 'other than it is'.[42] As we see in the next section, however, even Plato could not resist appealing to poets and literary techniques in the process of arguing that the latter have no place in the ideal state. Indeed the attempt to deny the relevance of aesthetic and emotional judgements is indistinguishable from the attempt to exclude Ariadne from the legal labyrinth. 'Truth' for Ariadne, I suggest in my closing chapter, does not have to come from, or not *only* from, knowledge and reason, and is not restricted to the visual, the empirical, and the material as legal positivists would have us believe: it can also come from listening to, from touching, and from travelling towards the other: *feeling*, not only *knowing*, is believing.

At the other extreme to Plato's condemnation of poets, the imagination, as Richard

---

[39] While philosophers from Plato to the stoics to Spinoza have dismissed emotions as false or irrelevant, Aristotle, as Martha Nussbaum has argued, shared the view that emotions have a place in the making of judgments and the search for truth about how things are and what is important: 'The Aristotelian conception contains a view of learning well suited to support the claims of literature. For teaching and learning, here, do not simply involve the learning of rules and principles. A large part of learning takes place in the experience of the concrete': Martha Nussbaum *Love's Knowledge: Essays in Philosophy and Literature* (Oxford: Oxford University Press, 1990), at 44.

[40] Here the 'narrower and more modest claim of these essays will be that with respect to several inter-related issues in the area of human choice [legislation, adjudication], and of ethics broadly construed, there is a family of positions that is a serious candidate for truth—and which deserves, therefore, the attention and scrutiny of anyone who seriously considers these matters—whose full, fitting, and (as James would say) 'honorable' embodiment is found in the terms characteristic of the novels here investigated'; *ibid.*, at 8.

[41] See, for example, Carol Gilligan, *In a Different Voice: Psychological Theory and Women's Development* (Cambridge, Mass.: Harvard University Press, 1982).

[42] Richard Kearney, *Poetics of Imagining: From Husserl to Lyotard* (London and New York: Routledge, 1991), at 3.

Kearney's study describes, has been celebrated for its ability to fashion rather than merely represent reality, for transforming the real into the ideal, and for enabling us to envisage new possibilities of thinking, being and living. In particular, fiction, by envisaging new forms of social organization, may enable us to envisage new forms of social justice. The apotheosis of the imagination with the Romantic movement is summed up by Shelley's declaration that poets are the unacknowledged legislators of the world and Baudelaire's assertion that, since the imagination 'created the world it is fit that it should govern it'.[43] Husserl went further, endowing the imagination with an ethical role and declaring it as a precondition to human freedom while Bachelard celebrated poetic images as transcending past and present realities, and acting as stepping stones to a renewed world by enabling us to listen to and discover what is different from ourselves: 'The imagination does not fabricate images of reality but forms images which surpass reality in order to change reality. It is the power of a sur-humanity'.[44] For Nietzsche, 'art is not an imitation of nature but its metaphysical supplement, raised up beside it in order to overcome it'; art and poetry do not reside in some realm outside reality but seek to express an 'unvarnished truth', untainted by 'the trumpety garments worn by the supposed reality of civilized man'.[45] In effect, rather than literature being an imitation of reality, in Aristotle's sense, it is reality that imitates, and indeed should *seek* to imitate, literature.

By creating alternative and autonomous worlds, the artist competes with God to be the sole creator and with the state's assumption of the power to regulate and name relationships.[46] It is also an attempt, I suggest, to compete with the life-giving powers of the mother: if we agree, as Eagleton puts it, that 'aesthetics is born as a discourse of the body',[47] in particular the body's revolt against the tyranny of the mind, the celebration of the creative powers of the imagination is an attempt to be what woman already is and to do through metaphors and images what woman can do materially, with her body. We must not forget that the romantic writers' exultation of nature and the imagination was also an appropriation of traditionally feminine qualities: as Anne Mellor has argued, 'By taking on the virtues of compassion, mercy, gentleness and sympathy, the male Romantic poets could claim to speak with ultimate moral as well as intellectual authority ... By usurping the mother's womb, life-giving power, and feminine sensibilities, the male poet could claim to be God, the sole ruler of the world.'[48]

---

[43] Quoted by Kearney, *ibid.*, at 4.

[44] Gaston Bachelard, *L'Eau et les rêves; essai sur l'imagination de la matière* (Paris: Gallimard, 1938), at 23, quoted by Kearney, *ibid.*, at 93.

[45] Friedrich Nietzsche, *The Birth of Tragedy* (New York: Doubleday, 1956), trans. Francis Golffing, at 142 and 53.

[46] See, for example, Cixous: 'He who will become the artist is in open opposition to the law and to authority'; Hélène Cixous, *Readings: The Poetics of Blanchot, Joyce, Kafka, Kleist, Lispector, and Tsvetayeva* trans. Andermatt Conley, (Hemel Hempstead: Harvester Wheatsheaf, 1992) at 3.

[47] Terry Eagleton, *The Ideology of the Aesthetic, supra*, at 13.

[48] Anne K. Mellor, *Romanticism and Gender* (London and New York: Routledge, 1993), at 23. See also Anne K. Mellor 'Romanticism and the Colonization of the Feminine' in Anne K. Mellor (ed.), *Romanticism and Feminism* (Bloomington, Ind.: Indiana University Press, 1988).

The celebration of the imagination as life-creating could not be further away from Plato's indictment of the imagination as falsehood; rather than being in opposition to truth, poetry is adduced as revealing what is most true. The relationship between truth and poetry is therefore not one of opposition but one of 'mutual interference'; without dismissing the relevance of religious language, for enabling us to express tidings of salvation, or legal language, for purporting to express what is right and what wrong, poetic language, claims Gadamer, 'bears witness to our own being'.[49] Here the imagination is celebrated for making what is absent present, for freeing us from the constraints of the empirical world and for projecting new possibilities of existence. For 'if there is a sense of reality', writes Musil, 'there must also be a sense of possibility . . . the possible includes not only the fantasies of people with weak nerves but also the as yet unawakened intentions of God. A possible experience or truth is not the same as an actual experience or truth minus its "reality value" but has something quite divine about it, a fire, a soaring, a readiness to build and a conscious utopianism that does not shrink from reality but sees it as a project, something yet to be invented.'[50] The power to surpass the self and the here and now invests the imagination with an ethical role: chief amongst its tasks, as I argue further in the chapter on *Beloved*, is to bear witness to forgotten or silenced voices, suppressed histories, and unsayable or unsaid past events.

The view that imagination is another mode of being disclosing new possibilities of existence is not to revert to modernist illusions of authenticity and originality, nor to the notion of final truths and meanings. The death of the author and the celebration of the reader in postmodern theory leads to the denial of the notion of an imagining subject as the origin of meaning, especially since the speaking subject is actually being spoken for by her unruly unconscious and the wiles of a language that does not belong to her. Instead, Gianni Vattimo's notion of 'weak interpretation' and acceptance of a 'reasonable amount of irrationality' is one answer to legal and scientific discourses' demand for univocal truths, unitary origins, and final answers.[51] In postmodern fiction in particular we have an attention to surfaces, signs referring to other signs, and images referring to other images; without a transcendental signifier to confer origin and validity to these signs, signs become our only hold on reality, indeed the only reality. This does not mean that the postmodern imagination is ahistorical or apolitical, as its critics often claim. The play of parody and pastiche, as Linda Hutcheon argues, contests the modernist insistence on artistic originality and authority and,

---

[49] Hans-Georg Gadamer, *The Relevance of the Beautiful and Other Essays*, trans. Nicholas Walker, (Cambridge: Cambridge University Press, 1986) at 105 and 115.

[50] Robert Musil, *The Man Without Qualities* trans. Sophie Wilkins and Burton Pike, (London: Picador, 1995), at 10–11.

[51] Gianni Vattimo, *The End of Modernity: Nihilism and Hermeneutics in Postmodern Culture* trans. J. Snyder (Oxford: Polity Press, 1988),: in contrast to the 'notion of cumulative development', Vattimo acknowledges a responsibility for the aesthetic which 'belongs not so much, nor only, to aesthetics as a philosophical discipline, but rather to the aesthetic as a domain of experience and as a dimension of existence that assumes exemplary value as a model for thinking about historicity in general'; at 95. I am grateful to Panu Minkkinen for bringing Vattimo's work to my attention.

through a mixture of complicity and critique, reflexivity and historicity, defamiliar-izes, disrupts and subverts the conventions and ideologies of the dominant cultural and social forces: '[T]hese entities that we might unthinkingly experience as 'natural' (which might include capitalism, patriarchy, liberal humanism) are in fact 'cultural', made by us, not given to us.'[52] To argue that meaning is not stable is therefore not to *deny* meaning but to *expand* it.

Not everyone of course is enthusiastic about the transformative potential of the aesthetic and the imagination. For some critics, the focus on an aesthetic revolution is to abandon political struggle and play into the hands of a system that already dero-gated the aesthetic to political impotence. Terry Eagleton comments on 'that heady celebration of instinct, intuition and spontaneity of which the aesthetizing lineage, at its most callow, must stand convicted.'[53] And Habermas, clinging to the 'unfinished project of modernity', dismisses literary language and the aesthetic in general as not 'serious' rational discourses which, in contrast to reason, cannot be appealed to in our search for philosophical 'truth' or legislative changes.[54]

Such criticism, however, assumes that the aesthetic and the political are both separ-ate and separable. This is to ignore the influence of the aesthetic on our understand-ing of ourselves and the world, an influence which is often stronger and more widespread than that of political and legal institutions. It is also to ignore, as historians such as Hayden White and Dominic la Capra have argued, the role of the literary in the creation of our identities and histories, past, present, and future.[55] It is to ignore, further, as Jonathan Culler and Stephen Connor have described, the fact that literature (and in particular, I suggest, the 'feminine' qualities associated with literature) has served philosophy (and law) as the repository onto which any untame-able aspects of language could be projected, thus enabling philosophy and law to guard their claim as guardians of the truth.[56] The same can be said not only of poetry but of art in general with law simultaneously rejecting and relying on images (often on images of dead women) in order to create and sustain its foundations.[57]

It is, further, to assume that it is possible to distinguish between literature and reality. But the very existence of art and literature blurs the distinction between the real and the imaginary, representation and referent, antecedent object and subsequent copy. And this is where I suggest the importance of literature lies: *the literary imagina-*

---

[52] Linda Hutcheon, *The Politics of Postmodernism* (London and New York: Routledge, 1989), at 1–2.

[53] Terry Eagleton, *The Ideology of the Aesthetic, supra*, at 269.

[54] Jurgen Habermas, *The Philosophical Discourse of Modernity: Twelve Lectures* trans. Frederick Lawrence, (Cambridge: Polity Press, 1987), at 205.

[55] I discuss this work further in chapter 9.

[56] See Jonathan Culler, 'Communicative Competence and Normative Force' 35 *New German Critique* (1985) 133–44, at 141; and further Steven Connor, *Theory and Cultural Value* (Oxford UK and Cambridge USA: Blackwell, 1992): '*literary discourse permits and promotes the analytic appraisal of the very distinction between valid and invalid discourse which traditionally has constituted it*', at 126–7 (emphasis in original).

[57] For a recent discussion of law's simultaneous 'fear and love' of images see Costas Douzinas and Lynda Nead (eds.), *Law and the Image: The Authority of Art and the Aesthetics of Law* (Chicago and London: Chicago University Press, 1999).

*tion creates alternative, fictional, worlds, but unlike the legal imagination, it does not
pretend, nor does it expect others to pretend, that those alternative worlds are 'real'.*

6 FEAR OF MIMESIS, FEAR OF DIFFERENCE, FEAR OF WOMAN

What is the relationship between literature and reality, representation and referent,
mimetic object and original subject? For Plato, mimesis implied an original which the
artist, poet, or actor imitates. As this so-called original was itself, in Plato's mind, an
imitation of the world of ideas, the artist is three times removed from the truth and
therefore at best superfluous, at worst dangerous. Behind Plato's distrust of appearances and imitations is what Nietzsche terms a will to truth, the search for a true
world of unchanging beings and essences. In imitating something other than oneself
the actor threatens the destruction of the original and deceives by appearance and
image the truth uttered by speech and logos.[58] At the heart of Plato's anxiety is the fear
that mimesis transgresses the boundary between self and other and threatens the loss
of truth and the loss of self in becoming another.[59]

But the argument against poets and mimesis is made not only poetically but also
mimetically. Plato the poet, imitator, and playwright summons Socrates and an array
of other actors to take part in a play which is used to condemn mimetic plays and
artists, poets, and actors as mimetes. More famously he rejects the image in favour of
speech by appealing to the image of the cave. In the process, he shows what Aristotle
appreciated, that man is a mimetic animal forever creating, exploiting, using, and
abusing signs. Mimesis, as Plato argues mimetically, is simultaneously a drug and a
poison, both necessary and dangerously addictive and therefore, in Plato's view, only
safe in the hands of philosopher-kings.[60]

The hierarchy of original versus representation maintains the notion of an essential
self versus the image or representation of oneself. Plato's insistence on essence, identity, and being assumes not only that there is a prior, original model or identity that
the act of mimesis repeats, but also that such an identity remains unchanged and
untouched by its reproductions. It is not contemplated that these prior, anterior selves
and actions may be in fact constituted by, or be the effects of, the signs and codes that
supposedly reflect them. Nor that the world, rather than an icon to be copied, is itself

---

[58] Plato makes the same arguments against the sophists, suggesting that his condemnation of theatre
extends to law as theatre; despite Plato's distrust of playwrights, this fear is shared and explored by playwrights as in Aristophanes' *The Birds*.

[59] My discussion of Plato's mimesis is indebted to Arne Melberg's analysis in *Theories of Mimesis* (Cambridge; Cambridge University Press, 1995).

[60] *ibid.*, especially at 10–36.

a phantasm, a world of simulacra.[61] The hierarchy between a primary idea and a secondary representation is the western malady Derrida dubbed the metaphysics of presence which ignores that the sign is never simply present but derives its character from the possibility of its repetition and re-presentation. Derrida reverses the notion of the present as real and its representation as fiction to suggest the fictionality of the present and the reality of the representation. In contrast to Aristotle's view of representation as mimetic of an original object, for Derrida representation mingles with the represented object; the latter is not a shadow or reflection of the former but the two play with, fuse, and seduce each other so that it becomes impossible to separate representer from represented, the seducer from the seduced, the dancer from the dance: it becomes impossible, in other words, to determine the point of origin.[62]

In representation, therefore, the distinction between original and copy, art and life, authenticity and imitation is blurred. By deconstructing the opposition between essence and appearance, between the world as object theorized and represented by a subject that is independent of the interference of time, language and, as I will argue, gender, one can uncover what Plato wanted to repress, that is difference. The main thrust of Platonic philosophy, as Irigaray argues, is towards unity and sameness, leading him to privilege philosophic discourse over genres like literature and theatre that may open language to difference and heterogeneity. Literature and theatre, Plato feared, poses the threat of difference because, like woman, it can dissimulate, form, deform, and reform and in the process express a different system and a different law. To challenge the distinction between original and representation is to question, further, the notion of mimesis as repetition or sameness. To open oneself up to the play of mimesis is to allow oneself to become not the same but another or different. Mimesis and theatre, as Plato feared, is a play with serious consequences, opening oneself to difference and in particular, gender difference.

Not only is so-called reality a representation, a phantasm, it is a sign, a text so endlessly repeated that its sources, interests, and assumptions are forgotten or go unquestioned. By recognizing itself as a system of signs, literature lays such signs open to play and display, in the process allowing us to question them, reorder, or appropriate them for different and competing purposes. Literature may reveal the repressed rhetoricity, production, and contingency of societal constructs that deny their own artificiality and reopen the gap between representation and reality to a time *before*

---

[61] Gilles Deleuze, *Logic of Sense* (New York: Columbia University Press, 1989 [1969]): 'It is a question of two readings of the world in the sense that one asks us to think of difference on the basis of pre-established similitude or identity, while the other invites us on the contrary to think of similitude and even identity as the product of a fundamental disparity. The first exactly defines the world of copies or of representations; it establishes the world as icon. The second, against the first, defines the world of simulacra. It presents the world itself as phantasm'; quoted and discussed in J. Hillis Miller, *Fiction and Repetition* (Oxford: Blackwell, 1982), at 1–21. Deleuze's view of repetition as difference rather than sameness is developed further in *Difference and Repetition* (London: Athlone Press, 1994 [1969]). Plato's project of the destruction of appearances in search for essences is rivalled, today, by Baudrillard's project of the destruction of essences in favour of appearances: 'On Nihilism' 6 *On the Beach*, 38–9.

[62] See especially 'The Double Session' in Jacques Derrida, *Dissemination, supra.*

existing practices, begun as myths and plays, became law and started to take themselves (extremely) seriously. Political society and legal discourse may not recognize
themselves as a production, legal discourse may not admit to its own rhetoricity but
literature may remind us of the time when we first, as children, started to imitate, of a
time when it was still possible to ask, why these practices, rules, principles, and
institutions rather than any others? In short, that 'the objects and institutions we
thought as natural are really only historical: the result of change, they themselves
henceforth become in their turn changeable'.[63]

For Jean Baudrillard the proliferation of signs, codes, and images in contemporary
media societies have led to the collapse of time-honoured distinctions between copy
and original, surface and depth, reality and representation. Signs no longer refer to
external referents but to other signs; indeed signs are the only reality we have, more
real or hyper-real than so-called reality. In contrast to Plato's insistence on the existence of essences behind the appearance, for Baudrillard appearances are the only
essences: whether in law, politics, economics, or history, it is now impossible to distinguish between the real and the simulacra, which means that '*it is now impossible to
isolate the process of the real,* or to prove the real'.[64] What has always been at stake, he
suggests, is 'the murderous capacity of images: murderers of the real': the contemporary murder of reality, the 'perfect crime' as he calls it, suggests further that the task of
the fiction writer is not to represent reality or even to interrogate reality but further to
create reality: 'it is no longer a question of imitation, nor of reduplication, nor even of
parody. It is rather a question of substituting signs of the real for the real itself'.[65]

Contemporary cyberfiction in particular, as the opening quote from J. G. Ballard
suggests, acknowledges that reality is infiltrated by fiction to such an extent that it has
become indistinguishable from fiction: 'In the past we have always assumed that the
external world around us represented reality, however confusing or uncertain, and
that the inner world of our minds, its dreams, hopes, ambitions, represented the realm
of fantasy and the imagination. These roles, it seems to me, have been reversed. The
most prudent and effective method of dealing with the world around us is to assume
that it is a complete fiction—conversely, the one small node of reality left to us is
inside our own heads.'[66] In this context the writer's role is not to preside, God-like,

[63] Fredric Jameson, *The Prison-House of Language* (Princeton, New Jersey: Princeton University Press,
1972), at 58.

[64] 'Simulacra and Simulations' in Mark Poster (ed.), *Jean Baudrillard: Selected Writings*, (Oxford: Polity
Press, 1988), at 179.

[65] *Ibid.*, at 170, 167. See further, Jean Baudrillard, *The Perfect Crime* (London: Verso, 1996), at 43–4: 'we are
currently manufacturing the prehistory of an age which will not even remember it, to the point where [our
culture's] remains will possibly even be suspected (as was the case with cave paintings in the eighteenth
century) of having been fabricated at some later date by twentieth century impostors, depicting an obscure
and, in the end, useless anthropological prehistory—that of a native wit happily now supplanted by Artificial
Intelligence'. I am grateful to Iain Grant for bringing this work to my attention, for his infectious enthusiasm
for Baudrillard's work in general, and for his expert translations of some of that work.

[66] J. G. Ballard, *Crash* (London: Vintage, 1995), at 4–5. Again I am grateful to Iain Grant for imparting his
enthusiasm for cyberfiction not only to myself but also to one lucky class of Bristol students. It seems to me
apt that *Crash*, like the sign on the cover of this book, charts a journey on the M4 motorway . . .

over the development of a linear narrative, omnisciently and authoritatively creating, representing, and judging characters and events. In a world where reality is a fiction, fiction becomes the *only* reality.

7 AN-OTHER LANGUAGE

The suggestion is that reality is itself a fiction maintained by language on which other linguistic constructs, particularly laws, social and legal, are superimposed to enforce and perpetuate the impression that it is 'real'. Art, on the other hand, by not claiming to be *real*, or the *only* reality, may in turn suggest our own *irreality*. Theatre can remind us that we are always playing a part to an audience of others who play at accepting us as being the role we play. Art may remind us, in short, to use an old shorthand, that all the world is a play: a play that is amenable to the same interpretive techniques we apply to literary texts and that give rise to similar horrors, fears, and pities. If, as Blanchot puts it, literature 'is a work of bad faith', bad faith on the part of the writer and bad faith on the part of the reader who both play at taking as real what is invented and fictional, 'these relations of bad faith are not unique to the novel nor to literature in general'.[67] Law also, as I have suggested and explore further in my reading of the *Oresteia*, started as, and continues to be, a play.

Where legal fictions and legal language, however, are concerned with concealing their own style in order to give the appearance of certainty and precision, for poets language need be neither static nor concerned exclusively with representation. While law aims at pan-signification, and hopes to reduce aberrant signs to unitary meanings, poetry is happy to play with signs, blur meanings, and is at home with contradiction.[68] Following Julia Kristeva, one may contrast scientific and legal language which aims to eliminate contradictions in the search for a single right answer, with poetic language which is heterogenous rather than homogeneous, dynamic rather than static and open to multiple rather than unitary meanings.[69] By putting signs under question,

---

[67] Michael Holland (ed.), *The Blanchot Reader* (Oxford: Blackwell, 1995), at 72.

[68] Legal language in that sense is like the language of myth, hiding its normative dimension behind an appearance of neutrality: see, for example, Roland Barthes: 'Whereas myth aims at an ultra-signification, at the amplification of a first system, poetry, on the contrary, attempts to regain an infra-signification, a pre-semiological state of language . . . This is why it clouds the language, increases as much as it can the abstractness of the concept and the arbitrariness of the sign and stretches to the limit the link between signifier and signified': *Mythologies* (London; Vintage, 1993), [1957], trans. Annette Lavers, at 133. The mythic status of law and legal language and law's own reliance on myths to secure its foundations is discussed further in chapter 2.

[69] '[S]emiotic practice breaks with this teleological vision of a science that is subordinated to a philosophical *system* . . . Without becoming a system, the site of semiotics, where models and theories are developed, is a place of dispute and self-questioning, a "circle" that remains open. Its "end" does not rejoin its "beginning", but, on the contrary, rejects and rocks it, opening up the way to another discourse, that is, another subject and another method; or rather, there is no more end than beginning, the end is a beginning and vice versa.' 'Semiotics' in Toril Moi (ed.), *The Kristeva Reader* (Oxford: Blackwell, 1986), at 78.

poetry can push the limits of language, and with them, the limits of law. Literature may point the way towards the transformation of political institutions, especially through its attention to the possibilities of language: 'there can be no socio-political transformation without a transformation of subjects: in other words, in our relationship to social constraints, to pleasure, and more deeply, to language.'[70]

Rather than insisting on a unitary and homogenizing language that hides its inconsistencies, gaps, and contradictions, literature can live with ambiguities and thus allow a space for the other without co-opting her through abstract rules.[71] Legal language resists doubt, gaps, and inconsistencies; poetry on the other hand can reopen the gaps, disrupt meaning and open it 'as a question, as a non-given, as a bafflement, as a possibility'.[72] For Julia Kristeva, literature is a prime location for such questioning because in artistic play the pre-oedipal articulations of the semiotic can intrude into, disturb, and unsettle the language of the symbolic order.[73] Hélène Cixous goes further to claim that rupture and subversion is more akin to female sexuality and female writing: women's writing, by eschewing masculinist binary oppositions, linearity, and hierarchical divisions, may encourage new ways of seeing and being and can serve as a springboard for transforming social and cultural meanings and values.[74]

The condemnation of mimesis and poetic language, as I suggest in my reading of the *Oresteia* and further in my closing chapter, is not dissociated from the attempt to exclude woman from the legal labyrinth. Plato's condemnation of mimesis is an attempt to expulse difference from the ideal state, and in particular gender difference; the attempt to guard an essential and unchanging identity from the perils of mimesis is an attempt to guard an essential and unchanging *masculine* identity. For women to enter the legal fortress and participate in its continuing growth they need not only different laws but a different language; one that acknowledges their different aspirations, languages, dreams, and journeys. In particular, journeys that are not solipsistic and return to oneself but which reach out toward the other. As Luce Irigaray argues, women's specificity can only be conveyed through a 'logic other than the one imposed

---

[70] Julia Kristeva, 'Woman can never be defined' in Elaine Marks and Isabelle de Courtivron (eds.), *New French Feminisms* (Brighton: Harvester Press, 1981), at 141.

[71] See, for example, Cixous: 'The difference with philosophical discourse is that I never dream of mastering or ordering or inventing concepts . . . All I want is to illustrate, depict fragments, events of human life and death, each unique and at the same time. Not the law, the exception.' in *The Hélène Cixous Reader, supra,* at xxii.

[72] Barbara Johnson, *The Feminist Difference: Literature, Psychoanalysis, Race and Gender* (Cambridge, Mass. and London, UK: Harvard University Press, 1998), at 174: 'legal editing is a resistance to opening up meaning as a question, as a non-given, as a bafflement, as the possibility that what is intended and what is readable might not be the same. The ideology of law review style attempts to create a world saturated with meaning, without gaps, and indeed, doubtless without lesbians.'

[73] 'In "artistic" practices the semiotic—the precondition of the symbolic—is revealed as that which also destroys the symbolic . . . no pure signifier can effect the *Aufheburg* (in the Hegelian sense) of the semiotic without leaving a remainder, and anyone who would believe this myth need only question his fascination or boredom with a given poem, painting, or piece of music': Julia Kristeva, *Revolution in Poetic Language, supra,* at 50–1.

[74] See especially 'The Laugh of the Medusa' in *New French Feminisms, supra.*

by discursive coherence . . . it would reject all closure or circularity in discourse—any constitution of *arché* or of *télos*; it would privilege the "near" rather than the "proper" . . . women's "liberation" requires transforming culture and its operative agency, language. Without such an interpretation of a general grammar of culture, the feminine will never take place in history'.[75] Poetic language in particular may reveal women's secret, unconscious, nocturnal selves: 'the enigmas of the body, the dreams, secret joys, shames, hatreds of the second sex'.[76]

The dreams available to us are also both enabled and constrained by the language we have at our disposal; language measures, contains but is also a tool that can be used to expand our dreams. Literary utterances, I suggest, can be less restrictive of the world's possible meanings than other forms of speech and especially legal speech that, for outsiders in particular, such as Ariadne in my closing chapter, resembles a monologue.[77] Though it constitutes and imitates, language also creates and recreates, it is constant *energeia*.[78] Literature in general and fantastic literature in particular, as Todorov argues, though constituted by words, can signify more than words, it is at once 'verbal and transverbal'.[79] Rather than destroying meaning and presence, poetic language can disrupt old meanings and create new ones; rather than denying identity, it can reveal identities in process, that express and are subject to the law but are also able to exceed, explode, and expand the law.

The imaginative writer's willingness to explore, bend, subvert, and explode existing linguistic tools gives us a glimpse of the possibilities afforded by other worlds, other selves and, in turn, other laws. To conceive of a different world or worlds, we need different words. The language employed by Ariadne, I suggest in my closing chapter, is seen by the legal labyrinth as far too perilous to be admitted. The same difference that is perceived as threatening by the law, however, also holds out the promise of opening more doors to a labyrinth that not only excludes outsiders but also imprisons those inside. Where Kafka's old man from the country dies without gaining admission to the law, the woman law and literature critic may help find new entrances to what has become, for insiders as well as outsiders, a forbidding and exclusionary edifice. In particular we need to investigate the limits of the language of reason to go back to a time *before* the word, the world, and its laws were invented. For in the beginning there was not the word, not logos, not law, but a feeling, an emotion called love.

Legal language tends to abstract and detach itself from everyday experience once it has spoken; literature on the other hand may reveal what law obscures by reopening the gaps and ambiguities that law necessarily distanced itself from in its insistence on

[75] Luce Irigaray, *This Sex Which Is Not One*, trans. Catherine Porter with Carolyn Burke, (Ithaca, New York: Cornell University Press, 1985), [1977], at 153–5.

[76] Julia Kristeva, 'Women's Time' in Toril Moi (ed.), *The Kristeva Reader, supra*, at 207.

[77] For the novel as dialogue see Michael Holquist (ed.) *The Dialogic Imagination: Four Essays by M. M. Bakhtin*, trans. Caryl Emerson and Michael Holquist, (Austin: University of Texas Press, 1981).

[78] Wilhelm von Humboldt: 'Language is not a work (*ergon*), but an activity (*energeia*); quoted in 'The Way to Language' Martin Heidegger, *Basic Writings*, (ed.) David Farrell Krell (London: Routledge, 1993), at 403.

[79] Tzvetan Todorov, *The Fantastic, supra*, at 156, 166–7.

speaking univocally, and forever. The law that in Kafka's universe hides its origins and mysteries, also takes on the role of the benevolent father, offering security and comfort and satisfying the human need for certainty and security. For those excluded from, or unconvinced by the benign nature of this paternalism, in particular women and marginalized groups, literature offers one way of reopening the world's complexity and thus unsettles both law and life. Ariadne, as I suggest in my closing chapter, welcomes literature because, like poetic utterances, and unlike legal texts, she is not frightened of contradictions, of displaying vivid emotions and of living with inexplicable causes.

In short, the fact that both legal and literary fictions are constituted in language means that it is in language that the artificiality of both literature and of law must be examined and uncovered. While much of contemporary literature, however, accepts, delights in, and explores its own constructedness, arbitrariness and artificiality, the writers of law are more concerned to disguise its status as a linguistic artefact. In that sense legal writers are like writers of realist fiction, trying to maintain the illusion of an omniscient narrator, chronological sequence, plot inevitability, and causal connection between events. Once such worlds, however, are shown to be not only artificial but also unfair or tyrannical, it is necessary to reveal the ways by which that artificiality is constructed. One of the aspirations, therefore, of law and literature analyses, is that the construction of literary texts may throw light on the construction and fictionality of the so-called real world, including that of the legal world, its values and conventions and of ourselves within it.[80] In that way, what we are accustomed to perceiving as the imaginary, challenges the so-called real and affirms Shelley's view that poets and for my purposes, poetesses, are the unacknowledged legislators of the world.

8 AN-OTHER REALITY

Though centuries of European literature privileged realism at the expense of magic and fantasy, though positivism in legal theory assumed that it is possible to abstract questions of what the law is from questions of what it ought to be, direct representation, in law or in literature, is also an illusion, the arrogant belief that law and the world is knowable, explainable, and objectively representable. That representation is an illusion is apparent as realism's and legal positivism's attempts to copy the original

---

[80] See especially Patricia Waugh's argument that fictional writing that draws attention to its own status as a linguistic artefact enables us to 'explore the possible fictionality of the world outside the literary fictional text ... If, as individuals, we now occupy "roles" rather than "selves", then the study of characters in novels may provide a useful model for understanding the construction of subjectivity in the world outside novels. If our knowledge of this world is mediated through language, then literary fictions (worlds constructed entirely of language) becomes a useful model for learning about the construction of reality itself': *Metafiction: The Theory and Practice of Self-Conscious Fiction* (London and New York: Routledge, 1984), at 2–3.

never entirely convince: gaps, cracks, inconsistencies, interested definitions continue to show through, shuttering their claim to objectivity. Rather than disguising the fact that their fictional universe is artificial or constructed, many contemporary writers draw attention to it: they answer, thereby, 'to a deep need in contemporary literary art—the need to confess the fact of artifice'.[81] Though film and literature have long experimented with breaking the illusion of continuity, shaking the audience out of their complacency that the narrative they are reading or watching is inevitable and could not have been otherwise, law has still to learn to confess to the fact of its own artificiality. It aims to preserve the illusion of order, consistency, and inevitability, to obscure the fact that its history, decisions, and stories could have developed in a different manner, taking in other experiences, other views, other voices.

The world, however, its origins and causes, are infinite, indecipherable, and ultimately uncontrollable; indeed it would be boring and flat if it was not. The attempt, therefore, to compete with, explain, represent, and thereby order the world is doomed to failure.[82] Rather than representing or imitating reality, and rather than negating or dissolving the mystery, art may intimate our failure to know reality: art may be less mimesis than mystery.[83] Indeed it is realism in literature, empiricism in philosophy, and positivism in legal theory, that, by identifying the knowable not only with what is observable but more damagingly 'with all there is', that have the effect of flattening our experiences.[84] It is being tied down to everyday circumstances that is poverty, suggests Borges, 'when one could be everywhere, when one could be in eternity! . . . Let's be endless',[85] he implores. If we abandon the assumption that reason can reason everything, then the concepts we rely on to ground and stabilize our experiences, such as the concepts of identity, time, law, are revealed as limiting and arbitrary. Fantasy on the other hand may enable us to suggest different experiences, what we have not expressed or experienced before. We are poor indeed, as Winnicot often said, if we are only sane. Artistic play may open the world, law, and language as a possibility rather than as a given. The effect is not to deny but to *expand* reality.

Such projections, can only ever take place in language, a language that speaks to us as much as we speak it; for this task language must correspondingly be stretched to intimate and allude to the ineffable and unrepresentable. Our business, Lyotard says, is to 'make visible that there is something which can be conceived and which can neither be seen nor made visible . . . not to supply reality but to invent allusions to the conceivable which cannot be presented.'[86] Fantastic literature in particular, as

[81] John Updike, 'The Author as Librarian', *New Yorker*, 30 October, 1968, at 223; quoted by Martin S. Stabb, *Jorge Luis Borges*, (Boston: Twayne Publishers, 1970), at 145.

[82] As Borges says, 'the machinery of the world is much too complex for the simplicity of a beast': Jorge Luis Borges, *Labyrinths* (ed.) Donald A.Yates and James E. Irby (London: Penguin, 1970), at 273.

[83] John Sturrock, *Paper Tigers: The Ideal Fictions of Jorge Luis Borges* (Oxford: Clarendon Press, 1977), at 127.

[84] J. Agassi, 'Philosophy as Literature: The Case of Borges', *Mind*, April 1970, 287–294, at 291.

[85] Richard Burgin (ed.), *Jorge Luis Borges: Conversations* (Jackson: University of Mississippi Press, 1998), at 196 and 209.

[86] Jean-Francois Lyotard, 'Answering the Question: What is Postmodernism?' in Thomas Docherty (ed.), *Postmodernism: A Reader* (Hemel Hemsptead: Harvester Wheatsheaf, 1993), at 43 and 46.

Todorov argues, questions the existence of an irreducible opposition between real and unreal and forces us to wonder whether there is such a thing as an external reality out there which it is literature's function to represent; we may need to accustom ourselves to the unsettling thought that reality is itself a fiction created by reason, and that so-called 'normal' man is himself the fantastic object.[87] A fantastic object that relies on law and language for security, identity, and finality.

True, as Blanchot acknowledges, literature is not the first 'discourse' to tell us that we are all deceived, that we live in a world where our laws, actions, thoughts, words, dreams are always already borrowed, always already loaded with values and meanings out of our control. True Marx warned us to beware of false consciousness, Freud of the pain of our unconscious desires, critical legal scholars of law's hidden designs on our bodies and our very souls. And still we do not listen, still we carry on as though we are our own true and only agents, and that language is at our disposal to help us express and fulfil our every purpose. Indeed, as Blanchot suggests, these disclosures may be 'part and parcel of the great hoax', covering up an even more dangerous and greater hoax.[88]

Since we are constituted by language, with words as its only weapon, poetry can murder our sense of self, our laws, and our worlds: murder reality itself. With one difference: while, as I suggest in my closing chapter, the legal Minotaur kills his victims and leaves their corpses lying where they fell, Ariadne and literature breathe new life into them for as many times as we read and reread old stories, write and rewrite old tunes. If, as Blanchot argues, literature succeeds in making of its lie, of its untruth, of its bad faith, a world that both writer and reader come to believe in, that success 'makes of the untruth of this world the element of emptiness in which, finally, there comes into view the meaning of what is most true':[89] 'This frail literature, scarcely existing', continues Blanchot, may not look like 'much to count on in the struggle against the great hoax'; but literature's perceived weakness may thwart the designs of the trickster more than those he perceives as strong and against whom he pits his energies.[90] As Baudrillard suggests, the repressive apparatus would be more ruffled by a *simulated* rather than a real hold up: 'For a real hold up only upsets the order of things, the right of property, whereas a simulated hold up interferes with the very principle of reality. Transgression and violence are less serious, for they only contest the *distribution* of the real. Simulation is infinitely more dangerous since it always suggests, over and above its object, that *law and order themselves might really be nothing more than a simulation.*'[91]

Frailer still Ariadne, I suggest in my closing chapter, may succeed where these 'great disclosures' stumbled and, rather than delivering the great revolutions they promised, became instead historical relics in the service of the great hoax. In that chapter, which

---

[87] *The Fantastic, supra,* quoting Jean-Paul Sartre, at 173.
[88] 'The Great Hoax' in *The Blanchot Reader, supra,* at 157.
[89] 'The Novel is a Work of Bad Faith' in *The Blanchot Reader, supra,* at 73.
[90] 'The Great Hoax' in *The Blanchot Reader, supra,* at 166.
[91] 'Simulacra and Simulations' *supra,* at 177 (emphasis in 'original').

is a sequel to this introduction and also a rebeginning, I try to invent such a reality by writing another sequel to the story and concept of finding oneself 'before the law', before representation, before logos. The story retells the Minotaur myth from the point of view of Ariadne and her successful negotiation of the law's attempt to deny her different languages. In revising the Minotaur myth it also invents another birth for law and literature that charts a journey that starts with the mother and rather than returning to oneself, or leading to death, reaches out towards others. *Herstory* suggests that in the beginning there was not logos but music, not utilitarian word but an image, not law but a feeling. That feeling promises continuity rather than closure, connectedness rather than competition, and eternity rather than death.

Like this book, Ariadne's journey is cyclical rather than linear, and along the way it suggests new entrances to the legal labyrinth and new ways of living with, without murdering, the Minotaur. While man, it suggests, has been hiding in self-created labyrinths variously called law, reason, knowledge, God, woman has travelled the world from the prison he imposed on her called home: 'to bring you', as P. J. Harvey sings it, 'my love'.

Ariadne appreciates that to gain entrance to the law she must begin by making her own laws which means devising not only new rules but a new language and a new style. By pushing the limits of what is sayable in the legal academy, she pushes the limits of language, and with them, the limits of law. Rather than expecting either law or literature to represent and order the world, her style hopes to allude to and preserve its mysteries. It also holds out the promise that the child born of the coming together of law and literature, of the marriage between 'the lawyer in his labyrinth and from her to eternity', need not necessarily be a boy; that it is a child, boy *or* girl, that, unlike Plato and generations of male philosophers, and lawyers, is not horrified at the idea of dressing up in women's clothes, that is, of performing and reperforming gender roles.

The freedom Ariadne enjoys from her long exclusion, her suspicious and playful approach towards both law and language, may point another way, one that does not suffer from the illusion of truth, that does not claim to deliver all the answers, let alone all the right answers, that does not, in other words, claim the last word. Rather than buttressing both law and literature as distinct disciplines, Ariadne's 'performance' may also suggest one way of writing not law, or literature, but law *and* literature.

2

MYTHS OF ORIGINS AND ORIGINS OF MYTHS: BEYOND OEDIPAL JOURNEYS[1]

For the Oracle leave at Junction 11
Sign on M4 motorway

1 MYTHOS AND LOGOS

To paraphrase Jean-Pierre Vernant, myths are not only present in a society but a society is present in its myths.[2] Myths do more than provide a source of entertainment or describe the society in which they are found; whether in ancient Greece or in contemporary society, myths are intrinsic to the process of naturalization and normalization. Their accessibility and dissemination means that they can be more important and influential than state laws in educating, unifying, and perpetuating a society and its cultural conventions and expectations. As Roland Barthes argued, behind the appearance of innocent story-telling and objective description, myths contain messages which are no less normative, value-laden, and didactic than those enunciated by law courts. Indeed, by being dressed as 'depoliticized speech', they can be more successful than legal language in making what is political, arbitrary, and conventional appear natural, factual, and inevitable.[3] For structuralists like Claude Lévi-Strauss, myths can express the underlying assumptions, structures and conventions of a society's political, religious, social, and sexual realms and where such realms are riddled with contradictions, they can perform the role of mediating, stabilizing, and

---

[1] Sophocles, *The Three Theban Plays: Antigone, Oedipus the King, Oedipus at Colonus*, trans. Robert Fagles, (Harmondsworth: Penguin Classics, 1984), all references in the text are to this edition.

[2] Jean-Pierre Vernant, *Myth and Society in Ancient Greece* (New York: Zone Books, 1988), trans. Janet Lloyd, at 10.

[3] Roland Barthes, 'Myth Today' in *Mythologies* (London: Vintage, 1993), trans. Annette Lavers, At 124–5: myth has 'an imperative, buttonholing character . . . it arrests in both the physical and the legal sense of the term', at 124–5.

ultimately overcoming them.[4] And for psychoanalysts, myths can express a society's unsatisfied, repressed, or unacceptable desires: if dreams are the royal road to an individual's unconscious, myths express society's collective unconscious, and just as the blocking of the unconscious by the ego leads to individual neurosis, so the blocking of collective desires leads to collective neurosis and the maintenance of a discontented civilization.[5]

The normative dimension of myths has not gone unnoticed by generations of western theorists who contrasted the murmurs of myth to the articulations of reason and found myths wanting: Plato denounced them as 'old wives' tales' lacking the logic and demonstrative power of rational discourse, or logos. In a similar fashion history scholars, in an attempt to limit the scope of what counts as history to empirically verifiable data, denied the value of myths in recounting the past. The same Plato, however, appreciated the myths' persuasive power sufficiently to warrant banishing poets from the ideal Republic and was not averse to appealing to myths and poets for inspiration when trying to express concepts such as the good and justice: 'And so, my dear Glaucon', Socrates concludes in *The Republic*, 'his tale was preserved from perishing, and, if we remember it, may well preserve us in turn'.[6] History scholars have similarly allowed for the importance of myths in understanding the past: as Bachofen put it, 'to deny the historicity of a legend does not divest it of value. What cannot have happened was nonetheless thought'.[7] The examination of modern law as itself a myth, relying for its origins, definition, and continuation on other myths, has also recently been the focus of attention by critical legal scholars.[8]

The suspicion with which myths have been treated suggests that the concept itself may have been invented to cater for as well as to denigrate aspects of otherness that the preferred tools of reason could not comprehend or countenance. Jean-Pierre Vernant inverts the priority between mythos and logos, suggesting that philosophy itself was an attempt to formulate truths that myth was already aware of and transmitted in the form of allegorical stories.[9] For the Greeks themselves, myths, as the society's shared cultural treasures, were both true and invaluable as a source of education of the young. Homer's epics were required teaching, habitually recited at feasts

---

[4] Claude Lévi-Strauss, *Structural Anthropology*, trans. Claire Jacobson and Brooke Grundfest Schoepf, (London: Allen Lane, 1968), at 244: 'mythical thought always progresses from the awareness of opposition toward their resolution'.

[5] For Jung's discussion of archetypal images and motifs from myths and legends see Carl Gustav Jung, *Two Essays on Analytical Psychology* (Princeton, NJ: Princeton University Press, 1972) [1943].

[6] Plato, *The Republic* trans. Desmond Lee (London: Penguin, 1987), at 393.

[7] J. J. Bachofen, *Myth, Religion, and Mother Right: Selected Writings of J. J. Bachofen*, trans. Ralph Manheim (Princeton, NJ: Princeton University Press, 1973), at 213; quoted in Peter L. Rudnytski, *Freud and Oedipus* (New York: Columbia University Press, 1987), at 190.

[8] See especially Peter Goodrich, *Oedipus Lex: Psychoanalysis, History, Law* (Los Angeles and London: University of California Press, 1995); Costas Douzinas and Ronnie Warrington, 'Antigone's Dike: The Mythical Foundations of Justice' in *Justice Miscarried: Ethics, Aesthetics and the Law* (Hemel Hempstead: Harvester Wheatsheaf, 1994); Peter Fitzpatrick, *The Mythology of Modern Law* (London and New York: Routledge, 1992).

[9] Jean-Pierre Vernant, *Myth and Society in Ancient Greece, supra*, at 222.

and symposia and served as a focus for Greek society's understanding of its past, its present traditions, and continuing self-definition. Coupled with rituals, myths 'made explicit what was implicit in social relationships', affirming social values and preferred ways of life.[10]

Myths have been called upon to mediate some of the more persistent categories and oppositions western societies have chosen with which to define themselves as well as to judge other societies: the contrasts between man[11] and god, man and beast, self and other, nature and culture, divine foreknowledge and meaninglessness, man and polis, public and private, order and chaos, man and woman. What if such oppositions, however, are cultural rather than natural and the discourses that constructed them as oppositions as contingent as the oppositions themselves? In that case, instead of myths revealing truths about the world, myths, and our readings of them, may help 'to make the world conform to the myth'.[12] The task would then be not only to unravel the oppositions that the myth is supposed to mediate but the oppositions themselves, and more importantly, the discourses that constructed them as oppositions.

Few myths can claim to have commanded such a long and pervasive presence in western societies as that of Oedipus, or loaded with a greater variety of meanings by generations of audiences and readers. While addressing a small number of these interpretations, my focus is less what the myth means, even less whether it is true, false, or constitutes part of a systemic unity with other myths, as who makes and who benefits from these meanings. What oppositions has the Oedipus myth served to mediate, how were the oppositions formulated, who decided, and who benefits from the form the mediation takes? If, as Freud believed, truth can only be glimpsed through its distortions, what truths does this myth distort and what do these distortions reveal about our society's unconscious? More importantly, what does the significance our society has accorded it reveal about ourselves? If the myth of Oedipus is not only over-determined but inexhaustible, then its meaning cannot be frozen but is ever open to reinterpretation and reappropriation by interested audiences and readers. In particular, if, as we have often been told, the Oedipus myth explores the origins and foundation of the human psyche, society, and law, what do the myth and its interpretations say about those excluded from its making and retelling, those representing the unconscious of the unconscious, the dark continent of the dark continent?

---

[10] Richard Buxton, *Imaginary Greece: the Contexts of Mythology* (Cambridge: Cambridge University Press, 1994), at 130.

[11] The masculine pronoun is used here deliberately for, as will be argued, 'woman' has been excluded, not from the text itself, but from its interpretations.

[12] Pierre Bourdieu, *An Outline of a Theory of Practice*, trans. Richard Nice, (Cambridge: Cambridge University Press, 1977), at 167.

2 MYTH AND TRAGEDY

Tragedy as enacted in ancient Athens was not divorced from other affairs of the city but was an integral part of city life, with structures and conventions analogous to those governing the law courts and political institutions. Tragedy emerged at the transitionary period between contrasting understandings of man and his place in the world, what Jean-Pierre Vernant and Pierre Vidal-Naquet have called 'the tragic moment'.[13] At this border zone, the contrast between heroic values on the one hand and civic values on the other, between legal and political thought and mythical and heroic traditions, between human autonomy and divine direction, between human justice and divine justice, were thrown open to question. Tragedy, as Charles Segal argues, highlights these oppositions by bringing heroes from the past into the world of the polis and confronting them with the contradictions within man, as well as the ambiguous nature of language that is called upon to reconcile these contradictions. However, in contrast to the Homeric poems, where the actions of mythical heroes provided lessons for human behaviour, tragedy does not yield easy answers. Once the Gods and heroes of the past are imported into the city-state, their actions become more an issue of debate at the hands of the dramatist with the participation of the audience-polites. Values once affirmed by the myths are reopened and questioned, as the fairness of the gods, the status, origin, and destiny of man, and the city's own structures and institutions are questioned, disrupted, and pushed to the limit. Rather than affirming the social order, tragedy countenances its contradictions and explores the possibility that conflicts may be neither resolved nor mediated.[14]

Charles Segal goes on to argue that the mask worn by the actors underlined the appearance of play, conferring on the participants a freedom that could be exploited to question society's rules and institutions. The hope is that by reopening pre-existing boundaries tragedy can provide a space from which one can perceive the contingency of existing rules and structures.[15] Indeed this is a form of self-reflection and interrogation that cannot be countenanced in institutions such as the law courts. But is the political effect of tragedy any more radical than a day in court? Can the questioning be maintained after the exit from the theatre? The converse fear is that tragedy may, as Augusto Boal denounced, quieten the will, and appease rather than provoke the

---

[13] Jean-Pierre Vernant, and Pierre Vidal-Naquet, *Tragedy and Myth in Ancient Greece* (Brighton: Harvester Press, 1981) [1972], at vii.

[14] See Charles Segal, *Tragedy and Civilization: An Interpretation of Sophocles, supra*, at 21 and 51; Jean-Pierre Vernant, *Myth and Society in Ancient Greece, supra*, at 214: 'Myth, in its original form, provided answers without ever explicitly formulating the problems. When tragedy takes over the mythical traditions, it uses them to pose problems to which there are no solutions'; and Roland Barthes: 'Myth starts from contradictions and tends progressively toward their mediation; tragedy, on the contrary, refuses the mediation, keeps the conflict open', quoted by Segal, *supra*, at 51.

[15] Segal, *Tragedy and Civilization, supra*, at 42.

audience, leading them to a passive acquiescence in the status quo rather than to questioning the human lot of suffering and inequality.[16]

Where questioning does take place, is it any more than a harmless diversion, a form of displacement that allows the polis and its polites to express doubts and contradictions about their laws and institutions that would be impossible, and painful, to interrogate in real life? In a psychoanalytic reading of tragedy, André Green argues that the disguises and exaggerations accepted in the theatre offer an ideal location for such displacements, portraying that 'other scene', the unconscious.[17] René Girard's analysis of the Oedipus myth as enacting the age-old ritual of scapegoating[18] can be extended to the experience of the theatre: the mechanism of scapegoating that is for Girard at the heart of human society, is itself a form of unconscious transference whereby everything felt to be dangerous or hateful in one's own psyche is projected onto another person. Tragedy, suggests André Green, may also be a form of scapegoating, getting rid of inappropriate emotions through witnessing the tragic spectacle: a substitute solution assuaging painful tensions and compensating for the lack of satisfaction of human desires elsewhere.

Furthermore, if the climax of tragedy, is, as Aristotle emphasized, the hero's anagnorisis, is this alleged resolution another master narrative that purports to resolve and contain conflict and difference? In particular, if tragedy assumes the existence of a 'permanent, universal and unchanging human nature'[19] do all members of the audience experience the same identification with the hero and thereby undergo the same cathartic experience at the hero's self-discovery and self-recognition? Do women readers and women members of the audience experience the same pity and fear at Oedipus' collapse and the same catharsis at his symbolic castration through self-blinding? Perhaps it is only by keeping the tragic ending open to a variety of interpretations, by highlighting conflicting views in our reading as well as the performance of the play, that tragedy may remain, as Nietzsche hoped, 'beyond good and evil'.

[16] Augusto Boal, 'Aristotle's Coercive System of Tragedy' in *Theater of the Oppressed*, trans. Charles A. and Maria Odilla Leal McBride (London: Pluto Press, 1979).

[17] André Green, *The Tragic Effect*, trans. Alan Sheridan (Cambridge: Cambridge University Press, 1979). Green goes further to assert that every hero and every spectator is in the position of the son in the Oedipal drama, entering into competition with the gods only to be quashed by them, assuring once again the triumph of the father: 'In the last resort every text springs from a murder (of the father) carried out with the intention of obtaining pleasure, sexual possession (of the mother)'; at 32.

[18] For René Girard, Oedipus' crime is to abolish the differences communities rely on for their order and stability; for order to be restored, 'Oedipus becomes the repository of all the community's ills . . . a prime example of the human scapegoat', serving to guard and cleanse the community from the consequences of their own violence and irreconcilable differences: René Girard, *Violence and the Sacred* (London and Baltimore: Johns Hopkins University Press, 1977), at 68–88.

[19] Raymond Williams, *Modern Tragedy* (London: Chatto, 1966), at 45.

3 HIDDEN SIGNS: DESTINY OR CHANCE?

Tragedy, says Holderlin, arises from the conflict between the simultaneous need for fusion and separation between god and man.[20] In the person of Oedipus we are at the border zone between nature and culture, natural and supernatural, civilization and savagery, order and disorder, autonomy and determinism. An issue of paramount concern in fifth century Athens, as new legal and political institutions were being established, was man's relationship to the gods and the relationship between human justice, law, and order to divine justice, law, and order. Law in fifth century Athens certainly appeared less autonomous than it does today, with large parts of it still in the process of being distinguished from religious and moral thought. While the law courts were busy disentangling it from other sources, its uncertainties and ambiguities were a rich source of inspiration for dramatists who addressed similar themes to those addressed by the law courts. With *Oedipus the King* even the form of the play, an investigation followed by judgment and punishment, resembles that of a law case. As Nietzsche noted, Sophocles 'presents us in the beginning with a complicated legal knot, in the slow unravelling of which the judge brings about his own destruction'.[21]

The ability of man to fashion language to express his thoughts and direct his own and others' actions also comes under scrutiny and is shown to be problematic: rather than a medium of communication, linguistic terms are displayed in all their ambiguity and indeterminacy. From the start words mean one thing for Oedipus and a different thing for the spectator who already knows the story. Thus Oedipus offers to fight for Laius 'as for my own father' since he and Laius, he says, possess a 'wife of common seeding' and children 'in common' (260). Such slips reveal a truth the speaker is unaware of. At the same time, no character can ignore the medium of language in their search for some underlying truth since that truth can only be expressed in, and indeed is constituted by, language. The very 'action' of the play consists almost exclusively of linguistic puzzles, that is the interpretation of oracles that (spoken, importantly, by a woman), were necessarily cryptic and mysterious.[22] Perhaps, as Jean-Pierre Vernant suggests, it is only when the protagonists, and the spectators accept that words, values, and men are themselves ambiguous, conflicting,

---

[20] 'Observations', quoted and discussed in Peter L. Rudnytsky, *Freud and Oedipus* (New York: Columbia University Press, 1987), at 127.

[21] Friedrich Nietzsche, *The Birth of Tragedy* trans. Francis Golffing, (New York and London: Doubleday, 1956), at 60.

[22] Cynthia Chase goes further to argue that Oedipus' crime, and his guilt, is read from a collection of texts rather than from empirical evidence. Oedipus' guilt is not in the original acts which were innocent because of Oedipus' ignorance, nor in the now of the play when Oedipus pieces together his story but somewhere in between: 'It is a story about the danger of storytelling; by telling a story Oedipus makes something happen': 'Oedipal Textuality: Reading Freud's Reading of Oedipus' in Maud Ellman (ed.), *Psychoanalytic Literary Criticism* (Harlow, Essex: Longman, 1994).

and problematical that we can talk of achieving a 'tragic consciousness' or the tragic experience.[23]

To acknowledge the limitations of human language is another way of acknowledging the limitations of human knowledge in the conflict between man and god. Tragedy opens the debate of human versus divine knowledge and debates the strength and limits of this knowledge. While the concept of hamartia depicted men as sick, doing wrong unknowingly, tragedy questioned the extent to which man is responsible for his actions. On the one hand for the tragic hero to engage our sympathies he must be seen as a free agent grappling with difficult decisions; on the other hand tragedy occurs because his actions are not fully separate from the designs of the gods. If the subject appears to have choice, autonomy, responsibility, and liberty, the power of superhuman forces looms just as large, and it is the conflict between the two that gives the drama its tragic dimension. In this context, the notion of free will assumed in western societies is anything but unproblematic; the view of the person as a universal, coherent, and continuous agent, responsible as the cause and source of his actions is itself a contingent and historical rather than a universal and immutable truth. If there is any scope for the will, Vernant notes, it is certainly not autonomous will in the Kantian sense, but a will bound by fear of divine powers, if not actually coerced by them.[24]

Sophocles' *Oedipus Rex* pitches the conflict between human choice and divine foreknowledge in stark form: Sophocles could not have failed to be aware of the influence the teachings of people such as Gorgias and Protagoras were having in contemporary Athens. These early sceptics celebrated man's capacity to reason and, asserting that 'man is the measure of all things', cast doubt on the relevance of prophesies and oracles. Oedipus, as praised by the chorus in the opening ode, is an embodiment of the contemporary man favoured by Pericles:

> You cannot equal the gods . . .
> But we do rate you first of men,

---

[23] Jean-Pierre Vernant, 'Ambiguity and Reversal. On the Enigmatic Structure of *Oedipus Rex*' in Jean-Pierre Vernant and Pierre Vidal-Naquet, *Tragedy and Myth in Ancient Greece, supra,* at 88.

[24] Jean-Pierre Vernant, 'Intimations of the Will in Greek Tragedy', in Vernant and Vidal-Naquet, *Tragedy and Myth in Ancient Greece, supra.* See also E. R. Dodds, 'On Misunderstanding the *Oedipus Rex*' in Harold Bloom (ed.), *Modern Critical Interpretations: Oedipus Rex* (New York: Chelsea House Publishers, 1988), at 42: 'The doctrine that nothing matters except the agent's intention is a peculiarity of Christian and especially of post-Kantian thought.' And R. P. Winnington-Ingram, 'The *Oedipus Tyrannus* and Greek Archaic Thought' in Michael J. O'Brien, (ed.), *Twentieth Century Interpetations of* Oedipus Rex (New Jersey: Prentice-Hall, 1968), at 89: Sophocles could simultaneously see man 'as free and as subject to determining powers, and so to produce that tension between freedom and necessity which seems essential to the tragic paradox . . . [he was] not tempted, as so many thinkers have been, to fudge the evidence in the interests of the autonomy of the will and the innocence of heaven'. Also Thomas Gould, 'The Innocence of Oedipus: The Philosophers on *Oedipus the King*' in Harold Bloom (ed.), *Modern Critical Interpretations: Oedipus Rex, supra,* at 51: 'the Greeks before the Stoics had not yet conceived of the will as we do and so did not see fate and free will as exclusive alternatives. That is, if we think away "our" notion of the will and accept Sophocles' idea of it, we will be able to see that Oedipus acted freely and was responsible for what happened even though the whole sequence of events is repeatedly said to be the work of the gods.'

> both in the common crises of our lives
> and face to face encounters with the gods.
> You freed us from the Sphinx, you came to Thebes
> and cut us loose from the bloody tribute we had paid
> that harsh, brutal singer. We taught you nothing,
> no skill, no extra knowledge, still you triumphed.
>   (*Oedipus the King*, 39–47)

This raised the problem of man's relation to the gods and specifically the issue of divine versus human knowledge. If god, the transcendental signifier that can confer meaning on our world and our existence cannot be trusted, then man's existence also lacks meaning, origin, or plan; the signs he clings to are as arbitrary and meaningless as they are consoling and reassuring. While praising Oedipus's capacities as a man, the chorus is careful to reserve higher knowledge to the gods. Jocasta, however, explicitly questions the value and truth of the oracles and does not shrink from accepting the possibility of a universe that is ruled by tyche, or chance: 'No skill in the world, nothing human can penetrate the future' (781–2), she asserts, and therefore man's fear of the future is absurd and nonsensical.

> Fear?
> What should a man fear? It's all chance,
> chance rules our lives. Not a man on earth
> can see a day ahead, groping through the dark.
> Better to live at random, best we can.
> And as for this marriage with your mother—
> have no fear. Many a man before you,
> in his dreams, has shared his mother's bed.
> Take such things for shadows, nothing at all—
> Live Oedipus,
> as if there's no tomorrow!
>   (*Oedipus the King*, 1069–78).

In proposing 'chance' as the force governing the order of the universe, Jocasta intimates the possibility of the existence of a different law, and a different truth, perhaps even a higher law and a higher truth, one that emanates not from conscious knowledge or reason but from unconscious impulses and the body. One can go further and suggest that Jocasta, and woman generally, is distrusted for intimating or understanding this higher truth and this higher law, and therefore her pronouncements need to be discredited and rejected: Jocasta, says Robert Fagles, 'thought there was no order in the design of the world . . . She was wrong; the design was there, and when she saw what it was, she hanged herself'.[25]

The chorus are also loath to countenance the possibility of a world ruled by chance. They repeatedly insist on the existence of immutable and eternal laws that lend a structure and meaning to the seeming randomness of life. The fulfilment of the

---

[25] Robert Fagles, Introduction in *The Three Theban Plays*, *supra*, at 153.

oracles in particular serves as a sign of gods' existence, omniscience, and omnipresence in men's lives.

> The skilled prophet scans the birds and shatters me with terror!
> I can't accept him, can't deny him, don't know what to say,
> I'm lost, and the wings of dark foreboding beating—
> I cannot see what's come, what's still to come . . .
> Zeus and Apollo know, they know, the great masters
> of all the dark and depth of human life
>
> (*Oedipus the King*, 550–62)

Conversely, the prospect that the prophecy may not be fulfilled fills the chorus with dread because it threatens society with chaos and meaninglessness. When Jocasta doubts the prophecy, the chorus pray that the prophecy be fulfilled and the divine governance of the world reaffirmed:

> Destiny find me always
> Destiny find me filled with reverence pure in word and deed
> Great laws tower above us, reared on high
> born for the brilliant vault of heaven—
> Olympian sky their only father,
> nothing mortal, no man gave them birth,
> their memory deathless, never lost in sleep:
> within them lives a mighty god, the god does not grow old.
>
> (*Oedipus the King*, 954–62)

> Never again will I go reverent to Delphi,
> the inviolate heart of Earth
> or Apollo's ancient oracle at Abae
> or Olympia of the fires—
> unless these prophesies all come true
> for all mankind to point toward in wonder.
>
> (*Oedipus the King*, 985–90)

As many commentators have argued, Sophocles also shrinks from espousing Jocasta's notion of a universe ruled by chance rather than a divine plan, and also from the sophists' celebration of man's ability to found a new order based on human rather than divine signs. The fulfilment of the prophecy represents the existence of a higher order and Oedipus's tragedy affirms the necessity for such an order, by denying man the power to be like the gods. The play's initial celebration of human reason and language is shown to be misplaced and the play asserts that man is ignorant and the gods are omniscient. It is said, further, that by recognizing the oracle's fulfilment and accepting his fate in the hands of the gods, Oedipus himself imposes order and closure on the play.[26] Oedipus, says Robert Fagles, is a man who tried to write his own story

---

[26] See, for example, Rebecca W. Bushnell, *Prophesying Tragedy: Sign and Voice in Sophocles' Theban Plays* (Ithaca, NY: Cornell University Press, 1988).

and avoid the fulfilment of the prophecy only to find that the prophecy was already fulfilled; 'The catastrophe of the tragic hero thus becomes the catastrophe of fifth century man . . . [man] is not the measure of all things but the thing measured and found wanting'.[27]

4 'MAN KNOW THYSELF'

In the face of this defeat, commentators have rushed to rescue Oedipus' nobility by celebrating a different virtue: Oedipus, it is said, is the embodiment of the human freedom to search, to *choose* to find out. As Dodds insists, 'what causes [Oedipus'] ruin is his own strength and courage, his loyalty to Thebes, and his loyalty to the truth. In all this we are to see him as a free agent . . . And his self-mutilation and self-banishment are equally free acts of choice'.[28] The play, after all, concentrates not on the oracle but on Oedipus' investigation and ultimate discovery that the oracle has been fulfilled. The cost of this knowledge is the suffering he undergoes, conferring on him a quality of heroism: 'nobody is capable of bearing this evil except me' (*Oedipus the King*, 1415).

The freedom to search belongs, of course, not to Oedipus but more relevantly to the critics who have rushed to celebrate Oedipus' quest as the culmination to Apollo's edict, 'Man, know thyself'. Hegel celebrated Oedipus as the embodiment of man's journey from east to west: Oedipus, like Adam, defies God's prohibition of eating from the tree of knowledge and challenges the gods on the right to speak the truth; such defiance signals the beginning of man's self-consciousness and freedom.[29] Oedipus is seen as a hero worthy of our respect and admiration because he has the courage to investigate and question the workings of divine prophecies. In assuming the power to define himself he manifests the beginnings of human freedom and responsibility in distinction to the gods.

Such celebration, however, is coupled with an awareness that absolute knowledge, of oneself or another, always eludes us and were we to have it, it would destroy us. Hölderlin warns of the perils of knowing too much, of 'having an eye too many'[30] and Heidegger describes how Oedipus can only bear the burden of knowing 'by putting

---

[27] Robert Fagles, 'Introduction' in *The Three Theban Plays, supra*, at 143.

[28] E. R. Dodds, 'On Misunderstanding the *Oedipus Rex*' in Harold Bloom (ed.), *Modern Critical Interpretations: Oedipus Rex, supra*, at 41.

[29] G. F. W. Hegel, *Phenomenology of Spirit*, trans. A. V. Miller (Oxford: Oxford University Press, 1977) [1807], but 'this knowing is, in principle, immediately a not knowing, because *consciousness*, in its action, is in its own self the antithesis. He who was able to solve the riddle of the Sphinx . . . [is] sent to destruction through what the god revealed to [him].' See further discussion in Rudnytsky, *Freud and Oedipus, supra*, at 51–74.

[30] *Poems and Fragments*, trans. Michael Hamburger (Cambridge: Cambridge University Press, 1980), at 603. See further discussion in Rudnytski, *Freud and Oedipus, supra*, at 121–30.

out his own eyes, i.e. by removing himself from all light'.[31] The urge for truth is therefore not a gift but a curse: 'It is as though the myth whispered to us that wisdom, and especially Dionysiac wisdom, is an unnatural crime, an abomination; and that whoever, in pride of knowledge, hurls nature into the abyss of destruction, must himself experience nature's disintegration'.[32] At best Oedipus teaches that the desire for self-knowledge can never be fulfilled as the 'self' under analysis is not static but a subject in process: 'to exist historically', as Gadamer puts it, 'means that knowledge of oneself can never be complete'.[33]

The same fascination with man's freedom to search and ultimately resolve seemingly intransingent riddles lies at the heart of detective fiction. Detective fiction celebrates, in the person of the ratiocinative investigator, the mind's ability to order reality and transform seeming chaos into order; normality and stability, briefly interrupted by the crime, are restored once the mystery is dissolved and the criminal punished. The guilt experienced by society at the presence of a corpse is attributed to a single individual, the criminal. In its focus on a crime, the investigation of the crime, and the identification of the criminal, *Oedipus* has been hailed as the first, and perhaps the best, detective story. The criminal who in the classic detective story is driven by a desire to repress knowledge of the crime and of his identity, in *Oedipus* is no other than the investigator driven by the reverse desire to find the criminal's identity and solve the mystery. Language is pivotal to the detective fiction in that the story does not end when we know who the criminal is but when the investigator gathers all the disparate clues together, reorders them and retells the story in a linear fashion to an awaiting audience. Throughout *Oedipus Rex*, however, language conceals rather than reveals the truth and in the end fails altogether: the discovery of parrincest, as Cynthia Chase puts it, is 'the unspeakable event . . . an unreadable palimpsest, the text that cannot be read out with a "single voice"'.[34]

However, is the injunction to know oneself a universal edict, or the preoccupation of only one half of humanity? Are we all, as Borges claims, Oedipus?[35] And are the answers such a search delivers universal or limited only to *man's* search? The view that the myth and tragedy of Oedipus reaffirm the basic polarities of human existence leaves such polarities intact, does little to question our ability to categorize life into such neat dichotomies, or aid our wish to reconcile them. If tragedy reveals the fragility of our social, legal, and moral structures, then the 'discovery' that such

---

[31] Martin Heidegger, *An Introduction to Metaphysics* trans. Ralph Manheim, (New Haven: Yale University Press, 1959) at 106–7. Again see further discussion in Rudnytski, *Freud and Oedipus, supra*, at 225–36.

[32] Nietzsche, *The Birth of Tragedy, supra*, at 61.

[33] Hans-Georg Gadamer, *Truth and Method*, trans. Garrett Barnett and John Cumming, (New York: Crossroad, 1982), at 269.

[34] 'Oedipal Textuality: Reading Freud's Reading of Oedipus' in Maud Ellman (ed.), *Psychoanalytic Literary Criticism, supra*, at 68.

[35] Jorge Luis Borges, 'Oedipus and the Riddle' in *Selected Poems 1923–1967*, (ed.) Norman Thomas di Giovanni, (London: Penguin, 1985), at 211: 'We are Oedipus; in some eternal way / We are the long and threefold beast as well—/ All that we will be, all that we have been. It would annihilate us all to see / The huge shape of our being; mercifully / God offers us issue and oblivion.'

structures contain irreconcilable oppositions leaves both the structures and the oppositions intact. Nor is the 'freedom to search' as disinterested and neutral an injunction
as it appears. To persist with the oppositions the myth interrogates, we may envisage
the discourses and interests that enacted, perpetuated, and purported to resolve these
oppositions.

5 HIDDEN ORIGINS: THE UNCONSCIOUS

In the manner of the detective, the analyst also gathers clues in an effort to discover
the repressed or hidden story behind a collection of disparate signs. It is no accident,
therefore, that psychoanalysis and detective fiction appeared at the same time in
Europe at the turn of the nineteenth century. It is Oedipus' determination to find out,
to solve the riddles of the Sphinx as well as of his origins that fascinated Freud. The
form of the drama, moving from repression to interpretation to revelation is as
important to him as the events themselves; the tragedy's unfolding, he writes, 'the
disclosure, approached step by step and artistically delayed, [is] comparable to the
work of psychoanalysis'.[36] Oedipus' self-interrogation and excavation of the past to
decode the present render him, like Freud, a self-analyst. As Cynthia Chase points out,
what Freud and Oedipus (what all of us?) share, is not, or not only, the drive to
commit parrincest, but the drive to self-scrutiny, interpretation, and resolution of a
seemingly intransigent enigma.[37]

For Freud, Descartes' confidence in the subject's ability to know, celebrated by
many critics in the person of Oedipus, ignores the effect unconscious processes and
the divorce between language and reality have on the subject's supposed unity, autonomy, and self-knowledge. Oblivious to such pitfalls, Oedipus claims the ability to
know but his tragic collapse reminds us that such knowledge is hidden from ourselves.
Where Hegel's Oedipus represented man's self-consciousness, Freud's Oedipus is the
representative of the unconscious. And in contrast to Hegel's teleological progression
into the future, Freud's quest is an archaeological excavation of the past:[38]

If the *Oedipus Rex* is capable of moving a modern reader or playgoer no less powerfully than
it moved the contemporary Greeks, the only possible explanation is that the effect of the
Greek tragedy does not depend upon the conflict between fate and human will, but upon the
peculiar nature of the material by which this conflict is revealed. There must be a voice
within us which is prepared to acknowledge the compelling power of fate in the *Oedipus* . . .
His fate moves us only because it might have been our own, because the oracle laid upon us

---

[36] *The Interpretation of Dreams* in *The Major Works of Sigmund Freud* (Chicago: Chicago University Press,
1952), at 246.

[37] Cynthia Chase, 'Oedipal Textuality: Reading Freud's Reading of *Oedipus*' in Maud Ellman (ed.), *Psychoanalytic Literary Criticism, supra*, at 57.

[38] Paul Ricoeur, *Freud and Philosophy: An Essay on Interpretation* (New Haven: Yale University Press, 1970),
at 461.

before our birth the very curse which rested upon him. It may be that we were all destined to direct our first sexual impulses toward our mother and our first impulses of hatred and violence toward our fathers; our dreams convince us that we were. King Oedipus, who slew his father Laius and wedded his mother Jocasta, is nothing more or less than a wish-fulfilment—the fulfilment of the wish of our childhood. But we, more fortunate than he, in so far as we have not become psychoneurotics, have since our childhood succeeded in withdrawing our sexual impulses from our mothers, and in forgetting our jealousy of our fathers. We recoil from the person in whom this primitive wish of our childhood has been fulfilled with all the force of the repression which these wishes have undergone in our minds since childhood'.[39]

In Freud's reading of this detective story, guilt is not dissolved by the attribution of the crime to one person, as in detective fiction, or as in Girard's account of the function of sacrifice, but universalized: nobody can escape blame for the crime of parrincest. The child's imaginary plenitude with and desire for the mother is severed during the Oedipal crisis by the intervention of the father threatening castration and the introduction of the universal taboo against incest. As in all father-son confrontations, the confrontation between Laius and Oedipus is along the lines 'I was here first';[40] although Oedipus defeats his rival, victory leads to guilt and to the formation of conscience, in Freud's term, the ego. Through the Oedipus complex, social structures are incorporated into the individual's consciousness and the subject learns to modify and control its desire in ways that are compatible with the social code. As the child internalizes and submits to the father's prohibition, it turns from the pleasure to the reality principle.

The prohibition of incest therefore forms an indissoluble link between desire and law with the Oedipus complex marking the beginning of morality, conscience, religion, and law. It signals the child's passage from the world of nature to the world of law and culture, and as I argue further later, from the mother to the father. This law is not founded on or sustained by some transcendental source (as natural lawyers would have it) or on rational authority (as social contractarians claim), but on desire. The fact that the subject has internalized such prohibitions facilitates policing and reduces opportunities for radical change. It is in the human psyche, therefore, that we must look if any meaningful and lasting social reforms are to be achieved.

We have come a long way from interpretations of *Oedipus* as the opposition between divine knowledge and human ignorance. For Freud, such ignorance does not arise from human limitations and divine omniscience; what is hidden from us does not reside with incomprehensible deities but in ourselves. In that sense, the will of the gods and the oracle are but 'glorified disguises of [Oedipus'] own unconscious'.[41]

---

[39] *The Interpretation of Dreams* in *The Major Works of Sigmund Freud, supra*, at 246–7.
[40] Peter L. Rudnytsky, *Freud and Oedipus, supra*, at 34.
[41] Freud, *A General Introduction to Psychoanalysis*, in *The Major Works of Sigmund Freud, supra*, at 582.

6 THE UNCONSCIOUS BECOMES THE LAW: THE LAW OF THE PHALLUS

The law instituted by the Oedipus complex is not a neutral law but unashamedly patriarchal: it is the father in the Oedipal structure who issues prohibitions and gives rise to social codes, while the super-ego polices the subject's repressed desires in accordance with the expectations of patriarchal culture. Freud's view that the little girl wants a penis takes male sexuality as the norm against which women are measured and found lacking; by confining women's sexual organs to the clitoris and measuring it against the male organ, he declares her deficient, wanting, already castrated. For Luce Irigaray the view that female desire springs from lack, absence, and envy of the male is itself a male defence against the overwhelming power of the mother. It also ignores that the little girl does not have only one organ but several. Do not little boys experience lack on realizing that they have no breasts or a womb? If little boys perceive a body without a penis as lacking, do not little girls regard the male body as lacking, if not, at times ridiculous?[42] And is not the birth of a child, supposedly, in Freud's terms, a substitute for women's lack of a penis, perhaps a replacement for men's lack of breasts and a womb? Freud's concept of female sexuality, Irigaray concludes, reflects what Freud wanted to see, woman as absence or hole serving as a mirror to reflect masculine fullness and appeasing male fears of castration.[43] For Melanie Klein it is not penis-envy but breast-envy[44] which describes sexual difference while for Karen Horney the decisive factor is men's womb-envy.[45] Furthermore, both Freud's and Lacan's account of gender are based on what can be seen rather than touched, tasted, or heard: a voyeur's theory, as Cixous calls it.[46]

For Irigaray it is not the little girl that fantasizes of seducing her father but the

---

[42] See, for example, Sylvia Plath, *The Bell Jar* (London: Faber and Faber, 1966), at 72: 'Then he just stood there in front of me and I kept on staring at him. The only thing I could think of was turkey neck and turkey gizzards and I felt very depressed.'

[43] These points are discussed in two of her major works: *Speculum of the Other Woman*, (Ithaca, New York, Cornell University Press, 1985), trans. Gillian C. Gill; and *This Sex Which Is Not One*, trans. Catherine Porter with Carolyn Burke (Ithaca, New York: Cornell University Press, 1985). Underlying her work is the view that 'Female sexuality has always been conceptualized on the basis of masculine parameters': *This Sex Which is Not One* at 23 and 'Psychoanalytic discourse on female sexuality is the discourse of truth. A discourse that tells the truth about the logic of truth: namely that *the feminine occurs only within models and laws devised by male subjects*': *This Sex Which is Not One*, at 86.

[44] In Maria Torok's phrase, Melanie Klein founds a 'religion of the Breast to replace Freud's religion of the Phallus' 'Melanie Mell by Herself' in John Phillips and Lyndsey Stonebridge (eds.), *Reading Melanie Klein* (London and New York: Routledge, 1998), at 57.

[45] Karen Horney, *Feminine Psychology* (London: Routledge, 1967).

[46] In contrast, Cixous says, 'the genesis of woman goes through the mouth': 'Extreme Fidelity' in Susan Sellers, (ed.), *The Hélène Cixous Reader* (London and New York: Routledge, 1994), at 133. See also Luce Irigaray: 'The sense which could invert things is basically *touch*, our body as tactile tool for apprehending and manipulating the world, ourselves, the other.' in Margaret Whitford (ed.), *The Irigaray Reader* (Oxford: Blackwell, 1991), at 141.

father who fantasizes of seducing his daughter and, refusing to recognize or realize his desire, legislates to defend himself from his desire for the daughter. The conception of law as arising from the child's Oedipal complex therefore misrepresents both the origin of law and the nature of human subjectivity. In short, contrary to Freud's dictum that 'anatomy is destiny', 'Anatomy is not really destiny. Destiny is what men make of anatomy'.[47]

While Freud's representation of sexuality is reductionist of both male and female sexuality, in practice men's abandonment of the pleasure principle and submission to the social law also makes them masters of that law. Freud was aware that paternal, unlike maternal, power is linguistic rather than corporeal; patriarchy, he says in *Moses and Monotheism*, represents the triumph of west over east, of intellectualism over faith and of the word over flesh. Invoking Aeschylus' *Oresteia* he argues that the 'advance' from matriarchy to patriarchy represents 'an advance in civilization, since maternity is proved by the evidence of the senses while paternity is a hypothesis based on an inference and a premise'.[48] Paternity is conferred instead by a law which marks the child as the property of the father, while the process of naming and baptism, introduce the child into the institution and compensate for the uncertainty of paternity. The father's authority, however, is never full or inviolable: in particular, women can subvert this law and the patriarchal structure it supports by being unfaithful.[49]

In *Totem and Taboo* Freud creates his own myth for the origins of law and culture in a fictional account of 'a memorable and criminal deed, which was the beginning of so many things—of social organization, of moral restrictions and of religion'.[50] The criminal deed is the sons' murder of the tribal patriarch who had monopolized the women of the horde. Being cannibals, 'it goes without saying', Freud continues, that they not only killed but devoured him in a totem meal that represents their complete identification with him. The father's murder however, leads to feelings of remorse, which in turn induce them to establish laws forbidding incest and murder.[51] The incest taboo therefore arises as a cultural rather than a natural law. The question left unresolved, however, is what gave rise to the feelings of guilt *before* the law? As Elizabeth Grosz points out, this so-called 'primal myth' does not explain patriarchy but presupposes it: if the father already has control of all the women and the sons are dominated by him, patriarchy must already exist.[52] The father's preeminent position

---

[47] Robert Stoller, in *Nouvelle revue de psychoanalyse* (Paris, 1973), No. 7, quoted by Christiane Olivier, *Jocasta's Children: The Imprint of the Mother* (London and New York: Routledge, 1989), at 53.

[48] *The Standard Edition of the Complete Psychological Works of Sigmund Freud*, Vol. 23, (ed.) James Strachey, (London: Hogarth Press, 1953–74), at 114.

[49] See, for example, Helga Geyer-Ryan, 'Adultery as Critique' in Helga Geyer-Ryan, *Fables of Desire* (Cambridge: Polity Press, 1994).

[50] *The Standard Edition of the Complete Psychological Works of Sigmund Freud, supra*, Vol. 13, at 203; see discussion in Costas Douzinas, *The End of Human Rights* (London: Hart, 2000), chapter 11.

[51] As Lacan elaborates, 'if this murder [of the father] is the fruitful moment of the debt through which the subject binds himself for life to the Law, the symbolic father is, in so far as he signifies this Law, the dead father': Jacques Lacan, *Écrits: A Selection*, trans. Alan Sheridan (London: Routledge, 1977), at 199.

[52] Elizabeth Grosz, *Jacques Lacan: A Feminist Introduction* (London and New York: Routledge, 1990), at 69.

can therefore only be explained by an earlier event which supplanted the immediacy of the child's umbilical connection with the mother with that of the father and that event, as Irigaray argues, was a matricide: matricide supplants the mother's authority with that of the father, and is a founding step towards the institution of the legal system. The myth of the *Oresteia* in the next chapter examines how the father's name and the institution of law were founded on this murder foreclosing 'this first body, this first home, this first love'.[53]

Juliet Mitchell's defence that '[h]owever it may have been used, psychoanalysis is not a recommendation *for* a patriarchal society but an analysis *of* one'[54] reminds feminists of the insights Freud's theory offers for understanding and challenging the hidden processes whereby patriarchal culture is internalized and reproduced in the subject and in society. This debt acknowledged, however, feminists must move beyond a theory that grounds women's marginalization on dubious anatomical measurements. To recognize further that Freud's interpretation of the Oedipus myth makes it a tale about boys' guilt and boys' anxiety may enable feminists to move beyond Oedipus to laws that are not governed by the phallus.

7 HIDDEN STRUCTURES: THE LAWS OF KINSHIP

If dread of the unknown, past, present, or future, motivates our desire to understand and thereby control our world, structuralism, perhaps more than any other school of literary criticism aims to deliver some answers and some reassurance. Assuming that a hidden order underlies our varied existences and experiences, they aim to uncover this order by decoding the structures allegedly lying beneath the surface. Where many see chaos, contradictions, and meaninglessness, structuralists hope to deliver the basic structures underlying our ways of thinking and being, in law, literature, and beyond. However, it is not at all obvious that such underlying structures exist, let alone that they are discoverable by us. The danger, moreover, is that the search will deliver 'truths' or 'meanings' that the researcher was already looking for, while suppressing or ignoring other structures, truths, and meanings.

As Charles Segal notes, to focus attention on structure rather than on the individual hero is at odds with the dominant tradition of Greek literary criticism.[55] But, he continues, the traditional approach rests on the assumption of an integrated personality, an assumption that is itself open to debate: tragedy in particular interrogates the concept of the self as well as its ability to exploit language to express and achieve its purposes. Structuralism denies that myth needs to have a message or meaning to

---

[53] 'The Bodily Encounter With the Mother' in Margaret Whitford (ed.), *The Irigaray Reader*, (Oxford: Blackwell, 1991), at 39.

[54] Juliet Mitchell, *Psychoanalysis and Feminism* (London: Allen Lane, 1974), at xv.

[55] Charles Segal, *Tragedy and Civilization*, *supra*, at 41.

convey: in contrast to the philosophers' logic of non-contradiction, myth brings into operation 'a logic of the ambiguous, the equivocal . . . not the binary logic of yes or no but a logic different from that of the logos'.[56] The function of the mythologist is not to understand the myth but to decode it, 'to show, not how men think in myths, but how myths operate in men's minds without their being aware of the fact'.[57]

For Lévi-Strauss, the most important factor in the passage from nature to culture, and from beast to man, are the structures regulating the combinations in human mating. Following Ferdinand de Saussure's method of unravelling the structures of language, he argues that kinship laws correspond to linguistic laws, aiding communication between individuals and groups. The most fundamental amongst such laws, common to all societies and marking the conquest of nature by culture, is the prohibition of incest. This prohibition leads to the creation of ties between unrelated groups, specifically groups of men: for women do not take part in such negotiations and function only as objects of exchange: 'We know what function is fulfilled by the incest prohibition in primitive societies. By casting, so to speak, the sisters and daughters out of the consanguine group, and by assigning to them husbands coming from other groups, the prohibition creates bonds of alliance between these natural groups, the first ones which can be called social. The incest prohibition is thus the basis of human society: in a sense it *is* the society.'[58]

What if the prohibition of incest, however, is Lévi-Strauss's own myth, a myth that, like Freud's penis-envy, has come to be presented as the natural and inevitable way culture came about? For post-structuralist critics, Lévi-Strauss' belief in and attempt to find a hidden Truth and a master meaning, is the ultimate delusion, trapped in logocentrism and the metaphysics of presence. This arch-meaning is not only illusory but dangerous when it is used to exclude or suppress alternative meanings and alternative cultural arrangements. In particular Lévi-Strauss's emphasis on the creation of homosocial bonds, necessitating the law against incest, takes for granted that society is founded on heterosexuality and suppresses the homosexual element of human sexuality. As Monique Wittig argues, 'the straight mind' continues to insist that incest, rather than homosexuality is the ultimate taboo.[59] Not only structuralists' but male psychoanalysts' emphasis on the Oedipal conflict presupposes that heterosexuality is the only possible mode of attachment to another human being. The incest taboo therefore presupposes a prior taboo, the taboo on homosexuality.[60] By privileging the creation of homosocial bonds, it further assigns women to the status of objects in exchanges made between men: just as in language systems words are circulated to

---

[56] Vernant, *Myth and Society in Ancient Greece, supra*, at 260.

[57] Claude Lévi-Strauss, *The Raw and The Cooked*, trans. John and Doreen Weightman (New York: Harper & Row, 1969), at 12.

[58] *Structural Anthropology, supra*, at 19.

[59] Monique Wittig, *The Straight Mind and Other Essays* (Hemel Hempstead: Harvester Wheatsheaf, 1992).

[60] See Gail Rubin, 'Traffic in Women: notes on the "political economy" of sex' in R. Reiter (ed.), *Toward an Anthropology of Women* (New York: Monthly Review Press, 1975) and Judith Butler, 'Melancholy gender— refused identification' *Psychoanalytic Dialogues*, Vol. 5(2) 1999, at 165–80.

enable dialogue between the speakers, in kinship systems the object of circulation is women: exchange 'provides the means of binding men together, and of superimposing upon the natural links of kinship the henceforth artificial links of alliance governed by rule . . . The law of exogamy applies to valuables—viz. Women—valuables *par excellence* from both the biological and the social point of view, without which life is impossible'.[61]

As Carole Pateman argues, the notion of the contract in general and the fiction of the social contract created by liberal theory in particular are in fact patriarchal constructs. The citizen in such exchanges is always male and women can only enter if they become men. In such contracts women's relationships with each other are not acknowledged with the result that, in a male economy, women are forced to play the role of rivals.[62] For Hélène Cixous the insistence on contractual exchanges and proper returns reflects a masculine obsession with proprietorship, an obsession that arises from man's fear of castration. Woman, she suggests, not suffering from castration anxiety, or a fear of ex-propriation, belongs to a different economy, that of the gift: 'if there is a self proper to woman, paradoxically it is her capacity to depropriate herself without self-interest: endless body, without "end"'.[63]

Irigaray goes further to envisage other social arrangements where the exchange of women does not form the basis of civilization. What would happen she asks, if women refused to enter the male economy as objects but insisted on entering as subjects? What if they created an alternative economy of their own, laying down their own rules and their own prices? Such a step does not mean rejecting the market but only taking part as retailers rather than as commodities. It does not consist in resolving her alleged desire for the father but in realizing her own desires which are independent from those of both her father and her lovers. For such new exchanges to take place, woman must attain her own identity distinct from her status as both mother and as man's double. It involves acknowledging women's difference from men, cultivating her relationships with other women starting with her mother, and rediscovering her own genealogies, laws, and myths. It involves acknowledging above all, 'the difference inscribed in nature and subjectivity: sexual difference'.[64]

---

[61] *The Elementary Structures of Kinship*, (Boston: Beacon Press, 1969), trans. James Harle Bell, John Richard von Sturmer and Rodney Needham, at 480–81.

[62] Carole Pateman, *The Sexual Contract*, (Cambridge: Cambridge University Press, 1988).

[63] 'Sorties: Out and Out: Attacks / Ways Out / Forays' in Hélène Cixous and Catherine Clément, *The Newly Born Woman* (I. B. Tauris: London, 1996), at 87.

[64] Luce Irigaray, *i love to you: Sketch of a Possible Felicity in History*, (New York and London: Routledge, 1996), trans. Alison Martin, at 45–7.

8 THE ORACLE BECOMES THE NAME:
THE NAME OF THE FATHER

Lacan draws on Lévi-Strauss's work on kinship structures to argue that the law against incest, superimposing the order of culture over the order of nature, is identical with the order of language. However, in contrast to Lévi-Strauss's hope to find a master meaning and a universal human nature behind the myths, Lacan denies the notion of a real or true identity in the first place. For Lacan the human subject is constructed in and through language, moreover a language that we do not possess but which possesses us.

Following Hegel, Lacan asserts that the self can only grasp itself through its reflection in and recognition by another person: 'the first object of desire is to be recognized by the other'.[65] The subject's sense of plenitude and imaginary unity with the mother is disturbed through its introduction to language during the mirror phase. The child's recognition of itself in the mirror marks the moment of alienation and division as the foreignness, emptiness, and arbitrariness of language mean that rather than experiencing plenitude the subject experiences a deep split, lack, and loss: 'the moment in which desire becomes human is also that in which the child is born into language'.[66] The inescapable gap between reality and language means that our experience of the world and our becoming subjects is an unending process and consists of a series of alienations.

On coming to recognize the impossibility of regaining its lost unity, the infant enters the symbolic order, an order of law and culture where the subject's position is already determined for, rather than by, him. The main centre of otherness and the instrument for the subject's introduction to the world of culture is the father who intervenes to break the subject's imaginary unity with the mother by prohibiting incest and threatening castration. The child recognizes that it cannot be its mother's lover but must subscribe to the social code, what Lacan calls the Law of the Father, symbolized by the phallus. The child emerges from the imaginary phase and becomes fully socialized by driving its desire for the mother into the unconscious. This subject, however, is far from the Cartesian autonomous, stable, and unified individual in control of its words and actions; instead it is unfixed, unsatisfied, contradictory, and perpetually in process. This divided subject, unable to regain the plenitude of the pre-Oedipal phase, is nonetheless condemned to an indefinite and impossible search for unity which is the very condition of desire. It seeks to find this in the recognition of another person; the other, however, is also hopelessly divided, and cannot respond unconditionally or forever. The search dooms the subject into an interminable relocation to words while the other remains unknowable and unreachable.

Language pre-exists the human subject who accedes to it when first learning to

---

[65] *Écrits: A Selection, supra*, at 58.
[66] *Ibid.*, at 103.

speak and assenting to its assigned name. In assenting to our name we also learn to differentiate ourselves from other named subjects, in particular those we are related to as daughter, son, sister, brother, niece, etcetera. For Lacan the laws of kinship and in particular the incest taboo are inextricable from the laws of language as incest is only possible once we recognize our assigned name: 'For without kinship nominations, no power is capable of instituting the order of preferences and taboos that bind and weave the yarn of lineage through succeeding generations'.[67] Oedipus only recognizes his crime when he is 'named' as Jocasta's 'son' in addition to his name as Jocasta's 'husband'; when he is named as Antigone's 'brother' in addition to his name as Antigone's 'father'; when he is named as Creon's 'nephew' in addition to his name as Creon's 'brother-in-law'. This inter-penetration of identities that society prefers to keep distinct leads to Oedipus' tragedy: 'What overwhelms Oedipus', as Edward Said puts it, 'is the burden of plural identities incapable of co-existing within one person'.[68]

If in Lévi-Strauss's schema the incest taboo is essential for separating culture from savagery, civilization from chaos, and human beings from animals, Lacan reminds us that the designation of names is intrinsic to this differentiation because without the names accorded by the rules of kinship human beings, like animals, would not be certain who their kin are and therefore who they can mate with as opposed to who they should refrain from mating with. The need for myths, laws, and names to help regulate social relationships and to designate identity arises, as Tom McCall summarizes, because blood is too 'inconspicuous and fragile' a means of conferring a sense of origin, continuity, and authority. The laws of human mating, particularly the law against incest, and the names following such laws ('father', 'mother', 'daughter', 'son') are not natural, obvious, or inevitable but ad hoc constructions superimposed on material bodies. Such signifiers, as Saussure showed, are arbitrary and unstable, hence the need for strong myths to keep them alive. Oedipus is one such myth, used to validate what constitutes a family in the western world. At the same time, however, the same myth, as told in Sophocles' tragedy, through the juxtaposition of extremes, opens the gap between cultural signifiers and material signifieds, reminding us of the artificial nature of family names and kinship laws.[69]

In a Lacanian reading of *Oedipus the King*, Pietro Pucci describes how Oedipus symbolizes man's search for a secure foundation and definition of himself in the Father, who stands for order, origin, and law, and away from the Mother who stands for false appearances, chaos, and chance.[70] The name of the father compensates for the father's absence from the birth by introducing an arbitrary signifier to replace the material presence of the mother. Parrincest is necessary to found the discourse of the father: 'transgression carves the father's presence in his real absence'.[71] The child's

---

[67] *Écrits: a Selection, supra*, at 66.

[68] Edward W. Said, *Beginnings: Intention and Method* (New York: Basic Books, 1975), at 170.

[69] Tom McCall, 'Oedipus Contemporaneous' 25 *Diacritics* 3–19 (Winter, 1995).

[70] Pietro Pucci, *Oedipus and the Fabrication of the Father* (Baltimore and London: Johns Hopkins University Press, 1992).

[71] *ibid.*, at 133.

connection with the mother's body is denied with the imposition of the father's name and the father's law; while the father's name is reinforced, the mother's name is denied or erased.

At the end of the play Oedipus has learned his own name and the father's law and has accepted his guilt in committing parrincest; names and laws, however, are arbitrary signifiers, and are not sufficient to endow him with a secure definition of himself or satisfy his desire: naming, a *word*, as Tom Mcall elaborates, cannot bring to presence the lost *body*. At the end of the play, there is still a lack of differentiation between Oedipus and his sons/brothers, daughters/sisters. The reader's parallel desire to grasp at reassuring terms such as 'the Father', 'telos', 'recognition', 'heroic endurance', 'self-knowledge', 'law' are themselves wishful responses to the uncertainty of identity. The law itself is created in response to an act that has already occurred and is retrospectively labelled unlawful: far from clarifying or creating order the law therefore betrays its own contingency, uncertainty, and arbitrariness.

9 WHAT'S IN A NAME?

Naming, Jeanette Winterson reminds us, is a difficult and time-consuming business; it concerns essences and it means power: 'Adam named the animals and they came at his call.'[72] There is no doubt that amongst these arbitrary signifiers the term father has achieved special status: the Father figure is the signifier of signifiers, the transcendental sign and origin of truth. The son's desire for a sense of origin, truth, and law leads to the search for his Father with the final revelation resolving the crisis of authority and affirming the father's name and the father's law. Oedipus' search leads to the father as the source of origin and law, rejecting Jocasta's advice to live at random, and thus making the son the father of the man.[73] The father's law therefore, depends not on blood, but on the act of naming. And there is no more powerful system of naming than that of the law. With the incest taboo—the law of laws—instituted, the law of the father may take effect.

The symbolic order Lacan describes is therefore not a neutral order but one structured around the transcendental signifier of the phallus and dominated by the law of the father. Where Saussure had drawn attention to the arbitrary relation between signifiers and signifieds, for Lacan the phallus provides the crucial link between the two, so that power, language, and law are identified with the phallus. Furthermore, since the Law of the Father, in this schema, is identical with the symbolic order, and the language of the father structures reality, patriarchy appears to be the inevitable cultural condition. Although Lacan insists that the phallus does not refer to the physical organ, the penis, but is a metaphor or signifier of our desire for wholeness,

---

[72] Jeanette Winterson, *Oranges Are Not the Only Fruit*, (London: Vintage, 1991), at 138.
[73] Pietro Pucci, *Oedipus and the Fabrication of the Father, supra*, at 63.

feminists need to insist that such restrictions in the realm of language can restrict women's opportunities of affirming a different language, a different law, and a different culture.

By eschewing Freudian biologistic assumptions and rereading Freud in terms of language, Lacan helped show that gender identity is not given in nature but is a product of specific cultural arrangements: 'I may be permitted a laugh', Lacan concludes, 'if these remarks are accused of turning the meaning of Freud's work away from the biological basis he would have wished for it toward the cultural references with which it is shot through'.[74] Lacan's laughter enables us to examine the mechanisms of patriarchal power in terms that are both personal (the Oedipal conflict) and public (language and law). However, to construe subjectivity, language, and law in terms of the phallus can also result in confining women within patriarchal discourse by fixing the debate around the phallus as the guarantor of meaning, subjectivity, and law. As Irigaray argues, the reliance on the phallus as a symbolic law and as the guarantor of meaning is the result of patriarchal culture and specifically patriarchy's attempt to efface the power of, and the debt owed to, the mother.

Lacan's view that woman, marked by lack and loss, stands outside language also comes close to denying her a language of her own. Instead of celebrating the symbolic order, Kristeva unearths an alternative language in the imaginary order. Whereas for Lacan entry to the symbolic implies a radical break with the imaginary order,[75] for Kristeva the semiotic continues to exert its influence on the subject, disrupting and subverting the symbolic order through tonal rhythms, slips, discontinuities, and silences.[76] The instability and polysemic nature of signs in the symbolic order, including the sign of the phallus, means that they are never immune from contestation and change. Since the effect of naming is retroactive, constituting, rather than labelling, a pre-existing subject, the activity of naming can be re-opened, re-performed, or, what official society fears most, allowed to float. For to allow names to be reopened, to go back to a time before signification, before naming, would be to admit that, as Angela Carter put it, 'a mother is always a mother since a mother is a biological fact, but a father is a moveable feast'.[77]

---

[74] *Écrits: a Selection, supra*, at 106.

[75] 'A brief aside—when one is made into two, there is no going back on it. It can never revert to making one again, not even a new one': Juliet Mitchell and Jacqueline Rose (eds.), *Feminine Sexuality: Jacques Lacan and the École Freudienne* (London: Macmillan, 1982), trans. Jacqueline Rose, at 156.

[76] 'Not only is symbolic, thetic unity divided (into signifier and signified), but this division is itself the result of a break that put a heteregenous functioning in the position of signifier. This functioning is the instinctual semiotic, preceding meaning and signification, mobile, amorphous . . . In the speaking subject, fantasies articulate this irruption of drives within the realm of the signifier; they disrupt the signifier and shift the metonymy of desire . . . fantasies remind us, if we had ever forgotten, of the insistent presence of drive heterogeinity.': Julia Kristeva, *Revolution in Poetic Language* (New York: Columbia University Press, 1984), trans. Margaret Waller, at 49.

[77] Angela Carter, *Wise Children* (London: Vintage, 1992), at 216.

10 FATHERS AND SONS

Oedipus' journey is akin, as Vladimir Propp has analysed, to the fairy-tale motif where a courageous and determined hero leaves home in search of adventure and is rewarded with money, power, a new home, and invariably a wife. Oedipus' story, however, represents a 'turning point' in the folktale scheme: his journey leads him not to a new home but back to his own home, not away from conflict with his father but to a renewed confrontation with the father who tried to kill him, and not to a new wife but to his father's wife. Rather than a linear progression, leading to knowledge of the world, his journey has been circular, leading back to himself.[78]

In Freud's analysis also, the 'resolution' of the Oedipus complex takes the form of the son *identifying* with the father who prohibits incest; the son kills the father in an acknowledgment of the father's authority and therefore parricide affirms rather than destroys that authority.[79] This leaves the field open for future antagonisms between future fathers and sons; the alleged resolution, marking the son's accession to the realm of the law, is therefore only the beginning of another journey for another son which gets repeated with each generation.

In Sophocles' tale Oedipus' journey does not end at Thebes; the end of *Oedipus the King* hints instead at the beginning of a new journey which takes place at Colonus. Unlike Freud, who declares the analysis closed at Thebes, Lacan pursues Oedipus beyond Thebes and argues that the Oedipus complex is not resolved at the end of *Oedipus the King* but in *Oedipus at Colonus* where Oedipus retells the story of his origins in his own words: 'the psychoanalysis of Oedipus is only complete at Colonus, when he tears his face apart. That is the essential moment, which gives his story its meaning.'[80] Oedipus' compulsion to repeat the traumatic events that led to his self-exile, hint at the possibility that language and narration are not only instruments of ambiguity, distortion, and concealment but can lead to understanding, disclosure, and healing. As in the psychoanalytic scenario, the ability to retell one's own story in language evokes the hope of some, albeit temporary and limited, cure. As when recounting a dream, the patient (Oedipus), says what he knows but also more than he knows, the words he chooses evoking more meanings than he himself glimpses. Theseus, like the analyst, urges Oedipus to 'Tell me all. Your story, your fortunes' (*Oedipus at Colonus*, 630) and like the analyst, becomes the 'recipient' of the symptom he diagnoses; the language Oedipus uses to recount his suffering, with all its limits, is the connecting instrument between the two and, for Lacan, 'the royal road to the

---

[78] Vladimir Propp, 'Oedipus in the Light of Folk-Tale' in Lowell Edmunds and Alan Dundas (eds.), *Oedipus, a Folk Lore Case-Book* (New York and London: Garland Press, 1984).

[79] See Mikkel Borch-Jacobsen, 'The Oedipus Problem in Freud and Lacan' *Critical Inquiry*, 20 (Winter, 1994), 267–82.

[80] Jacques Lacan, *The Seminar of Jacques Lacan: Book II; The Ego in Freud's Theory and in the Technique of Psychoanalysis 1954–1955*, (ed.) Jacques-Alain Miller, trans. Sylvana Tomarelli (New York and London: W. W. Norton, 1991) [1978], at 214.

unconscious'.[81] Through retelling Oedipus experiences self-exile for the first time and becomes foreign or 'other' to himself; the end of Oedipus' analysis takes place at the moment when he 'awaits—and indeed *assumes*—his death'.[82]

As Laura Mulvey points out, the fact that this retelling takes place in the presence of Theseus, the legendary founder of the Athenian state and its legal system, reinforces the Lacanian view that the Oedipus complex is resolved around the Name of the Father, the Law, and the symbolic order.[83] *Oedipus at Colonus* affirms this law by allowing Oedipus to repeat and close his narrative: the person who at the end of *Oedipus the King* was 'the worst of men' (*Oedipus the King*, 1568), becomes at Colonus 'someone sacred, someone filled with piety and power' (*Oedipus at Colonus*, 300). The 'truth' that Oedipus finds at the end of *Oedipus the King* is therefore not final but requires revision and retelling in *Oedipus at Colonus*. Sophocles' and Oedipus' retelling of the story suggests that truth needs to be constantly revised and presence, or meaning, cannot be located in language but is found only with death.

Oedipus, however, does more than retell his tragic past and accept his impending death: in line with his own father's attempt to kill him, Oedipus pronounces a thundering curse on his two warring sons:

> *You* Die!
>   Die and be damned!
>   I spit on you! Out!—
> your father cuts you off! Corruption-scum of the earth!—
> out!—and pack these curses I call down upon your head:
> never to win your mother-country with your spear,
> never return to Argos ringed with hills—
>   Die!
> Die by your own blood brother's hand—die!—
> killing the very man who drove you out!
> So I curse your life out!
>   (*Oedipus at Colonus*, 1567–1574)

Perhaps, as John Irwin suggests, Theseus' affinity with Theseus arises from Theseus' own 'accidental' killing of his father when neglecting to change the colour of the sails on his return from Crete after slaying the Minotaur. Oedipus curses his sons as Theseus will later curse his son Hippolitus, because, having recognized his own desire for the mother, he assumes that their sons will harbour the same desire for their wives. The myth therefore may be less about the desire for the mother than about the antagonism between father and son. Indeed, as Cynthia Chase points out, Oedipus is the one person in history *without* an Oedipus complex: 'the one person who actually

---

[81] Juan David Nasio, *Five Lessons on the Psychoanalytic Theory of Jacques Lacan* (Albany, NY: State University of New York Press, 1998), at 17 and 48.

[82] Shoshana Felman, 'Beyond Oedipus: The Specimen Story of Psychoanalysis' in Maud Ellman, (ed.), *Psychoanalytic Literary Criticism, supra* at 91.

[83] Laura Mulvey, 'The Oedipus Myth: Beyond the Riddles of the Sphinx' in James Donald (ed.), *Thresholds: Psychoanalysis and Cultural Theory* (London: Macmillan, 1991), at 41.

enacts parricide and incest completely misses the experience—until after the fact, when the parrincest is inscribed as a palimpsest and becomes readable for the first time'.[84] What is therefore the 'voice within us ready to recognize the compelling force of destiny' that Freud insisted we all hear? Perhaps the voice speaks less of the return to the mother but of the son's successful overthrow of the father's authority. That this return is couched in terms of destiny, accident, or chance, means that that authority is not discredited in the process of being overthrown and can be assumed by Oedipus intact.[85] The role of the mother or Queen in this rivalry is perhaps, as in a game of chess, of assisting the son in his fight to immobilize the King. As the antagonism between father and son cannot be eliminated by the simple assignation of kinship names and persists in subsequent generations, patriarchy's attempt to end conflict through legal rules and institutions is not successful. The antagonism persists amongst the analysts as much as the analysands: if Freud attempts to mimic Oedipus' solving the riddle of the Sphinx by solving the riddle of dreams and turns Sophocles' 'tragedy of truth' into a 'tragedy of sex',[86] Lacan repeats the parricide with his so-called 'return to Freud', the father of psychoanalysis. The tragedy of Oedipus is therefore repeated with each generation, perhaps explaining male critics' insatiable capacity to reread and rewrite it.

11 MOTHERS AND SONS

Naming, language, law, and culture have intervened to give us the illusion of knowledge. Such language, law, and culture, however, are no more neutral, natural, or self-evident than the knowledge they purport to confer. In the case of interpretations of *Oedipus* by Freud, Lévi-Strauss and Lacan, such knowledge has been unashamedly patriarchal, devising laws and models that allegedly pertain to humanity in general. In the process they create new myths of their own, purporting to *find* what they were already looking for, and their findings take the status of laws. The name of the father is one such legal fiction, instituting the father as the transcendental signifier and source of desire and law. Oedipus the mythical figure becomes the moral voice warning against crimes against the father.[87] Lacan's insistence that the phallus stands as the transcendental signifier guaranteeing other meanings in the symbolic order ignores the instability of linguistic signs and their openness for appropriation by other interested parties. It ignores further that female sexuality is not fixed, unified, or

---

[84] Cynthia Chase, 'Oedipal Textuality: Reading Freud's Reading of *Oedipus*' in Maud Ellman, (ed.), *Psychoanalytic Literary Criticism, supra*, at 62.

[85] John Irwin, *The Mystery to a Solution: Poe, Borges and the Analytic Detective Story* (Baltimore and London: Johns Hopkins University Press, 1994), at 201–28.

[86] Paul Ricoeur, in Jonathan Rée (ed.), *Talking Liberties* (London: Channel Four Publications, 1992), at 39.

[87] Freud, 'Dostoevsky and Parricide' in *The Standard Edition of the Complete Psychological Works of Sigmund Freud*, ed. James Strachey, (London: Hogarth Press, 1961), Vol. 21, at 188.

representable but ambiguous, multiple, and fluid, forever in process, and thus exceeding as well as escaping attempts at representation in accordance with laws and models devised by male theorists.[88] Male psychoanalysts' attempt to fix it, as in Freud's dictum that 'anatomy is destiny' or erase it, as in Lacan's declaration that 'woman does not exist' is itself an attempt to assert that what they fail to understand does not exist, is unknowable, or is not worth knowing. At the same time, by masking their theories as neutral, eternal and universal, such interpretations repress and efface the material fact of motherhood, her knowledge, her law, and her culture. Hence the struggle to de-essentialize the myth, the return of hidden, unrepresented myths to dissolve the facile identification between father, origin, and law; the return, in short, of repressed mothers and daughters to unsettle male culture, male law, and male identity and reclaim the dark continent of the dark continent.

Indeed the very notion of origin and the question 'where do children come from' may be more a masculine, than a feminine, question: the quest for origins that Oedipus and his male readers are obsessed by, suggests Cixous, is not a question that torments women's imaginary.[89] Could one go further and suggest that the search for self-knowledge is not only illusory but a vanity, a conceit? Is not the injunction to 'know thyself' also a form of self-love and self-absorption? Further, that it is a male conceit, that the journey back to oneself and the desire to know oneself is a male attempt to perceive oneself as self-made and self-created in an attempt to repress the debt owed to the mother? That, as Irigaray suggests, even the idea of God is a male strategy to suppress the debt owed by culture to the mother.[90]

Jocasta is the woman who marked the fate of Oedipus, first by giving birth to him, then by realizing her alleged desire for him. Jocasta's desire, however, is passed over by male psychoanalysts. Jocasta occupies the ambiguous position of a woman who is both a mother and a subject of her own desires. She inspires desire in men without being the antithesis of the maternal. Jocasta's desire however is either unknowable or at least unknown to male critics. In a lecture as late as 1932 Freud confesses that in spite of thirty years of investigation, the answer to the question 'what do women desire' still eluded him: 'Throughout the ages, the problem of woman has puzzled people of every kind . . . you too will have pondered over this question in so far as you are men; from the women among you that is not to be expected, for you are the riddle yourselves . . . you are now prepared for the conclusion that psychology cannot solve the riddle of femininity'.[91] The solver of the riddle of dreams, the seeker of knowledge,

---

[88] See Luce Irigaray, *This Sex Which Is Not One, supra,* at 28–9: 'Her sexuality, always at least double, goes even further: it is plural . . . not to mention her language in which "she" sets off in all directions leaving "him" unable to discern the coherence of any meaning'. Also, Hélène Cixous, 'The Laugh of the Medusa' in Isabelle de Courtivron and Elaine Marks (eds.), *New French Feminisms* (Brighton: Harvester Press, 1981), at 246: 'You can't talk about *a* female sexuality, uniform, homogeneous, classifiable into codes—any more than you can talk about one unconscious resembling another. Women's imaginary is inexhaustible, like music, painting, writing: their stream of phantasms is incredible.'

[89] Hélène Cixous, 'Castration or Decapitation?' *Signs,* 7, trans. Annette Kuhn, (Autumn 1981), 41–55.

[90] See Luce Irigaray *Speculum of the Other Woman, supra,* at 330–9.

[91] *New Introductory Lectures on Psychoanalysis* in *The Major Works of Sigmund Freud,* at 853–5.

is frightened of what he doesn't know: the dark continent of the sexual life of women. To conceal this fear he assimilates little girls to little boys, assuming that there is a symmetry between them. As Christiane Olivier points out, the assumption of sameness is not one made by Sophocles whose Oedipus bids Creon to take care of his little girls but 'the boys at least don't burden yourself. They're men.' (*Oedipus the King*, 1599–6000). Jocasta not only indicates the double standard of a culture that requires woman to be either a mother or a sexual object but explodes it and the price she exacts for the men around her and pays herself is death. Like the *femme fatale* of *film noir* she is associated with deception and irreverence; while male critics concede to her the nobility of fully accepting her fate by taking her own life, her suicide more importantly eliminates the threat caused by her presence. Dead, her excessive, shifting, and unknowable sexuality ceases to be a threat and enables the restoration of the social order.

Freud's analysis ignores women's difference and has led to an understanding of the play, and the origin of culture, in terms of models and laws that reduce woman to man's mirror. The work of feminist psychoanalysts has highlighted the need for different understandings of the play that acknowledge the need for 'different games, with different rules; games where the man's penis isn't necessarily the prize.'[92] Ideally these games will not be centred around the rivalry between father and son, and will not be concerned with annihilation and death but with life and love. Unlike Laius and Oedipus, Jocasta does not set off on a journey and therefore does not have the opportunity of encountering herself. In their attempt to escape their desire for the mother, however, both father and son encounter death. Can the journey lead to something else, not competition and death but communication and love? Woman's journey, more often than not taking place from the immobility that is her home, takes her not only to knowing herself but to knowing those other than herself. Woman doesn't go back to the origin, writes Cixous: 'A boy's journey is the return to the native land, the *Heimweh* Freud speaks of, the nostalgia that makes man a being who tends to come back to the point of departure to appropriate it for himself and die there. A girl's journey is farther—to the unknown, to invent.'[93] The language she employs in this journey is correspondingly other, not the language of reason or logic, but of the emotions, of desire, of love, and of the body. Refusing the mind/body distinctions, she relinquishes the language that builds walls and distances between the hell that is other people, and employs a language that aims to communicate with, connect, and reach out towards the other.

It may be suggested that Oedipus' attempt to find out his origins and order the world through language is also an attempt to evade the question of woman whose desire is unknowable and whose language cannot be contained or defined in his terms. Variously described as playful, seductive, or deceitful, Jocasta's language, like Ariadne's in my closing chapter, intimates a different truth and a different law that

---

[92] Christiane Olivier, *Jocasta's Children, supra*, at 29.
[93] 'Sorties' in *The Newly-Born Woman, supra*, at 93.

eludes Oedipus's as well as male critics' attempts to understand it. As Jocasta suggests, some things cannot be known linguistically, that is, they cannot be known at all.

12 HIDDEN MYTHS: THE LAW OF THE MOTHER

In 'The Bodily Encounter with the Mother' Irigaray argues that western culture is founded not on parricide, as Freud argued in *Totem and Taboo*, and as many intepretations of Oedipus claim, but on the murder of the mother. The denial of this 'more archaic murder' is used to deny the debt culture owes to the mother and to forbid 'the bodily encounter with the mother'. The story of Clytemnestra tells the installation of patriarchy following the sacrifice of the mother and her daughter while Orestes, the matricidal son emerges in *The Eumenides* to found the new social order. Society's, psychoanalysts', and literary and legal critics' continuing obsession with the Oedipus myth serves only to conceal the cutting of the umbilical cord to the mother: 'the whole of our culture in the west depends upon the murder of the mother'.[94]

The myth of Oedipus, generations of commentators have convinced us, is concerned with man's origins, self-knowledge, and self-recognition; in the stampede to provide answers to such weighty questions the question of how woman might search for who she is and where she has come from remains untold. More damagingly, where woman's origins and identity are not entirely ignored they are included only in so far as they are useful in conferring an identity on the man. In the figure of Jocasta the female reader encounters the choice of recognizing herself in this dangerous other: while it is Oedipus who commits parrincest Jocasta's impiety, dismissal of the oracles, and distrust of the gods are stressed both by the dramatist and his commentators.

If women participated in this myth-making in order to understand themselves and their place in the world, the traces have been erased or repressed. Instead we have myths where the male subject attempts to define himself by distinguishing himself from the other: gods, slaves, barbarians, animals, and, of course, women. The same Athens that denied women the status of citizen related myths depicting women as inhabiting the border zone between nature and culture, public and private, inside and outside, man and beast. Their closeness to biological processes, particularly through giving birth, rendered them a potential source of regression from the orderliness of city, family, and home to nature, savagery, and chaos. The view that women needed to be controlled for civilization to advance seemed an undisputed adjunct to this characterization. The continuing privileging of myths such as Oedipus means the continuing celebration of man's alleged origins and justice, and corresponding erasure of women's otherness.

We may ask, therefore, what happens when we change the archmyth? For Joseph Campbell the story of Perseus' slaying Medusa marked the overthrow of an earlier

---

[94] Margaret Whitford (ed.), *The Irigaray Reader*, at 47.

mythology where the Medusa was 'both the life and the death of all beings, the womb and tomb of the world: the primal, one and only, ultimate reality of nature, of whom the gods themselves are but the functioning agents'.[95] This led to the displacement, relegation or, in Freud's own terms, repression of female personages and the female imaginary from a patriarchal mythology. Medusa's gaze, feared for being deadly, or different, is denied her viewpoint, leaving Perseus with the power of representation. However, as Freud taught, what is repressed is bound to return, more powerful or more terrible than before: for Cixous, the Medusa is not only not deadly, she is beautiful and she is laughing.[96]

Woman's origins, woman's achievements, woman's justice continue to inhabit a silent dark continent. This silence perpetuates a vision of woman as devouring monster threatening madness and death, a hatred which finds outlet in negative depictions of women on other planes. The task is to bring these silences out of oblivion and to represent them outside the confines of masculine paradigms. The same interpretations that construe the myth of Oedipus and the murder of the father as the worst of all possible crimes and raise it to the status of a universal law conceal more than the figure of the mother. Irigaray wonders why law and community have to be founded on violence as in Freud's founding of culture on parricide in *Totem and Taboo* and symbolic sacrifice as in Girard's *Violence and the Sacred:* 'Why did speech fail? What was missing? Why kill, cut up and eat as a sign of the covenant?'[97] To conceptualize a different community, one which is not founded on violence but one founded on cooperation and love and in which women enter as autonomous subjects and not as men's inferior complements, we need, Irigarary suggests, new languages, new laws, and new myths.

The stakes for switching the myth are high. 'Death of the father', Barthes warns, 'would deprive literature of many of its pleasures. If there is no longer a Father, why tell stories? Doesn't every narrative lead back to Oedipus? Isn't story-telling always a way of searching for one's origins, speaking one's conflicts with the law, entering into the dialectic of tenderness and hatred?'[98]

Tell stories that do not return to origins perhaps? Tell stories that do not get repeated with each generation? Tell stories that are not obsessed with 'who got there first'? Tell stories that do not turn on a road rage incident? Tell stories that go beyond?

Tell stories about mothers perhaps?

---

[95] Joseph Campbell, *The Masks of God: Occidental Mythology* (London: Souvenir Press, 1974), at 25–6. See also Jean-Joseph Goux, *Oedipus Philosopher* (Stanford, Calif: Stanford University Press, 1993) where the myths of Jason and Perseus are taken as prior to that of Oedipus: 'Matricide is the great unthought element of Freudian doctrine', at 26.

[96] Hélène Cixous, 'The Laugh of the Medusa', *supra.*

[97] 'Women, the Sacred and Money' (1986), 8 *Paragraph,* 7.

[98] *The Pleasure of the Text,* trans. Richard Miller, (Oxford: Blackwell, 1975), at 47.

3

THEATRE AS WOMAN RE-PLAYING THE WORD: TOWARDS THE TRIUMPH OF THE FLESH IN AESCHYLUS' *ORESTEIA* [1]

I'm wary of Greeks bearing fables
Marilou Awiakta

So one day I just on my own decided I am going to walk in there and smash a myth.
Louisa Teish

1 FEAR OF MIMESIS, FEAR OF WOMAN

It may be that women who engage with male authors do so because of an unconscious desire to sleep with the father and a desire to abide by the father's law. If so, what will befall a Greek daughter who chooses to sleep with an old Greek father but, rather than following or celebrating the institution of the father's law, resurrects the ghost of a murdered and unavenged mother and the muffled voice of a favourite daughter? Two responses are possible. If, à la Althusser, we are all interpellated by ideology, it is clear that both the daughter and the father are constituted by this ideology but one has more to gain from it than the other. So, if Freud suggests that the daughter wants to sleep with the father, then every dutiful daughter responds 'So *that's* what I wanted to do!'.[2] Conversely, rather than the daughter wanting to sleep with the father and follow his law, it is the father, as Irigaray argues, who wants to sleep with the daughter and

---

[1] All references in the text are to Aeschylus, *The Oresteian Trilogy*, trans. Philip Vellacott (Harmondsworth: Penguin, 1956).

[2] See Slavoj Žižek: 'The function of ideology is not to offer us a point of escape from our reality but to offer us the social reality itself as an escape from some traumatic, real kernel', *The Sublime Object of Ideology* (London: Verso, 1989), at 45.

legislates to protect himself from his desire. Or, as I will suggest in this paper, the father wants to be the mother, to self-generate, to give birth first to his text and, through his text, to his law, to his city, and to himself. To do that, he not only denies but murders the mother who gave birth to him.

Rather than telling a story of order over chaos and of the triumph of justice as word and legality over justice as violence and revenge, my reading explores what is forgotten or repressed in such readings of the *Oresteia*, that is the murder of the mother and the silencing and sacrifice of a virgin daughter. It argues that these deaths are the founding images and myths of western law and tells a different story of the genesis of western law, one where the father wants to be the mother that he tried but failed to erase completely. This chapter continues the discussion of western philosophy's distrust of mimesis that I began in my opening chapter and suggests further that the fear of mimesis is aroused by male philosphers' fear of woman.

For Plato, impersonating someone other than oneself involved all too often, behaving like and thus becoming a woman. Plato's concern to guard an essential identity from the perils of impersonation was also a concern to guard an essential and unchanging *masculine* identity.[3] Although the imitation of good and brave men is encouraged, what one should avoid at all costs is the imitation of lower beings like madmen, women, slaves, and foreigners. For Plato and others before and after him, woman is the 'mimetic creature par excellence',[4] herself an imitation (of man) but also more prone to play and deceive and more susceptible to play and deception. For Nietzsche, woman 'does not *want* truth: what is truth to a woman! From the very first nothing has been more alien, repugnant and inimical to woman than truth—her great art is the lie, her supreme concern is appearance and beauty.'[5] 'Reflect on the whole history of women: do they not *have* to be first of all and above all actresses? . . . they 'put on something' even when they take off everything . . . they give themselves (that is, act or play a part) even when they—give themselves.'[6] One suggestion why women aroused such distrust and fear of dissimulation is that they are wet creatures and thus able, like other fluids, to form, reform, and transform themselves into different moulds and shapes.[7] This further renders woman less able than men to resist the assaults of eros and of other emotions which is why she must be controlled by others.

In western jurisprudence, the war against and fear of mimesis and images is

---

[3] See further, Karen Bassi, *Acting Like Men: Gender, Drama and Nostalgia in Ancient Greece* (Ann Arbor, Mich.: University of Michigan Press, 1998).

[4] Froma Zeitlin, *Playing the Other: Gender and Society in Classical Greek Literature* (Chicago and London: Chicago University Press, 1996), at 362. For a discussion of the depiction of woman as 'both the source and the exemplar of idolatry' in Renaissance and early modern English and French law see Peter Goodrich, 'Signs Taken for Wonders: Community, Identity and A History of Sumptuary Law', Vol. 23 (3), *Journal of the American Bar Foundation*, 707–28 (1998).

[5] *Beyond Good and Evil: Prelude to a Philosophy of the Future*, trans. R. J. Hollingdale (London: Penguin, 1973) [1886]), para. 232.

[6] *The Gay Science*, trans. Walter Kauffman (New York: Vintage, 1974 [1882]), para. 361.

[7] Anne Carson, 'Putting Her in Her Place: Woman, Dirt and Desire' in David M. Halperin, John J. Winkler and Froma I. Zeitlin (eds.), *Before Sexuality: The Construction of Erotic Experience in the Ancient Greek World* (Princeton, NJ: Princeton University Press, 1990).

therefore, as Peter Goodrich suggests, also a war against and fear of woman.[8] Indulging in mimesis is to give in to female seduction beyond the truth of presence, reason, and logos. In his harangue against mimesis, theatre, and role-playing in general, the worst scenario for Plato is that of a man imitating a woman.[9] It is no coincidence that Dionysos, the god of theatre, is associated with the feminine and endowed with feminine characteristics.

Conversely, by inverting the hierarchy between presence and representation, reality and fictionality, theatre, and woman as theatre can reveal law's dependence on theatre and on woman as theatre in order to create its own foundations. Woman, the source and subject of mimesis, its fascination and fear, can also take advantage of mimesis for her own ends. Women are not condemned to repeat their father's word and their father's law for the concept of mimesis is not homogeneous or unambiguous enough to resist its own imitation and impersonation. While Plato assumed that its movement was towards similarity, his fear that it would dissimulate and thereby destroy the original implied that mimesis depends on and is open to its opposite, that is, difference.[10] In Plato's account of mimesis, Irigaray reminds us, the concept is not univocal but vacillates between mimesis as production and mimesis as repetition; although the first has been repressed in favour of mimesis as sameness, in mimesis as production of difference lies the possibility of women's writing and writing for women.[11]

As I argued in my opening chapter, we need to question the distinction between representation and reality and explore the possibility that reality is itself a representation, fiction, or theatre. Further, that the insistence on the separation between representation and reality is political and that the fear and condemnation of mimesis is a fear of woman. As I suggested in that chapter, literature may reveal the production and contingency of societal constructs that deny their own artificiality and suggests readings of texts that reopen the gap between representation and reality to a time *before* existing practices began as myths or plays, became law and started to take themselves (extremely) seriously. By inverting the hierarchy between presence and representation, reality and fictionality, literature as woman and woman as literature may reveal law's dependence on literature and on (often dead) woman in order to create its own foundations. In the process, it appropriates mimesis from a device used

---

[8] See especially Peter Goodrich, *Oedipus Lex: Psychoanalysis, History, Law* (Berkeley and Los Angeles, Calif.: University of California Press), for a discussion of law's simultaneous rejection of and reliance on images.

[9] This would distract men from their pursuit of valour and glory; despite Plato's worries, dramatists like Aeschylus shared this view: 'do not with these soft attentions woman me' says Agamemnon to Clytemnestra shortly after his return from Troy: *Agamemnon*, 918.

[10] Although Arne Melberg does not discuss Irigaray, his analysis of Plato's mimesis insists on this point: Arne Melberg, *Theories of Mimesis* (Cambridge: Cambridge University Press, 1995), at 3: '*Mimesis is never* a homogeneous term and if its basic movement is towards similarity, it is *always* open to the opposite'; and at 13: 'Plato's mimesis is, in my reading, a movable concept, and every effort to make it reasonably unambiguous would be a betrayal of that floating ambiguity'. This point is discussed further, from a feminist perspective, by Elin Diamond, *Unmaking Mimesis: Essays on Feminism and Theatre* (London and New York; Routledge, 1997), at v: 'Mimesis, then, is impossibly double, simultaneously the stake and the shifting sands: order and potential disorder, reason and madness'. See further her discussion of Irigaray's mimesis of Plato, at x-xiii.

[11] 'Questions' in Margaret Whitford (ed.), *The Irigaray Reader* (Oxford: Blackwell, 1991), at 134.

to reflect male fullness, truth, and sameness into a tool through which to express difference, including gender difference.

Having revealed Plato's truth as a play or 'dream'[12] that denies the representation of woman, Irigaray does not retreat from the cave but enters it as the woman Plato feared: she playfully mimics, flirts with him, and seduces him into acknowledging his own dependence on her.[13] In this play by Irigaray, the concept of mimesis is turned from a device used to reflect male truth into a tool in the hands of women uncovering the political nature of representation, appropriating the available signs and creating new ones. Woman as play, literature, theatre thus disrupts the hierarchy between original and representation, exceeds the original and creates new representations in the imaginary that may in turn enter the symbolic order and become law.

2 CITIZENS' CLUB, MEN'S CLUB[14]

On examining the position of women in Greek society, legal, social, historical, and mythical sources serve to remind us what the index in Harrison's *Law of Athens* neatly sums up; as John Gould puts it, 'it reads, simply, "women, disabilities"'.[15] Legally a Greek woman of all ages and classes was no different from a minor or an animal, her legal status depending entirely on her relationship to males, whether as a daughter, sister, mother, wife, or widow. As in many societies, however, there is a paradox between on the one hand acknowledging woman's essential role of ensuring the continuation of the oikos and thereby, the polis, and her restriction to the domestic realm and exclusion from public affairs. Without expressing it, the polis and its politai knew that their present status and continuing existence derived from the women: indeed it is by distinguishing himself from the 'other', be that god, barbarian, animal or woman, that the adult male subject was able to achieve a definition of himself.[16] In

---

[12] *Speculum of the Other Woman*, trans. Gillian C. Gill (Ithaca, New York: Cornell University Press, 1985 [1974]), at 346.

[13] 'For she can only be known and recognised under disguises that denature her; she borrows forms that are never her own and that she must yet mimic if she is to enter even a little way into knowledge': *ibid.*, at 344.

[14] Terms used by Pierre Vidal-Naquet to describe the Athenian *polis*, 'Slavery and the Rule of Women in tradition' in R. L. Gordon (ed.), *Myth, Religion and Society* (Cambridge: Cambridge University Press, 1981), at 188. For analyses of the position of women in Greek society see, amongst others, John Gould, 'Law, Custom and Myth: Aspects of the Social Position of Women in Classical Athens' Vol. 100, *Journal of Hellenic Studies* 38–59 (1980); Roger Just, *Women in Athenian Law and Life* (Routledge: London and New York, 1989); Marilyn Arthur, 'Early Greece: The Origins of the Western Attitude Toward Women', Vol. 6 *Arethusa*, 7–58 (1973); Marilyn Skinner (ed.), *Rescuing Creusa: New Methodological Approaches to Women in Antiquity* (Texas: Texas University Press, 1987); John Peradotto and J. P. Sullivan (eds.), *Women in the Ancient World* (New York: State University of New York, 1984).

[15] As quoted and discussed by John Gould, *supra*, at 43.

[16] See Simon Goldhill: 'The male subject defines himself through a sense of the other: he distinguishes himself from the gods; the barbarians; the women'; *Reading Greek Tragedy* (Cambridge: Cambridge University Press, 1986), at 61.

the meantime, woman's subjectivity and powers, denied the power of reciprocity, aroused suppression and fear.

Women inspired fear as their powers of giving life means that they can also take it away. Women's sexuality, assumed to be voraciously promiscuous and insatiable, contained the threat of diminishing men's honour. Since women represent a threat to the stability and continuity of the civilized polis, like animals and earth, they must be controlled, tamed, and cultivated; the instrument for this task is the institution of marriage which was expected to tame young women for the production of legitimate children. Marriage was the culmination as well as end of a young woman's history, the point 'beyond which literally nothing happens'.[17]

Although the rules, rights, and definition of marriage vary from one society to the next, what remains constant, universal even, is the link between the rules of marriage and the rules of succession, citizenship, and the inheritance of property. Provided the rules of marriage were observed the polis could ensure its control over the principles of male descent, the transmission and inheritance of property and the rules of residence. Conversely property, inheritance, and citizenship, all came under threat if women strayed from the private realm of the house. Thus the exchange of women between men, as well as strengthening homosocial relations between men, as Lévi-Strauss describes,[18] was indispensable to the constitution and definition of their political status as Athenian citizens.

While legal rules provide us with one aspect of the role of women in Greek society much of what is hidden, suppressed, or unconscious behind the making and upholding of such rules may be glimpsed from the same society's myths. As I argued in the last chapter, myths are more important and influential than state laws in educating, unifying, and perpetuating a society and its cultural conventions and expectations. Indeed, the question whether such myths are true, false, or constitute a systemic unity (as structuralists like Claude Lévi-Strauss have claimed) are not as interesting as the question of what purposes and whose interests they have served. In looking at some of the myths enacted in the *Oresteia*, I am not, therefore, attempting to find out what those myths mean but who makes and who benefits from these meanings. Furthermore, if myths are, as Freud thought by analogy to dreams, expressions of a society's rather than an individual's unconscious, then they are also, like dreams, over-determined, loaded with a variety of meanings and uses, and thus open to reinterpretation and appropriation by interested parties, including feminists.

The ambiguity with which Greek society and law treated women is repeated in Greek mythology. In the male mythical imagination women are repeatedly associated with nature rather than culture, savagery rather than civilization, the wild rather than the tame. Women feature as sexually voracious, devious, and immoral, destroying

---

[17] Richard Buxton, *Imaginary Greece: The Contexts of Mythology* (Cambridge: Cambridge University Press, 1994), at 121; discussing Mary Lefkowitz, *Heroines and Hysterics* (London: Duckworth, 1981) and *Women in Greek Myth* (London: Duckworth, 1986).

[18] Claude Lévi-Strauss, *The Elementary Structures of Kinship*, trans. J. H. Bell and John von Sturner (Boston: Beacon Press, 1969), especially at 480–1.

men or diverting them from their pursuit of honour.[19] Woman's ambiguous position between outside and inside, public and private, city and family, nature and culture, civilization and chaos, repeat law's fears of the transgression of boundaries. By placing the danger and blame for such transgression at the site of woman, male fear of the loss of control and the dissolution of an ordered and hierarchical world can be allayed. The danger, it can then be argued, does not lie within oneself but with the other, with unruly woman. By going further and punishing the transgressive other with death, man and law can reaffirm the cultural order free of woman's disruptive presence.[20]

What if such oppositions, however, are cultural rather than natural and the discourses that constructed them as oppositions as contingent as the oppositions themselves? In that case, instead of myths revealing truths about the world, myths, and our readings of them, may help 'to make the world conform to the myth'.[21] The task is then not only to unravel the oppositions that myths are supposed to mediate but the oppositions themselves, and more importantly, the discourses that constructed them as oppositions. In other words, the order of culture is called upon to mediate oppositions that culture itself created;[22] the legal order, an order of culture, needs myths and rituals to sustain the oppositions it itself created. The *Oresteia* is one such myth, built to resolve the oppositions and distinctions culture itself created including the myth of the danger of the female other, her unbridled sexuality, and the necessity of her murder. The myth of Oedipus, perhaps the dominant myth in western culture's understanding of itself and its traditions, was itself sustained by repressing another myth, that of Orestes and the murder of his mother Clytemnestra. What is repressed, however, returns to claim its place alongside or instead of the myth of the murder of the father.

3 MYTH INTO THEATRE: THE TRIUMPH OF THE WORD

Looking at myths through the medium of theatre need not replicate but can problematize old myths. While myths repeat and reinforce societal values, theatre, by reopening the gap between mimetic object and original subject, may re-examine and question such values and structures. Tragedy, perhaps more than any other form of drama, through its insistence on conflict can keep the dilemmas open by emphasizing the grey area between existing categories, without the promise of resolution or

[19] The argument that this is the role of women in Homer's poems is made by Kakridis, *Homer Revisited* (Lund, 1971); quoted in John Gould, *supra*, at 56.

[20] For a beautiful analysis of this idea in western art and literature see Elizabeth Bronfen, *Over her Dead Body: Death, Femininity and the Aesthetic* (Manchester: Manchester University Press, 1992).

[21] Pierre Bourdieu, *Outline of a Theory of Practice* (Cambridge: Cambridge University Press, 1977), at 167.

[22] See James Redfield: 'The problems of culture can only be solved with the means of culture.' 'From Sex to Politics: The Rites of Artemis Triclaria and Dionysos Aisymnetes at Patras' in *Before Sexuality: supra*, at 122.

reconciliation.[23] In particular, tragedies problematize familiar myths, by confronting old dilemmas in the context of the new civil state. The *Oresteia* is representative of what has been called 'the tragic moment',[24] in its insistence on dramatizing and allegedly resolving the conflict between the mythical world of Homeric heroes on the one hand and the political world of the city on the other. Chief amongst issues to be discussed, as the Athenian polis was being established, was the notion of justice and its relationship to the individual, to civil institutions and to the gods. The trilogy, performed for the first time shortly after the creation of the court of Areopagus, the first court responsible for cases of homicide, addresses the relationship between justice and private vengeance, the will of Zeus, and the force of the old chthonian religion represented by the Furies: how did the new assembly and law courts fit into the system of revenge and retribution? Where did their authority stem from and what were the best means and procedures for achieving their aims?

The *Eumenides'* conclusion with the establishment and celebration of a court of law to end the cycle of revenge and violence as depicted in the *Agamemnon* and the *Coephoroi* has led to interpretations of the play as a narrative of law over vengeance and order over chaos.[25] It is certainly true that starting with the *Agamemnon*, characters from Clytemnestra, the chorus, Aegysthus, and Agamemnon refer to dike and the predominant meaning here is revenge or retribution. Agamemnon's and the Greeks' actions against the Trojans were thus in revenge of Paris's abduction of Helen, Clytemnestra's murder of Agamemnon was in revenge of Agamemnon's sacrifice of their daughter Iphigeneia, while Aegisthus' murder of Agamemnon was in revenge of another atrocity by Agamemnon's father Atreus against Aegisthus' father Thyestes. In the *Coephoroi* again references to justice imply punitive retribution as both Aegisthus' and Clytemnestra's murder are explained, in turn, by Orestes, Electra, and the chorus. The view of justice espoused by the Furies, although coming in for attack and ridicule in the *Eumenides* is no different from the view propounded and acted upon by the characters in the earlier two plays, with the understanding if not encouragement of the supposedly neutral chorus. Apollo describes this justice as a 'pit of punishments, where heads [a]re severed, eyes torn out, throats cut, manhood unmanned' (188–9), conveniently forgetting that his own advice to Orestes to avenge his father was based on just such a premise.

It is equally clear that its realization will prolong rather than resolve the conflict by encouraging further retribution and further revenge. Victims are faced with the obligation of revenge which in fulfilling they become perpetrators of a crime which in

[23] See especially Charles Segal, *Tragedy and Civilization: An Interpretation of Sophocles* (Cambridge, Mass.: Harvard University Press, 1981).

[24] Jean-Pierre Vernant and Pierre Vidal-Naquet, *Tragedy and Myth in Ancient Greece* (Brighton: Harvester Press, 1981) [1972].

[25] See for example James Boyd White: the forces represented by the Furies, Apollo, and Athena 'are here integrated into a new form and activity, an institution that will tell stories with authority, so that they will remain the same and not slide into other intolerable and mysterious meanings. The law will thus rescue us all from the unbearable incoherence of the world that has been presented to us—an incoherence of story, of intellect, of action, of the very self.' *Heracles' Bow* (Madison, Wis.: University of Wisconsin, 1985), at 180.

being avenged creates further violence, punishment, and transgression, and so on ad infinitum. By contrast, the view of justice espoused in the *Eumenides*, variously described as justice as 'legality', 'ordered propriety', 'due process', or 'law and order', conveys a move away from justice as administered by the victims of earlier injustices to justice administered centrally through the machinery of a court and legal system, following identifiable rules and procedures. In the play no less than in contemporary terms, this includes such appurtenances as pleas, hearings, prosecution and defence counsels, jury, judgment, and sentence.

We need to ask, however, whether it is our own preoccupation with the notion of justice as legality and its relationship to the state that has led to such readings of the *Oresteia* to appear natural and inevitable. Could it be that such readings say more about us than about Aeschylus, his characters, and audience, betraying, above all, a western pathological insistence on talking in terms of binary oppositions and dialectical syntheses? An alternative reading hopes to look at Athenian drama not in search for the truth of either law or justice but as constituting tragic accounts that avoid easy classifications and facile resolutions, and goes, instead, (as Nietzsche would hope), 'beyond good and evil'. This reading suggests that celebrations that legal procedure rather than individual revenge, and words rather than violence, have resolved the issue are both premature and misplaced.

First, the concept of legal justice espoused by Athene's court is no different from the old system of revenge as fear and retribution are retained to elicit respect for the law:

> And from your polity do not wholly banish fear.
> For what man living, freed from fear, will still be just?
> Hold fast such upright fear of the law's sanctity,
> And you will have a bulwark of your city's strength
> (*Eumenides*, 699–702)

The trial of course *appears* to be different because Orestes is acquitted; had the trial led to a conviction, the same punishment would have been inflicted on him, as he had inflicted on his victims, that is the cycle of revenge and violence would have continued, this time by *legal* means.

Second, Athene's court, for all its pomp and ceremony, procedural proprieties, and ordered speeches does not in the end resolve the conflict: the result is an impasse following an even split between the jurors. The reason Orestes is acquitted is not dictated by the notion of justice but by expediency: Athene, having warned the Furies against tainting 'pure laws with new expediency' (695) does exactly that by casting her vote with Orestes. Law thus triumphs not as an instrument of the illusory notion of justice but of force and politics or, in Foucaultian terms, of rationalization, normalization, and domination. The machinery of the trial serves to mystify law's sources of power which relies not only on logos and reason but on the power of the spectacle, on non-linguistic signs and images. Chief amongst such images, are images of defeated and dead women.

Third, the law's alleged reliance on language rather than force to resolve the conflict is shown to be chimerical. Language, as is shown by the array of characters appealing to the same word, dike, to express their different purposes, is an unsure foundation. Indeed language is at the forefront of the tensions explored in the texts, constituting rather then resolving the impasse depicted in the drama. Rather than a transparent medium of events, thoughts, and meanings taking place elsewhere, language creates, recreates, and as often distorts rather than reflects those events and meanings. As Aeschylus and other tragedians appreciated, words could be used to make what is false appear true and what was true false. Characters therefore say things they know to be false, while their listeners are shown to believe things that are untrue and disbelieve things that are true: Clytemnestra's words are successful in persuading Agamemnon to step on the red tapestry and commit blasphemy against the gods, an hamartia that leads to his immediate downfall; Orestes is able to deceive the servants and Clytemnestra into admitting him into the palace by appealing to the Greek rules of hospitality to strangers, while Cassandra's prophetic words fall on uncomprehending and disbelieving ears. Conversely characters seek to control events through their use of language but fail as language slips away from their control. The audience is therefore alerted to the fact that the speakers do not always say what they mean or mean what they say. In the end, rather than being a medium of communication between speaker and listener, or an instrument for conveying truth, language becomes a source of confusion, conflict, and ambiguity; rather than mediating between mind and reality, it creates, recreates, as well as distorts and obscures that reality. The audience's security in the veracity of language is thus replaced with a suspicion of the medium. From questioning the role of language it is only a short step to questioning the social order constituted by this language: the legal order, we are led to suspect, is built on a singularly unsure foundation.

Rather than follow the view of the *Oresteia* as a narrative of justice as legality, I want therefore to explore what is forgotten or repressed in these readings, that is the narrative of male over female. Rather than seeing the institution of the Athenian court as a superior solution to an intransigent cycle of revenge and retribution, it is a continuation of the problem by different means. In the end, the institution of the court is a political solution to a political problem and that problem, as ever, was sex.[26]

4 THE MURDER OF THE MOTHER

The struggles in the *Oresteia* stem, from the beginning, from the conflict between male and female. In a society where familial and kinship rules were paramount to the constitution of the polis, a woman's infidelity posed a strong threat. Agamemnon's

---

[26] See James Redfield, 'From Sex to Politics: The Rites of Artemis Tridaria and Dionysos Aisymnetes at Patras' in *Before Sexuality, supra.*

absence led Clytemnestra to leave the private realm of the oikos and turn her attention to the public affairs of the polis; in the *Agamemnon* she is described as having 'a man's will'(11), her 'words are like a man's' (350) and, unlike a woman, is 'combative' (940). Like a woman, however, she is accused of being false, guileful, and deceitful. More controversially she has broken the rules of marriage by taking a lover, Aegisthus, a man who is allegedly effeminate, not having joined the Greek army to Troy. If, in Lacan's schema, woman does not exist because her function is to reflect and support man's fantasy of wholeness,[27] Clytemnestra's infidelity and expression of her own autonomous desire ruins rather than reflects the sense of wholeness her husband relies on her to reflect. Between them the two lovers subvert and undermine the rules and roles expected of men and women in fifth century Athens; Clytemnestra's adultery and entry into the public realm reserved for men lead to the transgression of her society's sexual as well as political boundaries. Importantly, she shows no guilt or repentance for these transgressions: to the chorus's constant accusations of murder and deceit, her replies are consistent and unwavering: Agamemnon, she keeps reminding them, has killed our daughter.

The conflicting demands between the public and private realms, state and family, community and blood ties, were a frequent concern of Greek tragedies, arising most starkly again in Sophocles' *Antigone*. In both plays it is said, men privilege public affairs at the expense of the interests of the oikos while women privilege blood ties at the expense of societal ones. However, Clytemnestra is unique in Greek mythology in that her grief for her daughter does not lead her to disregard the affairs of the polis. Nor does she fit into the facile categorization of woman as irrational, and emotional for, as the chorus decry, she has been ruling like a man.

In the *Coephoroi* Clytemnestra's two children Electra and Orestes, bent on preserving their father's name, law, and honour, resolve to kill their mother. Electra does not mention her dead sister when she decries her mother as a 'blasphemer of motherhood' (190) or as 'fierce, flint-hearted' (430) and when she asserts that 'Children preserve alive a dead man's name and fame' (405). She thus confirms that in patriarchy, not only is the role of the mother devalued but that women, whether daughters, mothers, or sisters, are forced to play the role of rivals. At the same time, her woman's status denies her the facility to extract revenge for the wrong done to her by the murder of her father. For that task, she thinks, she must rely on her brother Orestes.

The abiding image from the *Coephoroi*, however, is the story invoked by the chorus: Clytemnestra has dreamt that she gave birth to a snake, wrapped it up in shawls, lulled it to rest like a little child and gave it her breast to suck; but with her milk the creature drew forth clots of blood (527–33). The dream of course does not dictate how it should be interpreted, leaving that task to interested parties for interested appropriation. Orestes is certainly quick to read the dream as an injunction to kill his mother. However, even when, or especially when, the association between the snake and

---

[27] Juliet Mitchell and Jacqueline Rose, *Feminine Sexuality: Jacques Lacan and the Ecole Freudienne*, trans. Jacqueline Rose (London: Macmillan, 1982), especially introduction by Jacqueline Rose.

Orestes is made, the violent unnaturalness of the image could have been used to suggest the abominable nature of the deed and served to dissuade rather than persuade him from carrying it out. Orestes, however, at this point at least, is quick to accept the role of the 'obscene beast':

> As I interpret, point by point it fits: Listen:
> First, if this snake came forth from the same place as I,
> And, as though human, was then wrapped in infant-clothes,
> Its gaping mouth clutching the breast that once fed me:
> If it then mingled the sweet milk with curds of blood,
> And made her shriek with terror—why it means that she
> Who nursed this obscene beast must die by violence;
> *I* must transmute my nature, be viperous in heart and act!
> The dream commands it: I am her destined murderer.
>
> (*Coephoroi*, 539–50)

The chorus is equally clear as to both the dream's meaning and what Orestes should do:

> I choose your reading of these signs, and say Amen.
>
> (*Coephoroi*, 551)

> Keep a bold heart, Orestes!
> When the moment comes to kill her,
> Thunder your father's killing;
> When she wimpers, 'Child, Orestes!'
> Answer, 'I am—my father's!'
> Finish your fearful deed;
> It is fate, and none condemns you
>
> (*Coephoroi*, 827–33)

The image that should have alerted Orestes of the horror of his proposed deed instead is interpreted as not only suggesting but commanding the deed with legislative force.

The chorus's view of woman's role in giving birth is of course spectacularly reiterated in the *Eumenides* by Apollo:

> The mother is not the true parent of the child
> Which is called hers. She is a nurse who tends the growth
> Of young seed planted by its true parent, the male.
> So, if Fate spares the child, she keeps it, as one might
> Keep for some friend a growing plant.
>
> (*Eumenides*, 657–61).

The goddess Athene continues in this vein, confirming that, born of Zeus, she has no need of a mother (735). Before the jurors cast their votes she warns them that, believing in 'the father's claim and male supremacy in all things' and that 'a woman's death who killed her husband is . . . outweighed in grievousness by his' (735–9) if the votes are equal she will cast her decisive vote on the side of the man. Clytemnestra, like Eve, is a fallen woman who must be defeated and killed in order to allow for the regeneration of the male order. As Irigaray argues, when 'Freud theorises and describes, notably in *Totem and Taboo*, the murder of the father as founding the primal horde, he forgets a more archaic murder, that of the mother, necessitated by the establishment of a certain order in the polis'.[28]

Another, less well-known, woman's death is the suicide of Aegisthus' and Clytemnestra's daughter Erigone following Orestes' acquittal. That her death is not often told may be another instance of Greek misogyny that seems to have been accustomed to girls committing suicide by hanging. In a particularly bizarre anecdote told by Diogenes Laertius one day Diogenes the cynic, whilst walking amongst an olive grove, saw several girls who had hanged themselves swinging from the trees. At this sight his reaction was to exclaim: 'If only all trees bore fruit like this!'[29]

Clytemnestra's avengers, the Erinyes, suffer a similar fate at the hands of male mythologists and Aeschylus. In contrast to young Apollo and Athena, the Furies represent the primitive past that needs to be defeated and tamed in order for civilization to progress. Like Clytemnestra, their sexuality causes problems, this time because they are barren and sterile and cause desolation to the lands they inhabit. Their defeat in the trial leads to their condemnation to an inferior position in the order of the polis, below the role assigned to the forces represented by Apollo. Athene's judgement also equates women's values with the forces of fear, punishment, and revenge and acknowledges an indispensable role for these emotions in the administration of justice;[30] the significance of blood ties and the family, associated with the female are also conceded. Athene, however, has no doubt that the forces of the polis and of rhetoric, argument and persuasion, (however sophistic) represented by Apollo should take precedence in a court of law.[31]

As Joan Bamberger argues, the myth of Orestes is another myth of the alleged existence and loss of matriarchal societies: such myths, by depicting women in authority as devious, destructive, and incompetent, are used to justify women's subsequent exclusion from positions of responsibility.[32] A parallel implication is that the overthrow of women was necessary for the progress of civilization. As in Freud's *Moses and Monotheism* the transition from female to male is presented as a triumph of the abstract over the physical: 'This turning from the mother to the father points

---

[28] 'The Bodily Encounter with the Mother' in Margaret Whitford (ed.), *The Irigaray Reader, supra*, at 36.

[29] Related by Eva Cantarella, 'Dangling Virgins: Myth, Ritual and the Place of Women in Ancient Greece' in Susan Rubin Suleiman (ed.), *The Female Body in Western Culture: Contemporary Perspectives* (Cambridge, Mass.: Harvard University Press, 1986), at 57.

[30] This point is discussed further by Paul Gewirtz, 'Aeschylus' Law', 101 *Harvard Law Review*, 1043–55 (1988).

[31] See Froma Zeitlin's seminal essay, 'The Dynamics of Misogyny: Myth and Mythmaking in *The Oresteia*', 11 *Arethusa*, 149–84 (1978).

[32] Joan Bamberger, 'The Myth of Matriarchy: Why Men Rule in Primitive Society' in Michelle Zimbalist Rosaldo and Louise Lamphere (eds.), *Woman, Culture and Society* (Stanford, Calif.: Stanford University Press, 1974).

in addition to a victory of intellectuality over sensuality—that is, an advance of civilization, since maternity is proved by the evidence of the senses while paternity is a hypothesis based on an inference and a premise.'[33] The power of the law, like the power of the father, is also linguistic rather than corporeal, based on word rather than flesh.[34] The triumph of male over female is therefore also a triumph of law over emotion and word over feeling. Nietzsche's *amor fati*, the love of the body and of fate, is replaced with the love of logos, of law, and of reason.

5 THE SACRIFICE OF A VIRTUOUS DAUGHTER[35]

So Agamemnon, rather than retreat,
Endured to offer up his daughter's life
To help a war fought for a faithless wife
And pay the ransom for a storm-bound fleet.
Heedless of her tears,
Her cries of '*Father!*' and her maiden years,
Her *judges* valued more
Their glory and their war.
A prayer was said. Her father gave the *word*.
Limp in her flowing dress
The priest's attendants held her high
Above the altar, as men hold a kid.
Her father *spoke again, to bid*
One bring a *gag*, and press her sweet mouth tightly with a cord,
Lest Atreus' house be cursed by some ill-omened cry.
Rough hands tear at her girdle, cast
Her saffron silks to earth. Her eyes
Search for her slaughterers; and each,
Seeing her beauty, that surpassed
A painter's vision, yet denies
The pity *her dumb looks beseech*,
Struggling for voice; for often in old days,
When brave men feasted in her father's hall,
With simple skill and pious praise
Linked to the flute's pure tone
Her virgin voice would melt the hearts of all,

---

[33] *Complete Psychological Works*, ed. James Stratchey (London: Hogarth Press, 1953–74), Vol. 23, at 113–14.

[34] See Richard Weisberg's study of 'characters who use words not only to avoid disturbing realities but to create them'. This verbal reorganization of reality, institutionalized in the courts of law, leads to the avoidance rather than realization of justice: *The Failure of the Word: The Protagonist as Lawyer in Modern Fiction* (New Haven and London: Yale University Press, 1984).

[35] My discussion of the sacrifice of Iphigeneia is inspired by and indebted to Elizabeth Bronfen's beautiful account of western representations of dead or dying women, *supra*.

> Honouring the third libation near her father's throne.
> *The rest I did not see,*
> *Nor do I speak of it . . .*
>   (*Agamemnon*, 225-45; emphasis mine).

In Mauss's terms, sacrifices and other gifts are occasions for the public display of wealth, an opportunity to gain prestige and honour by spending prodigally or at least more so than one's competitors.[36] Like men's exchange of women in marriage, women are sacrificed in exchange for symbolic capital; the hope again is the mainten-ance and solidification of homosocial relations and its hierarchical orderings. The imagery and rituals accompanying such sacrifices also resembled marriage proces-sions with the bride being passed over by her father to the bridegroom, in this instance Hades.[37] Iphigeneia, lured to Aulis with her mother on the pretext of mar-riage, is sacrificed by a group of men led by her father to affirm man's preference for the sport of war over the sport of love and courtship.[38] An act of violence, the sacrifice is intended to prevent violence within the group and, taken as a prelude to war, to be redirected against those outside the group, in this instance, the Trojans.

Jean-Pierre Vernant has disputed the view that violence and murder are at the core of sacrifice,[39] arguing that sacrifice 'plays among three terms, with the consecrated object serving as the intermediary between the sacrificer and the divinity'. Since the relations between 'these three partners vary from one civilization to another and from one case to another within the same culture', one cannot assume that the role of sacrifice remains constant.[40] Paradoxically Vernant goes on to argue that in Greek ideology, sacrifice is consistently distinguished from murder and therefore performs the constant function of distinguishing man on the one hand from animals (who devour each other) and on the other from the gods (who have no need to kill). Even if we accept this—Vernant himself acknowledges the existence of dissonant voices in Greek society who denounced sacrifices as murder—the portrayal of sacrifice in the *theatre*, rather than in *myth*, can, as argued earlier, problematize old categories and structures, including the distinction between god and animal that ritual sacrifices are supposed to preserve. The sacrifice of Iphigeneia, particularly if enacted *on*, rather than *off*-stage (as will be argued below), can serve to blur rather than enforce the carefully maintained boundary between humanity and bestiality.

[36] Marcel Mauss, *The Gift: The Form and Reason for Exchange in Archaic Societies*, trans. W. D. Halls (London and New York: Routledge, 1990), [1923–4] for a fuller discussion see Victoria Wohl, *Intimate Commerce: Exchange, Gender and Subjectivity in Greek Tragedy* (Austin, Tex.: University of Texas Press, 1998).

[37] See Nicole Loraux, *Tragic Ways of Killing a Woman*, trans. Anthony Foster (Cambridge and London: Harvard University Press, 1987), at 36–7.

[38] See Malinowski: 'No doubt the men were far too engrossed in the excitement of the fighting to turn any attention to the more usual and therefore, perhaps, less absorbing sport of love' in *The Sexual Life of Savages* (London: Routledge & Sons, 1929), at 414; quoted and discussed by Nancy Huston, 'The Matrix of War: Mothers and Heroes', in Susan Rubin Suleiman (ed.), *The Female Body in Western Culture, supra.* .

[39] As argued, for instance, by René Girard, *Violence and the Sacred* (Baltimore; Johns Hopkins University Press, 1977).

[40] 'A General Theory of Sacrifice and the Slaying of the Victim in Greek *Thusia*' in *Mortals and Immortals: Collected Essays*, ed. Froma Zeitlin (Princeton: Princeton University Press, 1991), at 293, 291.

Sacrifices also re-establish societal norms by turning bodies into signs:[41] the sacrifice of a beautiful and virtuous (in Greek thinking virtuous = virgin) woman is the means whereby man protects himself from the threat posed by both woman and death: the enigma of femininity is averted by turning its ambiguous and polyvalent nature into a fixed and secure sign, if only because it is immobilized by death. The fear and enigma of death is similarly avoided by placing it on the side of the ultimate other, of femininity, 'while masculinity is constructed as that which lacks death'.[42] By vanquishing woman associated with nature, men imagine that they vanquish nature and nature's demand, death. It is of course no coincidence that, as Jean Pierre Vernant has described, the masculine figure of death in the Greek language, Thanatos, is represented as a virile warrior enabling the hero's achievement of a glorious death and immortality while the destructive, unspeakable, and unthinkable finality and otherness of death are reserved for representation by feminine figures like Gorgo and Ker. In the Greek mythical imagination, 'it seems hardly necessary to point out that when women did not yet exist—before Pandora was created—death did not exist for men either . . . Death and woman arose in concert together'.[43]

Vernant points out further the striking similarity between descriptions of men succumbing to the seduction of the feminine gaze and of men succumbing to death; '[b]ecause of the desire that emanates from her . . . femininity acts like death' rendering Helen more deserving than her sister Clytemnestra of the appellation 'slayer of men'.[44] It is not surprising, therefore, that femininity, standing for both death and debilitating desire must be sacrificed for the social order to be re-established; following this collective act of aggression, the homosocial order is reinforced based on fixed and secure laws, free from the threat woman poses. The eroticization of Iphigeneia's sacrifice in the chorus's description is another instance of the 'pornography of death'[45] and the inextricability between death and desire: virtuous Iphigeneia thus grounds the symbolic order and law by becoming not only a martyr but a fetish in the cause of male narcissism.[46] Dead, the bodies of pure Iphigeneia and her impure mother Clytemnestra can reflect the fullness and wholeness man's narcissism demands free from the ambiguity and disruptive gaze they returned when alive.

[41] See Julia Kristeva, *Revolution in Poetic Language* (New York: Columbia University Press, 1984), at 75: 'sacrifice designates, precisely, the watershed on the basis of which the social and the symbolic are instituted: the thetic that confines violence to a single place, making it a signifier'.

[42] Elizabeth Bronfen, *Over Her Dead Body, supra*, at 218. See also Luce Irigaray: 'In this proliferating desire for the same, death will be the only representative of an outside, of a hetereogeinity, of an other; woman will assume the function of representing death (of sex/organ), castration and man will be sure as far as possible of achieving mastery': *Speculum of the Other Woman, supra*, at 27.

[43] 'Feminine Figures of Death in Greece' in *Mortals and Immortals, supra*, at 98.

[44] *Ibid.*, at 101–2.

[45] Title of a chapter in Emily Vermeule, *Aspects of Death in Early Greek Art and Poetry* (Berkeley, 1979); discussed by Vernant, *ibid.*, at 102–4.

[46] For a discussion of the fetishization of Euripides' sacrificial heroines see Nancy Sorkin Rabinowitz, *Anxiety Veiled: Euripides and the Traffic in Women* (Ithaca and London: Cornell University Press, 1993), at 31–102.

6 PREGNANT MEN[47]

If woman and the desire for woman threaten death and dissolution, they also, as the Greeks appreciated, offer immortality; women's generative power is the only sure way of guaranteeing and perpetuating a man's name. Indeed Odysseus rejects Calypso's offer not because he is averse to immortality but because eternal life as a god would also condemn him to eternal forgetfulness in the memory of humans. The desire for immortality and the desire for woman are thus indissolubly linked and, as Bataille explores, both linked with death.[48] The male writer, in his own search for immortality is also someone who, in awe and fear of the mother's generative power, both denies that power and attempts to give birth to his text and through his text, to his city and himself. The male attempt to dispense with the mother is encapsulated in the sign and concept of Athena who, born of Zeus, has no need of the mother. The persistence of myths of men born of fathers and even from stones leads us to ask, with Nancy Huston, 'with stones and dirt like that, one wonders, who needs women? And what must one conclude from these incredibly pervasive mis-conceptions?'[49]

One conclusion is that the desire to be the mother is, as Michelle Boulous Walker argues, psychotic, a perversion the symptoms of which Freud himself manifested through his persistent denial of the mother.[50] This repression is endemic to texts that went to define western culture's understanding of itself. In Irigaray's reply to Plato she points out that Plato's cave is a metaphor for the mother's womb, with Socrates the midwife assisting him in giving birth to truth and knowledge. The maternal body and woman's womb are thus turned into a metaphor that enable the male philosopher's journey towards truth. While woman becomes the stage for Plato's play, her role in giving birth is eclipsed so that Plato himself may take her place, engender himself as 'self-sufficient', without foundations and 'beyond all beginnings'.[51] Like Orestes who asserts that he is his father's child and Athena, born of a male in the male imagination, Plato kills the mother to assert his truth. As in Freud's *Moses and Monotheism* the male philosopher's journey into light is a move away from the material, physical body of the mother and the male subject's own gendered embodiment. Unfortunately it is not only woman's body but woman's *dead* body that seems to be necessary for the male search for truth.[52]

---

[47] The title of a motif in Claude Lévi-Strauss, *Mythologiques*, Vols 1–4 (Paris: Plon, 1964–71).

[48] Georges Bataille, *Eroticism* trans. Mary Dalwood. (London and New York: Marion Boyars, 1987 [1952]) I discuss Bataille's link between eroticism and death in chapters 4 and 5.

[49] Nancy Huston, 'The Matrix of War: Mothers and Heroes', in Susan Rubin Suleiman (ed.), *The Female Body in Western Culture, supra,* at 126.

[50] Michelle Boulous Walker, *Philosophy and the Maternal Body: Reading Silence* (London and New York: Routledge, 1998).

[51] *Speculum of the Other Woman, supra,* at 306–7; see further discussion in Michelle Boulous Walker, *Philosophy and the Maternal Body, supra,* especially at 11–16.

[52] For more examples of the pervasive (male) belief that the truth can be found over a dead woman's body see again Elizabeth Bronfen, *Over Her Dead Body, supra.*

The *Oresteia* may be the psychotic text par excellence. Writing the law and the law as word enables the male writer to take the place of the mother; once the mother has been killed and the sister silenced and sacrificed, it is possible for the writer and his city to self-generate, and those texts to be inscribed and embedded into, first myths, then tragedies, and finally laws.

7   CONTESTING GAZES AND EXCHANGES IN EXCESS OF MARKET RULES[53]

It is impossible to forget, however, that Plato's play depends on and is supported by the metaphor of woman. Plato's mis-conception only serves to reveal 'that blind-spot of conception'[54] and his use of woman's womb as an analogy becomes, in Margaret Whitford's phrase, a piece of 'anal logic'.[55] This logic, responsible for the contradiction and ambivalence with which Greek law, Greek myths, and Greek philosophers regarded women, can be discussed, explored, and questioned rather than affirmed by the tragedies. Although the performance of tragedies functioned as rituals of initiation into Athenian civic life and celebrated Athenian ideology, such ideology, was not, nor can ever be, sufficiently unambiguous, homogeneous, or univocal to evade the threat of interrogation.[56] The possibility for different conclusions can come, I will argue, first from within the text itself and secondly from the text's performance; in both cases our participation as readers and as spectators is intrinsic to the project of reading and of seeing otherwise.

First, it is because the demands of the oikos, the family and the private, come into opposition with the demands of the polis, the community and the public, that the conflict becomes the stuff of tragedy. In particular, by dwelling on extreme situations of women who escape the stereotypes, such as intelligent women who rule (Clytemnestra) or abandon the home for the wild (Phaedra), or sacrifice themselves for their brother (Antigone) or kill their mother (Electra), spurn marriage (Cassandra), imprudent wives (Pandora), the tragedies may point out the unsolved dilemmas and tensions in society's treatment of women. Furthermore, the neat oppositions between man and woman and culture and nature are opened for a glimpse of the grey area between them where issues are not so easily categorized or resolved. More ambitiously, one may hope for a glimpse of a female subjectivity divorced from male interests, imaginations, and laws.

---

[53] My discussion here is indebted to two expert analyses of the traffic in women in Greek tragedies: Nancy Sorkin Rabinowitz, *Anxiety Veiled: Euripides and the Traffic in Women, supra* note 55 and Victoria Wohl, *Intimate Commerce: Exchange, Gender and Subjectivity in Greek Tragedy, supra.*

[54] *Speculum of the Other Woman, supra,* at 353.

[55] Margaret Whitford, *Luce Irigaray: Philosophy in the Feminine* (London and New York: Routledge, 1991), at 107.

[56] See John J. Winkler & Froma Zeitlin (eds.), *Nothing to Do With Dionysos? Athenian Drama in its Social Contexts* (Princeton, NJ: Princeton University Press, 1990).

The *Oresteia*, by putting forward Clytemnestra's viewpoint, enables us to dwell on the predicament of Greek women, wives, mothers, and daughters whose desires are not only unrepresented but suppressed in that society's both legal and mythical imaginations. The text, and the performance, can insist on a powerful Clytemnestra who has been the ruler of Argos during her husband's long absence and who has taken a lover in response to her own desire. Unlike in Homer's *Odyssey* where the rights and wrongs of Odysseus' and Agamemnon's circumstances and returns are spelled out, in the *Oresteia* we are not asked to contrast adulterous Clytemnestra with patient and faithful Penelope. To acknowledge the need for myths imagining the sacrifice of beautiful virtuous girls and the murder of adulterous wives is also to acknowledge the threat and possibility of female power. The murder of Clytemnestra and the sacrifice of Iphigeneia rather than solidifying existing norms become the site where those norms can be reopened. The Furies' defeat at Athena's court is also only partially successful. It is no coincidence that the defeat of the Furies takes place at the site, as the text itself reminds us, of Theseus' defeat of the Amazons. The threat the new order feels from the return of the repressed allows a different re-telling of the story of defeat and a glimpse of the possibility of another order and another law.[57]

Again, although in sacrifices only a 'willing' offer was proper,[58] Iphigeneia, in Aeschylus' version, tries, in vain, to resist her powerful captors. She has to be tied and carried to the altar, like a goat, and her mouth is gagged lest she scream and curse her father's house and her father's law. Unlike Cassandra, who forgives and celebrates her captor Agamemnon, and unlike her sister Electra who follows her father's law and assists in her mother's murder, Iphigeneia does not go to her death willingly.[59] She therefore does not fulfil the male fantasy of a woman loyal to men or passively victimized by them. By looking back, Iphigeneia disrupts the desire of her captors (and spectators) that she reflect their fullness and totality; rather than a fixed sign, she is not only an ambiguous but a resisting one. Unlike her father's legislative 'word' that is issued to silence her, the text alludes to her 'virgin voice' that 'would melt the hearts of all'. Thus her death, rather than confirming social morality proves man's failure to expulse the 'other', death, and woman completely. In Nancy Rabinowitz's apt phrase, 'Texts can misfire'.[60]

In Lévi-Strauss's famous formulation the exchange of women between men guarantees the survival of the group; in Greek myth, theatre, and also life, women function

---

[57] See Sarah Bryant-Bertail, 'Gender, Empire and Body-Politic as Mise-en-Scene: Mnouchkine's *Les Atrides*' 46 (1) *Theatre Journal*, 1–30 (March 1993), at 25–7.

[58] *Ibid.*, at 20; discussing Nicole Loraux, *Tragic Ways of Killing a Woman*, *supra*.

[59] Both Electra and Cassandra affirm the view that in patriarchy women are forced to become rivals: thus Cassandra, despite being Agamemnon's captive and victim, celebrates his bravery and curses Clytemnestra as 'a lioness in human form'(*Agamemnon*, 1258). Similarly Electra celebrates and mourns her father but not her sister or mother. Clytemnestra too does not appreciate that the same forces that led to the sacrifice of her innocent daughter Iphigeneia lead to the sacrifice of another innocent outsider, Cassandra. In a production by Ariane Mnouchkine the part of Iphigeneia and Cassandra are played by the same actress, thus underlining this point: see Sarah Bryant-Bertail, *ibid.*

[60] Nancy Sorkin Rabinowitz, *Anxiety veiled*, *supra*, at 12.

as objects of exchange reinforcing male homosocial relations. More than a body to be exchanged, woman is also a sign, a lack, in Lacan's terms, reflecting to the male subject an imagined, albeit false and fragile, sense of fullness. What if women rather than signs themselves, used signs and themselves as signs for their own purposes, actively creating themselves and in the process creating new cultures and new laws? What if, as Irigaray suggests, the objects of exchange 'refused to go to "market"? What if they maintained another kind of commerce, amongst themselves?',[61] laying down their own rules and their own prices? If, as Lévi-Strauss theorizes, the rules on the exchange of women are analogous to linguistic rules governing the exchange of words then we may learn from the fact that words can both exceed, frustrate, and deviate from the speaker's intended meaning. In the same way that man may think he is in control of words but finds that such words control, constitute, and frustrate him, man may think he can exchange women but women may distract, override, and frustrate him from his purpose. When women refuse to be exchanged as war spoils, brides, or sacrifices, the system that was supposed to be cemented by these exchanges instead breaks down. The glimpse of a female subjectivity independent of male rules, once raised, remains in the consciousness of both readers and audiences.[62]

In the end, the social order affirmed by the sacrifice and murder of women is shown to have relied for its definition and continuance on the very disruption produced by women's otherness. The reconciliation offered by the plays' conclusion cannot ignore the sacrifice of Iphigeneia or Clytemnestra's avenging of it; again the return of the repressed ensures that such closure is only imaginary.

8 THE MURDER OF THE FATHER AND THE AUTHOR THROUGH PERFORMANCE

In the beginning of western theatre, as in the beginning of western law, there is the word. This logos/text written by an author/god/creator is paramount, interpreting and dictating what happens on stage to an audience of passive consumers. Such a theatre, however, is, in Antonin Artaud's words, a corruption or repression of theatre, turning the characters into 'puppets' and the audience into 'Peeping Toms'.[63] Reading the *Oresteia* as a text outside performance is already to accord primacy to the text, as well as to find, within the text, the assertion of the primacy of logos. I suggested above that there is a way of reading otherwise, of finding, within the gaps and contradictions in the text the assertion of feminist difference. A further possibility arises when the

---

[61]   Luce Irigaray, *This Sex Which is Not One* (Ithaca, NY: Cornell University Press, 1985 [1977]), trans. Catherine Porter with Carolyn Burke, at 196.

[62]   For a fuller discussion of this possibility see again Nancy Sorkin Rabinowitz, *supra*, and Victoria Wohl, *supra*.

[63]   Antonin Artaud, *The Theatre and Its Double* (London and Paris: Calder, 1993), trans. Victor Corti, at 64.

play is seen as a *play*, a site where meaning is made not by one author-god or one (ruly or unruly) reader but when the clustering of signs in the theatre are recognized and exploited. Such a possibility depends not just on reading but on looking otherwise. Freeing the theatre from the tyranny of the text and the author-god is to take us back to a time before the word was born and, in Derrida's words, requires not an incest but a parricide,[64] in this case of a Greek father by a Greek daughter.

When these myths and tragedies cease to be texts recited or read and become *theatre*, the female other can play and display herself to challenge existing structures and existing laws. By dwelling on the threshold between man and woman, Dionysos poses a threat to existing hierarchies and boundaries, introducing confusion and chaos. The body, often forgotten in readings of texts, is foregrounded in theatrical performance; if, as Barthes says, theatre is a celebration of the human body, women can use their bodies to trespass on ground previously forbidden to them and cross boundaries otherwise dictated by existing laws.[65]

As in the court-room, the clustering of signs in the theatre challenges the centrality of the word with signs other than the text contributing to the making of meaning. Although academically we read law as a text, in the court-room law is also a collection of images, performances, signs that influence if not determine the outcome. In this *con-text*, rather than *text*, the 'word' may be made to mean something different through the intervention and disruption by other linguistic and non-linguistic signs. In the theatre as in the court-room, musical, pictorial, and gesticular forms, the choice of actors, the choice of audience, stage-sets, costumes, lightings, not only illustrate, decorate, or accompany the written text but can disrupt the text, reveal its fragility, and deliver a different message.[66] The performance of the text can explore, exceed, and even explode the text, and dislocate the meanings suggested by any reading. It can explore the margins and limits of the text and of classical theatre, and in the process demystify, even kill the text and the author and his author-ity.[67]

As Laura Mulvey argued in a landmark article twenty-five years ago, women in western representations are the object of the male look or gaze, rarely being allowed to look back.[68] Although the subject and subject matter of the play, the text is not addressed to her, for she is herself the problem of the tragedy: as Freud said to his

---

[64] Derrida, 'The Theatre of Cruelty and the Closure of Representation' in *Writing and Difference* (London and New York: Routledge, 1978).

[65] See Froma Zeitlin at 14: 'using both transvestism (inter-sexuality) and parody (inter-textuality) as the means of trespassing on sacred female space forbidden to men, [*Thesmophoriazousae*] uses the feminine to cross a series of boundaries: between gender and genre, myth and ritual, theatre and festival, sacred and secular, and finally, life and art': *Playing the Other*, supra, and further discussion at 341–416.

[66] See Patrice Pavis 'what is fundamental to the stage, much more so than the signifieds of the text, is the *iconization (mise en vue)* of the word: the text is revealed in all its fragility, constantly menaced as it is by the gesturality which might at any time interrupt its emission, and which always guides the spectator in the rhythm of his reception' in *Languages of the Stage* (New York: Performing Arts Journal, 1982), 80.

[67] See Josette Feral: 'performance conscripts [the] subject both as a constituted subject and as a social subject in order to dislocate and demystify it. Performance is the death of the subject', 'Performance and Theatricality: The Subject Demystified', trans. Terese Lyons, Vol. 25(1) *Modern Drama* 170–81 (1982), at 173.

[68] 'Visual Pleasure and Narrative Cinema' 16(3) *Screen* 6 (1975).

audience in his lecture on femininity, 'from the women among you that is not to be expected, for you are yourselves the riddle'.[69] My reading assumes that women, generally watched as spectacles, are writing and directing the spectacles themselves.[70] While the moments where a challenge can be made are brief and transitory, it is up to creative readers, actors, directors, and audiences to highlight and stress them so that their impact may be lasting. Such moments include:

(a) The description of Iphigeneia's sacrifice and Clytemnestra's cries and tears when hearing them, in particular on hearing Iphigeneia's refusal to be sacrificed in the cause of the male order. We need a performance and a play or display where the disruptive quality of Iphigeneia's defiant look is not erased but where her death signifies a moment of control and power, a form of writing with her body.

(b) The image of Clytemnestra kneeling in front of her son and pleading with him not to kill the breast that gave him life:

> My own child, see this breast:
> Here often your head lay, in sleep, while your soft mouth
> Sucked from me the good milk that gave you life and strength.
> (*Coephoroi*, 897–99)

Unlike Homer's Orestes who shows no hesitation in killing his mother, Aeschylus' Orestes pauses to ask his friend's opinion. Unfortunately Pylades is as pathetic as Orestes and what's more a legal formalist who cannot see behind or beyond 'Apollo's words' (906). We need, instead, a performance that foregrounded Clytemnestra's pleas and Orestes' hesitation at the sight of his mother's breast.

(c) Ironically, the playing of women by male actors in ancient Greece may have disrupted gender ontologies more than contemporary insistence on female roles for women and vice versa. In Judith Butler's famous notion of gender as performative, drag disrupts our view of gender positions as coincident with the body. 'If the anatomy of the performer is distinct from the gender of the performer, and both of these are distinct from the gender of the performance, then the performance suggests a dissonance not only between sex and performance, but sex and gender and gender and performance . . . *In imitating gender, drag implicitly reveals the imitative structure of gender itself—as well as its contingency.*'[71] By reopening the gap between representation and referent, imitation and reality, in particular the gap between the performer's anatomy and the performer's gender, drag causes confusion, dissonance, or trouble. Rather than reflecting and reproducing the existing order, it can unsettle it by destabilizing the notion of identity and in particular gender identity, revealing its contingent,

[69] 'The Psychology of Women' in *New Introductory Lectures in Psychoanalysis* in *The Major Works of Sigmund Freud* (Chicago: Chicago University Press, 1952), at 854.

[70] See Loren Kruger, 'The Dis-Play's the Thing: Gender and Public Sphere in Contemporary British Theatre' in Helene Keyssar (ed.), *Feminist Theatre and Theory* (London; Macmillan, 1996), 49: 'Women have always made spectacles of themselves, as the saying goes. Only recently, and intermittently at that, have women made spectacles themselves.'

[71] *Gender Trouble* (London and New York: Routledge, 1990), at 137; emphasis in the original.

historical, and changeable status. While Clytemnestra is often depicted as large and dark, choosing a frail Clytemnestra might shatter expectations of her 'masculine' features and her alleged assumption of masculine roles.

(d) Finally, a comparison can be drawn between the association of women with the inside and men with the outside and the law's insistence that what happened inside must be put on stage, outside. Like legal judgments, tragedies chart an alleged path from ignorance to knowledge, deception to revelation, misunderstanding to recognition. While Iphigeneia's sacrifice and the murder of Clytemnestra are too ob-scene and therefore have to be perfomed off-scene, off-stage, a performance that foregrounded them and put them *on-stage* would elicit different audience responses.[72] Once what is inside is brought outside, it becomes hard to keep the boundaries intact.

9   REPRESENTATION WITHOUT END

If, as argued in my opening chapter, signs create rather than reflect reality and subjectivity, artists can use their power to create new signs, and thereby new selves and new laws. Plato unconsciously concedes the danger of this power by expelling poets and other mimetes from his ideal state; instead, he assigns the governance of his Republic to the hands of master poets and mimetes who had the forethought to call themselves not artists but philosophers and their plays not theatre but philosophy. In the theatre, the blurring between original and representation means that representation and repetition need not, and cannot, lead to identity or sameness but to iterability, to otherness, and difference. For Nietzsche this artistic will is not deceitful, as Plato thought, or imitative, as Aristotle thought, but creative and superior to the will to truth; rather than assuming a static world, it acknowledges a world subject to change and opens the writer, spectator, and reader to different identities and different laws.

The experience of the theatre in particular may remind us, further, that the body, socially and historically constructed, is itself a mask or masquerade, a spectacle on and off the stage. That it is itself the effect of signs it supposedly reflects and that the world, including the legal world, its norms and discourses, rules and hierarchies, is a stage. Theatre's capacity to regress us to childhood may also open the other scene, the unconscious, revealing repressed desires and forgotten fears. As the 'lawless space of displacements',[73] theatre can unsettle our ways of doing things, reminding us that such norms and practices are not only productions, representations, and contingent,

---

[72] See Ariane Mnouchkine's production of *Les Atrides*, discussed by Sarah Bryant-Bertail *supra*, where the staging of the *Oresteia* is preceded by the staging of Euripides' *Iphigeneia*, thus reminding the audience of the atrocity perpetrated by Agamemnon. (Of course great care has to be taken in how this is staged since Iphigeneia, in Euripides' version, accepts her role as martyr for the Greek cause and goes to her death willingly.)

[73] Hélène Cixous, *La Pupille* (Paris: Cahiers Renaud Barrault, Gallimard, 1972), at 47; quoted in Susan Sellers, *Hélène Cixous: Authorship, Autobiography and Love* (Cambridge: Polity Press, 1996), at 83.

they are also political: consciously or unconsciously they privilege some groups over others. In the case of the creation of the western legal system, such representations not only re-enact but enact or are based on the murder of the mother.

If the selves and actions depicted in the theatre are in fact constituted by the signs and codes that supposedly reflect them, the audience is similarly inscribed and created by signs reflected off the stage. Any everyday event and everyday utterance can be a theatrical performance or event.[74] As theatre producers and theatre spectators in the legal arena, we also rely on a tacit agreement between ourselves and other theatre-goers/producers, enabling thereby the legal spectacle to continue. What if this agreement is broken, what if it is not respected by some producers, actresses, audiences? If the theatrical performance begins and ends with the spectator, whose ability to recognize the performance *as a performance* permits the performance to go ahead,[75] what if the audience starts seeing otherwise, what if it denies or disrupts existing performances, asking for new stories and new endings? Rather than a passive, stolidly indifferent audience we can imagine an audience that, although inscribed and acted upon, also acts as agent and producer of new readings and meanings. A stark illustration of the power of the audience is a performance of the *Oresteia* which did not end when the director thought it would, but when the women members of the audience got up from their seats and untied the ropes that had been used to restrain the Furies.

Mimetic creature that she is, woman uses signs, and herself as sign, to express her desire and make it known to others. Time and language, however, laws and institutions, keep getting in the way, making sure there is always a distance between her desire and her expression of it. Hence the constant need for more representations, more mimeseis, more plays. The process is endless and in its wake she creates poetry and herself through poetry.

[74] See Richard Schechner: 'Context, not fundamental structure, distinguishes ritual, entertainment, and ordinary life from each other. The differences among them arise from the agreement (conscious or unexpressed) between performers and spectators.' *Essays on Performance Theory*, 1970–76 (New York: Drama Book Specialists, 1977), at 217–18.

[75] Keir Elam, *The Semiotics of Theatre and Drama* (London: Methuen, 1980), at 87 and 97.

4

THE MARRIAGE OF DEATH AND DESIRE IN *MEASURE FOR MEASURE*[1]

I'm yearning to be done with all this measuring of proof,
an eye for an eye and a tooth for a tooth,
and anyway I told the truth, and I'm not afraid to die.
Nick Cave and the Bad Seeds, *The Mercy Seat*

1 APPROPRIATING SHAKESPEARE

Shakespeare, Coleridge writes, 'is of no age. Nor, I may add, of any religion, or party, or profession'.[2] Instead, his work transcends time and place, justifying its continuing study and theatrical production, enlightening and delighting students and audiences on eternal problems about human nature and the human condition.

There is of course, a great deal of truth in this claim: Shakespeare speaks to different ages and different places as generations of actresses, audiences, and readers have looked and found in his work a way to relate and understand their own problems and dilemmas, loves and fears. In the rush to exalt the Bard's ubiquitous capacity to enlighten and delight, however, what tends to be underestimated is our insatiable capacity to incorporate and project our own problems and concerns in our interpretations of Shakespeare. In the course of over four hundred years of Shakespearian criticism what has remained constant are not Shakespeare's characters, themes, or concerns but the reader's enthusiasm for interpreting, or appropriating, the texts and making them speak her own problems and concerns. In this context, how could the author or his texts not remain a constant symbol or, what amounts to the same conclusion, fail to speak to every age?

That Shakespeare has yielded as many interpretations as readers have implored him

---

[1] Shakespeare, *Measure for Measure*, ed. N.W.Bawcutt (Oxford: Oxford University Press, 1994); all references in the text are to this edition.

[2] Quoted in Terence Hawkes (ed.), *Coleridge on Shakespeare* (Harmondsworth: Penguin, 1969), at 122.

to make should come as no surprise to those accustomed to, and comfortable with, the death of the author, the open text, and the celebration of the reader. Our continuing interest and ability to relate to Shakespeare have more to do with our conscious or unconscious willingness to transform those texts to our contemporary concerns than with claims concerning their timelessness or greatness. We need to remember, because it is most often overlooked, that neither Shakespeare nor his critics have a monopoly over the meaning that can be attributed to their words, nor do they write in a world where words have a one-to-one correspondence to reality. The fact that words do not offer an unmediated reflection of the world around us means that words can limit as well as enlarge our meanings and our worlds. If Shakespeare criticism has proved and continues to prove inexhaustible, this may be due less to the 'rhetorical excess'[3] of the texts than to the critics' willingness to find and exploit such an excess. This excess, and our willingness to pursue and exploit it, creates and maintains a space for alternative readings of the texts.

To recognize that texts are not written or read in a cultural vacuum and that every reader comes to literature with dirty hands means that my concerns are no more, or less, prejudiced than those of other critics in their parallel quest of making the text mean. The first step to any reading, of Shakespeare or any other author, is an admission of our own situationality and inescapable embeddedness in our historical and cultural circumstances; our personal views and histories cannot but influence our response to and interpretation of the characters and the action. In this chapter I aim, above all, to find out how some concerns have been privileged over others and how the issues of justice and mercy as interpreted by some critics have taken a predominantly male preoccupation with the affairs of the state and the machinations of the Duke. How Shakespeare's chief concerns have appeared to be 'the pathos of kingship and the decline of the great feudal classes'[4] while ignoring the audible but silenced cries of the dominated. In contrast to early critics' almost exclusive concern with male definitions and discussions of power, kingship, politics, and history, I address the concepts of justice and mercy as they pertain to issues of sexuality, desire, marriage, the home, and the mastered. By exposing and exploiting the rhetorical excess and ambiguities in the text and the play's final 'resolution', I hope to rebut facile interpretations of the play as teaching that 'the law must be tempered with mercy' or that marriage represents a just distribution of the play's ceaseless exchange of bodies.

Accepting the contingency of our own readings also means acknowledging the importance Shakespeare's texts and their readings have on the process whereby cultural meanings are created and sustained. Given the elevated position Shakespeare enjoys in our culture, his status as a major instrument by which we make meanings for ourselves and for other people, disputes concerning their interpretation can never be dismissed as merely academic. In the midst of a lucrative and active industry

---

[3] Christopher Norris, 'Post-structuralist Shakespeare: text and ideology' in John Drakakis (ed.), *Alternative Shakespeares* (London: Routledge, 1985), at 58.

[4] Michael Bristol, *Shakespeare's America, America's Shakespeare* (London: Routledge, 1990), at 13.

that Terence Hawkes has dubbed 'Bardbiz',[5] bent on re-enacting and recreating Shakespeare's works, Shakespeare has become, as Linda Boose puts it, 'a site of such competitive jostling because Shakespeare is a site of enormous cultural power'.[6] Moreover, we cannot ignore the view that many renaissance plays were 'fictional questions' which did not necessarily yield one answer or interpretation but were designed to encourage debate.[7] To attempt to fix Shakespeare's plays to a single, univocal meaning would therefore offend not just our postmodern suspicion of final truths and meanings but the dramatists' and audiences' desire to engage in debate about those truths and meanings. The political importance of finding out how those meanings are negotiated, defined, and used and for whose benefit cannot be overestimated.

2 DESIRE AND ITS PROHIBITION

The conflict between self and other, between our essential separateness from the other and our corollary need for the other, has plagued legal theorists in their quest to understand, justify, or challenge law's attempt to mediate this contradiction. Law's answers are in the form of rules that purport to define how far we may touch the other and how far the other may touch us before the contact becomes threatening to ourselves, to the other, and to society as a whole. Crossing the boundaries enacted by law is to risk punishment: law assumes the power to patrol the borders it creates by meting out pain and death on the objects of its command. The fact that this same contradiction is addressed, debated, but not necessarily resolved in literary texts like *Measure for Measure* forms the focus of my discussion.

In analysing this contradiction, the significance attributed to the human subject in liberal theories of law and state is parallelled in traditional literary criticism by an almost exclusive preoccupation with the intentions of the author as the guarantor of the work's meaning. In both fields, how the human subject is constructed, how it comes to know what it wants and more specifically to say what it means and mean what it says have only recently appeared problematic. By questioning the distinction between public and private, self and society, self and other, psychoanalysis from its early stages informed, or warned us, that we cannot properly understand the nature of the individual, her relationship with society, or talk about possibilities for social reform without understanding the nature of the human psyche.

For both Freud and Lacan the state of blissful plenitude and imaginary unity between self and other is the prerogative of the small baby whose proximity to another human being has not yet been severed by the intervention of the father and

---

[5] Terence Hawkes, *Meaning by Shakespeare* (London: Routledge, 1992), at 141.

[6] Lynda Boose, 'The Family in Shakespeare Studies; or—Studies in the Family of Shakespeareans; or—The Politics of Politics', 40 *Renaissance Quarterly* 707–42 (1987), at 708.

[7] See Joel Altman, *The Tudor Play of Mind* (Berkeley, Calif.: University of California Press, 1978).

social codes ascribing 'proper' behaviour. Such intervention, which in Lacan's case occurs through the medium of language, is the beginning of the subject's socialization into approved modes of behaviour. Such is its force that the subject learns to espouse and internalize these laws and prohibitions in her abandonment of pleasure and her submission to utility or reality. The negotiation of the Oedipus complex, however, achieves not just the socialization of the subject but also its condemnation to a state of emptiness, alienation, lack, and repressed impulses. For Lacan, the child's entry into language and the symbolic order is always painful as an arbitrary and external system of words and signs comes to stand in for its earlier sense of fullness and plenitude. The subject's accession to language and the alienation language entails is the birth of desire: 'Desire always becomes manifest at the joint of speech, where it makes its appearance, its sudden appearance, its surge forward. Desire emerges just as it becomes embodied in speech, it emerges with symbolism.'[8] The subject's yearning and search for that earlier sense of fullness becomes a demand for love and recognition by another person, a demand that is constant, unrealizable, and the very condition of desire. The attempt to regain a sense of unity and completion that we once had and have now lost, is an attempt that is also 'exasperated',[9] frustrating, and, in the end, futile: for 'language is as much there to found us in the other as to drastically prevent us from understanding him'.[10] As Žižek puts it, 'the Subject is always too slow or too quick, it can never keep pace with the object of its desire'.[11] Desire is constant energeia, always beyond our reach because it is a desire for the other's desire. The other, however, ridden by the same lack and divisions that plague the self, cannot respond to our call either unconditionally or forever. Desire therefore can never generate fulfilment; only more desire.

Eroticism, like religion and, for its staunch believers, law, offers one way of achieving this unity, by enabling us to open our selves to another human being, of transcending the boundary between our body and that of another's, even, for bodies in love, between our soul and that of another's. By denying or often ignoring society's other preferred methods of mediating the conflict between self and other, eroticism also becomes their rival and, from society's point of view, needs to be contained. In *Measure for Measure* desire is deemed to threaten Vienna's moral, social, legal, political, and religious orders. General lack of law enforcement has led to a situation, the Duke says, where

> liberty plucks justice by the nose,
> The baby beats the nurse, and quite athwart
> goes all decorum. (1.3, 29–31).

---

[8] Jacques Lacan, *The Seminar of Jacques Lacan, Book II: The Ego in Freud's Theory and in the Technique of Psychoanalysis, 1954–1955*, trans. Sylvana Tomaselli (New York and London: W. W. Norfolk & Co, 1991), at 234.

[9] Georges Bataille, *Inner Experience*, trans. Leslie Anne Boldt (Albany NY: State University of New York, 1988), at 89.

[10] *The Seminar of Jacques Lacan, Book II, supra*, at 244.

[11] Slavoj Žižek, *Looking Awry: An Introduction to Jacques Lacan Through Popular Culture* (London UK & Cambridge USA: October, MIT Press, 1991), at 110.

Although sexual transgression is only part of this lawlessness, both the Duke and Angelo see it as central to the project of restoring law and order; we are asked to agree that rampant sexuality is indistinguishable from disorder and chaos. An order is issued for 'all houses in the suburbs of Vienna to be plucked down'(1.2, 94–5) and Angelo's first decree on assuming the Duke's powers is to arrest and sentence Claudio to death for fornication.

Catherine Belsey's playful study[12] offers some suggestions why desire is viewed with suspicion by the state: sexual transgression is singled out as a major source of instability because its threat to the social order arises from the threat it poses to the rational subject's conscious control of herself. Amongst modernism's predilection for explanations based on binary oppositions, the distinction between mind and body is one of the oldest and most prevalent. Desire, associated with the body and the private, is also the site where the subject surrenders control of the mind to the body and where atavistic impulses challenge her sovereignty and identity. Desire, Belsey continues, is not a property of the mind or the body but subsists in the gap between the two, deconstructing the Cartesian opposition between mind and body and destabilizing the difference between them. If law insists that the human being is a rational animal, and religion that she is a spiritual animal, desire reminds us that she is also a sexual animal. Eros transgresses both the Platonic and Christian traditions: as Octavio Paz puts it, 'it transfers the attributes of the soul to the body . . . The lover loves the body as if it were the soul and the soul as if it were the body. Love conmingles heaven and earth: that is the great subversion'.[13]

Erotic play, by acknowledging primary or non-rational instincts, blurs the distinction between human and animal, nature and culture, even life and death: in Bataille's terms, to engage in the sexual act without thought for reproduction is to abandon oneself to pure expenditure without return and thus to challenge the utilitarian principle and the privileging of work over play. The sexual act allows us a glimpse of the possibility of blending with another human being, of dissolving into another, and achieving the union, continuity, and completeness we crave for. At the same time the promise of life and continuity of the sex act also gives us an intimation of death: 'the luxury of death is regarded by us in the same way as that of sexuality, first as a negation of ourselves, then—in a sudden reversal—as the profound truth of that movement of which life is the manifestation'.[14] If death is conceived not as discontinuity but as a return to a primary harmony and continuity with nature, then the erotic act offers a glimpse of immortality and eternity; the result is to blur the distinction not only between human and animal but also between human and goddess. However, the fact that Eros is erratic and insists on wandering from object to object, ignoring distinctions between night and day, between black and white, and between

[12] Catherine Belsey, *Desire; Love Stories in Western Culture* (Oxford: Blackwell, 1994).

[13] Octavio Paz, *The Double Flame: Love and Eroticism*, trans. Helen Lane (London and New York: Harvest, 1993) at 10.

[14] Georges Bataille, 'Consumption' in *Accursed Share: An Essay on General Economy*, trans. Robert Hurley (New York: Zone Books, 1991) [1967], Vol. 1 at 34–5.

social classes threatens society's preference for stability, permanence, and ordered hierachies.[15] This is the secret of Eros' strength: by countenancing change, instability, and dangerous precariousness it is a powerful site of resistance to society's cultural and institutional conventions. For the guardians of the law, the case for bringing it under surveillance is indisputable.

The Platonic and Christian separation between mind and body and subordination of body to mind is of course not gender neutral: the association of man with mind and woman with body, has led to female sexuality being viewed with special suspicion, linked to 'shame' and 'contamination'[16] and treated with 'disgust' and 'distrust'.[17] Indeed woman, or at least her perceived 'shame', is indispensable to the experience of transgression: in Bataille's words, 'ordinarily a man cannot have the feeling that a law is violated in his own person which is why he awaits the confusion of a woman, even if it is feigned, without which he would not have the consciousness of a violation'.[18] Law's fear of Eros, therefore, and the perceived dangers of unbridled sexuality is also a fear of woman. Woman, in Suzanne Guerlac's reading of Bataille, is 'at the center of eroticism . . . the paradoxical object which marks the limit between law and transgression or their interpenetration'; she is the object that renders eroticism '*saisissable*', presenting it 'to consciousness through the mediation of visual form'.[19] The law's attempt to restrict or regulate Eros' behaviour is therefore indistinguishable from attempts to rein and control woman, usually by keeping her inside the private or the house and outside the public or the law. If the subject's search for unity is the search for the lost unity with the mother, then the male subject tries to replace that lost paradise by being the one to regulate the conditions under which motherhood and reproduction may take place.

The Duke's attempt to regulate sexual behaviour and reproduction is inspired less by religion than by fear of the consequences unrestricted fornication would have for the political and social order. Illegitimacy would threaten the laws of property and succession for, as one historian put it, 'whatever ideological problems bastardy litigation might ultimately raise, jurisdiction over land was always at its center'.[20] Uncertainty over paternity would also increase the risk of the incidence of incest as men and women would not know who their parents or siblings are. In extreme cases such as that of Oedipus, this 'sexual and propertal communism' would lead to the

---

[15] See Terry Eagleton, *William Shakespeare* (Oxford: Blackwell, 1986), at 48–57.

[16] Carol Thomas Neely, *Broken Nuptials in Shakespeare's Plays* (New Haven, Conn.: Yale University Press, 1985), at 101 and Carol Thomas Neely, 'Constructing Female Sexuality in the Renaissance: Stratford, London, Windsor, Vienna' in Richard Feldstein and Judith Roof (eds.), *Feminism and Psychoanalysis* (Ithaca NY: Cornell University Press, 1989), at 225.

[17] Richard Wheeler, *Shakespeare's Development and the Problem Comedies: Turn and Counter-Turn* (Berkeley, Calif.: University of California Press, 1981), at 96, 114.

[18] Georges Bataille, *Oeuvres Complètes* (Paris: Gallimard, 1976), Vol.18; quoted in Suzanne Guerlac, '"Recognition" by a Woman! A Reading of Bataille's *L'Erotisme*', *Yale French Studies*, Vol. 78, 90–105, 1990, at 92.

[19] Suzanne Guerlac, '"Recognition" by a Woman! A Reading of Bataille's *L'Erotisme*', *ibid.*, at 104.

[20] R. H. Helmholz, 'Bastardy Litigation in Medieval England', 13, *American Journal of Legal History* (1969) 360–83; quoted in Marc Shell, *The End of Kinship: 'Measure for Measure' Incest, and the Ideal of Universal Siblinghood* (Baltimore and London: Johns Hopkins University Press, 1988), at 37.

dissolution of generational distinctions leading, finally, to a challenge to the distinction between ruler and subject.[21]

There is, however, not just an opposition but also an interdependence between desire and its prohibition, between liberty and restraint. Law polices desire through its prohibition of certain sexual behaviour but law also breeds desire because the stricter the restriction the stronger the desire for the forbidden act. While law's definition of abnormal sexual behaviour aims to dictate what is normal and acceptable, the same legal interventions in the individual's sexual life serve to create and enhance the value of the forbidden acts; the attempts to impose limits and punish transgression often make the forbidden acts more glamorous and precious. As Bataille comments, 'it is certain that the inhibition of love heightens the intensity of erotic pleasure'[22] and the subject comes to desire most what is most strictly forbidden. The risk of punishment certainly inflamed the Marquis de Sade's sexual imagination: as Blanchot comments, 'What can the law do against such power? It sets out to punish it and succeeds in rewarding it. When it reviles it, it exalts it.'[23] Law and punishment are therefore not simply repressive but can be instrumental in intensifying pleasure through transgression. At the same time, by knowingly and deliberately breaking the law, the Sadeian hero may be himself 'a closet Kantian', pushing the implication of Kantian ethics to its limits.[24] Rather than being antithetical, law and desire collude to create as well as enhance each other: the transgressor needs the law as much as the law needs the transgressor.

3 THE CREATION OF 'NORMAL' CITIZENS

A wealth of social, moral, religious, and legal conventions are summoned to police desire in *Measure for Measure*, with the play becoming a rich illustration of how the discourse of sexuality has been used to justify authoritarian control in modern western societies in ever wider and more pervasive spheres of the individual's life. Foucault thought Freud at least partly responsible for sexuality becoming a matter of science and hence, like other humanistic discourses, another discourse of power and domination of the modern subject. Prostitution and lechery, two recurring 'offences' in the play, are not simply threats to the law but more importantly serve to legitimate authority, their regulation becoming the excuse for stricter controls.

---

[21] These points are elaborated by Marc Shell, *ibid.*

[22] *Accursed Share: An Essay on General Economy*, trans. Robert Hurley (New York: Zone Books, 1993), Vol. II, at 167.

[23] Maurice Blanchot, 'Sade's Reason', in Michael Holland (ed.), *The Blanchot Reader* (Oxford: Blackwell, 1995), at 84.

[24] See Slavoj Žižek, 'Kant with (or Against) Sade?', in *The Ethics of Violence, New Formations*, Vol. 35, Autumn 1998, 93–7, at 95; discussing Jacques Lacan, 'Kant avec Sade' in *Écrits* (Paris: Editions du Deuil, 1966), 765–90.

The effectiveness of sexuality as a means of social control also rests at least partly on the fact that it is impossible to control completely. There will always be transgressions and so the need for surveillance and repression is justified. As Pompey suggests, 'Does your worship mean to geld and splay all the youth of the city?' (2.1, 219–20) while Lucio concludes that 'it is impossible to extirp it quite, friar, till eating and drinking be put down' (3.1, 365–6).

As in every society, Viennese law's definition of 'normal' sexual behaviour is determined by that society's version of a 'normal' or ideal social order. That order is embodied not only in social, moral, and religious rules but also in the laws of property and succession which work towards maintaining and reproducing the social order. In the regime enforced by Angelo this interest is greater where the upper classes are concerned: although members of the lower classes such as Mistress Overdone are occasionally punished for sexual offences, only Claudio is threatened with death. As Foucault puts it, the government's 'primary concern was not with the repression of the classes to be exploited, but rather the body, vigour, longevity, primogeniture, and descent of the classes that matter or the classes that ruled'.[25]

The play further demonstrates a change in the methods by which a ruler maintains power over his subjects from the medieval to the modern and from overt to covert means: the dissemination of legal and religious values achieve what overt coercion is unable to achieve, that is people's consent to their own domination and coercion. Such institutions, by defining and publicizing what is normal and acceptable behaviour enable governments to intervene in the private lives of their people.[26] By separating the public and private and assigning desire to the realm of the private, law's regulation of desire polices society more effectively and subtly. This is nowhere more evident than in the Duke's decision to disperse power among two deputies, enabling the application of power to take place surreptitiously and also to operate at all levels of society. His own withdrawal from the public eye, his disguise and descent into invisibility, are part of this surveillance operation, enabling him to gain access to people's innermost thoughts and feelings.

The dual role of the Duke as intermittently political ruler and pious friar exposes the operation and cooperation of religion in the task of social control. State law by itself is not enough for the success of the Duke's plans, restricted as it is to disciplining outward actions; religion on the other hand, works upon men's 'inward cogitations . . . the privy intents and motions of their heart'.[27] The discourse of religion, therefore, even more than other humanistic discourses, reinforces totalitarian control by gaining further control over the individual, his psyche as well as his body. Confession, an

---

[25] Michel Foucault, *The History of Sexuality: An Introduction*, trans. Robert Hurley, (London: Penguin, 1990), Vol.1 at 123.

[26] This point is discussed further by Kim Reynolds, 'Power and Pleasure: *Measure for Measure*' in L. Cookson and B. Loughrey, eds., *Measure for Measure* (London: Longman, 1991).

[27] Richard Hooker quoted by Jonathan Dollimore, 'Transgression and Surveillance in *Measure for Measure*' in Jonathan Dollimore and Alan Sinfield (eds.), *Political Shakespeare: Essays in Cultural Materialism* (Manchester: Manchester University Press, 1994), at 81.

instrument that the Duke uses, and unashamedly abuses, by emphasizing the subject's intention, what she thinks as well as what she does, performs the function of control and normalization. The Duke uses his confession of Mariana to elicit her respect and obedience, even whilst he plans to use her in the bed trick. As for Mariana, unresisting and accommodating as the text confines her to be, she appears to experience this exploitation as 'voluntary allegiance to disinterested virtue'.[28]

For their part Claudio and Juliet are only too keen to assume and repent their guilt, judging themselves more harshly than other characters in the play judge them: Claudio compares himself to thirsty rats (1.2, 128–30) while Julia confesses, repents, and bears her shame 'most patiently' (2.3, 28–9). It is hard not to detect in the Duke's dialogues with Claudio and Juliet two submissive subjects who admit and internalize their guilt. In this context, the religious extolling of marriage is another convenient form of propaganda for state control.

Only two characters in the play manage to resist the Duke's attempts at normalization; for that reason the roles of Barnadine and Lucio cannot be dismissed as purely comic. Indeed, as will be discussed in the next section, it is through comedy, farce, and carnival that elements of subversion and resistance can be glimpsed.

4 POLITICAL AUTHORITY

Attempts to regulate and constrain desire and sexuality through legal and religious instruments mean that binary oppositions between mind and body, public and private, the family and the state, desire and law are not as neat as the state would like them to appear. Desire affects the private as much as the public relationships of the citizen, particularly when it leads to children, hence the state's attempts to regulate and name both individuals and their relationships with each other. Political authority in the play becomes omnipresent with the Duke's descent into invisibility, intervening, overtly and covertly, in every sphere of the citizens' lives. What is the source and nature of this authority and does the play affirm or contest its existence and operation?

Critics have suggested that Vincentio bears many similarities to James I, some going further to argue that the portrayal of the Duke in the play is intended as a form of flattery to James I. Indeed the Duke's dislike of crowds, his delegation of authority to his deputies but continued reluctance to surrender control, his interest in the problematics of the concepts of justice and its relationship to mercy find many parallels in the then monarch's character and concerns. One of the most famous passages from *Basilikon Doron* has been quoted to sum up the play's themes: 'Laws', James I wrote,

---

[28] *Ibid.*, at 82. Directors have greater facility to register Mariana's disquiet at the Duke's plans than readers as in Steven Pomloy's 1995 production where Mariana's agreement is accompanied with a piercing, anguished cry.

'are ordained as rules of vertuous and social living, and not to be snares to trap your good subjects: and therefore the lawe must be interpreted according to the meaning, and not to the literall sense . . . Learn also wisely to discernce betwixt Iustice and equitie . . . . For Iustice, by the Law, giueth every man his owne; and equitie in things arbitrall, giueth every one that which is metest for him.'[29] Commentators have further charted the striking parallels between James's sentencing and last minute reprieve of Sir Walter Raleigh and his alleged conspirators with the Duke's meting out of pardons in the last scene of the play.[30]

Textual and thematic similarities, however, cannot by themselves determine whether Shakespeare intended them as a form of flattery to his King or as ironic if not subversive comparisons between the Duke and the ruler that Henry of Navarre dubbed the wisest fool in Christendom. Much of this uncertainty stems from the fact that critics are not quite sure what to make of the Duke: as A. P. Rossiter admitted, 'What one makes of the play depends on what one makes of the Duke . . . I do not quite know what to make of the Duke'.[31] This admission, the uncertainty and ambiguity of the text and the action, and the reader's inalienable prerogative of interpreting the text, mean that successive readers, actresses, and directors have used their freedom to find in the Duke qualities varying from those of an interfering fool to a wise and benevolent ruler.

Critics who see the play as a Christian humanist exploration of mercy's relationship to justice justify Vincentio's deceptive behaviour on the grounds that he is acting for the benefit of Isabella's spiritual growth, enabling her to recognize the value of mercy.[32] Other critics have seen the Duke as 'comparable with Divinity',[33] 'a kind of Providence directing the action from above' in 'a controlled experiment' in moral education,[34] or a secular analogy of the Incarnation.[35] Such interpretations are often accompanied with the view of the play as a Passion play in which sinful men are redeemed through God's mercy and conveying the Christian message that 'all men are pardoned sinners and must forgive'.[36]

The view that Shakespeare was somehow above or beyond the ideological disputes of his day does not, however, explain elements of the play that work towards affirming the

---

[29] Charles H. McIlwain, *The Political Works of James I* (Cambridge, Mass.: Harvard University Press, 1918), at 39.

[30] For example, Craig A. Bernthal, 'Staging Justice: James I and the Trial Scenes of *Measure for Measure*', 32 *Studies in English Literature* 247 (1992); Wilbur Dunkel, 'Law and Equity in *Measure for Measure*', 13, *Shakespeare Quarterly* 275 (1962).

[31] A. P. Rossiter, 'The Problem Plays' in Graham Storey (ed.), *Angels with Horns and Other Shakespeare Lectures* (London: Longman, 1961), at 164.

[32] For example, Roy Battenhouse, '*Measure for Measure* and the Doctrine of Atonement', *Proceedings of the Modern Language Association*, LXI (1946), 1029; Rosalind Miles, *The Problem of Measure for Measure: A Historical Investigation* (London: Vision, 1976)

[33] G. Wilson Knight, *The Wheel of Fire* (London, 1960), at 82.

[34] F. R. Leavis, *The Common Pursuit* (Harmondsworth: Penguin, 1962), at 170 and 164.

[35] Roy Battenhouse, *supra*.

[36] R. W. Chambers, *Man's Unconquerable Mind* (London: Methuen & Co, 1939), at 277–310.

re-imposition of centralized power. In particular, the Duke's absence and consequent abuse of power by one of his deputies serves to justify the return of full centralized authority in the last Act. As Leonard Tennenhouse puts it, *Measure for Measure* discovers 'what they would have us believe is a law of nature, that only the true monarch is the best form of political power'.[37] Stephen Greenblatt is similarly cynical about *Measure for Measure's* 'open, sustained, and radical questioning of authority before it is reaffirmed, with ironic reservations, at the close'.[38] And Jonathan Dollimore suggests that, 'like many apparent threats to authority this one in fact legitimates it: control of the threat becomes the rationale of authoritarian reaction in a time of apparent crisis'.[39] Moreover, in the midst of enjoying the 'happy' ending and the exposure and shaming of the corrupt deputy, the audience may easily forget that no law has been changed, or that political authority remains in the hands of the man who controlled the action throughout. The play's idealization of chastity and presentation of marriage as a resolution to every conflict further ignores that chastity and marriage are themselves ideological instruments at the service of the existing social order, in particular the laws of property and kinship. In that sense, as Dollimore and Sinfield argue, the theatre becomes a 'prime location for the representation and legitimation of power'.[40]

Less a disinterested attempt to temper justice with mercy, the Duke's underground manoeuvres are aimed at asserting his own, and the law's authority upon the bodies of his citizens. To do that he does not hesitate to substitute one body for another, as in the Isabella/Mariana bed trick, or one head for another, as in the Ragozine/Claudio beheading trick. 'The penalty', as Freud said, 'must be exacted even if it does not fall upon the guilty.'[41] The end-product of these exchanges, punishments, and pardons, is to mask naked violence and intrusive control as benign authority and protective rule. If the Duke's subjects, and indeed the audience, are convinced by these redefinitions, it is because the Duke and the law seduce them with words, images, and rituals into submission. When authority is presented as care, when power is presented as love, when violence is presented as reason, the will to resist becomes a will to submit, questioning becomes fascination, transgression becomes obedience.[42]

---

[37] Leonard Tennenhouse, 'Representing Power: *Measure for Measure* in its time' in Stephen Greenblatt (ed.), *The Power of Forms in the English Renaissance* (Norman, Okla.: Pilgrim Books, 1982), 139–56, especially at 140 and 143. See also Leonard Tennenhouse, *Power on Display: The Politics of Shakespeare's Genres* (New York and London: Methuen, 1986), at 156.

[38] 'Invisible bullets: Renaissance authority and its subversion, *Henry IV* and *Henry V*', in Dollimore and Sinfield (eds.), *Political Shakespeare, supra*, at 29.

[39] Jonathan Dollimore, 'Transgression and Surveillance in *Measure for Measure*', *supra*, at 73.

[40] Jonathan Dollimore, 'Shakespeare, cultural materialism and the new historicism' in Dollimore and Sinfield (eds.), *Political Shakespeare, supra*, at 3.

[41] *The Major Works of Sigmund Freud* (Chicago: Chicago University Press, 1952), at 711; this point is discussed by Jane Beverly Malmo who argues that while in the lawless brothels 'bodies are exchanged *for* money', the law's 'desire to have the body' means that in the Duke's court, 'bodies are exchanged *as* money': 'Beheading the Dead: Rites of Habeas Corpus in Shakespeare's *Measure for Measure*' in *The Ethics of Violence, New Formations*, Vol. 35, Autumn 1998, 134–44.

[42] See Peter Goodrich (ed.), *Law and the Unconscious: A Legendre Reader*, trans. Peter Goodrich with Alain Pottage and Anton Schütz (London: Macmillan, 1997).

5 COMIC SUBVERSIONS

Not every character in the play, however, and not every member of the audience is the child longing to submit to the father's law or is necessarily seduced by the law's semblance of love. The following sections identify characters and readers who succeed in remaining outside the Duke's and the law's spell. For, as always, the text provides us with material for readings that contest the Duke's authority, the choice between alternate readings and performances resting, as always, with the reader, director, and spectator. The critical unease the play's conclusion has caused explains partly its labelling as a problem play with the elaborate restitution at the end appearing more deception than confirmation of the Duke's power and the force of law.[43] Forced marriages and blanket pardons do not inspire confidence that justice has been achieved nor that it will last. The same show trials that can be seen as celebrating the Duke's wisdom and mercy can be read as demystifying the way in which political theatre is used to create state power, showing the Duke as an ordinary man pulling strings behind the scene to project an image mightier than himself.[44] By the end of the play few of the political assertions voiced at the beginning by the Duke and Angelo remain unchallenged by other characters or uncompromised by events.[45]

Once we abandon the view of the Duke as an allegory for Providence or divine justice, it is possible to see him too as a desiring subject who, like Angelo, claims not to be prey to desire (1.3, 2–3). It is in the Duke above all that one is expected to find the justification for law's existence and application and it is in the Duke again that one comes to abhor the use and abuse of such power. For it is hard not to agree with Lucio that the Duke is a 'seemer' manipulating the other characters for the perpetuation and exaltation of his own power.[46] The revelation of Angelo as a weak, desiring subject makes him a more sympathetic character than his master who having, like Angelo, professed indifference to the desires of the flesh seeks to use his position to write on Isabella. Productions that deny him this power offer more satisfaction than productions that have Isabella and the rest of the cast trailing after the Duke at the end.

In this reading, it is Lucio, not the Duke, who is the star of the play. He is 'a fellow of much licence' (3.2, 195), 'a kind of burr' (4.3, 175), a rebel, a realist, shrewd, relaxed, quick-witted, and practical. For Lucio, renunciation of sexual desire makes one akin to a saint:

---

[43] See Anthony B. Dawson, '*Measure for Measure*, New Historicism and Theatrical Power', 29 *Shakespeare Quarterly* 328 (1988).

[44] See Craig Bernthal, *supra*.

[45] See Paul Hammond, 'The Argument of *Measure for Measure*', 16 *English Literary Renaissance* 496 (1986).

[46] For support of this view see Thomas F. Van Laan, *Role Playing in Shakespeare* (Toronto: University of Toronto Press, 1978), at 98–100 where he describes the Duke as a writer/producer/director of his own 'carefully devised playlet', and who is 'like some film star, more interested in his own virtuosity than ideal representation of the script'. Also Marcia Reifer, 'Female Power in *Measure for Measure*', 35, *Shakespeare Quarterly* 157 (1984), at 161: 'His ultimate intention seems to be setting the stage for his final dramatic saving of the day—a day which would not need saving except for his contrivances in the first place'.

> I hold you as a thing enskied and sainted,
> By your renouncement an immortal spirit,
> And to be talked with in sincerity,
> As with a saint. (1.4, 34–37)

Lucio is a 'fantastic', one of the few characters in the play who refuses to be written on by the Duke, whether the latter is wearing his princely gowns or those of a holy friar. His punishment at the end helps shutter any inclination we might have to read this as a happy or just ending and undermine the view that the Duke is meting out 'justice tempered with mercy' in the last scene. Law remains, as Lucio understands and experiences it throughout the play, an external oppressive force that we should do our best to avoid. Unlike Claudio, Julietta, or Mariana, Lucio internalizes neither the Duke's legal codes nor the Friar's religious strictures.

The view that law is an external oppressive force rather than a positive force helping to constitute society is belied not only by Lucio but also Pompey: the latter is well aware that the law is a self-referential exercise, without a prior external source or justification other than the perpetuation of its own existence. Its prohibition of certain conduct justifies its existence as much as its existence depends on its prohibition of certain conduct:

Escalus: Is it a lawful trade?
Pompey: If the law would allow it, sir.
Escalus: But the law will not allow it, Pompey (2.1, 214–17)

The law, in other words, demands obedience not because it is based on truth or justice but simply because it is *there*. This conclusion has not changed much since Shakespeare's days: in Kafka's *The Trial* at first Josef K insists that something is a court 'only if I recognize it as such' but as the priest explains to him, 'it is not necessary to accept everything as true, one must only accept it as necessary'.[47] This 'melancholy conclusion', as K calls it, 'turns lying into a universal principle' and, like any tautology, allows the speaker to hide behind the language of authority and the absence that is law for want of a better explanation.[48]

In the same vein, the portrayal of Barnardine cannot be dismissed as an attempt to provide comic relief but as an important subversive sub-text in a play where the dominant text, or more accurately, the dominant reading of the text, supports autocratic authority. Barnardine consistently refuses to play the role of repentant man or display the anxiety which the criminal process aims to inspire.[49] His refusal to admit guilt or accept the verdict and sentence is in effect a refusal to perform the role of legitimating his own execution. Barnardine exposes the Duke's process as a sham by

---

[47] Franz Kafka, *The Trial* (Harmondsworth: Penguin, 1953) [1925], at 49 and 243.

[48] On tautologies, see Roland Barthes, *Mythologies*, trans. Annette Lavers (London: Vintage, 1993) [1957], at 152.

[49] See Stephen Greenblatt, *Shakespearean Negotiations* (Berkeley, Calif.: University of California Press, 1988), at 137.

using the only weapon available to the powerless, that is the refusal to take power seriously: 'I swear I will not die today for any man's persuasion' (4.3, 56–7). The element of laughter and the carnivalesque induced by Barnadine's brief appearances are just as effective a challenge to centralized authority as Claudio's more 'serious' protests. Barnadine's refusal to accord seriousness absolute power is itself, we must conclude, a serious matter: 'He who wants to kill most thoroughly—*laughs*.'[50]

6 AUTHOR-ITARIAN INSCRIPTIONS AND THE TRAFFIC IN WOMEN

In examining the role of women in the play one cannot but admit that the preoccupations of the reader will be more important than any alleged intentions the author may have had in promoting or discouraging equality between the sexes. Once again, such preoccupations are no less political than other issues explored by the reader. Indeed the very selection of this issue for consideration shows the sovereignty of the reader in the discussion of texts: early discussions and productions of the play found no problem with or cause for challenging the roles the play appeared to assign to its women characters.

It should therefore come as no surprise that just as some critics are able to enlist Shakespeare as a revolutionary challenging state authority while others see in his text a devout and loyal apologist for the Tudor myth, feminists have equally been divided between finding in Shakespeare an ardent proto-feminist on the one hand and a proponent of the patriarchal order on the other.[51] The text provides material for both views and it is for readers and producers to assume responsibility for their selection given the political importance of their enterprise. Negative representations of women in the cultural field, one must remember, can end up implying the inferiority and necessary subordination of women in the political field. For women readers it is imperative to expose the contradictions and ambiguities in the text and in readings and performances of it in order to uncover the operations of gender in literary discourse and women's exclusion from it. Such readings enable us to envisage new forms of social organization, including alternatives to the patriarchal family structure.

The view that Shakespeare can be enlisted as a liberal proto-feminist is not uncommon: Coppelia Kahn for instance suggests that, '[t]oday we are questioning the cultural definitions of sexual identity we have inherited. I believe Shakespeare

---

[50] Friedrich Nietzsche, *Thus Spoke Zarathustra*, trans. R. J. Hollingdale (London: Penguin 1961) at 324.

[51] For the former view see, for example, Irene G. Dash, *Wooing, Wedding and Power: Women in Shakespeare's Plays* (New York: Columbia University Press, 1981); for the latter see, for example, Ann Thompson, 'The Warrant of Womanhood': Shakespeare and Feminist Criticism' in Graham Holderness (ed.), *The Shakespeare Myth* (Manchester: Manchester University Press, 1988).

questioned them too.'[52] And Juliet Dusinberre refers to 'Shakespeare's concern to dissolve artificial distinctions between the sexes'.[53] Other critics are not so sure, worrying that Shakespeare's women, however strong or supportive of each other, are restricted by, or in the end submit to, the patriarchal structures that dominate their lives.[54]

Such assertions of course assume a god-like author whose intentions can be uncovered by a disinterested reader, ignoring that the latter's concerns will influence their interpretation of the characters and the text. They further have the effect of essentializing women by asking them to conform to one pattern of defying male authority. For this reader and spectator, the view that Shakespeare questioned patriarchal authority is hard to sustain in the context of a play where women form the main object of exchange and where contracts are negotiated by, and legal and political power is vested in the hands of, male actors like Vincentio and Angelo. The friendship between Isabella and Mariana, although used to outwit male authority is supplanted in the end with marriage. Isabella's chastity and Mariana's position as 'neither maid, widow, nor wife' (5.2, 80) could be read on the one hand as gestures of autonomy and female resistance but are in effect treated as abnormal and problematic. The play's preferred way of 'correcting' such problems is the institution of marriage. Isabella's silence at the end of the play does allow directors to read a gesture of feminist defiance at the Duke's attempt to co-opt her into his plans but no such opportunities are afforded to Mariana who is reduced to pleading forgiveness for her treacherous lover. As Kathleen Macluskie argues, within the parameters of the text, feminist criticism can do no more than expose its own exclusion from it; 'it has no point of entry into it because the dilemmas of the narrative and the sexuality under discussion are constructed in completely male terms'.[55]

Those wanting to co-opt Shakespeare to feminist concerns would also find it hard to explain away the recurring images in the play of women as blank pages waiting to be written on by the male pen/penis. In this image, which is not exclusive to Shakespeare,[56] the sexual act is likened to printing with the man reproducing copies of himself and the woman as the instrument or 'press' inscribed on or 'coined' by the man. The implication is that women are the passive objects of men's authority in legal and textual as well as sexual terms. The male pen or penis becomes not just the author but also the authority of women's bodies and lives. The relationship between Claudio and Juliet may be the most 'mutual' one in the play but it, too, is described in terms of contractual exchanges and male writing with woman as the object of exchange: 'Upon

---

[52] Coppelia Kahn, 'Man's Estate' in *Masculine Identity in Shakespeare* (Berkeley and Los Angeles: California University Press, 1981), at 20.

[53] Juliet Dusinberre, *Shakespeare and the Nature of Women* (London: Macmillan, 1975), at 153.

[54] See for example, Lynda Boose, *supra*; Kathleen Mcluskie, 'The Patriarchal bard: feminist criticism and Shakespeare: *King Lear* and *Measure for Measure* in Dollimore and Sinfield (eds.), *Political Shakespeare, supra*; Ann Thompson, 'The Warrant of Womanhood' in Holderness (ed.), *The Shakespeare Myth, supra*.

[55] Kathleen Mcluskie, 'The Patriarchal bard: feminist criticism and Shakespeare: *King Lear* and *Measure for Measure*' in Dollimore and Sinfield (eds.), *Political Shakespeare, supra*, at 97.

[56] Elizabeth Abel (ed.), *Writing and Sexual Difference* (Brighton: Harvester, 1982), at 73–93.

a true contract I took possession of Julietta's bed', Claudio explains and 'the stealth of our most mutual entertainment / with character too gross is writ on Juliet' (1.2, 154–5). Lucio is characteristically blunter, describing Claudio as the labourer who grows fruit from his property while Julietta's 'plenteous womb / Expresseth his full tilth and husbandry' (I.4, 43–4). The printing metaphor is extended to include the legitimacy of children with Angelo's likening the begetting of illegitimate children with the counterfeiting of coins (2.4, 42–9). Marriage in this context is the medium through which male authority is legitimized with the man acquiring true 'copyright' and ownership of the woman's body.[57] Women's passivity in these exchanges does not even exonerate them from blame: the Duke as Friar asks for and gets Julietta to agree that her 'sin' is of a 'heavier kind' than Claudio's (2.3, 28).

Verbal power, sexual domination, and legal authority support and reinforce each other throughout the play and most notably in the Isabella-Angelo and Isabella-Duke scenes. Both the Duke and Angelo use their authority to try to write on Isabella and although Angelo fails, it is far from clear that the Duke does. Everyone recognizes a wrong in Angelo's asking Isabella to choose between her chastity and her brother's life and Isabella has no problem recognizing Angelo as the 'devil' and his view of the nature of law and justice as perverted and insupportable. The real danger to her autonomy and capacity to choose, however, stems from the Duke; and here her ability to thwart his attentions is not as clear.

Even amidst the Duke's colonization of the voices and acts of the female characters there is, however, a slim opening for an alternative reading. The Duke may be the main character with the power to write on others, but Isabella's silence at the end has proved, for recent readers, more eloquent than any reply Shakespeare might have given her. As Jonathan Goldberg argues, 'it is not necessarily a sign of power to have a voice, nor necessarily a sign of subjection to lose it'.[58] At the same time it is not only the female characters that are silent or silenced in the last scene: Angelo's pleas for an 'Immediate sentence, then and sequent death' (5.1, 374), and 'I crave death more willingly than mercy. / 'Tis my deserving, and I do entreat it' (5.1, 479–80) are ignored by a Duke bent on inscribing his own language and his own law on the others. Claudio says little after the third act, even after his return from apparent death while Lucio's attempts to participate in his own future are repeatedly silenced by the Duke. Like other characters in the play, Angelo, Claudio, and Lucio also serve as empty signs to be inscribed on by the Duke for his own version of the nature of law and justice.

---

[57] See Meredith Skura, *The Literary Uses of Psychoanalysis* (New York: Yale University Press, 1981), at 243–70. Ann Thomson and John Thompson, *Shakespeare, Meaning and Metaphor* (Brighton: Harvester, 1987), chapter 5.

[58] Jonathan Goldberg, 'Shakespearean Inscriptions: The Voicing of Power' in Patricia Parker and Geoffrey Hartman (eds.), *Shakespeare and the Question of Theory* (New York and London: Routledge), at 130.

7 DESIRE AND THE INSTITUTION

Having charted a series of exchanges of bodies, the play concludes with the Duke meting out pardons and punishments. His chief instrument, or weapon, in these manoeuvres is the institution of marriage. Claudio is reunited with Juliet, Angelo with Mariana, he himself offers his hand to Isabella, and Lucio is forced to marry Kate Keepdown. Marriage as a solution to the threat posed by desire is preferred not because it is dictated by religion or only by religion; the legal, political and social order require it as a means of limiting fornication for the production of legitimate offspring. The fragile symbolic order, in other words, as Lévi-Strauss argues, uses the instrument of marriage to mediate the opposing forces of nature and culture: 'the rules of kinship and marriage are not made necessary by the social state. They are the social state itself.'[59] Through marriage society may recognize legitimate from illegitimate off-spring, it can limit 'accidents' of incest when offspring do not recognize each other as kin, and the law can restrict the inheritance of property to recognized heirs. Whether marriage is a just solution or a repressive mechanism hiding exploitation depends on the view one takes of the institution of marriage generally and of the marriages in the play in particular. These vary from seeing it as an interference with self-fulfilment, as a necessary institution for the maintenance of the social order, as an ideal dissolution of the contradiction between self and other, as an approximation of justice or as another form of social control silencing women.

In an early essay Eagleton proposed that marriage is the public sanctioning of personal passion, making personal life socially responsible without diminishing its authenticity. In this sense, he says, marriage serves as an image of the synthesis which the play struggles towards and is akin to language in bringing man into relationships and community by externalizing their private experience and making it open to public judgment and response. This conclusion cannot be separated from his view that marriage is a public commitment, a way of relating individual experience to society, and of resolving the contradiction between self and other by representing the true and mutual receiving of the print of the other.[60]

Such a sanguine view of the institution of marriage has not always found favour; amidst the changing views held by different cultures and different epochs on love and marriage, the opposition between passionate desire and utilitarian marriage is a dominant trope amongst historians and anthropologists of love. In the alternative jurisprudence delivered by the courts of love explored by Peter Goodrich, 'love and marriage were mutually exclusive . . . marital affection and true love were different in species and had their origin in radically distinct movements of the soul. They could

---

[59] Claude Lévi-Strauss, *The Elementary Structures of Kinship*, trans. J. H. Bell and John von Sturmer (Boston: Beacon Press, 1969) at 490.

[60] Terry Eagleton, *Shakespeare and Society* (London: Chatto & Windus, 1967), at 66–98; a similar view is expressed in his *William Shakespeare* (Oxford: Blackwell, 1986), at 48–57.

not, in consequence, be compared.'[61] In the domain of the courts of love as in many Shakespeare plays, marriage is, in addition, a means of asserting patriarchal authority over the danger of female desire which positive law perceived as excessive, insatiable, and unruly:

> Such duty as the subject owes the prince
> Even such a woman oweth to her husband

concludes Katherine in *The Taming of the Shrew*,[62] and for Luciana in *The Comedy of Errors*

> Men, more divine, the masters of all these,
> Lords of the wide world, and wild watery seas . . .
> are masters to their females, and their lords.[63]

In general, the view that marriage can be a tool to right social wrongs presupposes that marriage is a just solution, neglecting the realities of the power structures which inform social behaviour and in particular its patriarchal assumptions. For some, bourgeois marriage, by uniting procreation, sexuality, love, and a legal contract, functions as a moral legitimation of the political and social subordination of women. For Carol Thomas Neely 'women are defined and contained through their place in the marriage paradigm . . . These modes are in turn defined by the mode of sexuality appropriate to them: virginity for maidens, marital chastity for wives, abstinence for widows.'[64] Catherine Belsey also has no illusions that the transition from a dynastic view of marriage to a family founded on mutual love and consent leaves a lot to be desired: patriarchy reasserts itself in the affective family, she comments, as women do not achieve equality but acquire a sphere of influence which is restricted to the home, a place seen as outside politics and therefore outside the operations of power.[65] Marriage in this context becomes less an institution for ensuring mutual love and cooperation than a tool for reproducing patriarchal authority behind the guise of love and consent.

   Indeed, only one relationship in the play is not the result of deceit or exploitation, that between Claudio and Juliet; and they are both silent at the end of the play.[66] Angelo, although remorseful concerning his abuse of power regarding Isabella, is not moved to express any affection towards his new partner and Lucio makes no secret of

---

[61] Peter Goodrich, *Law in the Courts of Love: Literature and Other Minor Jurisprudences* (London and New York: Routledge, 1996), at 29–30.

[62] Shakespeare, *The Taming of the Shrew*, ed. Stephen Roy Miller (Cambridge: Cambridge University Press, 1998) at 5.2, 156–7.

[63] Shakespeare, *The Comedy of Errors*, ed. T. S. Dorsch (Cambridge: Cambridge University Press, 1988) at 2.1, 24.

[64] Carol Thomas Neely, 'Constructing Female Sexuality in the Renaissance', *supra*, 213.

[65] Catherine Belsey, 'Disrupting Sexual Difference: Meaning and Gender in the Comedies' in John Drakakis (ed.), *Alternative Shakespeares, supra*, at 166–90.

[66] In the Royal Shakespeare Company's 1995 production of the play in the last scene Juliet appears gagged and flagged by two police officers.

his distaste for the result. The Duke manipulates marriage as an instrument of punishment or forgiveness where the men are concerned (for both Angelo and Lucio
marriage is a substitute for threatened execution) while the women are thought to
be 'saved' by it from moral and very often financial destitution. Isabella's lack
of response to the Duke's proposal has allowed critics and directors to interpret
her silence as affirmation in earlier productions, blanket refusal in Jonathan Miller's
1975 production, to leaving the answer open to the audience in Steven Pimlott's 1995
production.

That marriage is an instrument of social control and that the Duke's primary
objective is the preservation of the social order is shown from the fact that the law is
used to repress the male characters, Angelo and Lucio, as much as the female characters. The panic over one-parent families in our own society and the Child Support
Agency's attempts to track down absent fathers shows that the Duke's preoccupations
in Shakespeare's Vienna are also shared by today's governments. The view that the
legal institution of marriage is a panacea for our social and personal problems of
course preceded and outlived Shakespeare. For Claude Lévi-Strauss the exchange of
gifts is the fundamental form of social intercourse, with the exchange of women
(mothers, daughters, or sisters) in marriage as the supreme gift. Such exchanges, by
forging artificial alliances between men, guarantee the survival of the group.[67] For
feminists, however, the view that culture depends on a form of gift exchange that has
the effect of ensuring hierarchical gender relations cannot go unexamined.[68] Isabella's
refusal to exchange her chastity for Claudio's life and her ambiguous response to the
Duke's proposal allows us to imagine an alternative form of family organization.

In the same way, as we saw in chapter two, the symbolic order Lacan describes is a
patriarchal order, structured around the transcendental signifier of the phallus and
dominated by the law of the father. Despite the patriarchal bias of this system, Lacan's
grounding of the subject in language, rather than, as Freud did, in biology, raises the
possibility of an alternative system of representations and an alternative system of
laws. Irigaray explains the law of the father as a mechanism for compensating for the
uncertainty of paternity as well as protecting the father from his desire for the daughter. Women must therefore resist the temptation of accepting male representations of
themselves and succumbing to the law of the father and to celebrate, instead, their
sexuality which, rather than singular, is plural, heterogeneous, fluid, and indefinite.
One site of female resistance is provided, of course, by the practice of adultery which
undermines the name of the father.[69]

[67] Claude Lévi-Strauss, *The Elementary Structures of Kinship*, (ed.) Rodney Needham, trans. James Harle
Bell, John Richard von Sturmer and Rodney Needham (Boston, Mass.: Beacon Press, 1969) especially at 480–1.

[68] See, for example, Gail Rubin, 'The Traffic in Women: Notes Toward a Political Economy of Sex' in
Robert Reiter, *Toward an Anthropology of Women* (New York: Monthly Review Press, 1975), at 157–210; Luce
Irigaray, 'Commodities among Themselves' in *This Sex Which Is Not One*, trans. Catherine Porter with
Carolyn Burke (Ithaca, New York: Cornell University Press, 1985) at 192–7.

[69] See Jane Gallop, *Feminism and Psychoanalysis: The Daughter's Seduction* (London: Macmillan, 1982), at
47–8; Helga Geyer-Ryan, *Fables of Desire: Studies in the Ethics of Art and Gender* (Cambridge: Polity Press,
1992), at 96–105.

Does Shakespeare's text allow room for such a celebration of female sexuality and power outside the confines of the law of the father as dictated first by Angelo and, later, and more surreptitiously, by the Duke? Mario DiGangi finds such a reading by focusing on a usually neglected character, Mrs Elbow, who defies the authority of both her physician and husband and enters a hot-house 'before due season', an action that was thought to risk premature birth. Marriage as portrayed in the play, he concludes, does not solve male anxiety about female sexuality and there is no guarantee that the marriages ordered by the Duke at the end will be less troublesome for the husbands: '[B]ecause none of the couples which crystallize at the end demonstrate mutual affection and commitment, they are no more the heralds of a renewed, redeemed society, than Elbow and his wife. Like the Duke's unanswered 'motion' to Isabella the motion of the final scene constitutes a deferment of resolution, a suppression of the dangers of unsanctioned pleasure through an institution which poses dangers of its own . . . Each woman may be economically and legally subject to her husband but her sexuality—as Luce Irigaray would have it, the 'sex which is not one'—slips away from his control. The play's focus on what Irigaray affirmatively calls the 'multiplicity of female desire', the plurality of female sexuality, thus opens the way for a feminist reading of female pleasure and the dangers it poses to male rule'.[70]

8 DESIRING SUBJECTS IN LAW AND LANGUAGE

The gap created by the instability and ambiguity of language on the subject's entry into the symbolic order, leaves the subject, Lacan tells us, in a state of lack, alienation, and, of course, desire for regaining her former fullness. This lack comes to be filled, in a patriarchal order (which for Lacan seems to be at times, an inevitable one) by the law of the father. Needless to say, different characters in the play negotiate this lack and this law in different ways, oblivious perhaps to the doomed nature of their quests.

For Angelo the law, literally as well as metaphorically, comes to supplant his desire for unity. He seems to have fully internalized the social and legal rules and thinks he has found a plenitude that the other characters are still seeking. Such is the difficulty of attaining this state that the others scarce believe his humanity. For the Duke

> Lord Angelo . . . scarce confesses
> That his blood flows, or that his appetite
> Is more to bread than stone. (1.3, 50–4).

Lucio mocks rather than admires this state of desireless contentment:

---

[70] Mario DiGangi, 'Pleasure and Danger: Measuring Female Sexuality in *Measure for Measure*' (1993) 60 *English Literary History* 589, at 604.

> They say this
> Angelo was not made by man and woman after this downright way of creation . . .
> Some report, a sea-maid spawned him. Some, that
> he was begot between two stockfishes. But it is certain
> that when he makes water his urine is congealed ice,
> that I know to be true.' (3.1, 366–73).

In other words, Angelo is a sad, desiring subject who identifies both with the law and the language in which it is expressed, claiming that there is no lack or ambiguity in either, as a means of filling the lack that is him. As Victoria Hayne puts it, Angelo adopts a legal absolutism according to which to be 'the voice of the recorded law' (2.4, 61) is to speak a transparent, absolutely referential language, the personification of justice itself.[71] In his first interview with Isabella he denies that it is possible to have more than one interpretation of the same law or that language is an unruly instrument whose meaning may change: 'It is the law, not I, condemns your brother' (2.2, 81), he tells Isabella, and he both 'will not' and 'cannot' rescind the sentence. He sees no ambiguities in language as he asserts that

> Your brother is a forfeit of the law,
> And you but waste your words (2.2, 72–3).

Not only law and language are unambiguous and coterminous but the meaning of justice, mercy and pity are also similarly constricted and come to inhabit the same ambit: 'I show [pity] most of all when I show justice' (2.2, 101).

Angelo is, in other words, the ideal Legendrian legal subject, erotically attaching himself to the labyrinth that is law in a desperate attempt to avoid confronting the labyrinth of female sexuality and his own desire for woman. As Isabella shows him, however, neither domain is as unambiguous and unproblematic as he would like to believe. He is terrified of seeing himself in woman's mirror because he suspects that, like the Minotaur in my closing chapter, he might see more than his preferred image of himself and might disintegrate. Isabella's presence does just that, first by showing him an unflattering image of himself and then by arousing in him desires that he sought to deny he had.

Angelo's views on the nature of the law, language, and desire are also amply contested in the play. As Terence Hawkes points out, for Angelo to be right, the legal text must be unified, objective, and coherent, and its meaning must be independent of the person reading it. Other characters in the play, however, do not share this view of the law or the language in which it is expressed. Conflicting readings of the law, notably the meaning of the marriage contracts between Angelo and Mariana and Claudio and Julietta, shutter its alleged unity and coherence as well as problematize the legality on which Angelo bases his terror.[72] Escalus provides another example of the representation of opposing views of the nature of law and justice in the play (3.2, 248) while

---

[71] Victoria Hayne, 'Performing Social Practice: The Example of *Measure for Measure*', 44, *Shakespeare Quarterly* 1–29 (1993).

[72] Terence Hawkes, *Meaning by Shakespeare, supra.*

Isabella points out the power as well as the instability of linguistic signs: 'I that do speak a word' she tells Angelo, 'May call it back again' (2.2, 58–9). Again unlike Angelo, and like Ariadne in my closing chapter, Isabella recognizes and empathizes with human weakness and instability in both the law and in language (2.2, 119–25). Her presence also awakens Angelo's repressed desires and leaves him perplexed. There is a big difference between this reading and Posner's dismissal of Isabella as 'a cold and priggish young lady' who becomes, at the end, with the Duke's proposal, 'a woman fit for a glorious marriage'.[73]

9 THE CULTURE OF DESIRE AND ITS END

Positive law, Peter Goodrich argues, is structurally unable to address the domain of intimacy, sexuality, or relationship; to address and rethink the plurality of sexual difference, we need 'an independent temporality, space or site . . . within which the sexuate person can dream, imagine or fantasize new forms of relationship and of expression'; such a task necessitates devising 'new procedures, novel jurisdictions and diverse and distinct forms of judgment' which cannot be provided by law alone.[74] If the tradition of courtly love, which provided one such space has been neglected, repressed, or dismissed as literature rather than law, this may be because literature is also to blame for inspiring expectations of everlasting love as a fusion and loss of oneself in another, that literature alone, not law or life, can satisfy. As even *literary* characters occasionally protest, '[novelists] won't represent the actual world; it would be too dull for their readers. In real life, how many men and women *fall in love*? . . . Not one married pair in ten thousand have felt for each other as two or three couples do in every novel.'[75] Rhoda Nunn forgets that, as we see in the next chapter, this longed-for absolute unity and fusion is fulfilled neither in law, nor in literature, but only in death.

Desire, celebrated and feared in equal measures, in law and in literature, is also, like law, culturally induced and historically contingent. Our understanding of love, passion, and desire, is not raw, authentic, or natural, but mediated by our position in history and geography, as well as by the language we have at our disposal to express it. The means by which we come to represent love and desire are prescribed and limited not only by social, religious, and legal codes but also by the forms and images afforded us by literature and art. However much we choose to deny it, both our understanding and our experience of passion is mediated by, and is as changeable as, fashion. Both law and literature as part and parcel of our culture's existing order of things, affirm and maintain, even when regulating and condemning, (in the case of law, affirm and

---

[73] Richard Posner, *Law and Literature: A Misunderstood Relation*, at 104. Coleridge also ignored her: Isabella, 'of all Shakespeare's female characters interests me the least' in Thomas Middleton Raysor (ed.), *Coleridge's Miscellaneous Criticism* (Cambridge, Mass.: Harvard University Press, 1936), at 49.

[74] Peter Goodrich, *Law in the Courts of Love, supra,* at 61.

[75] George Gissing, *Odd Women* (London: Thomas Nelson & Sons, 1893), at 86.

maintain most when regulating and condemning most), the notions of sexuality, desire, and love as natural, spontaneous, and instinctive. This is not just true of Shakespeare and the laws of Vienna but of the countless texts and laws that relate or dictate tales of desire, contained, in the end, by marriage. The implication is that the married couple and the nuclear family are the ideal form of societal organization and reproduction.

Law's, and literature's, preference for this form of organization are not, however, disinterested and certainly not gender-neutral. As Catherine Belsey argues, the religious vows of poverty and chastity were one response to the western anxiety about the lure of property on the one hand and passion on the other. Marriage is another way, ideally used to contain both property and sex.[76] The view that marriage is the ideal tool for society's problems assumes that marriage is a just solution. Since both law and much of literature, consciously or unconsciously, connive and exalt this view, it is up to resisting readers, male or female, to exploit any ambiguities in legal and in literary texts and contest this conclusion. The text of *Measure for Measure*, moulded and refined by generations of directors and readers, gives us ample room to argue with this conclusion. For contemporary audiences, overfed on a diet of promised desire, such an ambiguous ending is, by deferring satisfaction, paradoxically more satisfying than a neat resolution which, by satisfying, would also kill, desire.

The frequent equation of marriage with death in the play certainly offers no encouragement that the efforts of the western world to confine desire within the legal institution of marriage have been successful or that the unions ordered by the Duke are either just or happy. Lucio's exclamation that 'marrying a punk my Lord is pressing to death, whipping and hanging' (5.1, 525–6) reminds one of Claudio's earlier resolution that

> If I must die,
> I will encounter darkness as a bride
> And hug it in mine arms (3.1, 84–6).

Claudio's image eroticizes death and suggests the relationship between the sexual act and death that both the law and the Church attempt to deny. For, as Bataille says, 'it takes an iron nerve to perceive the connection between the promise of life implicit in eroticism and the sensuous aspect of death'.[77] The repression of this connection by law and much of literature, is to deny that eroticism is not a denial of, but lies at the heart of, the sacred. Indeed, in embracing death as a bride, Claudio could be said to have gone 'beyond the pleasure principle', 'given that', as Lacan puts it, '*jouissance* implies precisely the acceptance of death'.[78] The legal and religious authorities in *Measure for Measure* prefer to sustain the impression that marriage, not eroticism or

---

[76] Catherine Belsey, *Desire: Love Stories in Western Culture, supra.*

[77] Georges Bataille, *Eroticism* (London and New York: Marion Boyars, 1987) [1962], trans. Mary Dalwood, at 59.

[78] Jacques Lacan, *The Ethics of Psychoanalysis, 1959–1960: The Seminar of Jacques Lacan*, trans. Dennis Porter (London and New York: Routledge, 1992) at 189.

death, is the sacred rite, the mystery that all human beings must undergo. Barnadine, who, unlike Claudio, refused to embrace death earlier in the play, is the only character spared the punishment of both marriage and death at the end.

At the end of the play all 'unofficial' relationships are brought within the ambit of legal definitions with marriage representing the resolution to Vienna's social and moral problems. With desire channelled into the institutional, its threat to the social order is allegedly deflected. However, as Eagleton argues, no unblemished justice can ever be achieved from this final distribution of bodies as no two things are exactly identical; there is always some residue of difference, dislocation, or disparity which threatens to undo it.[79] One reason why the fusion between desire and the institution is not unequivocably harmonious, as this reading hints, is that for the illusion of such a fusion to be maintained, the union must at least appear to be one between equals. The women in the play, however, are not accorded that status and their resistance, though silent or silenced, can be heard in theatrical productions as well as read on the margins and between the gaps in the text.

'Marriage', writes Jeanette Winterson, 'is the flimsiest weapon against desire; you might as well aim a pop-gun to a python. You will still lie awake at night twisting your wedding ring round and round.'[80] For Freud, the institution of marriage, far from solving the problems posed by desire, was responsible for them. And for Lacan, the state of lack following the subject's entry into language cannot be satisfied by the institutional or legal; on the contrary, desire is 'autonomous in relation to this mediation of the Law ... it reverses the unconditional nature of the demand for love ... and raises it to the power of absolute condition'.[81] The promise of unity and fulfilment of desire promised by the institution of marriage is also undermined by both the characters and the events in this play. Even though the chess-master tries to make his pawns dance to a happy ending, there is 'a lot of creaking',[82] that is, desire and its corollary, law, persist. For the promise of a perfect and lasting union with another person, experienced by the infant in the womb, can be achieved neither in law, nor in literature, but in the tomb; 'when we wish to attain in the subject what was before the serial articulations of speech, and what is primordial to the birth of symbols, we find it in death'.[83] As we see in the next chapter, and as Shakespeare hints elsewhere, the absolute fulfilment of desire can be attained only by going beyond language and can happen only in death:

> I desperate now approve
> Desire is Death[84]

---

[79] Eagleton, *William Shakespeare, supra*.

[80] Jeanette Winterson, *Written on the Body*, (London: Vintage, 1993), at 78.

[81] Jacques Lacan, *Écrits: A Selection* (London: Routledge, 1977) [1966], trans. Alan Sheridan, at 311.

[82] A. P. Rossiter, *Angel with Horns, supra*, at 114.

[83] Jacques Lacan, *Écrits: A Selection, supra*, at 105.

[84] Sonnet 147 in William Shakespeare, *The Sonnets* (Cambridge: Cambridge University Press, 1996), ed. G. Blakemore.

5

WORLD BEFORE AND BEYOND DIFFERENCE: EMILY BRONTË'S *WUTHERING HEIGHTS* [1]

If it lasts forever, I hope I'm the first to die
James, *Laid*

1 A TEXT BY AND FOR A WOMAN?

Feminist theorists have been at the forefront of contemporary interest in cultural forms as a means of examining and challenging existing power structures. The deconstruction of the distinction between public and private, personal and political, has been accompanied with an insistence that contesting women's representation on the cultural and not just the political and legal planes is essential for achieving meaningful changes. For, as Arlyn Diamond put it, 'the parts we play in literature are not unconnected with the parts we are permitted to play in life'.[2] Since literature participates in making, and not just reflecting, our world and our understanding of ourselves, new ways of looking at literature may encourage new definitions of ourselves, our place in the world and thereby inspire changes in the structures and categories of that world itself.

While previous chapters have aimed to expose the impact of gender on the interpretation of texts written by male authors, in this chapter it is possible to see sexist values in literary criticism of a text written by a woman. To follow Elaine Showalter's chart of the progress of feminist criticism, feminist critics at first addressed depictions of women in literary texts by male authors only to find themselves excluded by a gallery of caricatures with women depicted as either angels or demons, whores or muses. Not only was such literature not addressing women but women, Elaine

---

[1] Emily Brontë, *Wuthering Heights* (Harmondsworth: Penguin, 1965) [1847]; all page references in the text are to this edition.

[2] Arlyn Diamond and Lee R. Edwards (eds.), *The Authority of Experience: Essays in Feminist Criticism* (Amherst, Mass.: University of Massachusetts Press, 1977), at 2.

Showalter argued, became its consumers and addressees, having internalized the assumptions of male criticism and the male system of artistic value.[3] The misogyny in many representations of female characters was adopted as the neutral point of view and while the diversity of women's experiences went unreflected in literary texts, women's powerlessness appeared to be part of the natural order of things rather than a patriarchal construct. To avoid this outcome a woman reader, Judith Fetterley argued, must become a resisting rather than an assenting reader, ridding herself of the male point of view inscribed in the text as well as in male literary criticism.[4]

One part of the feminist reading project is therefore the attack on male aesthetic criteria which, by pretending to be universal, conferred greatness on some books and put them beyond interrogation by inviting ever more sophisticated critiques of them. Male readers often dismissed women's writing as trivial or sentimental and where women's writing was praised, it was as a separate as well as a marginal category of literature, dealing with women's problems, in contrast to male authors' writing which allegedly addressed humanity as a whole: 'There must always be two literatures', Mary Ellman wryly comments, 'like two public toilets, one for Men and one for Women'.[5] Male critics' frequent inability to see past the author's gender consistently led to writing by women being praised (if praised at all) for showing sentiment, intensity of feeling, passion, romance, love, and the emotions, but lacking in intellectual judgment, abstract reasoning, originality, controlled plot, and breadth or intelligence.

Amidst this gendered criticism, *Wuthering Heights* presented the critics with a puzzle; while Ellis Bell's *Wuthering Heights* was admired for its original and strong depiction of violence and evil, Emily Brontë's *Wuthering Heights* was (less) admired for its depiction of a love story between two fated lovers.[6] The story has not changed much in the hundred and fifty years since the book's publication: 'The battle lines between the sexes may have been breached when it comes to jobs, sport, and even household', writes a recent newspaper article; 'But in the field of literature, men and women are still clearly at odds'.[7] A recent study on the impact of gender on reading habits, shows that men are 'turned off' by texts written by women, especially if the word 'love' or other 'emotional' term appears on the title or is suggested by the image on the cover.

To re-read and resist canonical texts like *Oedipus* and the *Oresteia* must therefore be accompanied with the search for a female literary tradition as glimpsed from the writings of women writers, what Elaine Showalter has termed 'gynocritics'. As the

---

[3] See especially 'Women and the Literary Curriculum', *College English*, Vol. 32, 855, (1972); *A Literature of their Own: from Charlotte Brontë to Doris Lessing* (London: Virago Press, 1978); 'Feminist Criticism in the Wilderness', *Critical Enquiry*, Vol. 8 (1981), 182.

[4] Judith Fetterley, *The Resisting Reader: A Feminist Approach to American Fiction* (Bloomington, Ind.: Indiana University Press, 1978).

[5] *Thinking About Women* (London: Macmillan, 1968), at 32–3.

[6] See Carol Ohmann, 'Emily Brontë in the Hands of Male Critics', *College English*, Vol. 32, No. 8, May 1971, 906–13; Nicola Thompson, 'The Unveiling of Ellis Bell: Gender and the Reception of *Wuthering Heights*', *Women's Studies*, Vol. 24, 341–67, 1995.

[7] Vanessa Thorpe, 'Women's books that turn men off', *Observer*, 19 March 2000, 8.

criteria by which artistic merit was judged was already loaded in favour of texts by male writers, feminist critics have had to reopen the definitions of what counts as serious versus trivial literature and point out the gendered nature of definitions of aesthetic value. Like Ariadne in my closing chapter, such criticism reopens the ambit of what counts as valid and valuable writing, and unsettles definitions of aesthetic merit, which, by purporting to be universal, privileged male writing and male concerns at the expense of women's writing and women's concerns. By celebrating women's writing and women's criticism without reference to male criteria, feminist readings of male authors and feminist readings of female authors, has encouraged a critical approach to literature where the role of gender in both writing and reading is acknowledged and investigated. It is thanks to such work that it is possible to appreciate that aesthetic criteria are not gender neutral and that the creation and perpetuation of the western literary canon is not gender blind. As a fundamentally 'suspicious' approach to literature[8] feminist criticism encourages the reader to delve beyond the surface of received conventions and investigates what assumptions are embedded in any literary text and readings of it, what interests such writing and criticism serve and how. This approach empowers both women writers and readers who had been previously excluded by a male literary establishment who encouraged them to view the male point of view as natural, neutral, and universal.

2 LEGAL AND OTHER VIOLENCES

From the time of *Wuthering Heights*' publication in 1847, critics have expressed both disgust and marvel at the author's capacity to envision and depict evil. 'Emily Brontë, of all women', writes Bataille, 'seems to have been the object of a privileged curse. Her short life was only moderately unhappy. Yet keeping her moral purity intact, she had a profound experience of the abyss of evil. Though few people could have been more severe, more courageous or more proper, she fathomed the very depths of evil.'[9] The text uncovers and dwells on individuals' capacity to inflict violence, a violence which takes a variety of forms from legal, physical, sexual, emotional, class, and economic. The text's indirect narration also means that there is no overt attempt by the author to judge or punish the perpetrators of this violence. Indeed, despite romantic writers' such as Wordsworth's injunction to writers to use literature for the purposes of moral education, the author of *Wuthering Heights* neither judges nor admonishes. There is no repentance by or reconciliation for those assumed to be villains; indeed, by casting

---

[8] This is the term used by Annette Kolodny; see especially Annette Kolodny, 'Dancing Through the Minefield: some observations on the theory, practice, and politics of a feminist literary criticism', *Feminist Studies*, Vol. 6, (1980), 1. 'A Map for Rereading: Or, Gender and the Interpretation of Literary Texts', *New Literary Texts*, Vol. 11, (1980), 451–67.

[9] Georges Bataille, *Literature and Evil*, trans. Alastair Hamilton (London and New York: Marion Boyars, 1990 [1957]) at 15.

some of those characters in a sympathetic light, the author was accused of endorsing this violence—a charge for which Charlotte Brontë in her 1858 Preface to the book was at pains to apologize. The idea that any author should have imagined and dwelled on such evil was bad enough; but the revelation that the author was a woman left critics perplexed: 'No woman could write *Wuthering Heights*' was one critic's conclusion.[10]

The most obvious candidate for the perpetration of violence is of course Heathcliff. At the start of the book we witness him hurling physical abuse and threatening physical violence on young Catherine and later he muses gleefully of hitting Isabella and 'turning the blue eyes black every day or two' (93). At various stages in the novel he imprisons both Isabella and the second Catherine in order to force them to comply with his plans. What renders him a true believer in and wielder of Evil, however, is his delight in inflicting pain irrespective of whether any material or other gain is likely to accrue: 'I can think of nothing which excites me more deliciously. There is no ecstasy similar to that which we experience when we yield to this divine infamy' he declares. 'It's odd what a savage feeling I have to anything that seems afraid of me! Had I been born where laws are less strict and tastes less dainty, I should treat myself to a slow vivisection of [young Catherine and his son Linton] as an evening's amusement' (302). As Bataille points out, this renders Heathcliff a perfect embodiment of the Marquis de Sade's definition of a sadist.

The infliction of violence, however, is not only Heathcliff's prerogative: repeatedly in the book those in a position of power, whether physical, legal, economic or social, wield it to abuse those who have less power than themselves because they are poor, orphans, women, children, or animals. Hindley threatens Nelly with a knife, inserts it in her mouth, and hurls his own son Hareton over the stairs. As a child, Hindley strikes blows at Heathcliff, and Nelly also confesses her 'injustice ' and 'inhumanity' towards Heathcliff, plaguing and pinching him almost as much as Hindley (78–9). Catherine pinches Nelly 'with a prolonged wrench, very spitefully on the arm' (111) and then slaps her suitor Linton when he reprimands her. Nelly witnesses, without apparent surprise, Hareton hanging a litter of puppies from a chairback in the door-way (217). Even kindly elder Earnshaw is easily 'vexed', and 'suspected slights of his authority nearly threw him into fits' (82). Lockwood, supposedly a product of polite society, is also not slow to attack Catherine's beseeching ghost: 'I pulled its wrist on to the broken pane and rubbed it to and fro till the blood ran down and soaked the bedclothes' (67).

Violence is not only perpetrated in the 'disorderly, comfortless' world of the Heights but also at the 'wealthy, respectable' world of Thrushcross Grange (119), home of magistrate Linton and his family. On the night of their excursion to Thrushcross Grange, Heathcliff and Catherine witness Edgar and Isabella Linton tearing their little dog apart trying to wrest it from each other. Education and wealth, it seems, were no barrier to violence in the parlours of the upper and middle classes any more than

---

[10] Quoted in Nicola Thompson, 'The Unveiling of Ellis Bell', *supra*, at 349.

among the lower classes. Old Linton stresses his role as a magistrate and the power this affords for protecting his property rights (particularly on evenings when he has just collected his rents), including setting the bull-dogs on suspected intruders. Edgar Linton, also a magistrate freshly returned from a justice meeting, is not slow to resort to physical violence, striking Heathcliff a blow 'full on the throat that would have levelled a slighter man' (154).

While turning to a mode of Victorian domestic realism with the union between Catherine and Hareton in the second part of the novel, both parts of the story show both Wuthering Heights and Thrushcross Grange as areas ridden with the threat of physical violence. The home and the family, far from being havens of domestic bliss and protection from the violence of the outside world are instead sources of conflict which erupts all too easily into verbal abuse, physical violence, and emotional exploitation. Though Nelly protests that 'There's law in the land, thank God, there is! though we *be* in an out-of-the-way place' (305) her intervention is greeted with derision by Heathcliff and she is powerless to prevent him from blackmailing young Catherine. Despite the Enlightenment's faith in the ability of law and reason to eradicate violence, Emily Brontë depicts an array of abuses that go unchecked by the legal system and whose officers are indeed at times responsible for perpetrating it. As critics have often pointed out, this violence does not stem from supernatural forces but from material, legal, economic, and social realities and inequalities.[11] For Marxist critics, the oppression endured by Heathcliff at the hands of Hindley who repeatedly flogs him, Nelly who confesses to pinching him, and Joseph who thrashes him 'till his arm ached' (87) leads to his determination and readiness to become a tyrant himself and take revenge on those who had been unjust to him once his physical and economic power allows it.[12]

The greatest violence explored in the book, however, is not the violence of the law, or of patriarchy, or of social and economic inequalities, but the violence of the love between Catherine and Heathcliff: from the time of the book's publication, critics accustomed to tales of love between young people framed by the climax of marriage at the end, were unsettled by the violent representation of the bond between Catherine and Heathcliff. For Bataille, Emily Brontë 'had the sort of knowledge which links love not only with clarity, but also with violence and death—because death seems to be the truth of love, just as love is the truth of death.'[13]

---

[11] See further discussion in N. M. Jacobs, 'Gender and Layered Narrative in *Wuthering Heights*' in Patsy Stoneman (ed.), *Wuthering Heights: Contemporary Critical Essays* (London: Macmillan, 1993).

[12] See especially Terry Eagleton who sees Heathcliff as both 'metaphysical hero' and a skilful exploiter of the values of the enterpreneurial class: *Myths of Power: A Marxist Study of the Brontës* (London: Macmillan, 1975), 97–121. For contemporary readers of the novel, William Godwin's, *Enquiry Concerning Political Justice* (1793) lent support to the argument that crime was the product of circumstances and of tyrannical institutions; see discussion in Nicholas Roe, *Wordsworth and Coleridge: The Radical Years* (Oxford: Oxford University Press, 1988), at 132.

[13] *Literature and Evil, supra*, at 16.

3 PATRIARCHY AND ITS VICTIMS

While social rules and conventions left women in a disadvantaged position in Brontë's society, such rules and conventions were buttressed, solidified, and maintained by the legal system. Contemporary law classified married and under-aged women as non-persons, their identities being subsumed under that of their husband or father. If, as Lévi-Strauss argues, the exchange of women as objects in marriage underpins the structure of all societies, in Victorian society such exchanges further maintained and replicated the system of capitalist exchanges. Edgar Linton appreciates the sanctity of the rules governing these exchanges and is 'appalled' at his sister's Isabella attraction towards Heathcliff: 'Leaving aside the degradation of an alliance with a nameless man, and the possible fact that his property, in default of heirs male, might pass into such a one's power, he had sense to comprehend Heathcliff's disposition' (139–40). Once Isabella marries Heathcliff, her higher social status is no match for the power the legal system confers on her husband. Their marriage makes him her legal protector which gives her no freedom beyond what he allows. Isabella's elopement from Thrushcross Grange puts not only her property, real and personal, in the hands of her husband but also her whole person. When Heathcliff imprisons her at the Heights he is acting within his rights and is happy to have a witness to his atrocities, knowing that the law will turn a blind eye to violence perpetrated within the home: 'Tell [Linton]', he tells Nelly, 'to set his fraternal and magisterial heart at ease, that I keep strictly within the limits of the law . . . If you are called upon in a court of law, you'll remember her language, Nelly; and take a look at that countenance—she's near the point which would suit me. No, you are not fit to be your own guardian, Isabella, now; and I, being your legal protector must retain you in my custody, however distasteful the obligation may be.' (188–9). Heathcliff also assumes legal control of young Catherine whose life, until Heathcliff's death consists of a series of imprisonments, first by her over-protective father at Thrushcross Grange, then by her feeble but demanding husband Linton and finally by her father-in-law Heathcliff. In the midst of a social and legal system that treated women as chattels even weak men who 'wanted spirit in general' (107) like Edgar Linton and Linton Heathcliff wield power over women, including strong women like the two Catherines.

As Gilbert and Gubar argue, in patriarchy men are encouraged to go out and seek knowledge that will lead to self-discovery while woman's education consists in self-denial and duty. Catherine's attempts to embark on a journey of self-discovery are doomed as her education, especially following her stay at Thrushcross Grange, leads her to believe that she should marry someone of her own or higher status; as she blurts out to Nelly whilst Heathcliff eavesdrops, 'It would degrade me to marry Heathcliff' (121). The contradictory demands made on her by society and her own instincts leave her frightened and confused. As Lockwood discovers in the margins of her books, she muses on whether she is or should become *Catherine Earnshaw*, *Catherine Linton* or *Catherine Heathcliff* (61). Her dilemma serves to underline that

'What Catherine, or any girl, must learn is that she does not know her own name, and therefore cannot know either who she is or whom she is destined to be'.[14]

The power Heathcliff wields over young Catherine is also one afforded to him by the legal system: Heathcliff calculates that his son, as Linton's nephew, is the prospective owner of Thrushcross Grange and 'I would not wish him to die till I was certain of being his successor' (243). In case Catherine is the heir, 'to prevent disputes' he resolves to bring about the union between Linton and Catherine (249). When young Catherine marries Linton Heathcliff, she changes from dependent daughter to becoming the legal property of her husband. When both her father and husband die she comes under the legal control of her father-in-law Heathcliff who has ensured that any property that might have passed on to her (personal as well as real) has gone to him. Although Edgar Linton on his deathbed sends for his lawyer to amend his will and settle some personal property on young Catherine for life, Heathcliff delays the attorney so that the personal property passes from Catherine to her husband Linton Heathcliff and from Linton Heathcliff to Heathcliff himself. It is still, as C. P. Sanger has carefully argued, not at all clear how Thrushcross Grange should have passed to Heathcliff on Linton's death. Under the law of trusts old Linton's estate passes to his son (Edgar Linton) in preference to his daughter (Isabella) and to his daughter's son (Linton Heathcliff) in preference to his son's daughter (Catherine Linton). Thrushcross Grange would therefore have passed from old Linton to Isabella's son Linton for the brief period when the young Linton outlived his uncle. It is unlikely, however, that young Linton, a minor, could have passed the title to his father Heathcliff:[15] '[Young Linton] had bequeathed the whole of his, and what had been her moveable property to his father. The poor creature was threatened, or coaxed into that act . . . The lands, being a minor, he could not meddle with.' Heathcliff's title is therefore dubious but, Heathcliff had claimed and kept them 'in his wife's right, and his also—I suppose legally' Nelly observes, but adds that 'at any rate, Catherine, destitute of cash and friends, cannot disturb his possession' (325).

The restriction of women by legal rules is matched by, allows and often also leads to the physical restriction of both Catherines; while they both long to explore the world outside Wuthering Heights and Thrushcross Grange their legal 'protectors', whether fathers, husbands, or fathers-in-law ban such excursions and enjoin them, through the threat of physical force (Heathcliff) or moral blackmail (Edgar Linton) to remain inside. The association of women with the inside and men with the outside is a dominant motif in western culture, as seen in our reading of Greek tragedies. For women to trespass the boundary between inside and outside is to pose a threat to the established order. That both Catherines manage to escape at various points in the novel and explore the world outside the home is, however, as important as the rules

---

[14] Sandra M. Gilbert and Susan Gubar, *The Madwoman in the Attic: The Woman Writer and the Nineteenth-Century Literary Imagination* (New Haven and London: Yale University Press, 1984), at 276.

[15] C. P. Sanger, 'Remarkable Symmetry in a Tempestuous Book' in Miriam Allott (ed.), *Emily Bronte: Wuthering Heights* (London: Macmillan, 1992) [1926], at 109–18.

forbidding them from doing so. It is the women's dissatisfaction, refusal to abide by these prohibitions, and the pivotal effect of such excursions that remain in the consciousness of readers: Catherine's visit to Thrushcross Grange leads to her meeting Edgar Linton and Catherine II's excursion to Wuthering Heights leads to her meeting Heathcliff and young Linton. Young Catherine, while aware of her physical weakness compared to Heathcliff is not afraid to defy him: 'I'll put my trash away because you can make me, if I refuse . . . But I'll not do anything, though you should swear your tongue out, except what I please!' (72). And Nelly's own dissatisfaction with her young mistress, Catherine, arises because rather than being passive and docile she is 'a haughty, headstrong creature' (106). The two heroines, despite their lack of economic and physical power, express their resistance to patriarchal rules, whether they are wielded by a potential lover or father. Within the constraints of the law, their physical confinement and financial dependence, the heroines of *Wuthering Heights* are therefore able to assert their own will and independence, a will that is more memorable than the prohibitions imposed on them.

4 PRE-LINGUISTIC DESIRES AND THE DISSOLUTION OF DIFFERENCES

Our western predilection of talking in terms of binary oppositions finds an array of contrasts to play with in *Wuthering Heights*. The distinction between nature and culture in readings of ancient Greek texts also returns to haunt readings of *Wuthering Heights* with Heathcliff appearing as the primary candidate for representing savagery and nature and Linton for representing civilization and culture. As Catherine puts it, Heathcliff is 'an unreclaimed creature, without refinement, without cultivation; an arid wilderness of furze and whinstone . . . he's a fierce, pitiless, wolfish man' (141). Heathcliff's association with nature means that the laws of culture, including Lévi-Strauss's primary law, the law of incest, hold no force for him. On the other hand, Linton appears to have not only accepted the Oedipal prohibition, but to be an embodiment of the ideal legal subject who upholds and respects the symbolic order, culture, and law. While Heathcliff has not abandoned the pre-Oedipal desire for unity and oneness with another person and uses all his energy to resist those preventing him from achieving it, Linton summons the institution and the legal power he wields as a magistrate to expel Heathcliff's untamed energies. While Heathcliff at the beginning is illiterate, and Catherine vows 'I hated a good book' (63), defaces books, or uses them 'not altogether for a legitimate purpose' in Lockwood's view (62), Linton is repeatedly associated with writing, reading, and books. As Catherine protests on her deathbed, 'What in the name of all that feels has he to do with books when I'm dying?' (122).

Heathcliff's alliance with the forces of nature repeatedly place him outside the law and on the side of nature's demands; when the world of the living cannot deliver the union he craves, he is not reluctant to use the same energy to destroy not only those who stand in his way but himself. Like Claudio in *Measure for Measure* he has recognized that for the ultimate *jouissance* one has to go beyond the pleasure principle and actively courts his own dissolution. Linton, on the other hand, strives not only to stay within the parameters of the symbolic order but personifies the legal institution through his role as a magistrate. Rather than embrace death, he pursues the ego's instinct for survival following his beloved wife's death. While Heathcliff refuses to grow up and abide by adult laws, Linton, like Angelo in *Measure for Measure*, has acceded to adulthood and hides his weaknesses, desires, and insecurities behind the law and language of the symbolic order. Heathcliff lives in Wuthering Heights 'a disorderly, comfortless house' while Linton lives in Thrushcross Grange, 'a wealthy, respectable one' (119). Although for a short time Heathcliff enters the law of culture and uses the capitalist system and the legal system in order to create wealth and buy Wuthering Heights, he does so less from a conviction in their rightfulness and inevitability but in order to beat Linton and his family at their own game. Nelly approves of Heathcliff's transformation,[16] thinking it not only good but permanent, without appreciating that Heathcliff's ability to adopt this role merely demonstrates the contingent nature of those roles, rules, and systems rather than their inherent truth or worth. Margaret Homans also contrasts the literal language preferred by Catherine and Heathcliff to the figurative language used by Linton, lawyers, and other characters in the book like Lockwood who prefer the security of the language of the symbolic order.[17] And as Gilbert and Gubar point out, against Heathcliff's and Catherine's preference for the energy and chaos of Hell, Linton and his supporters imagine a Heaven where hierarchical rules impose order on a difficult and painful narrative.

Of course Catherine and Heathcliff's pre-Oedipal language and games do not come to the reader raw and unmediated: they are related, and in the process inevitably reinterpreted, by Nelly and Lockwood through their own preferred lenses: reason, judgment, linearity, and progression. Their lives and desires can then be neatly explained and transcended through a narrative that insists on progress from chaos to order and that follows a seemingly inevitable path from beginning, middle, to end. A parallel urge towards a dialectical synthesis of these opposites is shown by the depiction of the romance between the second Catherine and Hareton. Their relationship in this case is closed in the symbolic order's preferred mode, that is, through the legal institution of marriage. As will be argued in the next section, however, even interested narration and a happy marriage are not sufficient to repress the energies depicted in the book, either fully, or finally. Amidst the violence depicted in the novel and the oppression allowed by, and even inflicted by legal structures, it is possible to glimpse an altogether different order that is repetitive and cyclical rather than linear, and

---

[16] 'He was the only thing there that seemed decent and I thought he never looked better. So much had circumstances altered their positions that he would certainly have struck a stranger as a born and bred gentleman and his wife as a thorough little slattern' (125).

[17] Margaret Homans, *Bearing the Word: Language and female experience in 19th century women's writing* (Chicago and London: Chicago University Press, 1986).

resides in eternity rather than in the time of laws, narrations, and institutions. This is the order imagined by, craved for, and occasionally enjoyed by Catherine and Heathcliff when they are able to escape the strictures of the adult world, the dictates of Hindley, and the religious fanaticism of old Joseph. As even Nelly appreciates, 'no parson in the world ever pictured heaven so beautifully as they did, in their innocent talk.' (85) This world is described only briefly yet it dwells on in Catherine and Heathcliff's and thus the readers' imaginations throughout the book. It is associated with nature rather than culture, consisting almost exclusively of the young children's forbidden forays onto the moors. It represents also, as Margaret Homans has argued, the law of the mother rather than of the father, the all too brief period in our lives where unity with mother and with nature was allowed and enjoyed, before the intervention of the law of the father and culture.

It is also a world where gender differentiations are irrelevant: the early relationship between the first Catherine and Heathcliff is one of equality where gender and class differences are not an issue. The first intervention to this pre-Oedipal existence occurs when Catherine arrives back from the Lintons acculturated into the dress and behaviour deemed appropriate for young women. Nelly approves of the change while Heathcliff retreats in both pain and contempt for her new 'part'; for the definitions of both femininity and masculinity, as we see again in my reading of Angela Carter's *The Bloody Chamber*, are not given in nature but are rules and principles created by culture and as such have to be learned and 'performed'. Catherine's willingness to play the role (learning 'to adopt a double character without exactly intending to deceive any one' (107)), to the satisfaction of the Linton family and their admirer Nelly causes the tragic split between her and Heathcliff who, for the time being at least, refuses to play the part insisted upon by polite culture.

That the world desired by Catherine and Heathcliff is impossible to survive the intervention of the order of culture is underlined by the narrators who frame, reframe, and retell the story and perhaps by Emily Brontë herself. That it is not allowed to subsist and results in tragedy is due to the fact that lack of differentiation, including gender differentiation is only possible in the state that ultimately dissolves all boundaries and oppositions, that is, death. That a world devoid of difference is craved for, and imagined however, enables us to consider what is lost by societal structures that insist on categorization and hierarchization; this glimpse subsists in the reader long after and beyond the lives and deaths of Catherine and Heathcliff.[18]

---

[18] David Musselwhite argues that Emily Brontë in her Gondal poetry imagined a world devoid of difference and full of energy where, as Deleuze and Guattari muse, 'I am God, I was not God, I am a clown of God, I am Apis, I am an Egyptian, I am a Red Indian, I am Negro, I am Chinaman, I am a Japanese. I am a foreigner, a stranger, I am a sea bird, I am a land bird. I am the tree of Tolstoy, I am the roots of Tolstoy . . . I am husband and wife in one. I love my wife, I love my husband.' Deleuze and Guattari, *Anti-Oedipus: Capitalism and Schizophrenia* (New York: Viking Press, 1972), trans. Robert Hurley, M. Seem, and H. R. Lane, at 77; quoted and discussed by David E. Musselwhite, *Partings Welded Together: Politics and Desire in the Nineteenth Century Novel* (London and New York: Methuen, 1987), at 75–108.

5 REJECTION OF CONVENTIONAL MORALITY

The threat to the law of the father comes from two parallel threads: Catherine's violent protest at its strictures once she finds herself inside it, and Heathcliff's systematic resistance to it. Catherine and Heathcliff are from the start the outsiders whose souls have not been captured by the legal, social, or moral law. In the beginning of the book the injustices perpetrated on Heathcliff and later on Catherine by Hindley serve to render them immune to and contemptuous of, the demands of social and familial conventions. But unlike *Measure for Measure*, where multiple weddings allegedly mark the end of disruptive passions and the restoration of law and order, Catherine's marriage to Linton only exacerbates her alienation from that law. Even though the law, personified in her magistrate husband and his orderly house, has captured her body, she has not submitted her desire to it and Heathcliff's return serves to underline her passionate resistance to its demands.

The book's exultation of romantic selfhood and all-consuming passion was another source of worry for Victorian critics. Heathcliff is the Byronic hero *par excellence* whose lonely egoism, anti-social manners, and single-minded pursuit of his goals were thought to be a recipe for the ills of anarchy and loss of community. The romantic movement, in exulting the powers and imagination of individual human beings also aimed to free human minds from the restrictions of social and moral conventions. Heathcliff, in common with other romantic heroes, eschews the dictates of society, law, religion, and family; as an outcast and an outsider such strictures hold no compelling force for him.[19] And although the case for Heathcliff as the villain of the text is often made, it is also clear that he appears more attractive, more interesting, and more intense than the more conventional Edgar Linton and Lindley. For the believers in society and community, however, such views raised the spectre of lawlessness and anarchic self-indulgence.

Catherine, rather than the passive, docile girl Victorian readers expected to find, is 'too mischievous and wayward for a favourite' (79), 'never so happy as when we were all scolding her at once, and she defying us with her bold, saucy look' (83).[20] Her friendship with Heathcliff provokes their polite neighbours' slight that old Earnshaw 'lets her grow up in absolute heathenism' (91). She is in marked contrast to the ideal of innocent, passionless, and preferably ignorant femininity whose sole role was to cater to the 'needs of her brothers, parents and husband'; at the same time, Linton, but not Heathcliff, fulfils the corresponding duties of the ideal male who would, as Gisborne taught in the same *Enquiry into the Duties of the Female Sex*, engage in 'the science of legislation, of jurisprudence, of political economy; the conduct of

---

[19] Eagleton points out that Heathcliff is probably also Irish and therefore less likely to want to abide by a system that oppressed his country and fellow countrymen: *Myths of Power, supra*.

[20] As Patricia Spacks puts it, Catherine is 'an anti-heroine, in every respect opposed to her century's ideal prototype of the adolescent woman': *The Female Imagination* (New York: Avon, 1972), at 17.

government in all its executive functions'.[21] Indeed, as Gilbert and Gubar argue, Heathcliff shares features of effeminacy as a result of being marginalized and oppressed by the same system that marginalized and oppressed women.[22] Like Ariadne in my closing chapter, and like a few other characters (men as well as women), we encounter in these texts, there is a bit of the feminine in him which ensures that he never surrenders his desire to the social law but to another, higher law, the law of love. Heathcliff is the untamed Minotaur Ariadne was looking for but never found.

More scandalizingly for some readers, both Catherine and Heathcliff show contempt for the Christian ideal of heaven; in a manner reminiscent to Blake's depiction of hell as full of energy, Catherine is convinced that heaven is not as desirable a place. Having dreamt that she was in heaven, she tells Nelly that 'heaven did not seem to be my home; and I broke my heart with weeping to come back to earth; and the angels were so angry that they flung me out, into the middle of the heath on the top of Wuthering Heights, where I woke sobbing for joy.' (120–1). The book itself offers no cause for admiration of a religious system that is embodied in the strictures of a hypocritical and superstitious Joseph; for Joseph, 'the wearysomest, self-righteous pharisee, that ever ransacked a bible to rake the promises to himself and fling the curses to his neighbours' (82–3), religion is not a means for love and forgiveness but of terror and punishment. Not surprisingly young Catherine and Heathcliff take every step to avoid his prolonged sermons.

Heathcliff's immunity to the demands of conventional religion continues until his death prior to which he expresses no remorse or repentance and refuses to accept the judgment of others or of God: 'as to repenting of my injustices, I've done no injustice, and I repent of nothing . . . No minister need come; nor need anything be said over me . . . I have nearly attained *my* heaven; and that of others is altogether unvalued and uncoveted by me' (363). Even worse, as early critics pointed out, Heathcliff's strength and energy invite both fear and admiration which the author, hidden behind a frame of narrators, is at best ambiguous about. The view that something that is 'as dark almost as if it came from the devil' (77), who has lived a 'selfish and unchristian life,' and displays such 'godless indifference' (363) arouses not only pity and sympathy but also admiration, worried critics that the author endorsed rather than denounced his transgressions. The legal system comes under similar attack as the instrument of those with social and economic power rather than a disinterested instrument of justice. Both old Linton and his son Edgar are magistrates and the implication is that social and economic power go hand in hand with legal power.[23]

---

[21] 1796; quoted in Kate Ferguson Ellis, *The Contested Castle: Gothic Novels and the Subversion of Domestic Ideology* (Urbana and Chicago: University of Illinois Press, 1989), at 12.

[22] *The Madwoman in the Attic, supra*, at 293–4: 'Heathcliff is somehow female in his monstrosity . . . on the level where younger sons and bastards and devils unite with women in rebelling against the tyranny of heaven, the level where orphans are female and heirs are male, where flesh is female and spirit is male, earth female, sky male, monsters female, angels male.'

[23] As Karl Marx noted, even if, and at times when, the government had wanted to improve working conditions, the magistrates whose job it was to apply the law made the implementation of any measures favourable to the workers ineffective: see especially chapter 10, *Das Kapital*.

At the other extreme, Heathcliff, in his refusal to abandon his desire, rejects not just the adult world of reason and law but more dramaticallly the ego's instinct for survival. His embrace of death is his ultimate rejection of a symbolic order that denies him, Catherine, and perhaps all of us, the realization of our desires.

6 SUBVERSIVE DESIRES

It is not only Heathcliff's romantic individualism and reclusive ways that threaten conventional morality and social rules; the unorthodox passion Emily Brontë depicted between Heathcliff and Catherine is the major source of threat to social harmony. The resemblance between Catherine and Heathcliff, starting with their childhood games to Catherine's declaration that 'I am Heathcliff' (180) remind us that in seeking the desire of the other we aim for an affirmation of ourselves. Catherine and Heathcliff's relationship is an extreme illustration of the self-reflexive nature of love; to seek a relationship with someone who is so similar to oneself that one *is* the other person, is to suggest that love is narcissistic or, at best, incestuous. Culture demands that in choosing partners we must choose someone who is different from ourselves, and at least someone outside the family group, albeit not so dramatically different from us as to upset distinctions based on race and class. Catherine and Heathcliff violate this demand by choosing someone who is so similar to themselves that they can both claim to be each other. The theme of incest is not only hinted metaphorically in the text: as her adopted brother who is also invested with her dead brother's name, the union between Catherine and Heathcliff may be also literally incestuous.[24] The union between Catherine and Heathcliff would therefore violate culture's earliest and most crucial taboo, the taboo against incest.

More so than in *Measure for Measure*, this desire appears detrimental to society and needs to be curbed by the institution and the system in the form of marriage. If, as Claude Lévi-Strauss claims, the incest taboo *is* society, then the metaphysical union Catherine and Heathcliff crave is not only pre-social but anti-social, threatening society's preferred kinship arrangement and thereby society's very existence. Catherine and Heathcliff's love, however, never takes society's preferred form of marital union. Indeed the idea of marriage seems both absurd and irrelevant to them; as for another outsider we encounter in the next chapter, the institution of marriage is beside the point. Heathcliff is contemptuous of Linton's love for Catherine as being based on 'duty, humanity, pity and charity' (190). Instead, they conceive their relationship as one of identification and spiritual union of their very souls: 'he's more myself than I am. Whatever our souls are made of, his and mine are the same . . . If all else perished,

---

[24] Eric Solomon, 'The Incest Theme in *Wuthering Heights*', *Nineteenth Century Fiction*, Vol. 14, 1959, 80–3, argues that Catherine and Heathcliff are half-brother and half-sister. See also William R. Goetz, 'Genealogy and Incest in *Wuthering Heights*', Vol. 14, *Studies in the Novel*, Winter 1982, 359–76.

and *he* remained, I should still continue to be; and if all else remained, and he were annihilated, the universe would turn to a mighty stranger . . . I *am* Heathcliff—he's always, always in my mind—not as a pleasure, any more than I am always a pleasure to myself—but as my own being—so don't talk of our separation again' (121–2). Heathcliff on his part expresses his torment at her death along lines that evoke that a part of him has died: 'I *cannot* live without my life! I cannot live without my soul!' (204), and dreams of 'dissolving with her' (320) to regain his lost self. The material, the physical, and the earthly, such as social conventions and legal institutions like marriage, only frustrate and delay this total union: 'I'm tired, tired of being enclosed here. I'm waiting to escape into that glorious world, and to be always there' (196). Catherine and Heathcliff's refusal to be described or restrained by societal rules and definitions means that fulfilment of their union only takes place in death. Their conception of love, however, persists beyond their death; it disrupts not only the lives of the fictional characters who knew them but all readers who become fascinated by, and identify with, their passions. This enables it to remain alive not just in myth but also in reality.

As Joseph Allen Boone argues, Catherine and Heathcliff conceive of their love as an identification with rather than a competition with each other. In contrast to the conventional presentation of love as a union of opposites, 'what one finds in the young Catherine and Heathcliff are states remarkably free of the constraints typically imposed by social construction of 'masculinity' and 'femininity'.[25] Their relationship is based not on antagonism but intimacy and friendship, inspired at first by their being the common victims of Hindley's oppression. Conversely, relationships in the book based on the understanding of love as the union of opposites, such as that between Catherine and Linton, Hindley and Frances and Isabella and Heathcliff are doomed, first because they are rooted in a 'basic inequality' and secondly because they are often also based on the male partner's oppression of the woman. Catherine and Heathcliff's relationship, on the other hand, threatens to dissolve all differences, including gender difference. In that sense Emily Brontë's tale pre-dates an understanding of relationships and love that is not couched in terms of opposition or appropriation of the other but in terms of being open to and receptive of the other. Rather than seeking to derive freedom, autonomy, and power from the encounter with the other, the encounter is envisaged as leading to relatedness, understanding, and intimacy. When pitched against the notion of love as competition against, or appropriation of, the other, this ideal also escapes masculine symbolism in preference of a feminine ideal of connectedness.[26]

The relationship between Heathcliff and Catherine is depicted as transcending sexuality, moral, social, and legal restrictions. This love, restricted by social and

---

[25] Joseph Allen Boone, *Tradition Counter-Tradition: Love and the form of fiction*, (Chicago: Chicago University Press, 1987), at 154.

[26] See especially Luce Irigaray, *i love to you: Sketch of a Possible Felicity in History* (New York and London: Routledge, 1996), trans. Alison Martin; I discuss this point further in chapter 6.

material circumstances, nevertheless subsists at a higher plane through the spiritual communion of Catherine and Heathcliff's souls after death. Catherine is certainly convinced of the existence of a spiritual dimension transcending the physical: 'I cannot express it; but surely you and everybody have a notion that there is, or should be an existence of yours beyond you. What were the use of creation if I were entirely contained here?' (122). Against this eternal love, the human notions of time and space need to be rethought: man-made concepts such as time and space are irrelevant as this love would persist 'always, always' just like 'the eternal rocks beneath'. Death is, for Catherine and later Heathcliff, an escape from the limitations of human time and space and they each come to long for and invite it. Catherine describes her body as a 'shattered prison' (196) from which she longs to be free into a disembodied existence with Heathcliff. The idea of the body as the prison house of the soul and of death as a liberator into a higher spiritual existence is of course prevalent in Christian thinking and invests Catherine and Heathcliff's love with a religious intensity.[27] As for many romantic poets, love is the agent for the fusion of souls, spiritual transcendence, and metaphysical existence. Such love subverts the boundary between self and other in favour of a primal condition of eternal union. Although, as we saw in the last chapter, the symbolic order seeks to deny it, this identification suggests that eroticism, as Bataille argued, lies at the heart of the sacred.

Heathcliff and Catherine believe this is a union they enjoyed in childhood; there is thus a similarity between romantic love and the child-like, pre-lapsarian existence imagined in the Garden of Eden. Before Catherine's stay at Thrushcross Grange, Heathcliff and Catherine enjoyed a childhood love that was both full of energy and oblivious to gender and class differences. The intervention of culture in the form of Thrushcross Grange introduced class and gender distinctions and taught Catherine a new set of social codes which Heathcliff has only contempt for. At her deathbed Catherine therefore longs to return to the days before she or Heathcliff grew up, that is before they were troubled by cultural codes and social expectations. According to Nelly 'her latest ideas wandered back to pleasant early days . . . "I wish I were a girl again"' she cries, '"half savage and hardy, and free . . . and laughing at injustices, not maddening under them"' (167), a place which she can only revisit in death.

For Bataille *Wuthering Heights* explores the link between eroticism and death, indeed illustrates that excessive sexual desire is the love of death: 'Eroticism, it may be said, is assenting to life up to the point of death . . . . eroticism is assenting to life even in death'.[28] From 'normal' society's point of view, such a desire needs to be curbed, silenced or denied and the taboo on necrophilia is one example of this fear which Heathcliff's insistence on reopening Catherine's grave violates. Such a relationship, ignoring cultural notions of time, space, the taboo against incest, and openly courting

---

[27] J. Hillis Miller, *The Disappearance of God: Five Nineteenth Century Writers* (Cambridge, Mass.: Harvard University Press, 1963): 'The love between Heathcliff and Catherine has served as a new mediator between heaven and earth, and has made any other mediator for the time being superfluous'; at 211.

[28] Georges Bataille, *Eroticism*, trans. Mary Dalwood (London and New York: Marion Boyars, 1962) at 11 [1957].

death, is, in cultural terms, doomed to fail. Brontë's tale therefore goes further than depicting an ideal relationship to show the perils attending its imaginary realization: Catherine and Heathcliff do not only identify with each other's needs and desires, they claim to *be* each other. They thus aim to transcend the ultimate boundary between self and other, a transgression that neither culture nor, in the end, the text can tolerate. That very failure, the ending in death, expresses a higher, albeit unattainable, truth or law and renders it for many critics the greatest love story ever told: '*Wuthering Heights*', writes Camus, 'is one of the greatest love novels because it finishes in failure and revolt—I mean in death without hope. The main character is the devil. Such a love can be maintained only by the final failure which is death. It can be continued only in hell.'[29]

The conception of love in terms of identification and relatedness rather than antagonism and competition is also more akin to a feminine ethic and aesthetic of love: explaining perhaps, to go back to my opening section, male readers' aversion to romantic novels, not only in Brontë's time but today. If we read in order to find ourselves in the characters of a book, to read Catherine and Heathcliff's narrative (mediated and diluted as it is by its tellers' interest in upholding the symbolic order), is to succumb to the threat of acknowledging the feminine, not only in the male hero Heathcliff, but also in oneself.

7 DEATH, OR WRITING WITH THE BODY

For Lacan, the child's entry into the symbolic order is marked by its departure from the semiotic or private language it enjoyed with the mother for the public world of a language that depends on differentiation and absence. The language of the symbolic order pre-exists the subject and its endless series of signifiers referring to other signifiers cannot be a substitute for the child's lost sense of plenitude with the now forbidden mother. The subject's subsequent and incessant search for this lost unity generates a ceaseless desire which language can never satisfy. As Margaret Homans has argued, Catherine refuses to live within the symbolic order marked by the law of the father and, like Heathcliff, prefers nature to the substitutions offered by linguistic signs.[30] Her brief stay at Thrushcross Grange as a teenager and later as a married woman has only served to strengthen her desire to remain outside the law. During that time her attachment to nature and to the mother was, as Margaret Homans suggests, not rejected but repressed. Such repression of the law of the mother and of

---

[29] Albert Camus, *Collected Essays & Notebooks* (Harmondsworth: Penguin, 1979), trans. Philip Thody, at 265.

[30] *Bearing the Word, supra*, at 68–93. For the view that *Wuthering Heights* is structured around the desire to return to a symbiotic oneness with the mother see also Philip L.Wion, 'The Absent Mother in Emily Brontë's *Wuthering Heights*' *American Imago*, 1985, Vol. 42 (2), 143–64.

nature is not only brief and unstable but returns to haunt her when Heathcliff reappears.

The cost of Catherine's refusal to enter the law of the father is, as Kristeva warns and Catherine enacts, psychosis or madness.[31] For Lacan, the loss of the mother is the precondition of language and representation while continuing adherence to the law of the mother can lead to psychosis and unintelligibility. At her deathbed Catherine has lost any sense of self and is unable to recognize her face in the mirror. If pregnancy, as Julia Kristeva argues, is experienced as a fragmentation of the self, this fragmentation is compounded in the case of Catherine who already experiences herself as divided. The prospect of motherhood, romanticized and often sentimentalized in Victorian fiction, in Catherine's case is perceived as likely to lead to further imprisonment and isolation. Her attempt to escape maternity, as Gilbert and Gubar argue, is a refusal to be a tool for the survival and continuation of the Linton line and the patriarchal society that confined her desires: 'Birth is, after all, the ultimate fragmentation of the self, just as 'confinement' is, for women, the ultimate pun on imprisonment'.[32] Her resort to anorexia and death is her only means of protest against a society whose demands she can only escape by 'relocating elsewhere'.[33]

Although this alternative space is interpreted as madness by the symbolic order, 'a permanent alienation of the intellect' (169), as Nelly calls it, her experience and despair also interrogate and lead us to suspect the alleged 'sanity' of that symbolic order. Catherine's refusal to be a mother and her resort to self-starvation, however, is not only a response to total powerlessness, but also a form of power, writing with her body the ending to her own story even at the cost of her body's extinction: 'If I cannot keep Heathcliff for my friend . . . I'll try to break their hearts by breaking my own. That will be a prompt way of finishing all when I am pushed to extremity!' (155).[34] In coming to long for her own death, and a total dissolution, Cathy, like Claudio in *Measure for Measure*, has gone beyond the pleasure principle, embracing and accepting her own death, the ultimate *jouissance*.

Catherine's death and her loss of language coincides with the birth of an heir and the return to the symbolic order, moreover an heir in the younger Catherine who appears more docile and accepting of the law of the father. The same fate befalls other mothers in the book such as Hindley's wife Frances and Heathcliff's wife Isabella. As in the *Oresteia*, the mother's death, murder, or suicide, appears to be a precondition for the birth of the symbolic order, language, and law. In Brontë's text, however, the

[31] See especially 'Stabat Mater' where pregnancy is described as the ultimate experience of the fragmentation of the self, and 'About Chinese Women': 'A woman has nothing to laugh about when the symbolic order collapses' in Toril Moi (ed.), *The Kristeva Reader* (Oxford: Blackwell, 1986), at 150.

[32] *The Madwoman in the Attic, supra*, at 286.

[33] The phrase is Barbara Johnson's in her reading of *The Yellow Wallpaper* in *The Feminist Difference: Literature, Psychoanalysis, Race and Gender* (Cambridge, Mass.: Harvard University Press, 1998), at 25.

[34] In that sense, Catherine's death lends authority to her view of love as 'the perfect identity of two bodies . . . which transgresses social laws, outside marriage, even outside the realm of the living', Elisabeth Bronfen, *Over Her Dead Body: Death, Femininity and the Aesthetic* (Manchester: Manchester University Press, 1992), 303–13, at 310.

memory of Catherine's protest is more eloquent than the substitutions offered by the second part of the book. Her death hints at a higher truth or law which cannot be fully erased and returns to haunt the surviving characters in the book as well as generations of readers. As Peter Goodrich puts it, 'Historically, at least within the western juridical tradition, the death which is courted, this desired demise or epistemically ostentatious threat of suicide, expresses a higher law and, being rendered in the name of love or truth, refuses the compromises that living brings'.[35]

8 TRANSGRESSIVE GENRES

The feeling that one is reading not one but several different books is not uncommon with *Wuthering Heights*; Emily Brontë seems to have used motifs and techniques from several different genres spanning several literary periods. On the one hand this has been seen as a mark of deficiency, an indication that Emily Brontë was inexperienced and unable to make up her mind what style to follow.[36] An alternative assessment is to acknowledge that 'within the heart of the law' that says that genres are not to be mixed, is lodged another law, 'a law of impurity or a principle of contamination' which makes it 'impossible not to mix genres'.[37] Moreover, if different genres can be, and have been, used to convey and serve different ideologies, what vision or visions does Emily Brontë propose through her appropriation, mixture, and exploration of disparate genres?

In common with other early nineteenth century literature, Emily Brontë's novel contains elements of romanticism, gothic, and fantasy. While eighteenth century Enlightenment emphasized the workings of the rational mind, romantic authors and poets privileged subjective experience, the passions, and the imagination. Childhood memories were one privileged area and Brontë's narrative is suffused with Heathcliff's and Catherine's memories of such childhood freedom. Gothic elements also abound in the first part of the novel where the description of Wuthering Heights as dark and isolated and its owner as inhospitable and dour introduce a familiar gothic setting. Heathcliff conforms to the archetypal gothic villain with his brutal behaviour towards Hindley, Hareton, Isabella, his own son, and even Isabella's dog. Like all gothic protagonists, he is contemptuous of hierarchies, values, and authorities whether they stem from the church, the legal system, or social status. His attractiveness stems at least in part from his willingness to defy established rules and privileges and challenge hierarchical institutions such as the church and the class system. Elements of gothic and

---

[35] Peter Goodrich, 'Courting Death' in Desmond Manderson (ed.), *Courting Death: The Law of Mortality* (London: Pluto Press, 1999), at 216.

[36] Q. D. Leavis, 'A Fresh Approach to *Wuthering Heights*' in Patsy Stoneman (ed.), *Wuthering Heights*, *supra*.

[37] Jacques Derrida, 'The Law of Genre' in *Acts of Literature*, ed. Derek Attridge, (London and New York: Routledge, 1992), at 225.

romanticism in the novel contrast the appeals of individual energy and creativity such as Heathcliff's and Catherine's to the stale world and values of Joseph and the Lintons. The source of the latter's authority is seen as questionable, oppressive and, compared to the hero's and heroine's raw energy, unattractive and outdated.

The main gothic motif, however, is the intrusion of the supernatural with the appearance of Catherine's ghost in Lockwood's sleep and Heathcliff's passionate response: 'I have a strong conviction in ghosts', he asserts. 'I have a conviction that they can, and do exist, among us!' (320). Although Lockwood and Nelly deny the possibility of a supernatural presence, as one critic puts it 'To deny Heathcliff's assurance of Catherine's presence is to deny the novel'.[38] As Nelly's story unfolds, the suggestion of incest between the young Catherine and Heathcliff is another gothic intrusion in the form of breaking civilization's ultimate taboo. Heathcliff's disturbance of Catherine's grave reverts to a well-rehearsed gothic motif that evokes the transgression of another taboo, necrophilia. After his own death the suspicion lingers that there is a communion between their spirits which appears amidst the world of the living. Ghosts of course disrupt the boundary between life and death, and as an attempt to portray death, they dwell on a subject which the dominant culture famously leaves unrepresented, obscures, or represses in the interests of stability. It is an attempt to represent what, as we see again in *Chronicle of a Death Foretold*, is beyond representation, even by imaginative writing.

'Incest, homosexuality, love for several persons at once, necrophilia, excessive sexuality . . . it is as if we were reading a list of forbidden themes established by some censor.' These are some of the frontiers Todorov suggests the fantastic allows us to cross; they are also some of the limits Emily Brontë's characters cross in order to articulate a different law: 'for the function of the supernatural', continues Todorov, 'is to exempt the text from the action of the law, and thereby to transgress that law'.[39] From women's perspective, the gothic motif of imprisoned heroines suggests further the real imprisonment of women within patriarchal structures and enables the depiction of the home as a place which is less a safe haven but, as both Catherines often experience it, a prison. Jane Austen's Henry Tilney in *Northanger Abbey* admonishes the heroine for reading gothic novels and imagining atrocities that could not possibly be perpetrated in 'the country and the age we live in': we are English, he protests, our laws, our education, our religion, could not possibly allow such things to take place.[40]

---

[38] Walter E. Anderson 'The Lyrical Form of *Wuthering Heights*', *University of Toronto Quarterly*, 47, (1977–8), 120.

[39] Tzvetan Todorov, *The Fantastic: A Structural Approach to a Literary Genre*, trans. Richard Howard (Ithaca, New York: Cornell University Press, 1975) at 158–9.

[40] Jane Austen, *Northanger Abbey* (Oxford: Oxford University Press, 1980) [1817], at 159: 'Dear Miss Morland, consider the dreadful nature of the suspicions you have entertained. What have you been judging from? Remember the country and the age in which we live. Remember that we are English, that we are Christians . . . Does our education prepare us for such atrocities? Do our laws connive at them? Could they be perpetrated without being known, in a country like this, where social and literary intercourse is on such a footing; where every man is surrounded by a neighbourhood of voluntary spies, and where roads and newspapers lay everything open?'

By juxtaposing gothic motifs with realistic narration, the reader of *Wuthering Heights* is led to question these assumptions and wonder instead whether the real world may be more disordered, nightmarish, and unjust than the so-called 'unreal' world depicted in fiction.[41] Kate Ferguson Ellis goes further to suggest that gothic novels not only expose the contradictions of the idealization of the home as a safe haven but also that it is the heroine whose rebelliousness and resourcefulness 'purifies' the fallen castle and enables the restoration of order. The fact that mothers are conspicuously absent in *Wuthering Heights* and from many gothic novels means that fathers rather than mothers serve as role-models, leading to more 'initiative-taking daughters'.[42] In *Wuthering Heights* the role of 'purifying the castle' and restoring stability and order falls on the younger Catherine.

Rosemary Jackson argues that fantastic fiction problematizes the distinction between self and other in an attempt to erase such separation and rediscover an original union between the two.[43] In that sense fantasy corresponds to the pre-Oedipal stage, before the intrusion of language and the law of the father when the baby enjoyed an undifferentiated union with its mother, a blissful state that, as Lacan says, can be recaptured only in death.[44] More generally, unlike realistic fiction that aims or assumes that direct mimesis or representation of reality is possible, fantastic fiction suggests that there are areas of experience that reason cannot understand, tame, or control: it acknowledges and rehabilitates the world of the passions, the emotions, and the irrational which were assigned a lower ranking in the hierarchy of knowledge.[45] In the process it hints at a different truth and a different law, perhaps even a higher law, that the world of reason is unwilling or unable to countenance. Fantasy literature eschews the emphasis on realistic representations and, by introducing another time and space, threatens conventional assumptions and expectations. In fantasy literature we encounter the suspension of all laws, human and natural, experience the merging of things perceived to be different, and witness the breaking of taboos. In this context, 'realism is but a bourgeois prejudice'.[46]

The desire for undifferentiation is close to what Freud identifies as the death instinct in *Beyond the Pleasure Principle*, a longing of perfect unity and bliss and the extinction of individuality and tension. Catherine and Heathcliff's separation in life and their belief in the certainty of their union after death is a prime example of this fantasy. Catherine's experience of herself as other in the mirror shortly before her

---

[41] Margaret Anne Doody, 'Deserts, Ruins & Troubled Waters: Female Dreams in Fiction and the Development of the Gothic Novel' *Genre*, Vol. 10, Winter 1977, 560.

[42] Kate Ferguson Ellis, *The Contested Castle, supra*, at 217.

[43] *Fantasy: The Literature of Subversion* (London: Routledge, 1981).

[44] 'When we wish to attain in the subject what was before the serial articulations of speech, and what is primordial to the birth of symbols, we find it in death': Jacques Lacan, *Écrits: A Selection*, trans. Alan Sheridan (London: Routledge, 1977), (London: Routledge, 1977) at 105.

[45] See also Eve Kosovski Sedgwick, *The Coherence of Gothic Conventions* (New York: Arno Press, 1980), elaborating on the value of the gothic as acknowledging the non-rational.

[46] Herbert Read, 'Foreword' in Devendra Prasa Varma, *The Gothic Flame: Being a History of the Gothic Novel in England: Its Origins, Efflorescences, Disintegration, and Residuary Influences* (London, 1957).

death, her inability to recognize herself, and her incoherent use of words are a reversal of Lacan's mirror stage and signals a return to the pre-Oedipal stage of unity and bliss, before the intervention of language and the law of the father. Although it is some years before Heathcliff can join her there, he has no doubt of his destination. Such desires and such aspirations threaten the symbolic order by negating the notion of stable and differentiated individuals, by seeking a return to the imaginary order, before language, before law, and before the differences inflicted by law, language, and culture. For the symbolic order, such a return is impossible and those who attempt it, such as Catherine and Heathcliff, are punished with madness or death. That both Catherine and Heathcliff crave for and indeed court this dissolution, is the ultimate transgression, defiance of, and revenge on the symbolic order.

There is nothing coincidental about the use of fantasy and gothic motifs to convey the flouting of social conventions. As Juliet Mitchell argues, the acceptance and persistence of social structures, laws, and conventions, the way we experience the world and live in accordance with certain moral, social, and legal structures is more unconscious than conscious; hence it is in the unconscious that we need to look in order to understand how the human subject and her society are created and sustained.[47] In fantasy literature we are shown a glimpse of such unconscious, silent, or silenced desires that are outside the law and outside the dominant ideology. Gothic fiction in particular submits the symbolic order to violent upheavals and the fact that this includes its patriarchal assumptions has made the genre attractive to women writers and readers. As Ellen Moers argues, gothic opens a space for the representation of women's fears of imprisonment and persecution, particularly the fear of birth, while also offering a space for the expression of female power, courage, and escape.[48] Although the women in *Wuthering Heights*, like their Victorian contemporaries, are powerless to influence the laws of marriage and property even as they have to endure their consequences, their resistance offers a glimpse of an alternative order where conventional structures are not observed and patriarchal laws are broken, albeit temporarily.

9 LOVE IN A SOCIAL SETTING

Although Catherine and Heathcliff eschew the dictates of conventional morality and the demands of the institution that the union between two human beings be framed in marriage, is it possible to imagine their love outside such constraints? In other words, would their love be able to subsist or achieve a definition of its otherness were it not for the competing demands made on it? Like all desire, Catherine and Heathcliff's love arises from, takes place in, and is defined by its existence in a social

---

[47] Juliet Mitchell, *Psychoanalysis and Feminism* (London: Allen Lane, 1974), at xvi.
[48] 'The Female Gothic' in Ellen Moers, *Literary Women* (London: W. H. Allen, 1977).

setting. Without their observation of Hindley's and Frances's relationship following their marriage, Catherine and Heathcliff would not have dreamed of a different relationship and a different mode of expressing it: '[Frances] went and seated herself on her husband's knee, and there they were, like two babies, kissing and talking nonsense by the hour—foolish palaver that we should be ashamed of' (63). Without the demands of polite society Catherine would not have denied Heathcliff, without the separation such a decision enforces their love would not have reached its depths and heights of intensity. In the same way that conventional morality needs transgressors in order to solidify itself, Catherine and Heathcliff need conventional morality to establish themselves as outsiders and their love as 'other'. Their demand for a different relationship is a response to the social conditions they observe, are conditioned by, and briefly, in both Catherine's and Heathcliff's case, abide by. As Heathcliff accuses Catherine, 'Because misery, and degradation, and death, and nothing that God or Satan could inflict would have parted us, *you* of your own will did it. I have not broken your heart, *you* have broken it' (197). Indeed the love between Catherine and Heathcliff only exists and can only be defined in opposition to social dictates; without those dictates they are at a loss to describe its nature or content. As J. T. Matthews puts it, 'The lovers themselves are unable to find a form of expression to explain or even name the nature of their relation . . . they are always on the threshold of fulfilment . . . They are in pursuit of a desire without nameable content . . . their longing cannot abide the congealment of representation'.[49] Such lack of fulfilment and absence of representation is the very condition of desire and the maintenance of a, however discontented, civilization.

Perhaps, as Bataille suggests, Catherine Earnshaw and Emily Brontë herself dreamt the same desires, the same evil that Heathcliff enacts. Catherine follows convention to the extent that she does not contemplate leaving her husband for her childhood dreams. But the dream and the desire persist in her refusal to abide by Nelly's 'steady, reasonable' (103) advice, including reason's demand that she eat to live. In endowing her characters with sympathetic features, Emily Brontë establishes them as tragic heroes in their doomed attempt to surpass and transgress laws and social conventions that insist on framing and regulating their relationship.

For some critics, Emily Brontë herself, unable to erase the twin dream of ultimate love and ultimate evil, attempts to deny them in the second part of the novel which appears to be a retraction from the violence of love and evil depicted in the first part. We must question, however, whether this compromise is successful in overcoming the subversive potential of the first part. The story of lost childish innocence and plenitude is different for Catherine II who is more willing to abandon childhood lawlessness than her mother. Following her first encounter with Heathcliff on her sixteenth birthday she gradually sheds her attachment to the mother (in this case, Nelly) and slowly enters adulthood and the father's law. By the end of the book she has espoused

---

[49] John T. Matthews, 'Framing in *Wuthering Heights*' in Patsy Stoneman (ed.); *Wuthering Heights, supra*, at 62.

the conventions of her society and is a happy, soon-to-be married, young woman. The subversive passions of Catherine and Heathcliff in the first half are replaced with the tamer affection between Catherine and Hareton to be contained by the legal institution of marriage. In contrast to the passion between Catherine and Heathcliff, the love between Catherine and Hareton is more successful but also more banal in that it can be assimilated to culture and described in a language that everyone can understand. At the same time, their common experience of oppression at the hands of Heathcliff means that, like the relationship between her mother and Heathcliff, this relationship begins and continues, as Joseph Boone argues, in intimacy and friendship rather than antagonism and competition. Again Brontë explores the ideal of love as identification with, rather than against, the other and creates a space that transcends social, class, and gender divisions.[50]

Society demands, however, not just the institution of marriage before it can endorse this relationship but also the affirmation of property rights and patrilinear inheritance. The new heir of Wuthering Heights, Hareton, bears the same name as that which was inscribed over the lintel of the house some three hundred years earlier. Heathcliff's arrival caused a break in the rules of primogeniture and Hindley's victimization of him following old Earnshaw's death is an attempt to insist on his role as his father's heir. Heathcliff further flouts the rules of inheritance by returning in the second half of the book as a man of means able to buy Hindley out of Wuthering Heights. The fact that he has used the rules of the capitalist system to achieve this does not render him a rightful owner as patrilinear succession harks back to the older feudal system.

Indeed gothic novels, while depicting evil aristocrats flouting law and convention, also betrayed a nostalgia for the feudal order and aristocratic values. The transgression of the social order, by inspiring fear of chaos and anxiety at the threat of total disintegration, also led to the welcoming of the return to laws and propriety. While the gothic novel has been linked to revolutionary power and energy, the punishment of gothic heroes at the end often leads to the enhancement rather than denial of the order threatened by revolution.[51] Further, by articulating and displaying revolutionary ideas, the gothic might have acted more as a displacement and escapism from their realization in practice.

The fantastic elements in the book are also eliminated in the second part as we witness a scene familiar from Victorian domestic fiction. Such fiction, as Nancy Armstrong has argued, while tolerating and even endorsing women's desire to write, does so on the condition that their writing is restricted to themes of domesticity and

---

[50] Joseph Allen Boone, *Tradition Counter-Tradition, supra*, at 169. As discussed above, this is also Irigaray's vision in *i love to you*: an interconnectedness that does not annul the other's difference, does not devour or appropriate the other and importantly where one's identity is not restricted to society's designation of what is proper 'masculine' or 'feminine' behaviour.

[51] For a fuller discussion of the gothic genre's double-bind between transgression and containment see Fred Botting, *Gothic* (London and New York: Routledge, 1996).

matrimonial bliss.[52] Women writing their experiences are tolerated because at the same time those experiences are interpreted as outside the public realm of politics.

However, while the second part of the book may be a prototype of domestic fiction, the energies and passions depicted in the first part are not easily effaced or repressed. The continuing presence of Heathcliff in the midst of the domestic plot ensures that the reader's memory of another order is not obliterated. The survival of the house Wuthering Heights is also a testament to an order that might have been defeated but not completely expulsed. Early critics' unhappiness with the novel for not affording clear moral instruction attests to the continuing power of the supernatural, the arational, and the asocial. Rather than being denied, the forces associated with Heathcliff and Catherine run parallel to and resist the comfortable closure of the second narrative. While Nelly claims that 'the dead are at peace', she admits that 'yet still I don't like being out in the dark now—and I don't like being left by myself in this grim house' (366) and that local folk and a young shepherd boy have seen the ghosts of Catherine and Heathcliff.

10 NARRATIVE LAWS

The subversive potential of fantasy literature must not be overestimated; on the one hand, fantasy literature uses the language of the dominant order, a language that assumes and constructs its own version of reality; using such language implies and can lead to an acceptance of its norms. Second, by expressing desires that are repressed, silenced, or lost, fantasy literature enables those desires to be experienced on paper, perhaps postponing or replacing their realization in practice.

In *Wuthering Heights* Catherine's and Heathcliff's otherworldly passion and uncultured energy are restrained by the text's conservative narrators Nelly and Lockwood. The urge to narrate is itself an urge not only to entertain but to understand, explain, and also to judge. In the hands of Nelly and Lockwood this urge takes the form of rationalistic explanations of desires and events that they do not understand or that indeed cannot be expressed linguistically. The fact that they share the same language means that communication between them leaves no room for what their language prefers to deny. Nelly, as Lockwood appreciates, is at pains to conform to and imitate what she perceives as her employers' values including their language: 'Excepting a few provincialisms of slight consequence, you have no marks of the manners which I am habituated to consider as peculiar to your class'(103). Nelly uses

---

[52] *Desire and Domestic Fiction: A Political History of the Novel* (New York and Oxford: Oxford University Press, 1987): 'the cultural sleight of hand that both granted women the authority to write and denied them the power to make political statements'. Charlotte Brontë's preface in particular encouraged readers to locate the novel's representations of the violation of the sexual contract in Emily's emotional life and thus remove it from political controversy, while the aggression of the first generation is replaced with a domesticated version of them at the end, especially at 36–58.

the standard language required by the bourgeoisie to mediate and dissolve any aberrant contradictions. From the start Nelly neither tries to, nor indeed can, limit herself
to a description of events; such so-called 'objective' narration is impossible as not
only fictional writers but lawyers and judges appreciate. Nelly's prejudices, preferences, and interests (in particular in achieving a union between her young mistress
and Lockwood which would establish her, once again, as housekeeper at Thrushcross
Grange) keep getting in the way. Prompted by the twin impulses of achieving what she
perceives would be good for herself and for those around her, and by 'idle curiosity'
(358) she arrogates to herself the power to decide 'what to hide and what to reveal'
(296).

But it is not only her narration of events that is affected by her interpretations and
judgements but the events themselves, as she occasionally concedes: 'I seated myself in
a chair, and rocked, to and fro, passing harsh judgment on my many derelictions of
duty; from which, it struck me then, all the misfortunes of all my employers sprang. It
was not the case, in reality, I am aware; but it was, in my imagination, that dismal
night and I thought Heathcliff himself less guilty than I' (308). Nelly thwarts
Catherine and Heathcliff's union by not alerting Catherine to Heathcliff's presence
when she is confessing her dilemma of choosing between Heathcliff and Edgar. Interpreting Catherine's illness as wilful and capricious, she does not alert Linton of its
seriousness and through what she claims to be 'pardonable weakness', does not warn
Edgar Linton of his prospective son-in-law's unpleasant character (297). Lockwood
also expels Catherine's ghost by rubbing its bare wrist on the broken glass until the
blood is running. Both Nelly and Lockwood reduce, by their commonsense approach,
the mysterious and the supernatural to the everyday and the empirical. For Leo
Bersani the neat circularity of Lockwood's narrative and the parallels between the two
love affairs 'create a structure in which events are repeated or return to their point of
origin . . . *Wuthering Heights* works towards a structural circularity and repetitiveness
which only Heathcliff might disrupt but which finally leaves no room for Heathcliff'.[53]
The 'otherness' of Catherine and Heathcliff, their excess and passion could not be
contained within the cultural, the social, the institutional or, in the end, the linguistic.
By suggesting an asocial relationship before the intervention of social roles, class, and
structures, it threatens to upset the existing order. More importantly, the language of
the symbolic order hints at, but fails to capture it. Only in death are their ghosts
allowed to roam Wuthering Heights without threatening the domestic peace of
Thrushcross Grange.

As 'patriarchy's paradigmatic housekeeper' Nelly is 'a man's woman' who not only
agrees with but takes up the task of 'keeping men's houses in order by straightening
out their parlors, their daughters and their stories'.[54] Like other real and surrogate
mothers we encounter in this book, perceiving herself as weak in a patriarchal culture,

[53] Leo Bersani, *A Future for Astyanax: Character and Desire in Literature* (London and New York: Marion
Boyars, 1978), at 222–3.
[54] *The Madwoman in the Attic, supra*, at 291–2.

she adopts and fiercely defends the forces that she perceives as both strong and superior: 'My heart invariably cleaved to the master's, in preference to Catherine's side', she admits without any compunction at choosing to side with the interests of patriarchy over those of her young charge (146). Her wish to see the continuation of the Linton family and their property leads her to condemn old Linton for leaving his estate to his daughter Isabella rather than to his sons: 'I mentally abused old Linton for . . . securing his estate to his own daughter, instead of his sons' (201). She worries that Heathcliff's marriage to Isabella would mean that the Linton property would fall in the hands of 'a stranger's gripe'. And in the midst of Catherine's illness her main preoccupation is again to see the continuation of the Linton family name and property: 'for on her existence depended that of another; we cherished the hope that in a little while, Mr Linton's heart would be gladdened, and his lands secured from a stranger's gripe, by the birth of an heir' (172). Importantly, the marriage between Catherine and Hareton assures not only their domestic bliss but that of Nelly's: 'there won't be a happier woman than myself in England' (268).

Lockwood also is at a loss to understand the tale he is listening to and periodically observes. To the end he denies the existence of ghosts and denies 'that anyone could ever imagine unquiet slumbers, for the sleepers in that quiet earth' (367). Emily Brontë's decision to frame the story through his narration could suggest an endorsement of his worldview, were it not for the fact that the reader is alerted to Lockwood's excessive concern with class, hierarchy, and convention and his pathetic inability to deal with emotions as well as cowardice concerning phenomena that are not susceptible to rational explanations and control. Early on he confesses how he found himself shunning the attentions of 'a fascinating creature, a real goddess' (48) that he was obviously attracted to. Although he is the only character in the novel to encounter Catherine's ghost he is brutally repressive of both the ghost's wish to be let in and the demands it makes on his faith in reason. More importantly, the explanations he clings to are those afforded to him by his position as a male subject with the prerogative of looking at and appropriating with his gaze the objects surrounding him. When these objects, like the 'real goddess', or the younger Catherine, defy his right to look at them, or, unlike Nelly who confirms his gaze, gaze back at him, he shrinks back to his shell 'like a snail' (48).[55]

Although Brontë adeptly mimics his phallocentric discourse, she also, through Lockwood's unsympathetic character, shows us the limitations of such a discourse. She thus successfully combines mimicry with critique, using Lockwood's words to imply and imagine different words and different worlds.[56] Our own urge to provide a closure, to understand and explain the novel can only ever take place in the language

[55] See Beth Newman, '"The Situation of the Looker-on": Gender, Narration and Gaze in *Wuthering Heights*' (1990), Vol. 105 (3), *Proceedings of the Modern Language Association*, 1029–41.

[56] Juliet Mitchell suggests that women's writing is that of the hysteric, simultaneously accepting and refusing patriarchy, both refusing and being trapped within femininity. Such 'hysteria' can be conformist, like Mills and Boon novels, or critical, like *Wuthering Heights: Women, the Longest Revolution* (London: Virago Press, 1982).

of the symbolic order. Language and logos promise to deliver what the subject needs, to close the gap of desire generated by the prohibition of incest and the separation from the mother. But language is a system of signifiers referring to other signifiers: the correspondence between words and reality that Nelly, Lockwood, and Zillah aim to achieve is fraught, as language slips away from their control, hinting at gaps and discontinuities in their representations of reality and ultimately in reality itself. In the same way the events of the past continue to intrude and disrupt their attempt to explain and master the present.

In its admixture of different genres, different languages, and different laws, Emily Brontë's novel remains simultaneously outside and within the symbolic order, using the symbolic order's laws and signs but at the same time questioning them through the intrusion of other languages, other laws, and other realities; the language of reason is threatened by Catherine's language of madness, the law of the magistrates is threatened by the law of love, the language of books and religion by the erasures, murmurs, and whispers of Heathcliff and Catherine, the 'reality' of the living by the world of ghosts. In this other world, distinctions between male and female, brother and sister, body and soul, even life and death, are blurred. It is a world that preceded our entry into the symbolic order and continues after our exit from it: as, for both Catherine and Heathcliff, and any readers who identify with their story, birth into the world of culture is not the beginning, nor is death the end. The text therefore exceeds and terrorizes the symbolic order and the law of the father that Lacanian theory would have us believe is the condition for its writing and reading.

6

LAW IN THE REALM OF THE SENSES: CAMUS' *THE OUTSIDER*[1]

The magistrate's expression seems to oscillate between pity and loathing, as he looks doon at me
n Spud in the dock.
—You stole the books from Waterstone's bookshop, with the intention of selling them, he states.
—Sell fucking books. Ma fucking erse.
—No, ah sais.
—Aye, Spud sais, at the same time.
—We turn aroond n look at each other. Aw the time we spent gitting oor story straight . . .

Irving Welsh, *Trainspotting*

1 BETWEEN NARRATIVE AND DISORDER

If all narratives are attempts to impose a semblance of order, however temporary, on a universe we cannot understand, predict, or explain, Camus' early novel *The Outsider* appears to embark on an impossible project: to assert, on the one hand, the world's meaninglessness and man's inability to derive meaning from it, through a narrative that necessarily imposes a semblance of order on it. As Sartre has commented, someone who experiences the world as absurd, who distrusts not only grand theories that attempt to impose meaning on it, but also the power of language to express both meaning and meaninglessness, has no other option but to remain silent. Or, and this is a question Camus himself posed in another work, if life is experienced as meaningless, why is it that we do not commit suicide, in the philosophical sense of ceasing to ask questions, or in the more basic sense of taking our own lives? In effect, Sartre argues, Camus has written a novel about the necessity of remaining silent. This conclusion, however, is reached only after examining and demonstrating the deficiency of other attempts to derive or, in some cases, dictatorially to impose meaning on our

---

[1] Albert Camus, *The Outsider*, trans. Joseph Lakedo (Harmondsworth: Penguin, 1982) [1942]; all references in the text are to this edition.

lives: whether these are based on the notions of romantic love, friendship, and the family, on social conventions that advocate economic and professional advancement, or institutionalized in religious and legal discourses. And not before arriving at an outlook of life that purports to reconcile us with, without evading, this meaninglessness. This meaning, if only an anti-meaning, can be derived from the hero's, or anti-hero's, attempt to write his own story and to close his life before his execution, in his own words.

Many readers remain unconvinced with both Camus' methods of arrival at this reconciliation as well as his conclusions. While acknowledging the validity of some of these criticisms, I argue that *The Outsider* continues to entice because of its insistence on confronting the persistent dilemma and accompanying perils of deriving and imposing meaning. Further, it illustrates the Nietzschean belief that, arbitrary or inconsistent as some of these attempts are, art can give form and closure to the meaninglessness of existence. It is an attempt to express life's meaning or meaninglessness not through reason—law's preferred arch-narrative—but through paying attention to the body and the senses in particular and to art, literature, and the aesthetic in general. In Nietzsche's words, art may be the only metaphysical activity open to us, our only refuge: 'Only as an aesthetic product can the world be justified to all eternity.'[2]

The full import of this insight, however, is not explored by Camus; in particular, I will argue, Camus, while according precedence to art, beauty, and the senses, neglects one factor that would make such meaning not transitory, not adhering only to the present moment, but lasting; that is the contribution woman can make to the discourse of the absurd. A contribution that is present but unacknowledged by the text because, 'women's time', to borrow Julia Kristeva's phrase, would introduce the dimension of continuity and eternity to a discourse that sees life as a series of isolated, discontinuous moments that lead only to death. One could go as far as to argue that, had Camus, metaphorically, been willing to listen to woman, had Meursault, literally, not returned to the beach as his way of escaping the sound of women's tears, none of this would have happened!

It is possible, Camus suggests in *The Myth of Sisyphus*, to live our lives without questioning its origins or meaning; Oedipus, as we saw at the start of the book, driven by the detective's urge to find out, is crushed by finding out too much. Despite the perils accompanying such a quest, human beings do sometimes find themselves, willingly or unwillingly, taking a break from following their routines and from bowing to convention, and questioning why it is they do what they do. At such points, our desire for meaning comes into conflict with our inability to find one, our desire to understand and explain is frustrated by the world's irrationality, our calls for clarity are resisted by the universe's deafening silence to our appeals. At such moments, we are struck by our solitude from other people and by an awareness of our own

---

[2] Friedrich Nietzsche, *The Birth of Tragedy* [1870], trans. Francis Golffing (New York: Doubleday, 1956) at 42.

mortality. Indeed the absurd can be summed up as the conflict between the human desire to live eternally and the realization of the inevitability of death: the 'divorce between the mind that desires and the world that disappoints'.[3]

Responses to this dilemma have often taken the form of posing an arch-signifier that will confer meaning and order to the multiple and seemingly chaotic signs the universe bombards us with. Sartre draws a distinction between Camus and Kafka on the basis of their different responses to the dilemma of the absurd: 'Camus's views are entirely of this earth, and Kafka is the novelist of impossible transcendence; for him, the universe is full of signs that we cannot understand; there is a reverse side to the decor. For Camus, on the contrary, the tragedy of human existence lies in the absence of any transcendence.'[4] There is no doubt that Camus rejects the concept of 'God' as the transcendental signifier that will confer order on disorder. The concepts of 'law' and 'reason', at least as manifested in the workings of the French Algerian courts, are similarly dismissed as potential foundations for anchoring our experiences. Are the concepts Camus seemingly attaches importance to, however, such as 'man', 'nature', 'the senses', and, as I will argue, 'art' and 'literature' less problematic? In particular, even if we are prepared to concede their importance, can they, by themselves, confer meaning to Meursault's life, and to his death, without also conceding importance to another neglected signifier, that is 'woman'?

2 THE WILL TO EXPLAIN AND THE ABSURD REFUSAL TO EXPLAIN

Seemingly drifting through a hot Mediterranean summer, Part I of *The Outsider* depicts through Meursault's laconic manner, an array of characters all clinging to their own version of what makes their lives valuable and meaningful. However tangentially and in passing, Meursault shares these observations with the reader: the young girls and boys of Algiers find diversion and amusement in courting, Salamano in his love-hate relationship with his dog (which we are led to believe follows the loss of a similar relationship with his wife), Marie in the promise of romantic love and marriage, his boss in the efficient working of his company, Raymond in asserting his power over those physically and socially weaker than himself like his Arab mistress. Meursault remains allegedly apart from these preoccupations, neither sharing them nor judging them.

The author of the absurd could be said to share the Nietzschean belief, which in some cases can be a despair, that in the absence of a transcendental authority, be that god or another dogma, all our values are equally arbitrary, meaningless, and

---

[3] Albert Camus, *The Myth of Sisyphus*, trans. Justin O'Brien (London: Penguin, 1975) [1942] at 50.

[4] Jean-Paul Sartre, 'An Explication of *The Stranger*' in Germaine Brée (ed.), *Camus: A Collection of Critical Essays* (Englewood Cliffs, NJ: Prentice-Hall, Inc., 1962), at 116.

contingent. There is no outside authority compelling us to choose one life plan rather than another, including no reason for protecting life, others' or one's own, rather than taking life. Though such values are presented to us as natural and inevitable, they are no more than cultural and conventional. They are, moreover, dangerous and enslaving, disabling us from creating and recreating our world, our values and ourselves and robbing us of the possibility of authenticity. It is only by recognizing the constructed nature of these values that human beings may become truly free to recognize their potential, choose their own values, and stand on their own feet without the support of faith or dogma. Camus has therefore created a literary model based on another literary model, Nietzsche's Zarathustra: 'To stand with relaxed muscles and unharnessed wills: that is the most difficult thing for all of you, you sublime men'.[5]

One attempt to confer meaning, however, seems to attract more than Meursault's customary indifference. In Part II the encounter with the examining magistrate and later the prison chaplain arouse in the usually untouchable Meursault something approaching contempt and even anger. The importance human beings attach to the existence of meaning is nowhere more starkly illustrated than by the examining magistrate's outburst against Meursault's obstinate refusal to attach importance to a transcendent authority, in this case God: 'Do you want my life to be meaningless?'(68) he protests. The view that because something is necessary for one's self-preservation it must necessarily exist attracted Nietzsche's contempt. For Nietzsche, man's propensity for consolatory narratives like religion was not only lacking in foundations but was positively harmful to man's capacity to be great. Christian morality, by preaching pity and compassion was responsible for diminishing and weakening man, imprisoning his body in the soul, making him sick and unable to stand on his own feet.

Like Nietzsche, Camus sees in Christianity a doctrine of injustice and privilege because it is founded on the sacrifice of innocent children and the acceptance of suffering as necessary for the acquisition of truth.[6] Worse still, by offering the illusion of future justice in another world, it fosters in believers an attitude of resignation and passivity and robs them of energies needed to fight present injustices: Christianity, Nietzsche writes, 'desires to dominate *beasts of prey*; its means for doing so is to make them *sick*. Weakening is the Christian recipe for taming, for civilization'.[7] With modernity, the impetus to understand was transferred from god to man, from religion to science, and from faith to reason and law. For Nietzsche however, such morality also appeals to the weak and the cowardly, those who prefer to adhere to the lowest common denominator and to follow herd values: 'the domestic animal, the herd animal, the sick animal man—the Christian'.[8] It is thus destructive of the instinct to explore and assert one's own greatness and distinctness from other people.

---

[5] Friedrich Nietzsche, *Thus Spoke Zarathustra*, trans. R. J. Hollingdale (London: Penguin, 1961) [1885] at 141.

[6] Albert Camus, *The Rebel*, trans. Anthony Bower (London: Penguin, 1971) [1951] at 50–6.

[7] Friedrich Nietzsche, *The Antichrist*, trans. R. J. Hollingdale (Penguin: London, 1990) [1885] at 144.

[8] *ibid.*, at 128.

Meursault shows a similar lack of a desire for transcendence and a similar indifference to conventional rules and standards. His very distrust of metaphysical explanations for man's existence poses a threat to would-be believers and adherents to these doctrines. Official society can only cope with this threat by destroying it and such destruction must be done by bringing it within its rules, that is without acknowledging Meursault's wider challenge to the arbitrariness and meaninglessness of these codes. Faced by this threat, the wielders of these doctrines are led to display them not only in all their ability to comfort and console, but also in all their dictatorial and dogmatic might.

3 WRITING THE ABSURD

As Sartre and other commentators noted, a disbelief in a unifying or totalizing system, means that the absurd hero cannot purport to be explaining the world, himself, or events and people surrounding him. All he can hope to achieve by speaking, and by writing, is to describe. Of course this is impossible, as Camus himself recognized: there is no such thing as a literature of despair because 'Despair is silent . . . if it speaks, if it reasons, above all if it writes, immediately a brother reaches out his hand, the tree is justified, love is born.'[9] Camus is therefore caught red-handed making meaning out of the experience of meaninglessness, of expressing the experience of not being able to express, of trying to understand our inability to understand. Like his creator, Meursault, try as he might, cannot avoid language, nor the fact that language is outside and beyond his control. Since words arrive to us always already endowed with meanings, Meursault cannot but make value judgments and interpretations each time he speaks, or each time, equally, when he remains silent.

In Part I Meursault attempts to tell a story that documents dialogue and events without making connections between them and without drawing conclusions or value judgments of either his own or other characters' words and actions. As Sartre commented, each sentence is isolated, frozen, self-sufficient; verbs do not act as bridges between the past and the present or suggest an order of causality; they appear to us 'like islands. We bounce from sentence to sentence, from void to void'.[10] If an order is suggested, it is no more than the order conferred by the succession of a series of discontinuous moments; since the narrator purports to attach equal significance (or, which amounts to the same thing, equal *in*significance) to each and every event, the fragments he relates are all, on the surface, seemingly equally indifferent and equally meaningless.

Camus was aware that realism in art is untenable: to write is to select, to judge, and

---

[9] 'The Enigma' in *Selected Essays & Notebooks*, ed. & trans. Philip Thody (Harmondsworth: Penguin, 1970) at 145.

[10] Jean-Paul Sartre, 'An Explication of *The Stranger*', *supra*, at 119.

to arbitrarily reduce: writers, therefore, he argued, should aim for 'invisible stylization, or rather stylization incarnate'.[11] Roland Barthes praised this style as 'writing
degree zero', as an innocent or neutral writing which 'achieves a style of absence
which is almost an ideal absence of style; writing is then reduced to a sort of negative
mood in which the social or mythical characters of a language are abolished in favour
of a neutral and inert state of form . . . it is the mode of a new situation of the writer,
the way a certain silence has of existing; it deliberately foregoes any elegance or
ornament'.[12] In contrast to the realist novel that, by pretending to be 'natural',
obscures the fact that it expresses the ideology and social values of the bourgeois class,
Camus' style, for Barthes, questioned the conventions by which bourgeois culture
orders the world and thereby drew attention to them. 'Neutrality', however, as Barthes
also came to recognize later, is itself a style, as historically and politically contingent as
any other style, and its revolutionary potential can be co-opted.[13]

Meursault's use of the perfect tense does not help achieve objectivity of recording
or immediacy of expression any more than the more commonly used past historic;
value judgments and interpretations, seep in, however unnoticed or unacknowledged,
each time one word rather than another is chosen for inclusion, each time one word
rather than another is chosen for omission. The account of events in Part I of the text
is therefore no more neutral or unmediated by value judgments than the explanation of events by the lawyers in Part II. Meursault's attempt to document events
without commenting on their significance, and seemingly without aiming to connect
or unify them into a complete whole, cannot hide the fact that he opts to register some
events rather than others, or that he chooses one narrative sequence rather than
another.

What appears to repel Meursault most, however, is other peoples' insistence that he
express his emotions. Whether he finds himself at his mother's funeral, in bed with
Marie, in the company of someone like Raymond who offers him friendship or
Salamano who extends sympathy, or in front of an accusing law court, he is consistently reticent. Such reluctance is due not only to his distrust of abstract feelings such
as grief, regret, love, or affection but to a suspicion of language as an adequate
medium for expressing these emotions. Aware of the fact that words cannot accurately
express his immediate experiences, Meursault often decides against saying anything at
all. His preference for silence for the distortion wreaked by words is the major aspect
of his adherence to the truth that made him such a favourite with his creator: he is a
man 'who, without any heroic pretensions, agrees to die for the truth.'[14]

His alleged indifference, however, his repeated assertion that 'it didn't matter' 'it
was all a bit pointless and I couldn't be bothered' (66), rather than being the mark of

---

[11] *The Rebel, supra,* 237.

[12] Roland Barthes, *Writing Degree Zero,* trans. Annette Lavers and Colin Smith (London: Jonathan Cape,
1967) [1953], at 83–4.

[13] See Roland Barthes, *Mythologies,* trans. Annette Lavers (London: Vintage, 1973) [1957], at 134–5 'it is
extremely difficult to vanquish myth from the inside'.

[14] Albert Camus, 'Afterword' to *The Outsider, supra,* [1955], at 119.

an uncomplicated, unthinking, or amoral cipher, is also the result of a studied choice. Living within the parameters dictated by the expectations of others and conventional morality is not only what most of us do but is also the easy option, easiest when adhered to unthinkingly. Far from being lazy, Meursault rejects the option of hiding behind values chosen by others in the name of consensus. In that sense, Meursault strives against the forces that tempt us to become copies of each other in search of authenticity.[15] It can equally be argued, however, that Meursault also opts for the easy option of shutting areas of his life and his emotions that he cannot understand, cope with, and even less express. For a psychoanalytic critic, such repression in language matches Meursault's parallel attempt to shut off part of his life (and of his flat) after his mother's death, and can not go unnoticed. In particular, I will argue his reluctance to acknowledge, express, or discuss his emotions, is a disavowal of the feminine in him, of the mother who died and whom he claims not to have mourned.

4 LAW'S WILL TO EXPLAIN

Meursault's attempt to avoid explanations and value judgments is in stark contrast to legal discourse's insistence on explanations and judgments. Legal discourse's faith in the ability of reason to explain characters and events set the examining magistrate and the prosecution and defence lawyers into an energetic search for the motive behind Meursault's action. Although legal doctrine can accommodate the notion of involuntary automatism, which would account for the trigger giving way when Meursault fired the first shot, Meursault's refusal to explain the four extra shots creates a lacuna of interpretation. Abhorring a gap, the lawyers set out to impose a meaning for this voluntary act that brings it within conventions that legal discourse can understand and thereby regulate.

The notion of intention in legal reasoning assumes that the legal subject can and does assess the pros and cons of present acts and relates them to past experiences and future effects. The notion of recklessness also presupposes the agent's ability to foresee, albeit also to ignore, the consequences of his or her acts. Meursault displays little propensity to analyse the meaning of his actions in the present or their likely future consequences. This is the case whether he is scripting a letter for Raymond's mistress, going to his mother's funeral, watching a film, or killing a man. Where calculations do enter his thoughts, he opts for the path that will create least inconvenience to himself: he will eat his meal out of the pan rather than go to the trouble of getting a plate and will marry Marie rather than go to the trouble of explaining why the institution of

[15] For a historical analysis of the concept of authenticity and its compatibility with social and moral codes, see Jacob Golomb, *In Search of Authenticity: from Kierkegaard to Camus* (London and New York: Routledge, 1995). Golomb argues that Meursault attains that state only on the eve of his execution when he reflects back on his life, that is, when it is the result of a studied, rather than an unthinking, choice.

marriage signifies nothing. As far as the notion of future or the abstract notion of time generally enters his thoughts, it is only as a continuation of the now, a repetition of a routine that, lacking an overall plan, he sees no good reason for changing: to his boss's offer of a promotion to Paris 'I replied that you could never change your life, that in any case one life was as good as another and that I wasn't at all dissatisfied with mine here . . . . none of it really mattered' (44).

The law is unwilling to acknowledge the idea of a life made up of discontinuous, isolated events without a logical sequence designed to conform to and achieve an overall plan. Meursault's past, therefore, needs to be rewritten in terms that the law can understand and to this end the prosecution choose to focus on Meursault's behaviour at his mother's funeral. Gradually but surely Meursault is transformed from the nonchalant lover of the sun and girls we encounter in Part I to a calculating monster with murderous impulses in Part II. His nihilistic denial of meaning and value are isolated in his person rather than risk them being characterized as a malaise that affects, and thereby threatens to undermine, society and its values as a whole. By construing Meursault as the exception to society's consensus on values, the prosecutor labels him a 'monster' whose 'empty heart would threaten to engulf society' (98–9); this explanation serves to found the elusive criminal subject with a criminal intention.

The ascription of the labels guilt or innocence to intentional acts assumes that a value judgment attaches to our activities, a judgment that can only be provided by an objective outside transcendent authority. Meursault's philosophy, or anti-philosophy, however, undermines not only reason's demand for motives but the significance and very existence of such concepts. Hence the examining magistrate's puzzlement at Meursault's refusal to acknowledge an outside authority sanctioning or forbidding human behaviour. The attempt to create a legal subject that can be brought within the confines of legal discourse is shared by both prosecution and defence lawyers; Meursault's lawyer tries to suggest to him responses that would be acceptable to the court: 'He made me promise not to say that at the hearing, or in front of the magistrate . . . The only thing I could say for certain was that I'd rather mother hadn't died. But my lawyer didn't seem pleased. He said, "That's not enough"' (65). As Roland Barthes puts it, 'The law is always prepared to lend you a spare brain in order to condemn you without remorse and . . . it depicts you as you should be, not as you are. This official visit of justice to the world of the accused is made possible thanks to an intermediate myth which is always used abundantly by official institutions . . .: the transparence and universality of language.'[16]

Even when the social, moral, and physical power of social norms in the form of the legal machinery is called in to destroy Meursault's difference, the destruction is not complete. Meursault remains impervious to their attempts to 'convert' him, and reconciles himself to both his crime and his punishment. He is indifferent to their attempts to judge him, conceding only their facility with words and remains obstinate in his refusal to show remorse or regret for his actions. In short, he does not

---

[16] Roland Barthes, *Mythologies, supra,* at 44.

internalize the values of the legal system and therefore annihilation is the only method of dealing with him. The punishment dealt him, without touching him in the way that the legal system and the chaplain hope it will, does, nevertheless serve as a springboard for his own form of self-understanding. Is this understanding as complete as Meursault claims when he opens himself to the 'benign indifference of the world' (117)? Or is it ridden by limitations that Meursault will not consciously acknowledge, but nevertheless the text hints at?

5 WRITING THE SUBJECT OF LAW; SILENT WITNESSES

No explanation of events, concurrent or retrospective, can take place outside the medium of language; it is language that gives form and constitutes one's conception of the world as well as of oneself. The language we have at our disposal enables or seduces us into believing that our thoughts, feelings, and explanations of our actions precedes the expression of those thoughts, feelings, and explanations. It seduces us further into believing that we exercise agency and free will, concepts without which no modern legal system would be able to assert its power to judge and to punish. Conversely, the personalities, values, and dreams we create through words are limited by the language we have at our disposal. The reification of language not only creates, but also stabilizes the human subject who would otherwise be in a constant state of flux. Once such a stabilization takes place, the human subject can be literally as well as metaphorically arrested by the law. Law's intervention takes place of course in the name of society and of justice, but serves, first and foremost, law's own interests, that is of securing its continuing existence.

The narrative of law cannot afford to admit to its own constructedness or arbitrariness: it cannot afford to confess that it is only one amongst many narratives created to impose order on chaos. For the legal narrative to attract both moral and political power, no allowance can be made for its human origins, or for the possibility of mistakes. Camus' portrayal of Meursault's trial, in some respects a parody of legal proceedings, nevertheless points out the law's unwillingness to admit to its own artificiality. In particular, by constrasting legal language with the language of Meursault and that of his friends, the text undermines law's self-appointed role to speak the truth on the concepts of guilt and innocence.

For Germaine Brée, Camus, torn by love and pity for a silent mother, undertook, as a writer, the duty of speaking 'for those who are silent either because, like his mother, they are unused to the manipulation of words, or because they are silenced by various forms of oppression'.[17] There is no doubt that at the trial Camus portrays an array of

---

[17] 'Introduction', in Germaine Brée (ed.), *Camus: A Collection of Critical Essays, supra*, at 6.

witnesses who, unable to understand legal discourse and what is expected of them to say in court, unused, in other words, to legal rhetoric and the skilful manipulation of words, repeatedly find themselves misunderstood or silenced. As Richard Weisberg has argued, *The Outsider* is another instance of a 'sensate, unsentimental and nonverbal' individual coming into conflict with 'a moralistic, intellectualized, and cognitively written legal procedure'; the latter, bent on investing events with its own narrative meaning, succeeds in distorting both the events themselves and the human subject it comes to analyse and thereby control.[18]

Marie's relationship to Meursault for example, is labelled by the prosecutor as an illicit casual liaison; her own appraisal of the meaningfulness of their relationship (albeit one that is not shared by Meursault) is, however registered by the text, if not by the law, as she finds, if not the words, then the sound, the voice, and the facial expression to communicate her frustration and articulate her difference: 'all of a sudden Marie burst into tears and said it wasn't like that, there was something else and she was made to say the opposite of what she thought, she knew me and I hadn't done anything wrong' (91). In a similar fashion Celeste's testimony, in particular his opinion that Meursault is 'a man of the world; and . . . that everyone knew what that meant' (89) is purportedly rendered irrelevant by the prosecutor. The memory of their protest, however, is more eloquent than the prosecutor's rhetoric, registering a resistance to the language of law and of authority.

Meursault's own silence is not imposed but the result of a conscious choice: unwilling, as ever, to say more than he feels, whether it is to please Marie, his boss, the director of the old people's home, or his friends, he similarly refrains from saying anything that might save his own life: 'There were times when I felt like breaking in on all of them and saying "Wait a minute who's the accused here? Being the accused accounts for something and I have something to say", but on second thoughts I didn't have anything to say' (98). This 'rigorous honesty', 'total sincerity', and lack of 'sham or pretence', as Germaine Brée calls it, has rendered him in Sartre's words, 'one of those terrible innocents who shock society by not accepting the rules of the game'.[19] For Camus himself Meursault is 'the only Christ we deserve'[20] while Alain Robbe-Grillet voiced many readers' readiness to identify with Meursault when he declared '*L'étranger*, c'est moi'.[21]

In the context of the legal arena, however, the unwillingness to talk or the inability to talk in an authorized fashion, is co-opted into further evidence of guilt. As an institution dependent on the veracity of words to express both character and action,

[18] Richard Weisberg, *The Failure of the Word* (New Haven and London: Yale University Press, 1984), at 114–23.

[19] 'An Explication of *The Stranger*' in Germaine Brée (ed.), *Camus: A Collection of Critical Essays, supra*, at 111.

[20] 'Afterword', *The Outsider, supra*, at 119.

[21] Alain Robbe-Grillet, 'Monde trop plein, conscience vide' in Raymond Gay Crosier and Jacqueline Lévi-Valensi (eds.), *Albert Camus: Œuvre fermée, œuvre ouverte?* (Paris: Gallimard, 1985), at 214; quoted by Ben Stoltzfus, 'Camus's *L'étranger*: A Lacanian Reading', *Texas Studies in Literature*, (1989), vol. 31(4), 514–35, at 516.

the law cannot afford to allow either Meursault's silence or his friends' inarticulacy to undermine its own faith in the power of language. The prosecutor having undermined the evidence of the defence witnesses, begins his oration which purports not to describe and evaluate but in effect construct a Meursault hitherto unknown to both reader, Meursault's friends, and Meursault himself. 'It seemed to me it was just another way of excluding me from the proceedings, reducing me to insignificance and, in a sense, substituting himself for me' (100). Such is the power of his oratory that even Meursault appears to be convinced: 'His way of looking at things certainly didn't lack clarity. What he said was quite plausible' (96).

The defence counsel on the other hand puts up a poorer show as Meursault himself appreciates: 'I thought my lawyer was ridiculous . . . he didn't seem to have nearly as much talent as the prosecutor' (100). As Jean H. Duffy, argues, drawing on Barthes' analysis of narrative in *S/Z*, 'Meursault is condemned to death not simply because his behaviour constitutes a challenge to social and ethical canons but also because the prosecutor team are better story-tellers than the defence lawyer.'[22] But as Meursault appreciates, there was not 'so much difference, anyway, between the two speeches' (95); the problem they share is that they both insist on talking about his 'soul'.

The abiding image of Meursault in the dock is that of an observer, an 'intruder' out of place (82), who experiences his trial, and his life on trial, from the same perspective of a spectator watching a stage production. For French lawyer and psychoanalyst Pierre Legendre, the aesthetics, poetry, and images at work in the legal system work to construct the identity of the subject and bind him to the law not only through fear but also through fascination and love: the legal subject becomes erotically attached to the law in the same fashion that the child becomes attached to its father. In Peter Goodrich's words, 'Law institutes an exterior limit or subjection but also an interior emotional structure which will bind the subject through fear and through love, through fascination and through fealty, to the theatre of justice and truth . . . The theatre of legal reason exists to cover over the violence and the madness of power, its function is to make believe that law is reason and to hide the fact that law is also power'.[23]

Does Meursault become captivated by the spectacle he is watching? Does he become erotically attached to the law and convinced by the benevolent paternalism its officers extend to him? In my view Meursault throughout the proceedings, during his court-room appearances as well as during his meetings with his lawyer and the examining magistrate, obstinately resists the seduction that is law. True, he finds the proceedings interesting, true he marvels at the lawyers' eloquence and deftness with words; but throughout his trial he remains stubbornly uncaptured. Like Ariadne in my closing chapter, he is interested and curious about the law, but never surrenders

---

[22] 'Narrative Code versus Truth: the Prosecution Case in *L'Etranger*', *Essays in Poetics*, Vol. 14, No. 2, (1989) at 28.

[23] 'Introduction: Psychoanalysis and Law' in Peter Goodrich (ed.), *Law and the Unconcious: A Legendre Reader*, trans. Peter Goodrich with Alain Pottage and Anton Scütz, (London: Macmillan, 1977) at 32.

his desire to it. Indeed it is when the law tries hardest to appear as his 'father' that, as we will see later, Meursault resists its advances most vehemently. There is, I suggest, a bit of the feminine in Meursault that ensures that his desire remains throughout with the mother.

Having failed to destroy Meursault's denial of a transcendent authority, having failed to seduce him with its reason, with its words and its images, having failed, in other words, to 'assimilate' Meursault's difference, the law has only one route left with which to assert its superiority: the ultimate punishment. In the name of justice, reason, and 'the French people', the law proceeds to take Meursault's life in a mirror act of Meursault's own transgression. In a manner that recalls, in Foucault's schema, early disciplinary societies, the law directs its force against the body of the criminal, having failed to touch Meursault's 'soul'. The law therefore, as we saw again in the *Oresteia*, does not abandon the will to violence but satisfies it by identical means. The spectacle of public executions will ensure that spectators will participate in the forbidden pleasure of inflicting violence. The spectacle will also serve as an act of catharsis, ridding the community of its own will to violence by targeting one individual, Meursault; in Girard's scheme, Meursault is the scapegoat whose sacrifice will rid society of other ills and restore order to the community.[24] That sacrifice is not alien to but a step towards the legal system, is shown by the fact that in the process of condemning Meursault the law betrays the transcendental values it claims to embody, and takes over rather than eradicates the violent impulses it purported to condemn in him.

6 AN ETHICS OF THE ABSURD

Is Meursault, as some commentators have claimed, amoral, a 'juvenile delinquent',[25] a selfish child, even a psychopath?[26] Is he so at the start of the novel, and if so, does he remain the same or change by the end of the book? There is no doubt that Meursault acknowledges the existence of social norms and values that are accepted by other people and strives, as far as his laziness allows, to live within and accommodate them.

Such an attitude, however, is not, as is sometimes alleged, unreflective, or spontaneous, but the result of a studied indifference to a world and its values that he has found to be equally indifferent and meaningless. 'When I was a student, I had plenty of that sort of ambition. But when I had to give up my studies, I very soon realized that none of it really mattered' (44). Meursault's alleged laziness is a response to

---

[24] René Girard, *Violence and the Sacred*, trans. Patrick Gregory (Baltimore: Johns Hopkins University Press, 1977). Girard himself, I should add, did not apply this analysis to *The Outsider*.

[25] René Girard, 'Camus's Stranger Retried', 79, *Proceedings of the Modern Language Association* (1964), 519.

[26] See J. G. Murray, 'Moral Death: A Kantian Essay on Psychopathy', *Ethics*, Vol. 82 (1972), 284–98 and A. Duff, 'Psychopaths and Moral Understanding', *American Philosophical Quarterly*, 14, (1970), 190. These are discussed and challenged by Robert J. Smith, 'The Psychopath as Moral Agent', *Philosophy and Phenomenological Research*, Vol. XIV, No. 2, Dec. 1984.

the world's own laziness in the form of consoling narratives of love, religious faith, friendship, and justice. Though he will admit to desiring Marie he cannot bring himself to tell her he loves her, as the concept of love is, for Meursault, an abstraction as consoling as any other metaphysical fiction. And while agreeing to marry her in order to please her, he adds that he would agree to marry any girl who asked him. For Meursault to think of an abstract notion such as romantic love in any other terms, would be to accord it the significance of a grand meta-narrative instead of seeing it as one consoling and artificial narrative among many. Its institutionalization by society in the form of marriage is a further attempt to confer a semblance of order and finality to our otherwise chaotic lives and guard us from our inability to be alone. As Nietzsche derided, 'Ah, this poverty of soul in partnership! Ah, this filth of soul in partnership! Ah, this miserable ease in partnership! . . . Well, I do not like it, this Heaven of the superfluous! No, I do not like them, these animals caught in the heavenly net!'[27]

In *The Myth of Sisyphus* Camus poses the question why, if life is meaningless, we do not commit suicide. For Camus physical suicide is a resignation to the paradox of the absurd existence, just as the leap of faith is a philosophical suicide. The solution is to live with the paradox, continually confronting its terms and consequences, rather than ignoring or caving in to it. The experience of the absurd does not put an end to moral thinking, condemning man to suicide, but is, for Camus, the beginning to all thinking, including the formulation of an ethic, for oneself and others, that acknowledges, without submitting to, one's inevitable death.

In the hot Algerian sun and the cool Mediterranean sea Meursault and Camus find not only the yearning for but also the acceptance of life that counteracts the pessimism and austerity encountered in northern philosophers such as Schopenhauer and Kierkegaard. Rather than offsetting despair by withdrawing from the world, or seeking solace by taking the leap of faith, Camus and his 'pagan hero'[28] find harmony and pleasure in the concrete experiences afforded by the kingdom of *this* world. Truth, he suggests, the 'secret of the world and the depth of the universe' can be witnessed as simply and as easily as 'the shadows of branches flowing on my white curtains'.[29] While the Greeks spent twenty years trying to recapture Helen, western thought, he admonishes, bears the responsibility of exiling beauty from man's life; and no man can live without beauty.[30]

In the face of the asexual and disembodied rights of religious and legal norms, Camus suggests an ethics of embodiment and of participation in the world.[31] In

---

[27] *Thus Spoke Zarathustra, supra*, at 95.

[28] Robert J. Champigny, *A Pagan Hero: An Interpretation of Meursault in Camus's* The Stranger (Philadelphia, Pa.: University of Pennsylvania Press, 1969), trans. Rowe Portis [1960].

[29] 'Betwixt and Between' in Albert Camus, *Selected Essays and Notebooks, supra*, at 63.

[30] 'Helen's Exile', *ibid*. For a recent example of Camus's influence beyond the realm of literature, philosophy, or law, and celebration of the senses and the present moment as another type of truth, see Ilse Crawford, *Sensual Home* (London: Quadrille, 1997).

[31] See especially Serge Dubrovski, 'The Ethics of Albert Camus' in Germaine Brée (ed.), *Camus: A Collection of Critical Essays, supra*.

contrast to Christianity's condemnation of the flesh as transient and sinful, Meursault denies the notion of sin: indeed the ultimate sin is to deny the riches offered by the body and the senses, and if Meursault is roused, or aroused, by anything at all, it is by his awareness of his physical existence. In contrast to Christianity's preference for an afterlife in a heavenly world, Meursault affirms the value of life in this world. In contrast to political ideologies' willingness to sacrifice the present for the sake of future goals, Camus denies the notion of history as progress. In opposition to Marxism and fascism, Camus asserts that 'real generosity towards the future means giving all to the present . . . it is the very movement of life and it cannot be denied without renouncing life'.[32] In his essays this perspective is linked to the Greeks' doctrine of moderation and the demand for a balance between the Apollonian and Dionysian forces.

For Camus the absurdity of life and the inevitability of death cannot be denied, but our awareness of beauty enables us to confront them with 'revolt, freedom and passion'.[33] Revolt derived from refusal to bow to consoling faith; freedom from actively and consciously maintaining the tension between man and the world; and passion from being in love with one's condition in all its limitations and experiencing each passing moment to the full. This joy is all the more intense because of our awareness of its transience: 'the present and the succession of presents before a constantly conscious soul is the ideal of the absurd man . . . the point is to live'.[34] Without hope and without resignation, life must be lived in its present moment, with the awareness afforded by immediate sensations rather than abstract doctrines or metaphysical consolations. As Nietzsche's Zarathustra says 'I entreat you, my brothers, *remain true to the earth* and do not believe those who speak to you of super-terrestrial hopes. They are prisoners, whether they know it or not'.[35]

It is a also an ethic of participation rather than withdrawal from the world and of resonance between man and nature. Meursault's description of swimming with Marie comes close to describing the body's openness towards and receptivity of nature: 'moving together and feeling content together' (52). At moments like this, Meursault experiences the harmony of abandoning oneself to nature that Camus himself experienced during the Algerian summers. Meursault's indifference to abstract notions such as love, friendship, and career, are in sharp contrast to his awareness of beauty and the joy derived from physical contact with nature. From the beginning of the book, Meursault clings to a life of the senses as the only joy man can experience in a world where the only certainty is death. His thoughts of Marie in prison are similarly limited to the joy he derived from her presence; 'now that we were physically separated, there was nothing left to keep us together or to remind us of each other' (110).

The inevitability of death does not diminish the value of this life, indeed it accords

---

[32] *The Rebel, supra,* at 268.
[33] *The Myth of Sisyphus, supra,* at 62.
[34] *ibid.,* at 63.
[35] *Thus Spoke Zarathustra, supra,* at 42.

it with value, with the only meaning it can have, and this is what Meursault appreciates at the end of the book. By being obliged to contemplate what it means *not to be*, Meursault appears to be awarded with the awareness of what it means *to be*. The certainty of his death, whether in a few days or in a few years, enhances both the value and the joy of each passing moment: the condemned man, writes Camus, accepts a universe 'in which nothing is possible but everything is given, and draws strength from his own refusal to hope and the unyielding evidence of a life without consolation'.[36] Acceptance of death increases the will to live without certainty and without hope. The attitude of revolt does not endow life with meaning but enables the absurd man to confront it without illusions: 'It was previously a question of finding out whether or not life had to have a meaning to be lived. It now becomes clear on the contrary that it will be lived all the better if it has no meaning. Living an experience, a particular fact, is accepting it fully ... One of the only coherent philosophical positions is thus revolt. It is a constant confrontation between man and his own obscurity.'[37] In that respect the alleged 'epiphany' Meursault experiences following the chaplain's visit in the last pages of the book is an affirmation, rather than a repudiation, of his supposedly unreflective and spontaneous approach to life in the earlier part of the book.

Meursault's affirmation of a sensual existence in the here and now in preference to the promise of an after-life, and his unconcern with lack of meaning, does not render him inhuman, as the prosecutor and the examining magistrate imply, but indeed superhuman: it asserts a Nietzschean delight in being 'free, fearless hovering over men, customs, laws and the traditional evaluations of things'.[38] To soar freely without illusions or hope, is, for Camus, courage, not despair: 'the absurd gives them a royal power. It is true that those princes are without a kingdom. But they have this advantage over others: they know that all kingdoms are illusory ... This absurd, godless world is peopled with men who think clearly and who have ceased to hope'.[39] Hope would undermine their courage to cope with their fate, and lead to a life of resignation rather than active participation and revolt. The positive acceptance of a negative condition—the lack of hope—enables the absurd man to confront and live with his own loneliness and affirm the uniqueness of the only life accorded him: 'The absurd is his extreme tension, which he maintains constantly by solitary effort, for he knows that in that consciousness and that day-to-day revolt he gives proof of his only truth which is defiance.'[40] 'One must imagine', he concludes, 'Sisyphus happy'.[41]

---

[36] *The Myth of Sisyphus, supra*, at 58–9.

[37] *ibid.* at 53.

[38] *Human, All Too Human* (London: Penguin, 1994) [1878], trans. Manon Faber and Stephen Lehmann, at 37–8.

[39] *The Myth of Sisyphus, supra*, at 85.

[40] *ibid.* at 55.

[41] *ibid.*, at 111. For a recent response to the challenge posed by nihilism that does not rely on philosophy, or art, or politics to redeem the world, but confronts it without giving up on the demand 'that things might be otherwise', see Simon Critchley, *Very Little ... Almost Nothing: Death, Philosophy, Literature* (London: Routledge, 1997).

7 OTHER SILENCES

In this courageous and undeluded fashion, Meursault faces his execution, and, via Meursault, universal man, we can infer, can face the inevitability of death. If the image fails to convince entirely, it is partly because the effect of Camus' appeal to Hellenic values is to create another myth, a myth of the Mediterranean man whose values and courage is worthy of emulation by stern northerners as well as by native North Africans. The response from the north is summed up by S. Benyon John: '[Camus] typifies that marriage of intense intellectual abstraction and moral passion which excites across the Channel, whereas, in England, it more frequently exhausts.'[42] To 'exhaust' northern common sense is, of course, no bad thing. But in the process of adducing the world as both tender and indifferent, and of nature as both hard and pacifying, Camus has also left other gaps, slips, and contradictions that allow readers to unsettle, supplement, and re-interpret the closure promised by the condemned man's death. One such gap is the reduction of the subaltern subject into an undifferentiated and silent mass, leading us to wonder whether the experience of the absurd is a universal human predicament, or restricted to the white western male. Is the spirit of revolt in the face of the absurd a solution or a suppression of other desires, conscious or unconscious?

The depiction of the legal system's adroit silencing of Meursault's working class friends registers both their difference and their resistance to law's attempt to discredit their values and their language. In particular, Marie's tears speak eloquently of her frustration at making herself understood by those wielding the power of the law. In effect, although the white working classes of Algiers are oppressed, silenced, or discredited by the text of the law, they are not silenced by Camus' text. Drawing attention to their oppression may indeed be one way of ignoring those silenced not only by legal discourse but by Meursault first and, however unconsciously, by Camus himself. For Edward Said, Camus' Arabs in *The Outsider* are no more than decorative background for Camus' exploration of western metaphysical angst: Camus 'incorporates, intransigently recapitulates, and in many ways depends on a massive French discourse in Algeria, one that belongs to the language of French imperial attitudes . . . [he thus] revives the history of French domination in Algeria with a circumspect precision and a remarkable lack of remorse or compassion'.[43] Viewing the Orient from the position of the outside observer, it is not surprising that the intricacies of its differences are denied, silenced, or subsumed in the race to answer western man's metaphysical quest: as Camus himself commented in *The Rebel*, the problem of revolt 'has no

---

[42] 'Albert Camus: A British View', in Germaine Brée (ed.), *Camus: A Collection of Critical Essays, supra*, at 85.

[43] Edward Said, '*Culture and Imperialism* (London: Vintage, 1993), at 223. See further, Edward Said, 'Representing the Colonized', *Critical Inquiry*, 15, Winter 1989, 205–25.

meaning outside our occidental society . . . [in other societies] Metaphysic is replaced by myth'.[44]

As Edward Said observes, the Arabs in *The Outsider* appear as nameless, depersonalized, objectified creatures, scarcely distinguishable from their physical surroundings: 'I saw some Arabs lounging against the tobacconist's window. They were looking at us in silence but in their own special way, as if we were nothing more than blocks of stones or dead trees' (50). John Ericson comments on the deft linguistic transference here whereby the perceiving colonial subject denies that it is its own gaze that petrifies the objects looked at;[45] in effect Meursault does not 'see' the Arabs, and when he does, they appear to him as silent and menacing as ghosts on whom even gunshots scarcely leave a mark (60).

In *The Wretched of the Earth* Frantz Fanon contrasts European representations of Arabs as dirty, lazy, and immobile with the colonizers' preferred models cast from Greco-Roman sources.[46] Camus' preference for these models, be they Greek or anti-Christian, shows at best a lack of curiosity about the traditions he was surrounded by in Algeria, that is, Judaism and Islam. While his lyrical descriptions of North Africa show an unquestionable love for the physical landscape, Camus seems unable to savour it other than through western, and specifically Greek lenses:[47] in effect, the country offers no more to Camus than what can be assimilated in his own discourse. Furthermore, as Conor Cruise O'Brien argues, the text, by depicting a hero who fails to show remorse for killing an Arab, and 'by suggesting that the court is impartial between Arab and Frenchman, it implicitly denies the colonial reality and sustains the colonial fiction'; Camus appears to imply that the Arab is 'not quite a man', and thus 'softens and distorts' the nature of colonial rule.[48]

At the same time, Camus, conscious of the injustices and inequalities perpetrated by the colonial system, was 'a colonizer who refuses'.[49] Neither Meursault nor any other characters in the book show any animosity towards the Arabs *as* Arabs. Raymond's quarrel with them arises from his quarrel with his mistress and Camus is at pains to portray Meursault's part in the quarrel as entirely motiveless. The first shot is triggered by the sun while the additional four shots, while intentional, are carried out without anger or hatred towards the victim, racial or otherwise. The only consequence Meursault registers is that 'I'd destroyed the balance of the day and the perfect silence of this beach where I'd been happy' (60). As critics have noted, Camus'

---

[44] *The Rebel, supra,* at 26.

[45] John Ericson, 'Albert Camus and North Africa: A Discourse of Exteriority' in Bettina L. Knapp (ed.), *Critical Essays on Albert Camus* (Boston, Mass.: G. K. Hall & Co., 1988), at 77.

[46] Frantz Fanon, *The Wretched of the Earth*, trans. Constance Farrington (London: Penguin, 1967) [1961], at 32–3: 'In fact, the terms the settler uses when he mentions the native are zoological terms. He speaks of the yellow man's reptilian motions, of the stink of the native quarter, of breeding swarms, of foulness, of spawn, of gesticulations.'

[47] For a study of Camus' reliance on Greek sources in all his work, see Paul Archbold, *Camus' Hellenic Sources* (Chapel Hill, NC: University of North Carolina Press, 1972).

[48] Conor Cruise O'Brien, *Camus* (London: Fontana, 1970), at 23.

[49] Albert Memmi, *The Colonizer and the Colonized*, 1957; cited by O'Brien, *supra,* at 13.

insistence on swiftly passing over the story of killing an Arab, is in itself telling of his reluctance to address the racism issue and Meursault's refusal at the trial to plead self-defence may be another concession to the Arab who is silenced not only by Meursault's gun but by Camus' text. Without lingering on the dead victim, the next part of the book finds Meursault in jail where he informs his cellmates that he has killed an Arab. At first 'there was silence. But a few minutes later it began to get dark. They told me how to lay out the mat I had to sleep on' (71). The text here suggests a bond between Meursault and the Arabs, a bond they share in opposition to the world of the law, rationality, and bourgeois morality that insists on causes and explanations. But as Michel Grimaud suggests, 'The point is that Camus protesteth too much; he too strenuously denies any hostility between his hero and the Arabs, thus suggesting that Camus was far from unaware of the racial overtones of his novel'.[50]

Racism, Slavoj Žižek argues, arises from the racist's fear that the racial Other has realized their desire better than oneself;[51] there are hints in Meursault's narration of this envy toward the Arab. As natives, Arabs are able to experience and enjoy the pagan values Meursault has to *learn* to enjoy, without angst and without fuss. They appear to know how to experience the joy of pure presence which can be communicated only with words that touch lightly, or, better still, with silence. Such a state is be perceived by Meursault and by Camus, as more authentic than the world of bourgeois society with its insistence on a hypocritical morality that emphasizes ambition, careers, social advancement, and financial benefits. Meursault's indifference and laconic manner may indeed be an attempt to resemble the world and the silence of the Arabs that he envies.[52] Meursault's own rejection of bourgeois values and his condemnation by a court that insists on the universality of those values suggests that Meursault's alienation resembles that of the Arabs.

This way of perceiving the colonized is of course solipsistic: the colonizer invents or projects onto the colonized the attributes he would desire but cannot have for himself. In Camus's evocation of the ideal mediterranean 'type' from whom austere northern Europeans have much to learn, the Arab is on the one hand Europeanized and the European Algerianized.[53] As Frantz Fanon argued, however, it is for the colonized to represent themselves, write and rewrite the songs and histories bequeathed to them by the colonized. Recreating the past through the imagination, is, as Toni Morrison

---

[50] Michel Grimaud, 'Humanism and the White Man's Burden; Camus, Daru, Meursault and the Arabs' in Adele King (ed.), *Camus's L'Etranger: Fifty Years On* (Macmillan: London, 1992), at 175.

[51] Slavoj Žižek, *The Sublime Object of Ideology* (London and New York: Verso, 1989), at 187: 'This supposed *jouissance* is one of the key components of racism: the other (Jew, Arab, Negro) is always presumed to have access to some specific enjoyment and that is what really bothers us.' See also Jacques-Alain Miller, 'Extimité' in M. Bracher, M. Alcorn Jr, R. Corthell and F. Massardier-Kenney (eds.), *Lacanian Theory of Discourse: Subject, Structure and Society* (New York: New York University Press, 1994), 74–87.

[52] See especially Jan Rigaud, 'The Depiction of Arabs in *L'Etranger*' in Adele King (ed.), *Camus's L'Etranger: Fifty Years On, supra*, at 189 and 191: 'Among the Arabs, Meursault finds real commiseration and justice' and Meursault's 'laconic manner brings out an "arabisme"'.

[53] Germaine Brée argues that this fusion was Camus's ambition, 'Climates of the Mind: Albert Camus 1936–1940' in Bettina L. Knapp (ed.), *Critical Essays on Albert Camus, supra*, at 91.

illustrates, essential for the task of forging new identities and building new nations. For such songs to be written, canonical texts including that of Camus need to be violated, dismantled, and disordered: textual violence, for Fanon, is an indispensable tool on the road to liberation.

8   SILENT DESIRES

Does Meursault consistently exhibit freedom from the demands of convention and other people's expectations? Or is the *conscious* revolt advocated in *The Myth of Sisyphus* a mask for silencing and ignoring other, *unconscious* desires? From the early pages of the book indifferent Meursault feels moved to express a disquiet about other people's opinion of him, expressing a sense of guilt, however vague, about what he says or does. When asking for some time off work to attend his mother's funeral, he is moved to protest to his boss, 'It's not my fault' (9) and has to stop himself making the same comment to Marie later. In his interview with the director of the old people's home, he says 'I felt as if he was reproaching me for something' (10) and when the old people come to join him by his mother's corpse he says 'For a moment I had the ridiculous impression that they were there to judge me' (15). It is no coincidence that the people present at the vigil, including the nurse and caretaker, make up a number of twelve, the same number as the jurors who will sit in judgment of him at his trial later. What does this guilt consist of, and does Meursault exculpate his guilt in the final pages of the book?

I suggested in the last section that this is, in part, the guilt of the colonizer aware of the inequalities and hardship inflicted by his rule.[54] Meursault's mixture of admiration for, envy of, and desire for the Arabs' otherness is also present in his ambiguity towards his ultimate other, woman and in particular his mother. Meursault, like Don Juan in *The Myth of Sisyphus*, is reluctant to express deep feelings for a woman. If there are feelings of love in *The Outsider*, they are adduced as emanating not from the 'heart' or the 'soul', but from the senses, from the skin, from the surface and contours of the body. These are the terms with which Meursault describes his fondness for Marie, and there is no doubt that Marie shares and reciprocates his enjoyment of the senses, as she swims towards and away from him under his admiring gaze. However, although sexual attraction is important for Marie, she expresses a desire to pierce the surface, to find out more about and to get to know Meursault. Whether one can generalize and suggest that for men love begins in erotic attraction while 'women rarely choose men solely on that basis',[55] we can agree that even if love starts with the

---

[54] As Albert Camus the journalist reported on the famine in Kabylia, 'if colonial conquest could ever find an excuse, it is in proportion to the help it gives the conquered populations to keep their own personality. And if we have a task to perform in this land, it is to allow one of the proudest and most human people in the world to remain faithful to itself and its destiny.' Quoted by Germaine Brée, *ibid.* at 96.

[55] bell hooks, 'Fools for Love', The *Guardian*, 14 February 2000.

surface, 'love goes beyond the desired body and seeks the soul in the body and the body in the soul. The whole person.'[56] Meursault, however, resists Marie's desire to know his 'soul', and displays a similar lack of interest in Marie beyond the visual pleasure afforded by her body and the sound of her laughter. 'A love?' Julia Kristeva asks; 'Or rather a feeling brought down to a sensation ... [which] does not dare reflect upon itself ... And into words, brief ones, dense, accurate. They capture an experience that claims to enter into speech without passing through the psyche.'[57]

In *The Outsider* the absurd man's hopeless desire to transcend the human condition must ignore that a relationship with woman may lead to fertility, procreation, and the surpassing of death. Woman's ability to procreate and thus lead to continuity and eternity, suggests that brave as the absurd man is, he lacks one form of courage, the courage 'not to be a man',[58] that is the courage to be a woman. Meursault's universe purports to be homosocial, a world where women's cries and tears are so many irritating noises which he is repelled by and tries to get away from. In running away from women's tears, however, Meursault both causes the death of another person and encounters his own death. In that sense the discourse of the absurd is another male journey that seeks, even in its affirmed denial of the expectation of a destination or a goal, an attempt to repress the feminine both within oneself and outside the self.

In an early Freudian reading of *The Outsider* Alain Costes suggests that Meursault's shooting of the Arab is a result of his unconscious wish to be reunited with the mother.[59] In a Lacanian analysis that pays close attention to the language of the text rather than to Camus' biography, Ben Stoltzfus suggests that *The Outsider* depicts the classic Oedipal triangle: the sun, masculine, is the father, the sea (*la mer*), feminine, is a homonym for the mother (*la mère*) and Meursault is the child in search of the 'spring' or 'la source', for water, the primordial mother element. The sun/father punishes this desire by appropriating Raymond's pistol, another phallic symbol, and the law of the father triumphs when the legal system condemns Meursault to the guillotine, his severed head symbolizing the ultimate castration.[60] As Stoltzfus points out, while Meursault remains calm throughout the court proceedings, he is roused to anger and indignation when the priest calls him his 'son' and refers to himself as his 'father': 'Then, for some reason, something exploded inside me. I started shouting at the top of my voice and I insulted him and told him not to pray for me' (115). It is

---

[56] Octavio Paz, *The Double Flame: Love and Eroticism* (London: Harvest, 1993), trans. Helen Lane, at 33.

[57] Julia Kristeva, *Strangers to Ourselves* (New York: Columbia University Press, 1991), trans. Leon S. Roudiez, at 25.

[58] See especially Anthony Rizzuto, 'Camus and a Society Without Women', *Modern Language Studies*, Vol. 13(1), 1983, 3–14: 'Not to be a man is to refuse everything which is given in life, including biological identity. This refusal in turn leads Camus to deny women any real status in his works'; at 6. See also Louise K. Horowitz, 'Of Women and Arabs: Sexual and Racial Polarization in Camus', *Modern Language Studies*, Vol. 17(3), (1987) 54–61, posing the question whether the discourse of the absurd is both 'misogynist (if not homoerotic) and racial', at 55.

[59] Alain Costes, *Albert Camus et la parole manquante* (Paris: Payot, 1973); discussed by Ben Stoltzfus, 'Camus's *L'étranger*: A Lacanian Reading' *supra*.

[60] Ben Stoltzfus, 'Camus's *L'étranger*: A Lacanian Reading' *supra*. See also Stephen Ohayon, 'Camus' *The Stranger*: The Sun-Metaphor and Patricidal Conflict', *American Imago*, Vol. 40(2), Summer 1983, 189–205.

also no coincidence that the case waiting to be tried after Meursault's is a case of parricide. For the prosecutor the link is all too obvious: 'you will not think it rash of me to suggest that the man who is sitting here in the dock is also guilty of the murder which this court is to judge tomorrow' (98–9). In Part II Meursault, like *Oedipus at Colonus*, accedes to language, tells his story, and like Oedipus, assumes his own alienation and accepts his death: 'I laid myself open for the first time to the benign indifference of the world' (117).

If, however, we take the *Oresteia* rather than Oedipus to be the founding myth of western culture, if the murder of the mother rather than the murder of the father lies at the basis of the symbolic order, then Meursault's crime is not that of parricide but his inability to effectively bury the mother. The dead mother is the only character consistently present in the text, and like the Arabs who gaze at him speechless or talking very quietly, is eloquent in her silence: 'When she was at home mother used to spend all her time watching me in silence' (11). The image of the dead mother keeps returning, like the repressed, throughout the book. If, as Camus says, 'the only paradises are those we have lost'[61] the nostalgia he feels for the fullness every subject once had with the mother takes the form of a longing for the sea: 'I wed the sea . . . Vast sea, forever virgin and forever ploughed, my religion with the night! . . . if I were to die, in the midst of cold mountains, unknown to the world, cast off by my own people, my strength at last exhausted, the sea would at the final moment flood into my cell, come to rouse me above myself and help me die without hatred.'[62] While the sun, the father, is the hostile element blinding Meursault (in another reminder of Oedipus and the parallelism between blindness and castration) and causing the trigger to 'give way', water, whether in the form of the spring or the sea, is a benign, warm, and welcoming presence that relieves the senses from the harshness of the sun and offers sanctuary.

It is Meursault's (and Camus') inability to leave or forget the mother that leads them to be condemned by a law that is intent on asserting its own values of reason over the mother's affinity to the senses.[63] Meursault's reconciliation with his mother at the end is an acknowledgment of what he was at pain to repress during the text: his staunch refusal to accede to the law of the father and the symbolic order signals his complete break from the world of men and the sterility of death. Rather than affirming the symbolic order and becoming erotically attached to the law of the father, Meursault at last consciously returns to the law, the language, and the silence of the mother. Indeed, for Hélène Cixous Camus is one of those rare male writers who are 'able to venture onto the brink where writing, freed from law, unencumbered by moderation, exceeds phallic authority and where the subjectivity inscribing its effects

[61] 'Between Yes and No', in *Selected Essays and Notebooks, supra*, at 38.
[62] 'The Sea Close By' in *Selected Essays and Notebooks, supra*, at 157 and 162.
[63] See especially Vicky Mistacco, 'Mama's Boy: Reading Woman in *L'Etranger*' in Adele King (ed.), *Camus's L'Etranger: Fifty Years On* (London: Macmillan, 1992); Vicki Mistacco also points out that Meursault's child-like language and elementary syntax recall the pre-Oedipal language of the mother while the language of the symbolic order is abstract, authoritarian and hierarchical.

becomes feminine'.[64] If the language of the father, the language of the law, dominates, determines, and alienates us, the pre-Oedipal language of the mother harks back to a lost fullness and oneness, before the separation inflicted by language. At the end of his life Meursault, like Ariadne in my last chapter, has resisted the lure of the legal labyrinth in preference for the unity and oneness with the mother.

9 NARRATIVE ORDER

'[A] life which disappears once and for all, which does not return', writes Milan Kundera, 'is like a shadow, without weight, dead in advance, . . . unbearably light, light as a feather, as dust swirling into the air'. Here on earth 'planet number one, the planet of inexperience . . . [w]e can never know what to want, because, living only one life, we can neither compare it with our previous lives nor perfect it in our lives to come . . . We live everything as it comes, without warning, like an actor going on cold. And what can life be worth if the first rehearsal for life is life itself?'[65]

If this is how Meursault, Camus, and Milan Kundera experience life, then why do Meursault, Camus, and Milan Kundera write? The reader must wonder why someone who claims to be indifferent to the world and its constructed values, bothers to overcome his physical laziness in order to record, and thereby inevitably, to analyse, interpret, and imbue value judgments on the events leading to his death. For all his studied indifference, Meursault and his creator, have by no means abandoned the desire for order, the human craving for unity, clarity, and closure. Death of course offers the only finality, the only promise of 'always'; it also guarantees Meursault's longed-for silence. The impulse to narrate, to close life and one's story for oneself before one is forever silent, does not escape even indifferent Meursault. In the midst of the temptation of nihilism and cynicism, Meursault affirms a law, and this law is not only expressed in but is constituted by art.

Meursault claims to understand why his mother, at the end of her life, was willing to relive it all again; while awaiting his execution, and while allowing himself to entertain hopes that his appeal has been granted, he finds that he himself is willing to relive his life all over again. As in Nietzsche's notion of the eternal return, man's powerlessness and the meaninglessness of his existence are transformed by the notion of an all-powerful man who recreates himself, his past and begets himself. Like Sisyphus undertaking his futile task over and over again, repetition accords value to an existence stripped of illusory hopes.

The description of Meursault's final hours are strikingly similar to that of other

---

[64] Hélène Cixous and Catherine Clément, 'Sorties: Out and Out: Attacks/Ways Out/Forays', in *The Newly Born Woman*, trans. Betsy Wing (London: I. B. Tauris, 1986), at 86.

[65] Milan Kundera, *The Unbearable Lightness of Being*, trans. Michael Henry Heim (London: Faber and Faber, 1984) at 3, 8, 223–4.

prisoners awaiting execution and the experience of an overwhelming feeling of reconciliation with the world. Arthur Koestler, contemplating the possibility of his execution responds: 'So what? Have you got nothing more serious to worry about?—an answer so spontaneous, fresh and amused as if the intruding annoyance had been the loss of a collar stud. Then I was floating on my back in a river of peace . . . Then there was no river and no I. The I had ceased to exist . . . [had] established communication with, and been dissolved in the universal pool'.[66] Though Camus, and Meursault, would deny the notion of a divine origin or faith in God to account for this sense of ecstasy, harmony, and acceptance of one's fate, transcendence is not absent from their writing.

In *The Myth of Sisyphus* the artist is one of the four heroes Camus singles out as finding a way of living with absurdity. Like the actor, Don Juan, and the explorer, the artist abandons the promise of 'always' and the desire for absolute knowledge. In the absence of an all-creating power like God, the artist accepts that human beings must face the task of giving birth to themselves and in the process transcend the limitations imposed by social laws and conventions. By creating and recreating himself, by being the author of one's own story, Meursault becomes the artist and the work of art at the same time: 'He is at once subject and object, poet, actor and audience'.[67] Writing furnishes the promise of unity, harmony, and cohesion denied by the world: as Camus argued, 'What, in fact, is a novel but a universe in which action is endowed with form, where final words are pronounced, where people possess one another completely and where life assumes the aspect of destiny? The world of the novel is only a rectification of the world we live in, in pursuance of men's deepest wishes'.[68] With one important difference: art, like the absurd hero, attains the promised unity, 'the reconciliation of the unique with the universal' without illusions: 'art disputes reality but does not hide from it'.[69]

The revolt against hope is therefore by no means full. Hope arises not from Meursault's awakening to the 'benign indifference of the world', nor from accepting the inevitability of his death and courageously facing up to his execution, but from the belief in the possibility of writing as a means of telling his own story. No writing takes place without the hope of communication, with oneself or with others, without, in other words, the abandonment of despair. As an interior monologue, Meursault's narrative serves the cathartic function of confessing to, understanding, and exculpating his, however unconscious, feelings of guilt. As a narrative addressed to others, Meursault's narrative aims to suggest another version of his story to that suggested, and bloodily enforced, by social institutions like the legal system. In the end, art gives form and closure to the meaninglessness of existence; in the world of words, even the 'outsider' finds a home.

---

[66] Arthur Koestler, *The Invisible Writing, Arrow in the Blue* (London: Hamish Hamilton, 1954), Vol. II, at 351–2.

[67] Nietzsche, *The Birth of Tragedy, supra*, at 42.

[68] *The Rebel, supra*, at 228.

[69] *ibid.*, at 223–4.

This hope and this possibility to write and to symbolize, may moreover, be linked to the mother and her generous promise of reconciliation, continuity, and eternity rather than to the foreclosures and executions dictated by a masculine economy and the law of the father. In the hours before his execution, Meursault's thoughts wander not to the law of the father that priests and lawyers tried in vain to captivate him with, but to the silence, love, and law of the mother. By reconciling himself with the memory of his mother, Meursault and the absurd man regain the lost fullness inflicted by the language and law of the father and link their lives, and their words, not to the abyss of death but to continuity and eternity.

Like the artist in *The Myth of Sisiphus*, Meursault perceives, however unconsciously, that 'to create is to live doubly'.[70] It is also an attempt to imitate the creative role of the mother, to give birth to words and to live and die anew, for as many times, and for as many readers, who read and reread Meursault's narrative.

[70] *The Myth of Sisyphus, supra*, at 87.

7

FANTASIES OF WOMEN AS LAW-MAKERS: EMPOWERMENT OR ENTRAPMENT IN ANGELA CARTER'S BLOODY CHAMBERS[1]

I was looking back to see
If you were looking back at me
To see me looking back at you
Massive Attack, *Safe from Harm*

1 INTERTEXTUALITY

A founding assumption of modernist art and literature is the notion of a work of art as the unique expression of an individual's originality and genius. As theorists such as Mikhail Bakhtin, Julia Kristeva, and Umberto Eco have shown, however, the production of meaning is not monologic but dialogic or intertextual.[2] A work of art is not original or unique but is part of existing discourses and texts; such texts, as Bakhtin argued, are constructed like mosaics from other texts with the resulting text resembling a patchwork of previous texts. The elitist, modernist insistence on artistic aura,

[1] Angela Carter, *The Bloody Chamber* (Harmondsworth: Penguin, 1979); all references in the text are to this edition.

[2] For a discussion of palimpsests and intertextuality see especially Umberto Eco, 'Casablanca: Cult Movies and Intertextual Collage' in *Travels in Hyperreality* (New York: Harcourt Press, 1986); Mikhail Bakhtin, 'From the pre-history of novelistic discourse' in *The Dialogic Imagination: Four Essays*, (ed.) Michael Holquist, trans. Caryl Emerson; Julia Kristeva (Austin, Tex.: University of Texas, 1981) 'Word, Dialogue and Novel' in *Desire in Language: a semiotic approach to literature and art*, ed. Léon S. Roudiez, trans. Alice Jardine, Thomas A. Gora, Léon Roudiez (Oxford: Blackwell, 1980).

autonomy, uniqueness, and separation of art from mass culture are closely allied to our notions of ownership and property. However, the author's ability to assign a single meaning to her work is undermined by the role of the reader in interpreting and using such texts. In particular, the death of the author challenges the view of the writer as god whose authority determines the meaning of the text.[3]

Contemporary writers undermine modernist assumptions of artistic autonomy through the use of parody and appropriation of existing representations, stereotypes, and conventions. Such texts acknowledge their own situationality and constructedness in language at the same time as they aim to subvert and critique the same conventions. By revealing the artificiality of what we perceive as everyday reality they enable us to see the constructed nature of our values, norms, and structures.[4] At the heart of such mimicry/critique is the belief that cultural representations are as unavoidably important as they are political.

Angela Carter was well aware of the political importance of art and impatient with the modernist insistence on the autonomy of art from politics: 'Fine art that exists for itself alone is art in a final stage of impotence' she admonished.[5] Instead, she brought political concerns to her writing and was keen to make use of art's capacity to envisage new worlds by dismantling old laws and structures and creating new laws in the realm of the imaginary.

Perhaps no genre exemplifies the death of the author, intertextuality, and every text's debt to previous writers and texts than the art of fairy tales. The same motifs have been the subject of interested appropriations, imitations, and re-workings for hundreds of years from peasants' hearths to the salons of eighteenth century Paris, to Victorian nursery rooms, to the twentieth century studios of Walt Disney. That fairy tales should be the subject of such political exercises is not a coincidence: like all literature, fairy tales operate in the realm of ideology, sustaining and promoting their own moral and political messages. Although such messages vary with both audience and tellers, the ubiquity and appeal of fairy tales to children and adults alike make them a powerful source of ideological value systems.

One recent such appropriation is by feminist writers concerned at the patriarchal bias of some of these re-tellings. By juxtaposing new stories on old texts feminist writers can reveal the oppressive nature of previous stories as well as uncover new voices, new possibilities and new roles for women within them. The use of prior texts is not, however, a simple matter of appropriation or imitation. All texts and languages, legal or literary, are the carriers of ideas and ideologies and it is the task of the new writer to use and abuse the genre to best suit her new purposes. The problem,

---

[3] See especially Michel Foucault, 'What is an Author?' in *Textual Strategies* ed. Josue V. Haran (Ithaca, NY, 1979): 'The coming into being of the notion of "author" constitutes the privileged moment of individualization in the history of ideas, knowledge, literature, philosophy and the sciences', at 141 and Roland Barthes, 'The Death of the Author' in *Image-Music-Text*, trans. Stephen Heath (London: Fontana Press, 1977).

[4] See especially Patricia Waugh, *Metafiction: The Theory and Practice of Self-Conscious Fiction* (London: Routledge, 1984) and discussion in my opening chapter.

[5] Angela Carter, *The Sadeian Woman* (London: Virago: 1979), at 13.

however, is whether such musings appease by offering imaginary solutions to real problems.

This issue can only be investigated by interrogating the genre of the fairy tales as a whole before addressing Carter's use of the genre in *The Bloody Chamber*. In this chapter I examine the motifs of three well-known tales, 'Bluebeard', 'Little Red Riding Hood' and 'Beauty and the Beast' in sources such as Charles Perrault and Madame de Beaumont[6] before contrasting Carter's interested and interesting appropriation of the same motifs.

2 THE LEGISLATIVE ALLURE OF FAIRY TALES

If stories play a part in structuring our world, fairy tales whose ubiquity, longevity, and dissemination is stronger than that of other stories play a crucial role in our understanding of ourselves, anxieties, and dreams. Such tales have an inescapable normative dimension, providing a strong mythology of moral examples for children and adults to follow. For, as Tolkien protested, 'the association of children and fairy-stories is an accident of our domestic history . . . Children . . . neither like fairy stories more, nor understand them better than adults do'.[7]

For Bruno Bettelheim, such stories provide a safe place for the resolution of fears and dilemmas involved in the passage from childhood to adulthood.[8] More than easing this passage, however, fairy tales help to cultivate appropriate roles and modes of behaviour for entry into the adult world. In fairy tales there is an abundance of stereotypes of good versus evil, strong versus weak, rich versus poor, man versus woman, and boy versus girl. These binary oppositions help inculcate what behaviour is socially acceptable and will lead to reward in contrast to what is unacceptable and will lead to harm or punishment. Above all, the tales affirmed that there is such a thing as a moral order and that in that other world of the tales goodness is invariably rewarded and evil punished.

For groups outside the dominant ideological and power systems fairy tales also represent what is outside mainstream culture and history. Their lack of elitism, eccentricity, and malleability offer a way of inscribing oneself in an alternative history and culture. Oral folktales often expressed the hopes and aspirations of a peasant class where paupers became princes and virtuous girls princesses. Through such myths a disadvantaged class faced with poverty and sickness could express their dreams for a

---

6 These are collected in Jack Zipes (ed.), *Beauties, Beasts and Enchantment: Classic French Fairy Tales* (Harmondsworth: Penguin, 1989).

7 J. R. R. Tolkien, *Tree and Leaf* (London: Allen & Unwin, 1964), at 34.

8 Bruno Bettelheim, *The Uses of Enchantment: The Power and Importance of Fairy Tales* (Harmondsworth: Penguin, 1978).

different, a happier, and more just world.[9] Such reworkings of the myths, developed and adapted with each generation of tellers and listeners, further undermined the bourgeois notion of art as a unique one-off and the modernist distinction between high and low culture and hierarchies between literary genres.

In the nineteenth century, however, the myths of the poor were appropriated and rewritten for the education and entertainment of the bourgeoisie. Although such tales were traditionally told by women, those versions were denigrated by mainstream culture as 'old wives' tales' while the successful dissemination of the versions by Charles Perrault in France and the Grimm brothers in Germany had the effect of concealing rival writings by women. The writings of the *précieuses* in seventeenth century France were indeed undertaken in direct rebellion to the strictures of the established academies with their emphasis on Greek and Latin classics; their favoured form for expressing their views for the equality of women and the perils of arranged marriages was the fairy tale. As in Carter's collection of fairy stories for Virago Press, 'the qualities these stories recommend for the survival and prosperity of women are never those of passive subordination' but show 'the richness and diversity with which femininity, in practice, is represented in "unofficial culture" and the richness and diversity of women's response to their predicament—being alive—its strategies, plots and hard work'.[10] Here, female initiative is rewarded rather than punished. However, such versions were forgotten or suppressed in favour of tales that asserted the need for conformity and the danger of female desire. Hence the importance for women writers to wrest the fairy tale back from Perrault and the Brothers Grimm and exploit their possibilities and power.

Carter allies herself with predecessors like the *précieuses* and aims to render the fairy tale once again an instrument of change with women as masters rather than slaves of history-making and law-making. Myth, she thought, 'is more malleable than history' and therefore provides one way of claiming women's fair share of the future by staking their claim to their share of the past.[11] By inscribing women in history, women writers may explore and advocate new perceptions, new structures, and new roles for women in society's marital, economic, and legal arrangements.

Furthermore, fairy tales are a writing of excess, Carter's own version of Bakhtin's carnivalesque with its irreverence, improprieties, laughter, and resistance to hierarchies and the symbolic; such writing undermines official culture, laws, and conventions by creating an alternative to established values and structures. Dwelling in the realm of fantasy, fairy tales also disrupt classical unities of time and space and subvert the dominant order by intimating the existence of another place, another time, and another law. As we saw in *Wuthering Heights*, the presence of supernatural elements functions 'to exempt the text from the action of the law, and thereby to transgress

---

[9] See the work of Jack Zipes for the view that fairy tales may enable disadvantaged groups to inscribe themselves into history: *Breaking the Magic Spell: Radical Theories of Folk and Fairy Tales* (London, 1979) and *Fairy Tales and the Art of Subversion* (London, 1988).

[10] Angela Carter (ed.), *The Virago Book of Fairy Tales* (London: Virago, 1990), at xiv.

[11] *ibid.*, at xvi.

that law'.[12] Fantasy literature in general can threaten cultural stability with disorder and illegality by exploring what lies outside dominant norms and values.[13] By countenancing fragmented, fluid selves and character metamorphoses, it also departs from our culture's reliance on subjects that are unified, whole, and essential and points out the limits of what we are accustomed to seeing as real and inevitable. As Rosemary Jackson argues, fantasy literature dreams of a return to a state of unity in the imaginary, before the intervention of the father, culture, and law. In the world of fantasy there is a dissolution of cultural differentiations between self and other, human and animal, human and god, male and female, day and night, even life and death. In short, fantasy releases signs from their orthodox uses and thereby disrupts a culture's ways of creating and institutionalizing meaning. The liberation of the sign from signifying practices means that women writers in particular can use fantastic literature as a tool with which to subvert the dominant patriarchal order.

Jackson privileges the writing of fantasy as subversion but is there also a danger that such writing may be escapist, filling the hearer with dreams and illusions that prevent them from taking action to improve their lot? Do such explorations provide imaginary appeasement, compensating, in literature, for the lack experienced by writer and reader in everyday life? The fact that such literature has to use the language of the dominant order increases the danger of complicity masquerading as critique.[14]

3 LEGISLATING SEXUAL DIFFERENCE

In nineteenth century re-tellings of the tales as in the versions created by Perrault, the Brothers Grimm, and in Victorian nurseries the moral or didactic aspect of fairy tales became paramount. Writers recognized the legislative allure of fairy tales and rewrote them to accommodate the developing notion of childhood as a time of innocence and education. Such differences were reinforced with Perrault's insistence on attaching a summary of the alleged moral of each tale while the Grimm brothers added Christian expressions and eliminated sexual references from their version of German tales. In short, fairy tales were domesticated and the sexual dimension of human experience denied or suppressed.[15] However, such censorship, aimed at the 'pedagogisation of

---

[12] Tzvetan Todorov, *The Fantastic: A Structural Approch to a Literary Genre*, trans. Richard Howard (Ithaca, New York: Cornell University Press, 1975), at 159.

[13] Rosemary Jackson, *Fantasy: The Literature of Subversion* (London: Routledge, 1981).

[14] The notion of 'complicitous critique' as a political strategy in postmodern cultures is developed by Linda Hutcheon, *A Poetics of Postmodernism: History, Theory, Fiction* (London: Routledge, 1988) and *The Politics of Postmodernism* (London: Routledge, 1989).

[15] Mary Cadogan and Patricia Craig: 'the tendency to emphasise the joys ('the fun') of childhood was part of a deliberate attempt to counter teenage precocity . . . girls' writers were by implication in the awkward position of having to deny the nature of adolescence': *You're a Brick, Angela!* (London: Gollancz, 1986), at 170.

children's sex', is, as Foucault reminds us, a tactic of no more than local significance, leading not only to repression but also to 'a regulated and polymorphous incitement to discourse'.[16] By rejecting 'the repressive hypothesis' Foucault encourages us to examine the incidence, resourcefulness, and polyvalence of power in fields previously regarded as free from its operation.

Fairy tales are one such area, constituting themselves as a field of knowledge with their own legislative effects and moral messages. Such lessons, including what constitutes good and evil, virtue and vice, reward and punishment were not gender neutral but imbued with the values of a patriarchal culture.[17] Sexual difference was inscribed and emphasized with the assignation of separate roles for boys and girls and the use of stereotypical male heroes who are brave, strong, and resourceful and female heroines who are pure, virtuous, docile and, like Sleeping Beauty, endlessly patient. In stories such as 'Cinderella' and 'Sleeping Beauty' the role model presented to young girls suggested the virtues of patience, selflessness, silence, purity, and docility. Invariably the greatest asset for a girl is beauty for which she is rewarded with a prince, wealth, and marriage. Such girls need not do anything apart from wait, often in a remote tower, to be rescued by a brave prince. Fairy tales also re-enact Greek myths warning of the danger of female speech by suggesting that the less a female character speaks the nicer she is.[18] Domesticity is such characters' reward for their beauty, passivity, and uncomplaining helplessness.

In contrast, girls who attempt to take charge of their lives by showing initiative, wit, or resourcefulness are rare amongst the well-known stories; where they do appear they are denounced as ugly and wicked and their lack of conformity to community expectations is severely punished. Girls are thus led to believe that meekness, suffering, and self-pity will be rewarded and the greatest reward of all is marriage to a rich man. Boys on the other hand are invited to identify with the young prince who rescues the helpless heroine out of her predicament and to admire his courage, perseverence, and thirst for adventure. The same stories provoked competition and suspicion between women (who are all, after all, vying for the attentions of the prince) and between mother and step-daughter (who are both vying for the attention of the father).

It is such conventions that are interrogated in Angela Carter's playful retellings of familiar folktales. Forever conscious of the immense power of myths, old and new, Angela Carter was concerned to identify, expose, and explore them: 'I'm in the demythologising business', she said, that is, investigating how certain ideas, theories, fictions, come to regulate our lives and become invested with a semi-religious coating

---

[16] Michel Foucault, *The History of Sexuality, Volume 1: An Introduction*, trans. Robert Hurley (Paris, 1976; New York, 1978), at 34.

[17] See Andrea Dworkin, *Our Blood: Prophesies and Discourses on Sexual Politics* (London: The Women's Press, 1982) and Jack Zipes, (ed.), *Don't Bet on the Prince: Contemporary Feminist Fairy Tales in North America and England* (London: Gower Publishing, 1986), especially at 185–260.

[18] Marina Warner, *From the Beast to the Blonde: On Fairy Tales and their Tellers* (London: Chatto & Windus, 1994), at 387–408.

that prevents us from interrogating them.[19] And what better weapon do we have against such myths, than, à la Barthes, to mythify them in their turn and produce other *artificial myths*?[20]

4 WOMAN-BORN BUT MAN-MADE

Writing in the 1970s, Carter was swift to play with Foucault's notions of sex and the body as malleable, material, and constructed in history. For Carter, human nature and the human body are not timelessly natural but constructed and inscribed by historical and cultural signs so that we cannot speak of a pre-cultural nature, (male or female), sex or gender: 'flesh comes to us out of history . . . we may believe we fuck stripped of social artifice; in bed, we even feel we touch the bedrock of human nature itself. But we are deceived. Flesh is not an irreducible human universal.'[21] Such signs are not only fictitious and culturally contingent, they are also dangerous as they are invested with the norms and expectations of a patriarchal society and have been used to confine women to restrictive roles or archetypes.[22] Art and literature is as, if not more, responsible in this respect as law in creating models that reproduce stereotypes of women as madonnas or whores or, in fairy tale terms, wicked witches and sleeping beauties.

The notion of the pure virgin and Jung's maternal archetype come in for special denunciation from Carter as 'consolatory nonsenses':

If women allow themselves to be consoled for their culturally determined lack of access to the modes of intellectual debate by the invocation of hypothetical great goddesses they are simply flattering themselves into submission . . . All the mythic versions of women, from the myth of the redeeming purity of the virgin to that of the healing, reconciling mother, are consolatory nonsenses; and consolatory nonsense seems to be a fair definition of myth anyway . . . mother goddesses are as dangerous as father-gods.[23]

The exaltation of woman's role as mother collapses the feminine into the maternal and female sexuality to reproduction. This threatens women's confinement and exile from history and law-making into a hypothetical world of eternal essences while

---

[19] Anna Katsavos, 'An Interview with Angela Carter' 14(3) *Review of Contemporary Fiction* (1994) 11, at 12.

[20] Roland Barthes, 'Myth Today' in *Mythologies* (London: Vintage, 1993) [1957], trans. Annette Lavers, at 135.

[21] *The Sadeian Woman, supra*, at 9.

[22] Carter was insistent on this point: 'The feminine character, and the idea of femininity on which it is modelled, are products of masculine society': Angela Carter, *Shaking a Leg: Collected Journalism and Writing* (London: Vintage, 1997), at 110. Also, 'The notion of universality of human experience is a confidence trick and the notion of a universality of female experience is a clever confidence trick': *The Sadeian Woman, supra*, at 12.

[23] *The Sadeian Woman, supra*, at 5.

father is assumed to be the guarantor of autonomy and action within history and law. As in Irigaray's 'And the one doesn't stir without the other',[24] the mother must resist the threat of losing her identity in an identification with the daughter while the daughter must achieve autonomy, if necessary, in Carter's view, by destroying the mother.[25]

The confinement of women to stereotypes is illustrated by the Marquis de Sade's twin heroines, the egocentric and aggressive Juliette versus her passive and submissive sister Justine. In psychoanalytic terms the two women conform to Freud's model of female sexuality as either masculine (with the clitoris as substitute penis) or feminine (with the emphasis on vaginal passivity). The striking point of this contrast is not that Juliette is bad and Justine is good but that Juliette is bad and Justine is good '*according to the rules for women laid down by men*'.[26]

Carter bravely analyses the two heroines in order to show the pitfalls and limitations of both models. Juliette, guided by Enlightenment reason, attains the 'lonely freedom of the libertine' who has learned that 'to escape slavery, she must embrace tyranny'. She knows that 'in a world governed by God, the King, and the law, that trifold masculine symbolism of authority, it is useless to rebel'[27] and therefore imitates male rules and causes rather than suffers pain. Her self-definition assumes the Cartesian dualism between self and other and espouses an economic theory of sexual pleasure. According to this model 'pleasure consists in the submission of the partner; but that is not enough. The annihilation of the partner is the only sufficient proof of the triumph of the ego.'[28] Juliette's and Eugenie's denial and abuse of the role of the mother aid the project of the demystification of motherhood. But such fear of the mother and adoption of possessive individualism and masculinist reason is not, in the end, seen as a challenge to patriarchal norms. Rather than changing the master's rules, Juliette understands them and uses them to her own advantage; this strategy, however, leaves both the rules and the hierarchies they inscribe intact:

The Sadeian woman . . . subverts only by her own socially conditioned role in the world of god, the king and the law. She does not subvert her society, except incidentally, as a storm trooper of the individual consciousness. She remains in the area of privilege created by her class, just as Sade remains in the philosophic framework of his time'.[29]

If Carter is unhappy with Juliette's 'rationality without humanism', she is even more impatient with Justine's self-pity, 'unreason of the heart', and 'false logic of feeling'. Justine is the passive victim, the innocent, suffering martyr who, while hoping to be rescued, does nothing to resist oppression; rather than helping herself, she is a party to her own victimization. Such a figure is defined negatively, as the mirror image

---

[24] (1981) 7 *Signs* 1.
[25] *The Sadeian Woman, supra*, at 124.
[26] *ibid.*, at 38.
[27] *ibid.*, at 80.
[28] *ibid.*, at 143.
[29] *ibid.*, at 133.

of a male economy that itself created the myth of female passivity and submissiveness. 'That is why', Carter comments, 'there have been so few notoriously wicked women in comparison to the number of notoriously wicked men. Our victim's status ensures that we rarely have the opportunity. Virtue is thrust upon us.'[30] Such virtue is celebrated and sustained by a patriarchal culture for its own interests:

> To be the object of desire is to be defined in the passive case.
> To exist in the passive case is to die in the passive case—that is, to be killed.
> This is the moral of the fairy tale about the perfect woman.'[31]

Since both the categories and characteristics of Juliette and Justine, masculine and feminine, are not changeless essences, the task of the storyteller is to combat traditional myths about the nature of women and to construct alternative roles.[32] Fairy tales are one site where patriarchal fictions were created and sustained and it is there that Carter begins to inscribe her differences.

5 CARTER REMAKES

(A) BLUEBEARD

In Perrault's retelling of this remake of the tale of Psyche and Cupid, death is impliedly an apt punishment for Bluebeard's wife's curiosity and disobedience of her husband's command. As in the tales of Pandora, Eve, and Lot's wife, curiosity in women is seen as threatening in a masculine culture that praises the search for knowledge in men but urges women not to look but only to be looked at.

In Carter's version the protagonist, poor and innocent like Sade's Justine, is flattered and seduced by the Marquis' attention, sexual knowledge, and wealth. For him she is, as she realizes, a beautiful object, a commodity, a prize, whose poverty and innocence entitles him to legislate and control her. Catching him looking at her in a mirror during their engagement, she sees herself as he sees her, 'with the assessing eye of a connoisseur inspecting horseflesh, or even of a housewife in the market, inspecting cuts on the slab'. He is the 'purchaser' and she is 'his bargain' which he unwraps slowly and deliberately in his own time. However, while this heroine is the object of the male gaze, unlike Justine she retains a sense of her own identity that is separate from her husband's attempt to reduce her to an object of his desire. Her seduction and objectification by his gaze and wealth horrifies and appals her: 'for the first time in my innocent and confined life, I sensed in myself a potentiality for corruption that took my breath away' (11).

---

[30] *ibid.*, at 56.
[31] *ibid.*, at 76–7.
[32] Angela Carter, 'Notes from the Front Line', in Michelene Wandor, (ed.), *On Gender and Writing* (London: Pandora Press, 1983), at 77.

When the heroine disobeys the Marquis' law by looking into the bloody chamber she attains knowledge, not only of his murdered previous wives but of her own sexuality and independent desire. For this reason she must be punished that is, pay the price for opening and finding the secret to Pandora's box. Unlike Justine, however, this heroine is no longer innocent and does not surrender to the role of the victim. The instrument for her rescue is not a chivalrous prince, as in previous versions, or her brothers, as in the Grimms' version, but her mother who, through a form of maternal telepathy, realizes her daughter's danger and gallops, gun in hand, to her rescue. This wild mother stuns the monstrous Marquis motionless before 'administering a furious justice by aiming a single irreproachable bullet into his head':

The puppet-master, open-mouthed, wide-eyed, impotent at the last, saw his dolls break free of their strings, abandon the rituals he had ordained for them since time began and start to live for themselves; the king, aghast, witnesses the revolt of his pawns. (39)

Although unusual in Carter's work, the appearance of the mother is a significant departure from fairy tale motifs where the mother is either dead, powerless or, if powerful, a wicked stepmother bent on destroying her daughter. The heroine's admiration of, and positive relation with, her mother is a rare representation of the mother/daughter relationship. Such a relationship, Irigaray's *'dark continent of the dark continent'* is 'an extremely explosive kernel in our societies: To think it, to change it, amounts to undermining the patriarchal order'.[33]

Significantly it is the gaze of the mother who, like Medusa, objectifies and annihilates the monstrous patriarch. It is the mother rather than the father who acts to guarantee the law and return the daughter to the symbolic order while the father/lover breaks the law and dismembers its subjects. The symbolic order the protagonist enters is not, however, one ruled by hierarchical or patriarchal expectations. Following the mother's extraordinary feat the protagonist, her mother and her new lover, the blind piano tuner, set up a modest home away from the seductions of the castle. Her relationship with the blind piano tuner is one of accommodation and understanding of each other's needs rather than of antagonism and devourment of one by the other. His blindness ensures that she does not, once again, become the object of the male gaze. Furthermore, the daughter-mother relation that enables entry into the symbolic and into history is not an essentialized relation of mythical great goddesses but, one that by retaining a sense of humour and self-parody, understands its own identity as performance.

(B) BEAUTY AND THE BEAST

In Freud's view, the daughter's attraction to the father is one of the obstacles to be overcome in the child's successful passage into adulthood. 'Beauty and the Beast' tales

---

[33] *Le Corps-a-Corps avec la mère,* quoted in Margaret Whitford, *Luce Irigaray: Philosophy in the Feminine* (London: Routledge, 1991), at 77.

enact this incestuous attraction by dramatizing the daughter's love for her father and reluctance to leave him for any one of her many suitors. Her decision to go to the Beast is another act of self-sacrifice as she resolves to die in her father's place. For Bruno Bettelheim the tale depicts the daughter's successful negotiation of the Oedipal complex when she learns to relinquish her attraction for her father in return for a relationship with a stranger member of the opposite sex.[34]

However, in such versions Beauty's progress from father to Beast is not a journey of self-exploration and understanding but the trading of one patriarch for another. The Beast's transformation into a handsome prince is her reward for obedience and servility to their values and expectations. In Victorian re-tellings of the tale the focus is, as Carter put it, 'on housetraining the *id*', that is, instructing young women on how best to conform and survive arranged marriages by suggesting the illusion that inside the beast there is a handsome prince. For Irigaray, rather than the daughter desiring the father, the father desires the daughter and legislates to protect himself from the consequences of his desire. The focus on the possessiveness of the father rather than the daughter's weakness for the father is also the angle taken by Carter.

In 'The Courtship of Mr Lyon' Beauty is her father's 'pet' who is made an item of bartering in the deals between two men. Beauty herself has not attained an understanding of herself as separate person, feeling herself, in the presence of the Beast as 'Miss Lamb, spotless, sacrificial'. She has dinner with the Beast

because her father wanted her to do so . . . For she knew with a pang of dread, as soon as he spoke, that it would be so and her visit to the Beast must be, on some magically reciprocal scale, the price of her father's good fortune.

Do not think she had no will of her own; only, she was possessed by a sense of obligation to an unusual degree and besides, she would gladly have gone to the ends of the earth for her father, whom she loved dearly (45–6).

The Beast is no better than her father at exploiting Beauty's weak (alias 'good') nature; by exalting Beauty's 'goodness' they confine her in a stereotype of sentimental femininity, deprive her of choices and ensure that such goodness is directed towards serving them rather than herself. Like her father, the Beast is ruthless at extracting Beauty's pity and ultimately love:

'I'm dying Beauty,' he said in a cracked whisper of his former purr. 'Since you left me, I have been sick. I could not go hunting, I found I had not the stomach to kill the gentle beasts, I could not eat. I am sick and I must die; but I shall die happy because you have come to say goodbye to me' (50).

Beauty complies and offers him not only her pity but also her love and her whole self: ' "Don't die, Beast! If you'll have me, I'll never leave you".' (51)

Carter is impatient with Beauty's tolerance of her subordinate status in the deals between the two men and spurs her to grow up as a separate person. The tale, she says, is 'an advertisement for moral blackmail: when the Beast says that he is dying because

---

[34] Bruno Bettelheim, *The Uses of Enchantment, supra*, at 303–9.

of Beauty, the only morally correct thing for her to have said at that point would be, "Die, then".[35] Although this Beauty lacks the initiative to respond in such a way, another Beauty in the next story is wiser in the ways of men and more adept at asserting her independence from both her father and her suitor.

In 'The Tiger's Bride' Beauty, like her mother before her, is again the object of exchange in the relationship between two men. Her father loses everything, including Beauty, in a game of cards with the Beast: 'You must not think my father valued me at less than a king's ransom; but at *no more* than a king's ransom' (54). This Beauty, however, is aware of her position as object of exchange and instead confronts and renegotiates the terms of the contract:

I was a young girl, a virgin, and therefore men denied me rationality just as they denied it to all those who were not exactly like themselves, in all their unreason . . . . I meditated on the nature of my own state, how I had been bought and sold, passed from hand to hand. That clockwork girl who powdered my cheeks for me; had I not been allotted only the same kind of imitative life amongst men that the doll-maker had given her? (63).

Like Sade's Juliette and unlike Justine she is determined not to remain a victim but to exploit her situation to her own advantage: 'For now my own skin was my sole capital in the world and today I'd make my first investment' (56).

Beauty divests of her role as the 'cold, white meat of contract' when she confronts and alarms the Beast with her own desire and demand to be his sexual equal. Not only does she refuse to undress for the Beast but she contests and returns his gaze, with the Beast becoming the object of her look and her desire. And rather than Beauty being frightened of the Beast without his mask, she has to reassure the Beast that she will not harm him: 'The tiger will never lie down with the lamb; he acknowledges no pact that is not reciprocal. The lamb must learn to run with the tigers' (64).

In running with rather than away from the tiger, Beauty offers the Beast the possibility of a different relationship between self and other, 'the key to a peaceable kingdom in which his appetite need not be my extinction'. (67). The Beast's otherness is not construed as frightening or engulfing but as positive and creative. It is not the Beast who is transformed into a handsome prince when she kisses him but she is transformed into a tiger when he licks off her skin. Stripped of her skin and he of his man's mask, they are free to reinvent themselves outside cultural stereotyping and enjoy a relationship that is reciprocal rather than exploitative. Beauty's transformation from girl to woman and from object of exchange to a subject making her own contracts and laying down her own laws is complete when she dispatches her clockwork twin, a wind-up doll, to her father: 'I will dress her in my own clothes, wind her up, send her back to perform the part of my father's daughter' (65). Rather than desiring the father the daughter constructs her own identity independent of his laws and his desires. The Beast is also seen as constructed in a male economy that dictates that men should be predatory and women victims. Confronted with her active rather

---

[35] John Haffenden, *Novelists in Interview* (London: Methuen, 1985), at 83.

than passive sexuality the Beast reveals his own wish and ability to be tender, released from having to play the role of the aggressor. The happy dénouement is not the result of Beauty's patient inactivity but her discovery of her own animality and independent desire, free of fear and inhibition.

(C) THE COMPANY OF WOLVES

The oral tale that preceded Perrault's retelling of the story of Little Red Riding Hood is no longer well known. In that version, faced with the threat of engulfment, a shrewd and brave Red Riding Hood devises a plan that outwits the wolf and succeeds in saving her own life. In the better known version by Charles Perrault, Little Red Riding Hood is of course consumed by the wolf, a fit punishment, Perrault implies for disobeying her mother, straying off the main path, and talking to strangers. The Grimms were only slightly more charitable to Little Red Riding Hood by providing a strong man who appears just in time to save her from the trouble she gets herself into. In both cases the young girl is discouraged from being independent and exploring, let alone realizing, her capacities including her awakening sexuality. If she does, it is implied, there will be pain and tears instead of the safety and protection provided by the father-patriarch. At the same time, while the blame is placed on Little Red Riding Hood's rebellion and thoughtlessness, the wolf is excused from blame for his voracious appetite; as Susan Brownmiller argues, in such tales the heroine is made to bear the responsibility for rape by implicitly 'asking for it' while the male figure is represented as power, whether as offender (giving in to female temptation) or protector (of helpless females).[36]

Unlike the Grimm's version, in Carter's retelling, the sexual connotations are explicit:

Her breasts have just begun to swell; her hair is like lint, so fair it hardly makes a shadow on her pale forehead; her cheeks are an emblematic scarlet and white and she has just started her woman's bleeding, the clock inside her that will strike, henceforward, once a month. . . . She does not know how to shiver. She has her knife and she is afraid of nothing (113–14).

This Little Red Riding Hood is 'strong-minded', 'wise', and sexually defiant; far from seeing herself as a victim, she is not frightened by the wolf's predatory sexuality and does not flinch when he threatens to eat her: 'The girl burst out laughing; she knew she was nobody's meat. She laughed at him full in the face, she ripped off his shirt for him and flung it into the fire, in the fiery wake of her own discarded clothing' (118).

This Red Riding Hood is good not because she is patient and innocent but because she is resourceful and brave; as such she is the active agent in her own sexual development. In turn the wolf is not terrifying as a masculine economy would dictate; like other beasts in Carter's tales he suffers from 'atrocious loneliness' 'and would love to

---

[36] See Susan Brownmiller, *Against Our Will: Men, Women and Rape* (New York, 1975). Also Jack Zipes, *The Trials and Tribulations of Little Red Riding Hood: Versions of the Tale in Sociocultural Context* (London, 1983).

be less beastly if only [he] knew how' (112). Faced with the heroine's active sexuality he reveals his own ability to be tender and a companion rather than an antagonist: 'See! Sweet and sound she sleeps in granny's bed, between the paws of the tender wolf.' (118).

6 APPROPRIATING THE PORNOGRAPHIC IMAGINATION

For commentators like Patricia Duncker what we are witnessing in this retelling is the ritual disrobing of Little Red Riding Hood as the willing victim of pornography.[37] As 'the high priestess of postgraduate porn'[38] Carter, like Red Riding Hood, would have laughed at this interpretation. For the notion of pornography, like the notion of sexuality, is not intrinsic or immutable, but, like beauty, lies in the eye of the beholder. Further, pornography relies on its definition and existence on a supposed 'natural' or 'normal' sexuality which it supposedly exceeds.[39] Since sexuality is itself culturally constructed, the boundaries between what is normal and what is pornographic shift from one generation and from one culture to the next. No wonder it is so difficult to legislate on pornography or separate it from eroticism which is, again, in Carter's words, no more than the pornography of the elite.[40]

Far from seeing pornography as unambiguous violence against women, Carter instead appropriates the genre and reuses its signs with a view to empowering her female heroines. She puts forward the notion of the 'moral pornographer who might use pornography as a critique of current relations between the sexes'[41] and reveal that sexuality is not timeless or fixed but constructed by social, economic, and historical circumstances. More controversially, she enlists the help of Sade in demystifying the concepts of femininity and motherhood, for separating female sexuality from repro-duction and thus contributing to the emancipation of women. Although Sade is seen at the end as in complicity with the forces of law and state, Carter sees him as putting pornography in the service of women or perhaps allowing it to be invaded by women.[42]

---

[37] 'Re-Imagining the Fairy Tales: Angela Carter's *The Bloody Chamber*' 10(1) *Literature and History* (1984), 3. See also Robert Clark, 'Angela Carter's Desire Machines' (1987), 14, *Women's Studies*, 147–61 for the view that the ideological power of fairy tales cannot be overcome.

[38] *New Statesman*, 1987; quoted in Merja Makinnen, 'Angela Carter's *The Bloody Chamber* and the Decolonization of Feminine Sexuality' (1992), 42, *Feminist Review*, 2, at 3.

[39] See Susan Sontag's reading of pornography as a writing of excess; rather than a monolithic conception of pornography, Sontag stresses its varying styles: 'The Pornographic Imagination' in Susan Sontag, *Styles of Radical Will* (New York: Farrar, Strauss & Giroux, 1969).

[40] *The Sadeian Woman, supra*, at 17.

[41] *Ibid.*, at 7.

[42] *Ibid.*, at 37.

Western art and literature affirm the myths of patriarchy by assigning and implicitly prescribing certain roles for men are others for women. Traditionally, in such pornographic/erotic representations '*Men act* and *women appear*. Men look at women. Women watch themselves being looked at. This determines not only most relations between men and women but also the relation of women to themselves'.[43] Laura Mulvey's landmark essay 'Visual Pleasure and Narrative Cinema'[44] showed how Hollywood cinema renders women the objects of male desire and the male voyeuristic gaze, thus inscribing gender difference. Fairy tales are no exception, instructing young girls how to make themselves desirable to men while the narrative, textual, or cinematic, sees desire from the point of view of the male.[45] The range of roles afforded female heroines in Perrault's retellings is predictably limited and limiting, consistently advising young girls to be beautiful rather than clever, passive rather than active. Here, women heroines do not look but are looked at, serving to confirm, express, and reflect male desire and male identity. Conversely women who arrogate to themselves the power of the look are punished for their rebellion and impertinence.

Carter's reply to this scenario is to create heroines who do not subscribe to gender stereotypes and who look and choose, rather than passively allow themselves, to be looked at. This look, as immortalized by one of Carter's screen heroines, Lulu, 'is not so much a "come hither" look as a look that says, to each and every gender, "I'll come to you". (If, that is, she likes the look of you, a big if, in fact).' Like Lulu, Beauty in 'The Tiger's Bride' defies the Beast's right to look at her and instead looks at him back, 'with interest . . . [she] is not presenting herself as an object of contemplation so much as throwing down a gauntlet . . . Essentially, her attitude is one of: "Now show me what *you* can do".'[46]

In a manner that forecast Judith Butler's work on gender as performance, Carter shows that femininity and sexual difference are spectacles created by and conforming to male definitions of women; when women refuse the role of passive victim, the spectacle is revealed for what it is, thus opening the possibility for change and reinvention. Carter creates heroines that delight in the liberating potential of the construction of self in history and who recreate themselves outside the law of the father and the confines of the Oedipal complex. Such women stop performing the roles assigned to them by traditional fairy tales, showing that gender roles are 'a kind of persistent impersonation that passes as the real'.[47] Aware of the performative nature of gender, they create and recreate versions of themselves for their own advantage. By being in charge of what the male sees, they elude male scripting and avoid objectification.[48]

---

[43]　John Berger, *Ways of Seeing* (Harmondsworth: Penguin, 1972), at 47.

[44]　(1975) 16(3) *Screen* 6.

[45]　As for example in Jean Cocteau's film 'Beauty and the Beast'.

[46]　*Shaking a Leg, supra*, at 377.

[47]　Judith Butler, *Gender Trouble* (London: Routledge, 1990), at viii.

[48]　Patricia Palmer, 'From coded mannequin to bird woman: Angela Carter's Magic Flight' in S. Roe, (ed.), *Women Reading Women's Writing* (Brighton: Harvester Press, 1987) and 'Gender as Performance in the Fictions of Angela Carter and Margaret Atwood' in J. Bristow and T. L. Broughton, (eds.), *The Infernal Desires of Angela Carter: Fiction, Femininity, Feminism* (London: Longman, 1997).

The men benefit from a similar freedom to remake themselves outside masculinist stereotypes thus showing that the roles ascribed by any culture to beasts, men, and women are not fixed and immutable but open to negotiation.

Such heroines, moreover, undergo changes through the course of the narrative: human nature is not fixed in either men or women so that both men and women may appear, in turn predatory, violent, and aggressive as well as passive, inert, and victims. As Rosaleen's mother says in Neil Jordan's film version: 'If there's a beast in men it meets its match in women too.' In the story 'Lady in the House of Love' it is the lady vampire who is the aggressor while the man is an innocent, virgin victim. While in Sade Juliette and Justine represent unchangeable and continuous essences, in Carter's stories gender roles are relative so that a man may be a lamb and a woman a tiger or may change through the course of the narrative from lamb to tiger and vice versa.

The result is that Carter appropriates the pornographic imagination from an instrument where unequal gender relations are inscribed to a tool through which women can express their difference. Furthermore, her picture of female sexuality is more complex than the dichotomies allowed by Sade as well as her feminist critics, acknowledging that women, like men can be violent, actively desiring, unruly, danger-ous, and polymorphously perverse. Desire for 'this sex which is not one' is not, as Irigaray famously explored, singular or unified, active or passive, but all at once, fluid, ambiguous, and excessive[49]. The subject, male or female, is multiple rather than uni-tary and open to self-reinventions through play and display. Forever changing, it eludes the control of patriarchal scripting (pornographic or otherwise) and of male economies. By exposing gender roles and categories as the *effects* of laws and power rather than their cause or origin, Carter enables us to rethink them for a new, feminist imaginary and a feminist symbolic order.

7 ETHICS OF ALTERITY

The symbolic order on which previous versions of Beauty and the Beast rest is unashamedly homosocial: Beauty is the object of exchange between two men, the guarantor of their promises and contracts, that is of capitalism itself. Madame de Beaumont's version illustrates Lévi-Strauss's view that the exchange of goods in the contract called marriage takes place between two groups of men with the woman being the circulating object of that exchange.[50] However, as Carole Pateman showed, the notion of the contract in general and the fiction of the social contract created by liberal theory in particular are in fact patriarchal constructs. The citizen in such

---

[49] Luce Irigaray, *This Sex Which is Not One*, trans. Catherine Porter (Ithaca, New York: Cornell University Press 1985) [1977] especially 23–33.

[50] Claude Lévi-Strauss, *The Elementary Structures of Kinship*, trans. James Harle Bell, John Richard von Sturmer and Rodney Needham (Boston: Beacon Press, 1969) especially at 480–1.

exchanges is always male and women can only enter if they become men. In such contracts women's relationships with each other are not acknowledged with the result that, in a male economy, women are forced to play the role of rivals.[51]

Carter's revisions and reversions of the tales shows us what would happen if, as Irigaray suggests, commodities like Beauty, 'refused to go to market? What if they maintained another kind of commerce, among themselves?',[52] laying down their own rules and their own prices? Such a step need not mean refusing to take part in exchanges at all, as some of Carter's critics would prefer, but only taking part as an autonomous subject rather than an object of the exchange. It does not consist in negotiating the Oedipal complex and her alleged desire for the father as previous versions of Beauty and the Beast suggested, but in realizing her own desire which is equal to but also independent of that of the Beast. For such new exchanges to take place, however, woman, as Irigaray argues, must attain her own identity distinct from her status as mother and as man's complement. It involves acknowledging women's differences and relationships with each other, her own genealogies, her own laws, myths, and histories.

Creating a social organization that is based on contiguity and fertility rather than death and sacrifice, as Irigaray argues, involves devising structures and norms that transcend binary oppositions of man and woman as predator or victim, active or passive, submissive, or aggressive, conqueror and conquered, rational or feeling. Instead they need to acknowledge the possibility of being one or the other or both at once or changing from one to the other.[53] Such norms resist the dualism between the sexes and rest on reciprocity rather than coercion, mutual communication, and recognition rather than antagonism: 'the object of a reciprocal desire which is, in itself both passive object and active subject. Such a partner acts on us as we act on it.'[54]

In relationships where one is consumed by the other, as in Sade's monsters and in previous retellings of these tales, the result is, in Freud's terms, cultural cannibalism. In the same way that a hungry person tries to satisfy his/her hunger by the possession of an object, the lover hopes to satiate his/her desire by the possession of the love object.[55] Such cannibalism is reinforced by representations in legal and literary fictions that construe woman as man's other rather than acknowledging her identity and difference.

In Irigaray's economy, however, women not only refuse to be man's inferior other, 'dark as the negative of a photograph'[56] or 'dressed meat'[57], but enter society and

---

[51] Carole Pateman, The Sexual Contract (Cambridge: Cambridge University Press, 1988).

[52] This Sex Which is Not One, supra, at 196.

[53] The Sadeian Woman, supra, at 79.

[54] ibid., at 146.

[55] Emmanuel Levinas, Existence and Existents (Dordrect: Kluwer Academic Publishers, 1988); for an excellent analysis of this point see Susan Sandford, 'Writing as a Man; Levinas and the Phenomenology of Eros' 87 Radical Philosophy 6(1998).

[56] Angela Carter, Heroes and Villains (Harmondsworth: Penguin, 1981), at 137.

[57] Angela Carter, The Passion of New Eve (London: Virago, 1992), at 31.

exchanges in their own space and their own time. Irigaray describes this relationship as an 'amorous exchange', 'acceding to another energy, neither that of the one nor that of the other, but an energy produced together and as a result of the irreducible difference of sex'.[58] In this ethics of alterity the relationship between the sexes is not defined by competition and overcoming but by each subject respecting the other's irreducible difference. It is a relationship where, as The Tiger's Bride learns, 'his appetite need not be my extinction'.

A certain degree of cannibalism, of absorbing the other within the self, does of course take place; our own existence and self-definition depend on the existence of the other. As the emotions of anger, jealousy, desire, and above all love, constantly remind us, the boundaries between self and other are fluid. For Derrida infringement of the other is inevitable: 'One eats him regardless and lets oneself be eaten by him . . . The moral question is thus not, nor has it ever been: should one eat or not eat . . . but since *one must* eat in any case . . . how for goodness sake should one eat well?'[59]

Irigaray's 'j'aime à toi', rather than 'je t'aime', attempts to negotiate this problem by reaching out towards the other as subject rather than assimilating him/her as object. It accepts and benefits from our interconnectedness but tries not to subordinate the other to the self. Possession of the other, it is suggested, is impossible as the other always eludes and exceeds our attempts at incorporation. Successful relationships, therefore, are founded on equality and recognition of the difference of the other, where one does not assimilate the other but allows her/him to grow.[60] This is a relationship of love where each lover confronts the other with admiration and while crossing the boundary between self and other the encounter does not lead to loss of identity but to creativity:

[We] need to reach another dimension, another level of consciousness, a level not of mastery but one that attempts to find spiritual harmony between passivity and activity . . . It would entail . . . becoming capable of giving and receiving, of being active and passive, of having an intention that stays attuned to interactions, that is, of seeking a new economy of existence or being which is neither that of mastery nor that of slavery but rather of exchange without preconstituted object . . . What we would be dealing with, then, is the establishment of another era of civilization, or of culture, in which the exchange of objects, and most particularly of women, would no longer form the basis for the constitution of a cultural order.[61]

Part fantasy, part utopia, such imaginings or imaginaries are nevertheless

---

[58] Luce Irigaray, 'Questions to Emmanuel Levinas', in R. Bernasconi and S. Critchley, (eds.), *Rereading Levinas* (Bloomington Ind.: Indiana University Press, 1991), at 113.

[59] Jacques Derrida, *Points . . . Interviews, 1974–94* (Paris: 1992; Stanford: Stanford University Press, 1995), at 282. On this point I am indebted to Patricia Deutscher's 'Irigaray anxiety: Luce Irigaray and her ethics for improper selves', 80, *Radical Philosophy*, 6 (1996).

[60] See also Kaja Silverman, *Male Subjectivity at the Margins* (New York: Routledge, 1992) where a similar distinction is made between *idiopathic* identification which cannibalizes the other and *heteropathic* identification which respects the other *as other*.

[61] Luce Irigaray, *i Love to You; Sketch of a Possible Felicity in History*, trans. Alison Martin (London: Routledge, 1996), at 45.

indispensable for beginning to envisage an alternative form of social organization, that is a new symbolic order.

8 AUTHORESSES: COLLUSION OR APPEASEMENT?

What is the importance of an aesthetic revolution to political problems and aims? A revolution, moreover, which utilizes the language and genres of the existing system? Can such a strategy avoid the values implicit in that language and those genres? Can mimicry of male language and male discourses avoid being absorbed by male values and male norms? Furthermore, is fantasy an adequate political tool or does it lead writer and reader to forget material circumstances whilst indulging in a fairyland where all difference and struggle are dissolved and they all lived happily ever after? Is Carter, in other words, creating new consolatory myths of her own?

By choosing to use the genre of the fairy tale Carter is aware that she is treading dangerous ground: 'It is after all very rarely possible for new ideas to find adequate expression in old forms.'[62] Her hope, instead, is that by 'putting new wine in old bottles, the pressure of the new wine may make the old bottles explode'.[63] Fantasy as a subversive instrument of change is also not a panacea for women's politics: while using the power of fantasy to tell new stories, Carter 'kept her feet firmly on the ground'[64] confronting material conditions and contemporary issues on sexuality and social justice; abortion law, access to further education, equal rights, the position of black women. 'I'm a socialist damn it; how can you expect me to be interested in fairies?'[65] At the same time, fantasy enables us to find a space for the articulation of alternative or suppressed stories, interrogating, distorting and also changing existing stories and beliefs. In this sense fantasy and literature in general are not marginal to mainstream culture but contribute towards what Kristeva termed the semiotic's revolt against the symbolic.[66]

Of course such articulations can only take place from within existing language and existing discourses. Aware of this limitation, Carter adopts a strategy that consists of challenging patriarchy with its own techniques, knowledges, and discourses. This strategy, familiar from Irigaray,[67] consists of borrowing from male discourses, deliberately parodying and exaggerating them, in order to say something new. Like the hysteric, Irigaray argues,

---

[62] Angela Carter, 'The Language of Sisterhood' in L. Michaels and C. Ricks, (eds.), *The State of the Language* (Berkeley and Los Angeles: University of California Press, 1980), at 228.

[63] Angela Carter, 'Notes from the Front Line', *supra*, at 69.

[64] Marina Warner, *The Independent*, 17 February 1992, at 25.

[65] M. Harron, *The Guardian*, 25 September 1984, at 10.

[66] Julia Kristeva, *Revolution in Poetic Language* (New York: Cornell University Press, 1984) [1974], trans. Margaret Waller.

[67] 'the option left to me was to *have a fling with the philosophers*': *This Sex Which is not One, supra*, at 150.

one must assume the feminine role deliberately. Which means already to convert a form of subordination into an affirmation, and thus begin to thwart it . . . To play with mimesis is . . . to try to recover the place of her exploitation by discourse, without allowing herself to be simply reduced to it. It means to resubmit herself to . . . ideas about herself, that are elaborated in/by a masculine logic, but so as to make 'visible', by an effect of playful repetition, what was supposed to remain invisible: the cover-up of a possible operation of the feminine in language.[68]

Irigaray's engagement with male philosophers is a prime example of intertextuality, flirting with male philosophers, writers, and pornographers, seducing them and imitating them whilst saying the opposite or something different to what they said.

The problem is, how does one distinguish the person who mimes phallocentric discourse strategically from one who speaks and believes in it? How can one tell the dancer from the dance, the seducer from the seduced?[69] The answer, partly, is that such mimesis is not blind parrotry but ironic parody, moving from imitation of the dominant discourse to creation and celebration of one's own language and discourses. For such language and such a system is not monolithic or homogeneous but a process. Although Carter's critics worry that it is impossible to escape the sexist ideology of fairy tales, fairy tales and the language they are expressed in are not univocal but polysemic. The result is that linguistic signs, although dominated by certain groups at any one time, can also, through struggle, be the object of appropriation by interested groups including feminists.

Angela Carter's imaginative retellings of traditional fairy tales partakes of the freedom available to a parodist when engaging in the task of mimicry combined with critique. While retaining many of the conventions of traditional fairy tales she creatively substitutes new images, characters, and plots, subverting old conventions and ideologies at the same time as repeating and borrowing from them. Without destroying the original tales, Angela Carter steals liberally from them reusing the signs for her own very different purposes. Strategic theft is, perhaps the only available option:

Today, there is no area of language exterior to bourgeois ideology; our language comes from it, returns to it, remains locked within it. The only possible answer is neither confrontation nor destruction but only theft: to fragment the old texts of culture, of science, of literature, and to disseminate and disguise the fragments in the same way that we disguise stolen merchandise.[70]

Such parody, as Linda Hutcheon argues, is not nostalgic but ironic and critical,

---

[68] *ibid.*, at 76.

[69] Patricia Palmer 'Gender as Performance', *supra*, asks whether the idea of gender as performance is 'a sell-out to society's current obsession with stylizing the body and the erotic'; at 27. Also in the same volume, Christina Britzolakis, 'Angela Carter's Fetishism', wonders whether the emancipation promised by the notions of theatricality and masquerade is more apparent than real.

[70] Ihab Hassan, *The Right Promethean Fire: Imagination, Science and Cultural Change* (Chicago and London: Chicago University Press, 1980), at 17.

problematizing dominant values and ideologies and laying bare the political nature of all representation.[71]

The reader is also free to construct her own meanings from the available signs; in intertextual texts such as *The Bloody Chamber* such participation is indispensable. The reader's memory of previous texts and representations plays an intrinsic role in the text's engagement in the politics of representation. While such engagement is restricted to readers familiar with the earlier text and has therefore attracted the criticism of elitism, the high currency of fairy tales means that most readers can fruitfully compare and learn from the differences between the two texts. While some readers have found Carter's retellings complicit with patriarchal ideology, the freedom and responsibility for finding alternative stories and alternative ideologies rest with the reader's engagement with the text, not the writer's prescriptions.[72]

The result for both writer and reader is to encounter female heroines who do not subscribe to the patriarchal mould but restore the forgotten voices; while they necessarily repeat the original violence, the original trauma, they do so with a different purpose.[73] Here one cannot overestimate the power of irony and humour as a tool for subverting earlier texts and cultural orthodoxies. Although humour has the effect of 'blowing up the law, breaking up the "truth" '[74] it is itself absent from legal discourse, an institution notoriously unable to laugh at itself. Such deconstruction reveals the sexist values implicit in fairy tales at the same time as redefining their ideological position. As Marina Warner puts it, 'Carter snatches out of the jaws of misogyny itself 'useful stories' for women. 'There she found Sade' a liberating teacher of the male-female status quo and made him illuminate the far reaches of women's polymorphous desires. The effect is to lift Beauty, Red Riding Hood, and Bluebeard's last wife out of the pastel nursery into the labyrinth of female desire.[75]

Of course changes in legal, social, and economic conditions are necessary for achieving women's autonomy; such changes however need to be accompanied if not preceded by a transformation in language and representational norms as negative representations of women on the cultural plane contribute to the denigration of women on the political and social plane. Carter represents women and femininity in terms that are not dictated by phallocentric culture and constructs alternative models that respect women's difference. The Marquis de Sade's model of the virtuous victim Justine and of the aggressive Juliette are both shown to be unhelpful. Instead woman must find her own voice and her own sexuality in order to begin writing/creating herself. The heroines in *The Bloody Chamber* extricate themselves from objects of

---

[71] *Supra.*

[72] See Merja Makinen, *supra*: 'Narrative genres clearly do inscribe ideologies (though that can never fix the readings), but later re-writings that take the genre and adapt it will not necessarily encode the same ideological assumptions.'

[73] See Judith Butler, *Excitable Speech: A Politics of the Performative* (London, 1997), especially 37–8.

[74] Hélène Cixous, 'The Laugh of the Medusa', in Elaine Marks and Isabelle de Courtivron (eds.) *New French Feminisns: an Anthology* (Brighton: Harvester Press, 1981), at 258.

[75] Marina Warner, *The Second Virago Book of Fairy Tales*, ed. Angela Carter (London: Virago, 1992), at x.

male desire and male laws, discover their own desires and write their own endings to old stories. Following Irigaray's strategy of mimesis, they take up the role of law-making and recreate themselves independently of male scripting. That these new selves are fashioned on the back of previous well known texts enables the reader to appreciate the contrast with irony, wit, and humour.

Fantasy, to extend Gillian Beer's phrase, may remake the world in the image of female desire.[76] Envisaging new imaginary orders enables us to envisage new laws for what is the symbolic order but another imaginary that has become law?

---

[76] Gillian Beer, *The Romance* (London: Methuen, 1970), at 79.

8

ARCHIVE FEVER THAT MISSES THE FIRE: LEGAL AND OTHER TEXTUAL MEMORIES IN *CHRONICLE OF A DEATH FORETOLD*[1]

The past is a notional construct, a hypothesis, a poem . . .
It is not so much a document as it is a brand or a scar.
Luc Sante, *The Factory of Facts*

1 STORIES AND HISTORIES

'Chronicle', according to the *Oxford English Dictionary* is 'a register of events in order of their occurrence; a narrative, a full account; (*Chronicles*) the name of two of the historical books of the Old Testament or Hebrew books; to record (events) in the order of their occurrence.' A term and a definition that the reader (male *and* female?) soon forgets on wading in and, often after one sitting, out of Gabriel García Márquez' *Chronicle of a Death Foretold*. Seduced, as s/he is, by the promised climax in the title, the foretold and inescapable closure afforded only by death.

On multiple readings and re-readings, however, the irony of the title begins to emerge, upset, and unsettle. The inexorable fate promised to the reader and related with such seeming inevitability for one hundred and twenty-two pages, does anything but satisfy and foreclose the desires she brought to her reading. The promised climax is not only continually repeated in order to be repeatedly deferred, it is also radically and cruelly denied. On one level, the death bloodily described on the last page is 'foretold': Santiago Nasar 'brush[es] off the dirt that was stuck to his guts' (122) before collapsing on his face in the kitchen where less than two hours earlier he had

---

[1] Gabriel García Márquez, *Chronicle of a Death Foretold*, trans. Gregory Rabassa (London: Picador, 1982), all page references in the text are to this edition.

witnessed with horror the steaming guts of a rabbit being pulled by the roots and thrown to the dogs (8). The intervening pages, purportedly 'chronicling' the short time between 5.30 a.m., when Santiago Nasar got up, and 7.05 a.m., when he was 'carved up like a pig'(2), rather than reassuringly explaining, cataloguing, or fully narrating the intervening events, succeed only in opening other truths, other spaces, arousing rather than fulfilling the reader's multiple dreams and desires. These desires not only remain unappeased at the end, but can only be hinted at by the text, glimpsed, but not captured by the narrator/creator and even less so by his many readers.

'After thirty years', says Gabriel García Márquez, 'I discovered something that we novelists often forget—that the best literary formula is always the truth'.[2] He would also have us believe that '[W]hat I am interested in, and what I believe ought to interest the critics is the comparison between the facts and the literary work'.[3] These claims however, like Bayardo's way of talking in the book, 'serve more to conceal than to reveal' (25), and create more tensions than offer appeasing solutions. Just like the text, rather than revealing the creator's elusive intentions, or delivering the text's 'meaning', they succeed only in drawing attention to the fact that the boundaries between fact and fiction, literature and journalism, literature and history, literature and law, biography and projection are always already blurred.

It is well-known that the story is based on events that took place in Sucre, Colombia, on 22 January 1951. 'Real' people inhabit the text like the narrator's mother Luisa Santiago and his future wife, Mercedes. The narrator also purports to divorce himself from novelistic accounts of similar events, excusing himself for relating an event that would fill the shelves of literature, even trashy literature like dime-novels (11) and claiming that 'I couldn't bring myself to admit that life would end up resembling bad literature so much' (89). To the investigating judge, it 'never seemed legitimate that life should make use of so many coincidences forbidden literature, so that there should be the untrammelled fulfilment of a death so clearly foretold' (100). Such asides tease and confuse the reader, on the one hand claiming to distinguish the text from fiction while drawing attention to the fictionality of the work. The narrator thus lays bare, indeed confesses to, the falsity of the distinctions he claims to rely on.

Chronicle of a Death Foretold, by self-consciously blurring the genres of literature, law reporting, journalism and history, not only transgresses the law that 'Genres are not to be mixed. I will not mix genres. I repeat: genres are not to be mixed. I will not mix them.'[4] It also illustrates Derrida's point that the law which tries to institutionalize and preserve the purity of genres always fails because genres inevitably exceed their boundaries and are open to contamination by other genres.

---

[2] Quoted by Gonzalo Díaz-Migoyo, 'Truth Disguised: *Chronicle of a Death* (Ambiguously) *Foretold*' in Julio Ortega (ed.), *Gabriel García Márques and the Powers of Fiction* (Austin, Tex.: University of Texas Press, 1988), at 77.

[3] *ibid.*, at 75.

[4] Jacques Derrida, 'The Law of Genre' in *Acts of Literature*, ed. Derek Attridge, (New York and London: Routledge, 1992), at 223.

In what sense then, is the literary work, as Márquez claims, telling the 'truth'? In *Chronicle of a Death Foretold*, the 'truth' the narrator has been allegedly searching, rather than being found, becomes as elusive as the 'reality' he fooled us into thinking he was trying to depict. My suggestion is that the 'truth' comes not from a reality that is somehow 'out there' waiting to be captured by the law report or the literary text but is a different truth, perhaps even a higher truth than the one expressed by competing genres and discourses, whether they are religious, historical, legal, or literary. It is the intimation of a kingdom ruled not only by literature but by woman as literature, of a truth uttered not by a God but a Goddess, not by law, religion, or history, but by a woman who writes, and through writing, creates herself, herstory, and her law.

2 TEXTS OF LAW AND HISTORY

Throughout the novel the reader is never certain what part of the narrative belongs to literature, what part to history, what part to the legal chronicle or to the transcription of the legal chronicle by the narrator. The borders between fact and fiction, history and fable, art and reality are opened to investigation and, thereby also to contestation. It is impossible to say, legislate, or judge which is the more real, the more true, depiction. Literature, law, and history dissolve into each other while the text creates its own law, and its own history which in turn rewrites the history of the event and the town depicted in it. Not surprisingly, following the publication of *Chronicle of a Death Foretold* in 1981, Sucre was invaded by journalists eager to interview and report on the 'real life' incident; a development that served further to compound the interrelation and inter-penetration between fact, law, history, and literature.

Such a development was also the outcome of Gabriel García Márquez' depiction of the events surrounding the famous banana strike in *One Hundred Years of Solitude*. As Márquez admits, 'Nobody has studied the events around the real banana strike—and now when they talk about it in the newspapers, even once in the congress, they speak about the *3000* who died! And I wonder if, with time, it will become true that 3000 were killed.'[5] It is not difficult to believe that with *Chronicle of a Death Foretold* again recollections of the 'real' event will hereafter be coloured, if not superseded, by their fictional rewriting; the 'real' event, will be impossible to be imagined, let alone retold, outside the contours of its retelling by literature. Particularly since, as Márquez again assures us, 'I'm pretentious enough to believe that the 'drama' in my book is better, that it's more controlled, more structured'.[6]

---

[5] *Playboy*, interview with Claudia Dreyfus, February 1983, Vol. 30(2), 65, at 76.

[6] 'An Interview with Gabriel García Márquez', *Cencrastus*, 7, quoted in Bernard McGuirk, 'Free-play of fore-play: the fiction of non-consummation: speculations on *Chronicle of a Death Foretold*' in Bernard McGuirk and Cardwell (eds.), *Gabriel García Márquez: New Readings* (Cambridge: Cambridge University Press, 1987), at 171.

For some historians this development is anathema:[7] in a fashion similar to legal theory's resort to positivism in the nineteenth century to explain the binding quality of legal norms, historians affirmed the possibility of a scientific knowledge of the past. The desire for the 'scientization' of history is no different from that of the scientization of law and is shared by the metaphysicians these schools decry: by distinguishing law and history from extraneous elements, the aim is to base law, and the past, on a secure foundation with its promise of pure presence, fullness and essential, final meanings. The historian, like the lawyer, searches and imagines can discover, like the detective or the archaeologist, the origin and the truth of the past. This origin, truth, or meaning, it is claimed, is not 'made' but 'found', and once found, it is possible to believe in it in the same way that one believes in one true God. In the words of one historian, 'Everything must be recaptured and relocated in the general framework of history, so that despite the difficulties, the fundamental paradoxes and contradictions, we may respect the unity of history which is also the unity of life'.[8]

The work of critical legal scholars has alerted us to the fallacies involved in the positivist enterprise and the losses incurred by their insistence on law as fact divorced from politics, morality, and literature. In the same fashion, the fetishism of facts has, as Hayden White argues, led history to 'lose sight of its origins in the literary imagination'.[9] The work of historians like White and Dominic la Capra has served to remind us that history, like law, is also a text, textually constructed. The analytic tradition's attempt to eliminate metaphor from human discourse ignores that style is intrinsic to content and academic empiricism is one style among many, chosen rather than inexorably dictated from above. Though historians crave for a reality that is outside or beyond interpretation, history does not exist 'out there' ready for us to appropriate. It arrives, if at all, through the traces it leaves in other, already textualized, sources. Archives, the testimonies of witnesses, law reports, political documents, are not transparent forms of representation but depend always, and already, on other symbols and codes.[10]

The historian's attempt to accord these diverse sources with meaning cannot take place without the activity of selecting, hierarchizing, supplementing, suppressing, and subordinating some facts to others. This process cannot be other than literary and the historian's tools are the same as those of the literary critic and writer: as Hayden

---

[7] Eduardo Posada-Carbo, 'Fiction as History: the bananeras and Gabriel García Márquez's *One Hundred Years of Solitude*', *Journal of Latin American Studies*, Vol. 30, 1998, 395–414 expresses concern that *One Hundred Years of Solitude* contains today's 'official version' of the developments in the banana zone in the 1920s and that since the book's publication, Colombia's perceptions of the banana strike resembles not the Colombia in which they live but the history written by the novelist.

[8] Fernand Braudel, *On History* (Chicago, Illinois: University of Chicago Press, 1980), trans. Sarah Matthews, at 16; quoted by Linda Hutcheon, *The Politics of Postmodernism* (London and New York: Routledge, 1989), at 63.

[9] Hayden White, *Tropics of Discourse: Essays in Cultural Criticism* (Baltimore: Johns Hopkins University Press, 1978), at 99.

[10] Dominic LaCapra, *History and Criticism* (Ithaca, New York: Cornell University Press, 1985), at 128: 'the past arrives in the form of texts and textualized remainders—memories, reports, published writings, archives, monuments and so forth'.

White says, the historian's instruments 'for endowing his data with meaning, of rendering the strange familiar, and of rendering the mysterious past comprehensible, are the techniques of *figurative* language . . . history . . . is made sense of in the same way that the poet or novelist tries to make sense of it, i.e. by endowing what originally appears to be problematical and mysterious with the aspect of a recognisable . . . form. It does not matter whether the world is conceived to be real or only imagined; the manner of making sense of it is the same.'[11]

The losses incurred from the empiricist's attempt at disciplining the past are as great: the attempt to distinguish history from fiction, the suppression of the literal, the rhetorical, and the speculative has led to the exclusion of alternative ways of looking at both the law and the past. In the legal academy, the work of theorists like Peter Goodrich, has alerted us to 'minor jurisprudences' that have been forgotten, ignored, or repressed in the law's drive toward 'oneness'.[12] In a similar fashion, 'Since the second half of the nineteenth century', decries Hayden White, 'history has become increasingly the refuge of all those 'sane' men who excel at finding the simple in the complex and the familiar in the strange'.[13] For White, history's status as a text means that the past cannot be captured, only interpreted. This does not render history meaningless nor does it deny the existence of the past. On the contrary, it affords new opportunities for understanding and living with the past. This is a gain to those suspicious of claims to single, univocal, and eternal truths: for the effect is not to *deny* but to *expand* past and present laws and histories.

3   APPROPRIATING HISTORIES

The dismay with which some historians have greeted these arguments is akin to the reception of critical legal scholarship by the legal establishment and understandable for the same reasons. Just as legal stories are constitutive of our identities as legal subjects, the stories we tell about the past are constitutive not only of our past but also of our present identities, individual and collective. We remember, or try to remember, in order to understand ourselves as subjects living in time and with others. The texts and images we employ to tell these stories do not present themselves neutrally but in codes that are always and already political. To lay bare the political nature of these representations is also to lay them open to interpretation and appropriation by different groups.

The political nature of representation, explored and exploited as we saw in the last chapter, to retell old stories by and for women, is also the starting point for post-

---

[11] Hayden White, *Tropics of Discourse, supra*, at 94–8.

[12] See especially Peter Goodrich, *Law in the Courts of Love: Literature and other minor jurisprudences* (London and New York: Routledge, 1996).

[13] Hayden White, *Tropics of Discourse, supra*, at 50.

colonial writers. The stories inherited from the past, presented as final and definitive often obscured the voices of the colonized or the losers, robbing them of the opportunity to tell and thereby create their identities for and by themselves. As Márquez put it in his Nobel Prize acceptance speech, 'The interpretation of our reality through patterns not our own serves only to make us ever more unknown, ever less free, ever more solitary'.[14] Increasingly post-colonial writers have taken up the task of recreating the past through the imagination, to reopen and question old stories, so as to create not only new stories but new histories and new identities for individuals, communities and nations. This 'chutnification of history'[15] as Salman Rushdie calls it, denies neither the notion of the past, nor that of identity; on the contrary it affirms that both history and the identities it creates are a never-ending process and inseparable from the political process.

As in Angela Carter's *The Bloody Chamber*, in *Chronicle of a Death Foretold* we find a denial of the modernist notion of originality and uniqueness. The text is self-consciously compiled from a collection of other texts, who mingle with and jostle each other, and whose vacillating interactions thwart any attempt at a final or closed meaning. Well-known existing texts are appropriated and imbued with new significances, the consecrated texts of the west being a prime candidate for such 'complicitous critique'.[16] Interpreted in the past so as to confer a sense of history as linear progression, and as revealing universal truths, they are now reopened to reveal other truths, conflicting voices, and suppressed contradictions. The 'truths' inherited from the inherited models are paid lip-service to only to be questioned and, just as often, ridiculed.

The first and major western archetype to be reopened and repositioned is the Bible; we know that the solemnity of that text will be undercut from the book's first pages as the narrator relates how Santiago's father's gun accidentally went off: the bullet, he relates, 'wrecked the cupboard in the room, went through the living room wall, passed through the dining room of the house next door with the thunder of war, and turned a life-size saint on the main altar of the church on the opposite side of the square to plaster-dust' (4). Humour, irreverence, outrageousness, and exaggeration here deflate the seriousness with which the Church treats its emblems. The value and significance of the Church and its dignitaries are similarly challenged and undermined. Rather than acting to prevent the tragedy, the church officials, the narrative implies, are indirectly responsible for it. Had it not been for the bishop's visit, Santiago would have been wearing his hunting outfit, that is, he would have been armed when he turned to face his attackers. At the same time, the townspeople, preoccupied with the

---

[14] 'The Solitude of Latin America' in Julio Ortega (ed.), *Gabriel García Márquez and the Powers of Fiction*, *supra*, at 89.

[15] Salman Rushdie, *Midnight's Children* (London: Picador, 1988), at 459.

[16] This is Linda Hutcheon's term and approach: *The Politics of Postmodernism*, *supra*, at 11: 'my own paradoxical postmodernism of complicity and critique, reflexivity and historicity, that at once inscribes and subverts the conventions and ideologies of the dominant cultural and social forces of the twentieth century western world'.

visit, forget or delay warning Santiago, his mother and his friends of the plans of Pablo and Pedro Vicario (the names could not be more ironic). The priest, Father Amador, though warned of the impending tragedy, like Pilate, washes his hands of the crime, contenting himself with the view that 'it wasn't any business of mine but something for the civil authorities' (70); he tells the narrator he had planned to tell Santiago's mother but forgot to do so because he was distracted by the bishop's visit. The bishop himself does not even get off the boat to give his obligatory blessing, despite the townspeople's fervent anticipation of his visit, because 'he hates this town'(6) and is more interested in collecting their offerings, 'coxcomb soup', to which he is known to be partial.

The analogy with the behaviour of Pilate before Christ's crucifixion is only one of many indications of Santiago as a Christ-figure. Santiago Nasar's name as well as fate evokes the sacrifice of Christ the Nazarene: the stab on his right hand, according to the report, 'looked like a stigma of the crucified Christ.' (76) More provocatively, the truth of the Church's teachings are themselves reopened. Santiago's sacrificial death does not lead to understanding or salvation for the community but suffering that is compounded by their inability to understand the tragedy: Pedro Vicario suffers 'the frightful certainty that he wouldn't sleep ever again for the rest of his life. "I was awake for 11 months", he told me, and I knew him well enough to know that it was true' while Pablo Vicario unlooses 'a pestilential cholerine' (80).

In a further parodying of western canonical texts, and another transgression of the law of genres, biblical undertones are re-worked alongside motifs from Greek myth and classical tragedy.[17] The foretold nature of the crime, 'announced' by the title of the book, evokes the doomed fate of Oedipus Rex, a fate that Santiago cannot escape any more than Oedipus. People who see Santiago on that morning describe him as a 'ghost', an 'angel' they do not dare touch; those he touches, find that his hand 'felt frozen and stony, like the hand of a dead man' (12). In another reminder of motifs from Greek epic poetry Angela, like Helen of Troy, is the cause of the conflict that results in tragedy, and, later, like Penelope, sits at home with her embroidery, shunning the outside world and waiting for the husband who abandoned her to return. The humour and hyperbole, however, with which these motifs are reworked in the text unsettle rather than reinforce the foundations the canonical texts purported to inscribe. As we see later, Angela does more than wait for Bayardo and, unlike Penelope, feels no need to lie about her past or her present to strangers or suitors.

As with Oedipus, it could be argued that Santiago is guilty of arrogance, ('he thought that his money made him untouchable', (102)) and further hubris in his enthusiasm for calculating the cost of Angela and Bayardo's wedding. But while in Greek tragedy the fate of men like Oedipus was dictated by the inexorable wisdom

---

[17] See John Carson Pettey 'Nietzsche's *Birth of Tragedy* and Euripides' *Bacchae* as Sources for the Apollonian and Dionysian Aspects of Gabriel Márquez's *Chronicle of a Death Foretold*: A Speculative Reading' *Hispanofila*, 1997, Vol. 121, 21–34. Also Arnold Penuel 'Echoes of the *Iliad* in *Chronicle of a Death Foretold*' in his *Intertextuality in García Márquez* (York, SC: Spanish Literature Publications Co., 1994).

and foreknowledge of the gods, Santiago's death leaves us with no such certainties. The accidents and coincidences that led to him being publicly butchered despite the entire town's knowledge of his attackers' plans, shake, rather than affirm, our belief in a universe ordered by a divine order. Unlike Oedipus, Santiago's death is not preceded by anagnorisis, indeed he dies confused and bewildered, unable to decipher his attackers' motives: 'I don't understand a Goddamned thing,' are some of the last words we hear him say (116).

Nor does Santiago's death lead to catharsis for the community that stood by and watched. Instead, the town for years later remains 'an open wound' (99), unable to forget the crime or get on with the future. We are told that Hortensia Baute falls into a penitential crisis and runs out naked into the street, Santiago Nasar's fiancée runs away with a lieutenant of the border patrol who prostituted her among the rubber workers, the midwife suffers a spasm of the bladder, and Clothilde Armenta's husband does not survive the shock (98). The abiding guilt experienced by the community retains one of the hallmarks of tragedy but in contrast to Sophocles' *Oedipus*, this guilt is not framed by a redeeming and reassuring belief in an all-powerful divinity that dictates and watches over the fate of humans.

4 FOILING THE DETECTIVE

'The dead body', writes Žižek, 'is the object of desire *par excellence*, the cause that starts the interpretive desire of the detective (and the reader): How did it happen? Who did it?'[18] The Greek text that first straddled the genres that we have now come to call tragedy and detective story is *Oedipus Rex* where the investigator turns out to be the criminal. The classical detective story, as analysed by Tzvetan Todorov, consists typically of two stories: the story of the crime, involving action and often blood, followed by the story of the investigation, involving enquiry, revelation, and knowledge.[19] Such stories chart the progress from a community whose order and stability are temporarily disrupted by a crime that breaks the rules, and that society was unable to prevent, back to order and stability once the criminal has been identified and his or her crime explained by a suitable motive.[20]

The assumption that all signs, those of the criminal as well as of the detective, are capable of being deciphered and explained into one true meaning is shared not only

[18] Slavoj Žižek, *Looking Awry: An Introduction to Jacques Lacan Through Popular Culture* (London, UK & Cambridge, USA: October, MIT Press, 1991), at 143.

[19] 'The Typology of Detective Fiction' in Tzvetan Todorov, *The Poetics of Prose*, trans. Richard Howard (Oxford: Basil Blackwell, 1977) [1971].

[20] See Stephen Knight, *Form and Ideology in Crime Fiction* (London: Macmillan, 1980); Stephen Knight argues that as the society depicted, and whose values are threatened, is typically middle class, the success of the lone, private detective, reasserts bourgeois values, in particular the importance of the principle of individualism in maintaining and preserving those values.

by the detective genre but by the legal system. Law cannot tolerate indeterminacy, gaps or contradictions when faced with an act that challenges its supremacy. Since murder is 'dirt', 'matter out of place'[21] the law and the detective-hero seek to clean up the mess, to reduce aberrant signs into a single and coherent meaning. Like the detective story, the law assumes that this meaning can be achieved through narrative. Law puts its trust in language as the instrument through which polyvalent signs can be reduced to a single truth and deliver both justice and narrative closure.[22] The ability of reason and of language to explain and dissolve mysteries delivers the reassuring message that, with enough effort and perseverance, order and meaning will prevail over chaos and ignorance. In the best examples of the genre the reader also experiences the pleasure of believing that s/he has participated in the solving of the mystery, that the credit for solving it is owed as much to him/her as to the writer. Conversely, a crime that remains unsolved challenges the coherence and validity of the system by refusing to be assimilated into society's system of approved signs.

Márquez is not oblivious to the attractions offered by the detective story and indeed claimed that 'Chronicle of a Death Foretold is structured as carefully as a clockwork'.[23] The text is awash with hallmarks familiar from the detective genre from motive, plot, place, time, crime, victim, investigation, and punishment. The reader who picks up these hallmarks, however, soon realizes that his reading of the text as a detective story is, if not a *mis*reading, at least only a partial reading. For the traits of detective novels are evoked only to show that they are irrelevant to both understanding and to coping with the tragedy. In *Chronicle of a Death Foretold* everything that the detective seeks to find is well-known before the crime has taken place: 'Someone who was never identified had shoved an envelope under the door with a piece of paper warning Santiago Nasar that they were waiting for him to kill him, and, in addition, the note revealed the place, the motive, and other quite precise details of the plot' (12). Furthermore, although the narrator sets out to find the one true meaning of the crime, his investigation leads not to understanding and closure but to multiple truths and meanings which cannot be reconciled with each other. Having set out to 'put the broken mirror of memory back together from so many shattered shards' (5) he succeeds only in finding new fragments, that break into smaller pieces and into more discontinuous narratives; the effect is not to dissolve the mystery, but to compound it.

This is because the secret the detective/narrator is looking for does not concern causes and effects. He does not assume himself to be the source of truth, like a Sherlock Holmes or a court of law, that can authoritatively rewrite and retell the stories of the criminal, the victim, and the other participants in the tragedy. Where these stories are told, the narrator is insistent that they are again more fragments, more unfinished messages. The secret he wants to confront and share with the reader

---

[21] David Trotter, 'Theory and detective fiction' *Critical Quarterly*, Vol. 33(2), 66–77, (1991), at 70.

[22] See further, Peter Hühn, 'The Detective as Reader: Narrativity and Reading Concepts in Detective Fiction', *Modern Fiction Studies*, Vol. 33(3), (1987), 451–66.

[23] *Playboy*, interview, *supra*, at 70.

is his own, and the reader's, need to ask 'why'; more importantly to teach us 'to accept the burden of our need to ask why'.[24] For years, we are told, the narrator and inhabitants of the town recount obsessively the events that led to Santiago's absurd murder 'and it was obvious that we weren't doing it from any urge to clear up mysteries but because none of us could go on living without any exact knowledge of the place and the mission assigned to us by fate' (97). The task, in other words, is not to explain or dissipate the mystery, for that is impossible, but to learn to live with it.

The detective novel, as Dennis Porter has argued, solicits in the reader a desire to know, while controlling and intensifying that desire by deferring its fulfilment. The reader is kept in an anticipatory state of excitement which is gratified only in the release afforded by the final solution in the last pages.[25] The legal subject also, Legendre argues, is erotically attached to, fascinated by, and captivated by the power of the law, as the child is to the father it both fears and loves.[26] However, the law or detective novel that not only defers but refuses answers and leaves loose ends untied, does not perform this therapeutic function and fails to assuage the anxieties of the reader and the legal subject. Only she who has reconciled herself to the impossibility of arriving at a single and final 'truth', of who is content with living with disorder and instability, who does not need to have every mystery dispelled and every riddle explained, may derive pleasure from the closure afforded by this novel; a pleasure that can perhaps be summed up by Nietzsche's aphorism, *amor fati*.

5 LEGAL AND OTHER MEMORIES

The officers of the law, in the form of policeman Leandro Pornoy, having had, and having missed, the opportunity of preventing the crime, reappear after the event to impose order on the events, to retell them in a fashion that can be accepted by legal discourse and by the community, and thereby to justify the punishment meted out to the perpetrators. Despite the fact that 'No-one could understand such fatal coincidences', the investigating judge, while sensing them, does not have the luxury of admitting to them; his, and the law's, 'interest in giving them a rational explanation was obvious in the report' (10–11). Although the events themselves elude meaning, there is no shortage of attempts to find, and failing finding, creating such meaning. The narrator, however, does not let us forget that this meaning is invented rather than found, imposed rather than detected. Each attempt to endow them with a final meaning is therefore doomed to failure.

---

[24] Graham Swift, *Waterland* (London: Heinemann, 1983), at 93.

[25] Dennis Porter, *The Pursuit of Crime: Art and Ideology in Detective Fiction* (New Haven & London: Yale University Press, 1981).

[26] Peter Goodrich (ed.), *Law and the Unconscious: A Legendre Reader*, trans. Peter Goodrich with Alain Pottage and Anton Schütz (London: Macmillan, 1997).

Ill at ease with the present, narrator and community hope that by piecing together the fragments of the past they may form for themselves a more secure identity for the future. The emphasis on the importance of memory for the creation of identity follows a tradition where memories are perceived to be spontaneous, instinctive, or unconscious, in contrast to the writing of history which is self-conscious, purposive, and artificial. The assumption is that while history is textual and abstract, memory works through concrete images and sensations and, as Horace Walpole put it, can see more than the eye. Through his own and other survivors' memories the narrator attempts to make the absent past present. But memories do not exist in the past or merely repeat or refer to it; as Bertrand Russell suggested, as memory of the past can only ever take place in the present, it is not logically necessary that the past should have existed at all.[27] Memories therefore serve the function of creating, recreating, inventing, and reinventing the past for the benefit and interests of the present.

'For years', the narrator says, 'we couldn't talk about anything else. Our daily contact, dominated then by so many linear habits, had suddenly begun to spin around a single common anxiety' (97): members of the community compulsively repeat the painful events hoping that if they can assign a meaning to them, their memories will cease to torment them and they can start 'living' again.[28] The same drive to knowledge that led to the scientization of law and the scientization of history that we explored earlier, emerges here, as Ian Hacking has argued, as a drive to 'scientize the soul through the study of memory': 'When the family falls apart, when parents abuse their children, when incest obsesses the media, when one people tries to destroy another, we are concerned with defects of the soul. But we have learned how to replace the soul with knowledge, with science. Hence spiritual battles are fought, not on the explicit ground of the soul, but on the terrain of memory, where we suppose that there is such a thing as knowledge to be had'.[29]

Proceeding on the assumption that oral testimony of memories of the past is both valuable and reliable, indeed more reliable than the official records, the narrator sets out to interview the surviving witnesses of the event. He thus follows the tradition, or prejudice, espoused by western philosophy and Anglo-American legal systems, that the presence of the speaking subject will confer origin, unity, and authority to their utterances whether the latter concern their past actions or future purposes. This assumption, however, is undermined from the first pages when it is obvious that the memories the survivors relate are both fragmented and contradictory. The problem is

---

[27] Bertrand Russell, *The Analysis of Mind* (London: George Allen & Unwin Ltd, 1929), at 159: 'memory of past sensations seems only possible by means of present images. It is not logically necessary to the existence of a memory-belief that the event remembered should have occurred, or even that the past should have existed at all. There is no logical impossibility that the world sprang into being five minutes ago, exactly as it then was, with a population that 'remembered' a wholly unreal past.'

[28] Cathy Caruth describes this as 'the absolute inability of the mind to avoid an unpleasurable event that has not been given a psychic meaning in any way': *Unclaimed Experience: Trauma, Narrative and History* (Baltimore: Johns Hopkins University Press, 1996), at 59.

[29] *Rewriting the Soul; Multiple Personality and the Sciences of Memory* (Princeton, New Jersey: Princeton University Press, 1995), at 5–6.

not so much that witnesses want to conceal or distort their role in the events in order
to escape moral or legal censure; indeed they are only too keen to confess any blame-
worthy action or omission on their part. Their urge to tell and retell the events leading
to Santiago's murder is a form of therapy but the cure and final catharsis are not
forthcoming. The problem is that even where the questions relate to seemingly trivial
matters, their testimonies are at best ambiguous, and often contradictory. Thus many
people recalled that 'it was a radiant morning . . . But most agreed that the weather
was funeral, with a cloudy, low sky and the thick smell of still waters, and that at the
moment of the misfortune a thin drizzle like the one Santiago had seen in his dream
grove was falling' (2–3) while 'Victoria Guzman, the cook, was sure that it hadn't
rained that day' (7). If the witnesses cannot remember or agree on the state of the
weather, their memories seemingly coloured by their own perception of what the
weather on that tragic day should have been like, then how much less likely it is that
they will be able to enlighten us on other matters. The narrator and thereby the reader
are quickly disabused of the illusion that the speaker's presence will deliver the 'truth'.

To paraphrase John Sturrock, if history 'is one damned thing after another, then
historiography is one damned thing *causing* another'.[30] But the diverse 'facts' the
narrator is able to collect do not magically connect to each other in the preferred
narrative of cause and effect. Instead, each fact, each memory, written or oral, throws
light but also dims, reinterprets, and forces us to rethink other facts and other memories. The written evidence collected by the investigating magistrate is similarly fragmentary, only partly because the ground floor of the building it was kept in, had been
flooded so that the narrator was only able 'to rescue some 322 pages filched from the
more than 500 that the brief must have had' (99). This partial brief contains notes
scribbled in red by the judge on the margins which are, the narrator appreciates, more
eloquent than the collection of diverse accounts gathered from eye-witnesses. The
investigator, 'a man burning with the fever of literature' (99), cannot resist allusions to
Greek tragedy when he refers to the door in front of which Santiago was butchered as
'the fatal door'. If the accumulation of facts is aimed at arriving at an empirical
explanation of the events, the Appolonian impulse towards rationality is continually
subverted by the notes on the margin that hint at a different truth inspired less by
Apollo than by Dionysus, less by reason than by imagination, and less by fact than by
literature.

The narrator's tale therefore, is a *construction*, not a *reflection* of the past, dictated
not by the events themselves which are now irretrievably lost, but by his interpretation
and retelling of those events. Such a retelling, moreover, despite the privileging he
assumes should be accorded to oral testimony, can only take place *textually*. His
preference for speech over writing, following a long western tradition that depicts
speech as truth and presence, can itself only be communicated *in writing*. Despite the
resulting accumulation of evidence, written, and oral, simultaneous and retrospective,

[30] John Sturrock, *Paper Tigers: The Ideal Fictions of Jorge Luis Borges* (Oxford: Clarendon Press, 1977),
at 139.

the 'truth' remains elusive and the events absurd and meaningless. The narrator is only too aware of this, as another text extends his metaphor of the mirror: 'I am forced to reflect that world in fragments of broken mirrors . . . I must reconcile myself to the inevitability of the missing bits'.[31] Even this absence of meaning in texts, however, can only be communicated textually, that is, with more writing.

If writing the events is an attempt to confer meaning on them, to capture the truth and make it permanent, the narrator continually defers delivering such meaning. The promised closure never arrives, as the narration circles around and repeats the one event we are certain about from the title of the book. If the preoccupation with linear plots in nineteenth century realist fiction was a symptom of a faith in order and legality as able to deliver not only knowledge but also justice, then the insistence on a circular and open-ended plot undeceives us from the promise of both knowledge and justice. As Hayden White puts it, 'The historian serves no one well by constructing a specious continuity between the present world and that which preceded it. On the contrary, we require a history that will educate us to discontinuity more than ever before; for discontinuity, disruption and chaos is our lot'.[32] However, as we saw again in Camus's *The Outsider*, no writing, whether in history, law, or literature, can evade the attempt to impose a semblance of order on chaos; even if, as in *Chronicle of a Death Foretold*, this order is delivered only by death.

6 THE STAIN OF HONOUR

As their name suggests, the Vicario family are enacting and defending a social code that is outside their making or control. This code is part of a system of rules that assumes that while men's sexual activities are a matter of personal pride, entertainment, or, occasionally, reprimand, the sexual behaviour of women is a political matter and concerns society as a whole. The honour code, demanding that girls offered by their families for marriage must be virgins, is one area where sexual politics, bourgeois morality, and Christian religion combine and consolidate each other. When the code is broken, the whole community and not just the immediate parties has an interest in seeing the 'guilty' punished so that the social order temporarily disturbed by its breach may be restored.

As the head of a family that has lost its social and economic power, Poncio Vicario has dedicated himself to maintaining 'the honor of the house' as the only remnant to the family's claim to respectability. On this, as in many matters, public appearance is more important than substance so that when one daughter dies, the family's mourning 'was relaxed inside the house but rigorous on the street' (60). In the Vicario

---

[31] Salman Rushdie, *Shame* (London: Picador, 1983), at 69.
[32] Hayden White, *Tropics of Discourse, supra*, at 50.

household the brothers are brought up to be men 'while the girls are brought up to get married by being taught embroidery, sewing, weaving bone lace, wash and iron, make artificial flowers and fancy candy and write engagement announcements'. Unlike the girls of the time who had forgotten 'the cult of death', the four Vicario girls were 'past mistresses in the ancient science of sitting up with the ill, comforting the dying, and enshrouding the dead' (30). In short, as the narrator's mother approvingly puts it, 'They're perfect . . . Any man will be happy with them because they've been raised to suffer' (31).

In this context, the codes governing gender roles for the twentieth century society of Sucre are no different to the social rules, laws, myths, and rituals of ancient Greece or those recommended by traditional fairy tales: proper conduct for women again extols silence and staying inside, caring for the ill and presiding over burying the dead. The ideal for Latin American women, as in so many other societies, past and present, is to be 'religious and pious, focused on family, secluded at home and the moral force of their families'.[33] Writing is passed over in favour of embroidery, speech is restricted within the confines of the home, and then only to other women and straying outside is actively discouraged and condemned. Virginity for women is not only the desirable state but one whose maintenance is rigorously patrolled by vigilant fathers, brothers and, importantly, by other women, especially their mothers. For men on the other hand, it is not only desirable but necessary that they should engage in sexual activity in order to reach maturity and the town brothel caters to this demand.

Woman's sexuality is again perceived to pose a threat to society because she is allegedly unable to subject her passionate emotions to rational self-control. As Freud declared, 'A thinking man is his own legislator and confessor, and obtains his own absolution, but the woman, let alone the girl, does not have the measure of ethics in herself. She can only act if she keeps within the limits of morality, following what society has established as fitting. She is never forgiven if she has revolted against morality, possibly rightly so.'[34] The means by which this threat can be contained in a homosocial society is the institution of marriage whereby women are exchanged as gifts between men. As depicted in the fairy tales explored in the last chapter, again the contractual exchange called marriage is established not between a man and a woman, but between two groups of men and the woman is only the object, not subject of the exchange.[35]

---

[33] Susan Hill Gross and Marjorie Wall Bingham, *Women in Latin America: The Twentieth Century* (St Louis Park, Minnesota; Glenhurst, 1985), at 141; quoted in Irvin Solomon, 'Latin American Women in Literature and Reality', *Mid-West Quarterly of Contemporary Thought*, Vol. 34(2), 1993 192–205, at 199.

[34] P. Grosskurth, Review of Ronald W. Clarke, *Freud the Man and the Cause*, Times Literary Supplement, 8 August 1980, 887–90.

[35] Irigaray in 'Commodities Amongst Themselves' questions what would happen if women refused to play the game of being the passive objects of their own exchange: '*what if these "commodities" refused to go to "market"*? What if they maintained "another" kind of commerce, among themselves?' in *This Sex Which is Not One* (Ithaca, New York: Cornell University Press, 1985), at 196. That Lévi-Strauss's normative man uses the woman as a conduit of a relationship in which the true partner is a man is also the subject of Eve Kosovski Sedgwick, *Between Men: English Literature and Male Homosocial Desire* (New York: Columbia University Press, 1985).

The cult of virginity, demanding that brides be 'like blank white sheets on which nothing is written'[36] or 'purity infinite, spotless bloom' like fresh garden produce,[37] is, as Christopher Hill argued, indispensable to the system of capitalist exchanges: 'in the world of capitalist production expensive goods must not be shop-soiled or tarnished'.[38] The townspeople recognize this economic basis, describing 'affairs of honour' as 'sacred monopolies with access only for those who are part of the drama.' (98). In this fashion they console themselves for failing to prevent the crime.

Significantly, they also refrain from blaming Angela for her loss of virginity, thus denying her even the autonomy accorded to the criminal. Angela is denied the freedom to transgress, responsibility for the 'wrong' being placed instead on the man who 'deflowered' her, allegedly Santiago. In a similar fashion, the injured party is not Angela but other men: her husband and the men in her family. The responsibility for repairing the wrong falls again not on her but on the men, in this case, her brothers. If Pura Vicario, her mother, is the only person to punish Angela, this is not because the community acknowledges her independent desires or sexual freedom but because the honour code, like other laws, was made by men in order to legislate affairs between men. For the community the victim of the tragedy is not Angela, not even Santiago, but the man whose pride was injured by a woman who reflected back to him not his greatness but herstory that began before and without him: 'For the immense majority of people there was only one victim: Bayardo San Roman. They took it for granted that the other protagonists of the tragedy had been fulfilling with dignity, and even with a certain grandeur, their part of the fortune that life had assigned them. Santiago Nasar had expiated the insult, the brothers Vicario had proved their status as men, and the seduced sister was in possession of her honor once more' (84).

As Peter Goodrich has argued, modern law 'is initially and predominantly a masculine enterprise and a homosocial profession'.[39] By denying her ability to transgress, by not bringing Angela but only her brothers to account, the law succeeds in ignoring and erasing her own desire and role in the drama. In Goodrich's words again, 'Where law judges death to be the moral retribution of unfaithful acts or hermeneutic deceit between men, and leaves no place for a woman other than as the empty space through which the communication of masculine desire passes, then we are close to the modern concept of positive law and correlatively to a derisive or negative expression of the laws of love'.[40]

---

[36] D. H. Lawrence, 'A Propos of *Lady Chatterley's Lover*' in T. Moore (ed.), *Sex, Literature and Censorship* (New York: Viking, 1959) [1929] at 85.

[37] Meredith, *The Egoist* (Harmondsworth: Penguin, 1968), [1879] at 152: 'the devouring male egoist prefers them as inanimate overwrought polished pure metal precious vessels, fresh from the hands of the artificer, for him to walk away with hugging, call all his own, drink of and fill and drink of, and forget that he stole them.'

[38] Christopher Hill, 'Clarissa Harlowe and her Times', *Essays in Criticism*, Vol. 5, (1955) 315–40, at 331.

[39] 'Gynaetopia: Feminine Genealogies of Common Law', 20, *Journal of Law and Society* (1993), 276.

[40] Peter Goodrich, 'Courting Death' in Desmond Manderson (ed.), *Courting Death: The Law of Mortality* (London: Pluto Press, 1999), at 227.

7 SCAPEGOATS AND COLLECTIVE GUILT

While women like Angela are the objects not subjects of these laws, her brothers also fall short of the macho image expected by their society. Though 'brought up to be men' as the 'girls were reared to be married' (30), and though conscious of the weighty duty the honour code demands of them, they are desperate for an exit route. As Clothilde Armenta realizes, 'they looked like two children' (55) and thinks the mayor should have arrested them 'to spare those poor boys from the horrible duty that's fallen on them . . . she was certain that the Vicario brothers were not as anxious to fulfil the sentence as to find someone who would do them the favour of stopping them' (57).

Since a wrong is perceived to have been inflicted, however, since the Vicario family's reputation is tarnished by Angela's inability to display 'open under the sun in the courtyard of her house the linen sheet with the stain of honor' (38), since the rule is part of the code that the whole community has chosen, and wants to continue to abide by, it is the community as a whole that requires reparation. The brothers' reluctance to act as the conduits of society's code has to be ignored and, if necessary, resisted. The women like Clothilde Armenta and the narrator's mother who try to challenge the code, are prevented from doing so, or dismissed as mad. The community's insistence, however unconscious, for the rectification of the order Angela's deflowerment is perceived to have unsettled, turns Santiago's murder, in Girard's terms, into a sacrifice in the cause of reaffirming the social order.

For Girard, sacrifice is a deliberate collective act of violence inflicted on a surrogate victim, a form of displacement for the internal feuds, tensions, and rivalries pent up in a community and serves to protect the community from its own violence. Preceded by elaborate communal rites and rituals, its end is to restore harmony and reinforce the social fabric. Santiago's murder is indeed preceded by an elaborate and extravagant wedding. In another parody of the romantic novel, however, the wedding in *Chronicle of a Death Foretold* is not the climax that centres the protagonists' lives and unifies the threads unravelled by the text, but a reckless display of excessive expenditure and leads to death. Girard insists that for the sacrifice to work the scapegoat, or substitute victim, must be incapable of propagating further violence. Angela's choice of Santiago for victim is therefore not arbitrary: as the only child of a mixed marriage whose father is dead, the violence inflicted on him does not contain the risk of provoking further vengeance which would continue the cycle of violence. The only candidates for avenging his death, members of the Arab community, are either alienated from Santiago because of his superior wealth or peaceful people who are reluctant to intervene.

For most readers the code Santiago's sacrifice is used to reaffirm is the code of virginity and the text does not hide the hypocritical nature of a code that derogates women to the level of objects in an exchange between men. A persuasive argument has also been made, however, that the community is guilty for turning a blind eye to the real perpetrator of Angela's deflowerment, that is her father Poncio Vicario; Poncio's blindness in this context marks him, like Oedipus, as a perpetrator of incest.[41] Angela's mother and brothers, and the community as a whole, unable to countenance this possibility, dissociate themselves from its truth. The unconscious motivation, Rohana and Sieberh suggest, is to repress the suggestion that incest was taking place in their midst as well as to conceal their own unconscious desire for the murder to occur. But their unwillingness to confront the truths of the past prevents them, as the narrator describes, from dealing with the present or planning for the future. For Rahona and Sieburth Angela's choice of Santiago as the victim is not fortuitous because the text hints that he is also engaged in an incestuous relationship with his mother. More interestingly, Rahona and Sieburth suggest that this dissociation is shared by readers who, unable to countenance the possibility of incest, prefer to blame 'Fate' for the tragedy.

If incest, the ultimate taboo, has indeed been broken, then the stakes for avenging the wrong, cleansing the community, and restoring order and stability, cannot be stronger. In that respect, as Girard argues, the community ignore all their differences and unite against a surrogate victim; this 'violent unanimity' enables them to forget or repress knowledge of their own violence and participation in a death that, as the narrator says 'we all could have been to blame' (82). As we saw in the *Oresteia*, the legal system also arises not to put an end to violence, but to satisfy man's seemingly unappeasable desire for violence and to disguise it as knowledge or justice. As Girard argues, sacrifice is no different from, but a step

in the direction of a legal system. But the evolution, if indeed evolution is the proper term, is not continuous . . . the system functions best when everyone concerned is least aware that it involves retribution. The system can reorganize itself around the accused and the concept of guilt. In fact, retribution still holds sway, but forged into a principle of abstract justice that all men are obliged to uphold and respect . . . As soon as the judicial system gains supremacy, its machinery disappears from sight. Like sacrifice, it conceals—even as it also reveals—its resemblance to vengeance . . . In the judicial system, violence does indeed fall on the 'right' victim; it falls with such force, such resounding authority, that no retort is possible . . . The procedures that keep men's violence in bounds have one thing in common: they are no strangers to the ways of violence . . . Centuries can pass before men realize that there is no real difference between their principle of justice and the concept of revenge.[42]

Though the victim in this ritual sacrifice is a man, we must not forget that the community, and above all, her mother, demand that Angela must also be sacrificed by being 'buried alive', that is by being ostracized, before order, cleanliness, and stability can be restored to the community. As I argue later, however, Angela, unlike Iphigeneia

[41] Elena Rahona and Stephanie Sieburth, 'Keeping a Crime Unsolved: Characters' and Critics' Responses to Incest in García Márquez's *Crónica de una muerte anunciada*', *Revista de Estudios Hispanicos*, Vol. 30(3), 433–59; and John S. Christie, 'Fathers and Virgins: García Márquez's Faulknerian *Chronicle of a Death Foretold*' *Latin American Literary Review*, 21, (1993) 41.

[42] René Girard, *Violence and the Sacred*, trans. Patrick Gregory (Baltimore and London: Johns Hopkins University Press, 1977) [1972] at 21–4.

in the *Oresteia*, succeeds in walking away from the sacrificial altar and being written on by men, by starting to write her self. That writing is a reminder of that other favourite daughter's eloquent, but silenced, protest against dying in the name of patriarchal law and the symbolic order. As in the case of Iphigeneia, it is because women are used as objects of exchange to cement relations between men that sacrifices are perceived to be necessary for the stability of the social order. For women to enter into relations as independent subjects and on their own terms, like Angela Carter's heroines in the last chapter, it is also to avoid the necessity, as Irigaray argues, of sacrificing, of cutting up, and of killing.[43] In my closing chapter I re-invent the story of Ariadne as a heroine who, like Angela, writes herself and is at ease with a world of chance, uncertainty, and defeat as an antidote to a male and conceited search for knowledge that so often leads not to truth and enlightenment but to violence and death.

Furthermore, in an inversion of the theme of sacrifice in Greek tragedy, Santiago's sacrifice does not bring catharsis to the community who are unable either to understand or forget the event. True that, aware of the impending tragedy, the townspeople take up positions like an audience about to watch an execution: 'The people had stationed themselves on the square the way they did on parade days. They all saw him come out, and they all understood that now he knew they were going to kill him' (116). The spectacle reassures the audience of their own survival but reminds them also of their own mortality. To witness a death is of course not to experience it; the only death they, and we, can ever witness is not our own death but the death of another. The survivors therefore need to reconcile themselves to the fact that understanding death is something that will always be denied them.

8 MOTHERS AND DAUGHTERS

If in *One Hundred Years of Solitude* we witness men trying to counteract their fear of solitude by going out and making war, in *Chronicle of a Death Foretold* it is the women whose lives are marked and marred by solitude, a solitude that is the result of frustration and impotence in a social structure dictated by men. The narrator's mother, Luisa Santiago, ignoring her husband for the first time in her life, declares that men are 'Lowlifes . . . shitty animals that can't do anything that isn't something awful' (22) but in her attempt to stop their madness she is declared mad. Clotilde Armenta similarly tries to convince the Vicario brothers and the town officials to stop the murder but is repeatedly ignored: 'That day', she concludes, 'I realised just how alone we women are in the world!' (63).

Placida Linero, is the 'solitary mother' (6) locked in a loveless marriage of

---

[43] Luce Irigaray, 'Women, the Sacred and Money', *Paragraph*, 8, October 1986, 6–18.

convenience 'that hadn't had a single instant of happiness' (5) from which Santiago is the only child. We have a brief glimpse of the 'beautiful woman asleep' shortly before Santiago's murder, arousing the desire of his friend Cristo Bedayo as he passes through her bedroom in search for Santiago. Her own description of Santiago as 'the only man in my life' (5) hints at other illicit desires and frustrations. Twenty-seven years later, her solitude intensified, the narrator finds her in the exact same position in her hammock, her multiple desires and solitude seeking impossible solace in an addiction to chewing pepper cress seeds.

On the surface, other women in the story seem to enjoy a community based on gossip and their common distrust of men: the Vicario women in particular are 'predisposed to find hidden intentions in the designs of men' (32). The narrator's mother, without going out of the house, is able to keep a watchful eye over the town's activities and cast a seemingly fair judgment on characters and events: '[she] seemed to have secret threads of communication with the other people in town, especially those her age, and sometimes she surprised us with news that was ahead of time which she could only have known through powers of divination' (19). Angela also has girlfriends and confidantes who advise her how to ensure that her loss of virginity is not discovered by her husband.

However, although women form a separate community within the world of men, their community is not aimed at escaping from, changing, or demolishing the structures they find themselves born into, but is directed towards maintaining, or at best surviving, the patriarchal culture they are constrained by. Prudencia Cotes, Pablo Vicario's fiancée, treats the honour code with more reverence and faith than any men in the book: "I knew what they were to do', she told me, 'and I didn't only agree, I never would have married him if he hadn't done what a man should do!' [she] stood waiting in the kitchen until she saw them leave and she went on waiting for three years without a moment of discouragement until Pablo Vicario got out of jail and became her husband for life' (62–3).

The criticism levelled at men's machismo in the book, therefore, cannot fail but be directed at women's collusion with these values and therefore their participation in their own oppression. Pura Vicario hides her iron will behind a 'meek and somewhat afflicted look' (30) because, like Nelly in *Wuthering Heights*, perceiving herself as weak in a society run by men, she identifies with the strong and assimilates male ideology as her own. When Bayardo returns Angela to her as soiled goods, Pura Vicario directs her strength, both physical and moral, against, rather than in support of her daughter, hitting her with such rage that Angela thought she was going to kill her. Without recognizing it, Pura Vicario here follows a pattern whereby the mother reproduces in the daughter the same acceptance of the society that marginalizes them both.[44] In

---

[44] See Angela Carter, *The Sadeian Woman* (London: Virago, 1979), at 124: 'If the daughter is a mocking memory to the mother—"As I am so you once were"—then the mother is a horrid warning to her daughter—'As I am, so you will be', mother seeks to ensure the continuance of her own repression, and her hypocritical solicitude for the younger woman's moral, that is, sexual welfare masks a desire to reduce her daughter to the same state of contingent passivity she herself inhabits, a state honoured by custom and hedged by taboo.'

bringing up her daughter in her own image and her sons to be as different as possible from her, Pura Vicario perpetuates the same values in the next generation that are used to exile her daughter. The struggle faced by women like Angela, therefore, and the antagonism she must understand, and distance herself from, is not with men but with her mother.[45]

Angela breaks out of this cycle when she recognizes that her own mother is as much trapped by the patriarchal system as she is. When Pura Vicario smiles at Angela with her new glasses 'In that smile, for the first time since her birth, Angela Vicario saw her as she was, a poor woman devoted to the cult of her defects' (93). As Irigaray argues, mothers and daughters live as each other's images and women should seek an identity that is separate from being a mother, as well as independent of men's norms and expectations.[46] As Pura Vicario was the agent communicating patriarchy's myths to her daughters, Angela's understanding and acceptance of her mother's limitations enables her to separate herself both from her mother and from male rules. On that day Angela accedes to a subjectivity that is not a denial of the mother, nor acquiescence to her values, but a sympathetic understanding of her mother and the values that a patriarchal system projected onto her. The same day, we are told, Angela 'was reborn'. An event that significantly she marks by starting to write.

9   WOMAN AS LITERATURE

If the text, from beginning to end, is unable to uncover 'the truth' or satisfactorily explain the distinction between fact and fiction, history and literature, reality and fantasy, this is because, I suggest, at its core lies the unresolved enigma of femininity. Woman, the arch-simulator we encountered in the *Oresteia* reappears in her multiple guises and disguises in *Chronicle of a Death Foretold* endangering and frustrating the narrator's as well as the reader's efforts at 'mastering' her and declaring the text closed.

We know that while the murder is being committed, while male law is being asserted, another law is being affirmed, at another space and another time. The goddess presiding over this law is not reason but passion, not law but literature, not the 7.05 a.m. time of the murder but that of eternity. The narrator is not at the scene of the murder because, he tells us, he is with Maria Alejandrina Cervantes, whose name recalls the scene of literature and presents a challenge to male law and its attempt to deny and suppress literature. Maria's 'apostolic lap' (3) has been host to a whole generation of young men who lost their virginity to 'the quicksand of her tenderness' (78). While the other law, as I suggest in my closing chapter, has become a labyrinth,

---

[45] This argument is developed by Rosalind Coward, *Our Treacherous Hearts: Why Women Let Men Get their Way* (London: Faber & Faber, 1992).

[46] 'And the one doesn't stir without the other', *Signs*, 7(1), (1981), 60–7, trans. H.V.Wenzel.

keeping its doors hidden and confusing those who try to enter it, Maria Alejandrina keeps a 'house with open doors'; there they learn other laws, 'more that they should have learned, but especially that there's no place in life sadder than an empty bed.' (65). The presence of Maria Alejandrina reminds us that, as Irigaray suggests 'it was once otherwise, that there was an era in which it was the women who initiated love. At that time, woman was goddess and not servant, and she watched over the carnal and spiritual dimensions of love. In her, love and desire were indivisible'.[47] As Peter Goodrich has argued, this is 'a separate and superior law originating from and administered by women under the feminine sign of fate or justice, fortune or phronesis'.[48]

At Maria Alejandrina's kingdom there is play rather than action, sensuous abandon rather than guilt, confused rather than stable identities. Santiago, I would go further and suggest, is an ideal candidate for a scapegoat not because he deflowered Angela's virginity but for compounding the mystery that is woman rather than dissolving it, *like a man*. The narrator remembers him as a magician whose favourite trick is getting the mulatto girls to swap clothes 'so that they all ended up feeling different from themselves and like the ones they weren't. On a certain occasion, one of them found herself repeated in another with such exactness that she had a crying attack. 'I felt like I'd stepped out of the mirror,' she said' (66). It has already been suggested that Santiago's relationship with his mother is ambiguous and his relationship with the town madam also blurs the distinction between client and prostitute. He shares with Maria Alejandrina a deep affection unadulterated by the 'disorder of love' and she finds she cannot make love to his friend after his death because 'you smell of him'.

The mystery the narrator and townspeople who gather to talk repeatedly about Santiago's death are seeking, is therefore not the mystery of the crime but the mystery of woman's sexuality, the enigma of femininity. This mystery remains both unsolved and untamed. It lies beyond the means of scientific knowledge and positivistic methodologies, including, as we saw in the chapter on *Oedipus*, the attempts of male psychoanalysts. Angela continues to elude and frustrate the critics' attempt to 'capture' both her, her text, and her law. If, as male theorists like Lacan have concluded that woman does not exist, if, like Baudrillard they are forced to suggest that the feminine is always absent, and it 'is and always has been, somewhere else', then they also confess that this is 'the secret of her strength'.[49] It is also the reason why she poses a threat to the text of the law: as the unconscious, forgotten, or repressed face or icon that can never be present or appear in itself, it threatens, in Peter Goodrich's words, male law by reminding it that it 'was never one'.[50]

---

[47] *i love to you; Sketch for a Felicity Within History* (New York & London: Routledge, 1996), trans. Alison Martin, at 135.

[48] Peter Goodrich, *Oedipus Lex: Psychoanalysis, History, Law* (Los Angeles and London: University of California Press, 1995), at 147.

[49] Jean Baudrillard, *Seduction* (New York: St Martin's Press, 1990) [1979], trans. Brian Singer, at 6.

[50] Peter Goodrich, *Oedipus Lex, supra*, at 155–7.

10 HERSTORY: WRITING THE SELF

Angela is not the only woman to remain a mystery in the text but she inhabits the superior position of both knowing the identity of her first lover as well as rising above the 'open wound' her mother worked so hard to instil in her. Though the narrator describes her as having 'a helpless air and a poverty of spirit' (31), traces of her courage can be seen from the start, in her protests against being forced to marry the most eligible bachelor the town has ever seen, her distaste of arrogant men like Bayardo and of men, like Santiago, who are over-fascinated by money and, finally in her refusal to follow her girlfriends' instructions on how to deceive her husband in order to be able to display 'the stained sheet of honor' on the morning after. The narrator's mother again, Luisa Santiaga, 'was the only one who appreciated as an act of courage the fact that she had played out her marked cards to the final consequences' (41).

Angela's pronouncement of Santiago as her perpetrator, or, in the Spanish, 'her author' (101), follows the same tradition that perceives women as being written on or inscribed by the male pen and penis that we encountered in Shakespeare's *Measure for Measure*. But unlike her mother who forces the whole family to flee town after the 'disgrace', Angela is happy to tell the story to anyone who wants to listen without regrets, violence, or shame. Angela therefore rises above the 'aesthetics of silence' that patriarchal culture insists on for women. There seem to be two things, writes Barbara Johnson, that women are expected to be silent about: 'their pleasure and their violation. The work performed by the idealization of this silence is that *it helps culture not to be able to tell the difference between the two.*'[51] Angela resists her culture's expectations by not attempting to hide her 'violation' from Bayardo, and later by insisting on writing her desire whether Bayardo is willing or brave enough to read it or not. Although the narrator's description of her as waiting patiently by the window self-consciously evokes motifs from fairy tales like Sleeping Beauty, and from epic poetry like Homer's Penelope, unlike them, Angela does more than sleep, weep, or weave. She does not find it necessary to lie about her story and instead takes charge of it by writing. Though physically confined, she is able to write herself and discover herself as the only 'author' of her own life. If part of the content of those letters are confessions about her past—'the bitter truths that she had carried rotting in her heart ever since that ill-fated night' (95)— including about her illicit first affair, then Angela appropriates that past and thereby also writes her future.

If in reading we passively lose ourselves in the lives of others, identify with, or become others, even find, as Freud said, the plurality of lives we need, each time we write we actively create ourselves anew. In writing we become dispossessed or exiled

[51] Barbara Johnson, *The Feminist Difference: Literature, Psychoanalysis, Race and Gender* (London UK & Cambridge USA: 1998), at 137.

from ourselves, we can be one person or every person. Abandoning ourselves to the limitless blank space or page, we lose ourselves in an instant that becomes an eternity and become infinite and immortal. In Peter Goodrich's words, 'To write is in this sense the most powerful of ethical activities, it is both the construction of a space of possibility for the self and a positioning of the self within that space and in relation to the other. Writing inserts the self in history, in the domain of the other, and it is that relation of the self to writing which suffuses both law and the other genres of correspondence.' For women in particular writing is a 'movement beyond the self into politics and into law'.[52] For a woman to write about love and her own love story is a further movement towards independence: as Octavio Paz puts it, 'the history of love is inseparable from the history of the freedom of women'.[53] This ambition has been voiced by post-colonial women writers in particular: as Elena Poniatowska puts it, 'We write in Latin America to reclaim a space to discover ourselves in the presence of others, of human community—so that they may see us, so that they may love us—to form the vision of the world, to acquire some dimension—so they can't erase us so easily. We write so as not to disappear'.[54]

For Angela writing becomes not a substitute for living, but living itself. Significantly this writing takes place at night when, away from the dictates of the law of the father and the watchful eyes of its staunch upholder (her mother), she sits down to write. Writing, words, love is not an end in itself but a means towards the constitution of herself as separate and at the same time in relation to another person. Through writing, Angela 'became lucid, overbearing, mistress of her own free will . . . and she recognized no other authority than her own' (94). If in writing Angela seeks to be recognized by the other, to find in Bayardo's desire a recognition of herself, she appears to appreciate that Bayardo is, like herself, also divided and therefore her own desire or the lack that is desire, cannot be filled by the lack or desire of another. She therefore seeks no response, and his silence does not deter her. That she continues her soliloquy for 2000 letters over half her lifetime, is an acknowledgment not only of the fact that the other exceeds her and cannot reply either unconditionally or forever; more importantly it testifies to the fact that the other is an extension of herself. As Legendre puts it, 'the love letter does not seek a response, the lover does not await a letter . . . *lovers write themselves*. They are bound up in their letters.'[55] Like all writing, her writing is narcissistic: with very little knowledge of the real Bayardo, she has created a fantasm of a Bayardo who is an extension of the image she is creating, through writing, of herself.

---

[52] Peter Goodrich, 'Epistolary Justice: The Love Letter as Law', *Yale Journal of Law and Humanities*, Vol. 9(2), (1997), 245–95, at 273, 281.

[53] Octavio Paz, *The Double Flame: Love and Eroticism* (New York: Harvest, 1993), trans. Helen Lane, at 93.

[54] Bell Gale Chevigny, 'The Transformation of Privilege in the Work of Elena Poniatowska', *Latin American Literary Review*, Vol. 13, (1985); 49–62, quoted in Irvin Solomon, 'Latin American Women in Literature and Reality', *supra*, at 199.

[55] Legendre, 'Protocol of the Love Letter', in Peter Goodrich (ed.), *Law and the Unconscious: A Legendre Reader, supra*, at 82.

Bayardo, however, is 'insensible to her delirium; it was like writing to nobody' (95). If Angela is driven to pour her heart out, and tell her life story, Bayardo, in contrast, is at pains to reject the language of the emotions, of sentiment, and of tears. His abrupt ending of the marriage and disappearance without discussion or questions is at once aggressive and defensive: he is furious with Angela for not reflecting back to him his own exalted sense of self which in his schema is the proper function of a wife. It is also defensive in that he is protecting himself from becoming like the woman whose qualities he appreciates only in so far as they reflect back to him his own sense of fullness: 'If the love letter marks the threat or possibility of change or of becoming other, then for the masculine it represents the threat of self-abandonment, the threat of love, of becoming a little feminine, a little alive, a little mad'.[56]

Unlike Bayardo, Angela is not afraid to express her emotions and indeed 'The more letters she sent the more the coals of her fever burned'(94). Bayardo, who was noted for saying little even before his perceived humiliation, who built so many defences and walls around him that none of the townspeople could ever claim to have understood him, resists the space of intimacy offered by Angela's correspondence. Faced with her demanding, incessant, perhaps insatiable desires, he retreats into silence and, as we find out later, he not only did not write, but did not read, or even open Angela's torrent of letters. Forever true to his determination to keep his distance from women that, perhaps, he perceives as devouring, forever determined to limit his words as much as his emotions, he returns to Angela twenty-seven years later and cannot bring himself to say more than: 'Well, here I am' (96).

No writing, not even love letters can achieve an escape from loneliness. Angela's writing, however, unread and unreciprocated, enables her to express, understand, and survive her loneliness. The narrator in *Chronicle of a Death Foretold*, on the other hand, though purportedly having returned to piece together the broken mirror of memory, steadfastly ignores or refuses to address the possible content of these letters. Like generations of historiographers, as Peter Goodrich has argued, he chooses to ignore 'the unconscious or repressed domain of positive or secular law'. This omission comes at a high price: 'to read those love letters, to recoup that history, not as reality but as fantasm, not as truth but as a possibility, opens up an ethical-political space— perhaps a space of the feminine—within the public sphere . . . That space or forgotten domain is one of ethics and not of rules, of love and of love's law'.[57] Angela remains guardian of this ethics and this law, a 'truth' that continues to elude narrator, writer, and countless readers.

---

[56] Peter Goodrich, 'Epistolary Justice: The Love Letter as Law' *supra*, at 281.
[57] *ibid.*, at 294.

11 DEATH AND CLOSURE

Telling and retelling tales about the past is not, as historians like Hayden White and Dominic La Capra have argued, about finding the 'truth' of that past. At most, if not repetition, such re-tellings are entertainment, affording the aesthetic pleasure derived from a story well told. By couching the trauma of Santiago's murder in language, retelling is also a form of therapy, albeit temporary, and albeit, like any analysis, interminable. For neither the narrator nor the witnesses he calls upon can bear the burden of what they witnessed. In the same way, throughout the narrative, the reader, rather than deriving satisfaction from 'mastering' the text, and imposing a meaning on it, is left frustrated and anxious. The desires that prompted the searching, writing, and reading remain unappeased: for 'there would be no archive desire', as Derrida says, 'without the possibility of a forgetfulness . . . and no archive fever without the threat of the death drive, the aggression and destruction drive'.[58]

In *Chronicle of a Death Foretold* readerly satisfaction, deferred and postponed during the circuitous textual excitation, reaches erotic *jouissance* in the only possible climax: death. For Freud, the human craving for immortality, faced with the fear of and inevitability of death, leads us to suspend, ignore, or eradicate our knowledge of its inescapability from our lives. Although representations of death abound in both legal and literary narratives, they are in effect displacements: our fear of our own death is negotiated through our representation of the death of another. The other's death, while confirming our mortality, confirms simultaneously our successful survival of the other: '[o]ur own death is indeed unimaginable, and whenever we make the attempt to imagine it we can perceive that we really survive as spectators. Hence the psychoanalytic school could venture on the assertion that at bottom no one believes in his own death, or to put the same thing in another way, in the unconscious everyone of us is convinced of his own immortality'.[59]

In *Chronicle of a Death Foretold* death is certainly understood as inevitable: it is announced, expected, foreseen. But its 'meaning' eludes the narrator, the towns-people, and, ultimately, the reader. The narrator embarks on a process of detection for the 'truth' about Santiago's death, in the hope of deciphering its causes and of fixing it with a meaning. He finds, however, that the tragedy is not only open to a plurality of meanings but resists meaning altogether. Neither the characters nor their motivations nor their stories are complete, unified, or continuous. The ending does not convey narrative closure or resolution but catapults us violently back to the beginning. The trial narrative also tries to give an appearance of causality, significance, order, and closure. The judicial process in this story as with every story the law attempts to

---

[58] Jacques Derrida, *Archive Fever: A Freudian Impression* (Chicago and London: Chicago University Press, 1995), trans. Eric Prenowitz, at 19.

[59] 'Thoughts for the Times on War and Death', in *The Major Works of Sigmund Freud* (Chicago: Chicago University Press, 1952), at 761.

adjudicate, aims to be the 'author', the origin, the source of meaning, just as Angela claimed Santiago was her 'author'. But the text undermines and ridicules this pretension. The death of Angela's 'author' leaves a gap that others try to fill with their authority but their narratives neither explain it nor console the survivors: the town continues to experience the event as 'an open wound'.

The language of religion that is often used to ascribe meaning to death is also undermined by the text where the religious leaders are almost complicitous in the massacre. Does the language of poetry succeed where legal and religious language fail? Poetry aims to speak death through metaphors but metaphors also defer rather than confer meaning. The story cannot be told, the cause cannot be found, because the community, and the reader, would need to admit their collective guilt and complicity in perpetuating a system that turns women into objects of exchange to be written on by desiring men. Angela alone, unlike the other people in the town, who continue living and reliving Santiago's death, is 'reborn' by losing herself and creating herself anew in writing. In the same fashion that Angela writes herself, readers may *read themselves* outside the dictates of a masculine politics of closure and death. Significantly Angela's writing like Ariadne's in my closing chapter, eschews the masculine discourse of death in favour of writing on love, continuity, and eternity. For no language is adequate for talking about death. Once the climax of death is reached, words run out. Literally.

9

LANGUAGE, ETHICS, AND THE IMAGINATION IN TONI MORRISON'S *BELOVED*[1]

> *i is a long memoried woman.*
> *I have crossed an ocean*
> *I have lost my tongue.*
> *From the root of the old one*
> *a new one has sprung.*
>   Grace Nichols

1 THE SPECTRE OF POSTMODERNITY

For critics of postmodernism, the war on grand narratives, the claim that we cannot get outside our own history and make judgements, the denial of the possibility of objective truth outside the constraints of language, and the lack of faith in historical progress raises the spectre of nihilism and passivity. If no one system reveals the entire truth but, at most, *a* perspective, if power is everywhere rather than in the hands of one class, if there is no pattern to history, if the present is no better or worse than the past, then why try to resist or change existing institutions? In particular, if the notion of one truth is neither possible nor desirable how does one identify and remedy past and present injustices? Is it possible to develop principles of justice in a world where there is no context-free standard of truth? The teachings of neo-pragmatists like Rorty[2] and neo-conservatives like Bell[3] have not helped by appearing to invite their readers to a passive acquiescence in the status quo and an acceptance of the values of

---

[1] Toni Morrison, *Beloved* (London: Picador, 1988), all page references in the text are to this edition.
[2] Richard Rorty, *Consequences of Pragmatism* (Minneapolis: University of Minnesota Press, 1982). Similar disquiet has been expressed concerning Stanley Fish's *Doing What Comes Naturally: Change, Rhetoric and the Practice of Theory in Literary and Legal Studies* (Oxford: Clarendon Press, 1989) and *There's No Such Thing as Free Speech and It's a Good Thing Too* (New York and Oxford: Oxford University Press, 1994) where we appear to be left with making only one point: that there is no point.
[3] Daniel Bell, *The Cultural Contradictions of Capitalism* (London: Heinemann, 1976).

present day American society.[4] As Christopher Norris further warns, Jean Baudrillard's fusion of the real and the imaginary ignores that 'for many reality remains resistant and harsh: they need to sink their teeth into some quite real bread before abandoning themselves to munching images'.[5] For those with a clear political programme and an agenda, such injunctions are anathema: as Catherine MacKinnon impatiently puts it, 'epistemologically speaking, women know the male world is out there because it hits them in the face . . . It has all the indeterminacy of a bridge abutment hit at sixty miles an hour'.[6]

While at times postmodernity seems to have abandoned the possibility of both theory and practice, changes in the conception and possibility of theory can and have led to the rethinking, not the abandonment, of political goals and methods. To question the idea that history has a cause or goal or that it represents evolution and progress, raises doubts about the legitimacy of the present. This is especially the case if one suspects, with Foucault, that the Enlightenment's ideal of Order is in fact best secured in a prison and its realization was accompanied by the suppression of other views, other races, other nations, and other genders. Schools, churches, hospitals, factories, and of course courts and judges, participated in this suppression by enabling the production of the 'normal' individual. The 'human' sciences in particular asserted control over the individual's soul by defining the 'normal' individual in distinction to the insane and the deviant. For Foucault, however, Unity and Sameness are myths and claims to naturalness a way of justifying the disciplining of those who deviate from the norm. They are part, therefore, of the struggle not for truth and freedom but for power, discipline, and domination of the human subject.[7]

On the theoretical level, the view that what gets taken as truth and meaning is historically contingent means that the logic by which the western system of thought and western political and social institutions maintain their force come under question. Reason itself is a specific historical form and like everything else, is not self-validating; its claim to legitimacy must therefore be explained. This is not, as Norris explains, to repudiate the Kantian project but to push it to its limits by demanding a reason for reasonableness itself and forcing us to rethink old premises.[8] The point is that the modernist desire for closure led to settlements rather than resolutions, constructions rather than facts, provisional rather than final truths. Postmodernity is not therefore destructive but, by demolishing false certainties, pretensions, and unjustified illusions about truth, forces us to face the contingency of the criteria we use with

---

[4] 'The political consequence of such a relativism can only be quietism': Tony Bennett, *Outside Literature* (London: Routledge, 1991), at 55. See further, Christopher Norris, *What's Wrong With Postmodernism: Critical Theory and the Ends of Philosophy* (London: Harvester Wheatsheaf, 1990) and *Uncritical Theory: Postmodernism, Intellectuals and the Gulf War* (London: Lawrence & Wishart, 1992).

[5] Christopher Norris, *Uncritical Theory, supra* at 155.

[6] Catherine MacKinnon, *Toward a Feminist Theory of the State* (Cambridge, Mass.: Harvard University Press, 1989), at 123.

[7] Especially Michel Foucault, *Discipline and Punish: The Birth of the Prison*, trans. Alan Sheridan (London: Allen Lane, 1977), 1979.

[8] Christopher Norris, *Derrida* (London: Fontana, 1987), at 160.

which to evaluate our world. This 'site-clearing operation',[9] by revealing hidden assumptions in our philosophical, ethical, juridical, and political structures leads to closer attention to detail, context, and perspective. This does not need to mean chaos, but creativity.

On the political level, aims and goals also change: the concern is no longer with abstractions, such as 'the masses', but with the individual; not with a single determinant, such as the economy, but with multiple processes and factors; not with the objective, the institutional, and the universal but with the subjective, the heterogeneous, the particular, and the relative. Not with grand narratives, revolutions, global processes, and large scale political change but with micro-narratives, local, diffused, and neglected struggles. Not with one ultimate, unifying, and dominant meaning and the hope for a single ordered community but with micro-politics, multiple voices, and mini-communities.[10]

2 POST-FOUNDATIONAL ETHICS

In modernist thinking, justice was defined in terms of universal laws emanating from the individual; the search for equality or symmetry was conducted by those in power who placed themselves in the position of enunciator of the universal prescription. As Douzinas and Warrington have argued, in practice this often meant absolute *injustice*: to interpret the other in one's own terms meant suppressing what is different or alien to oneself.[11] Such homogeneity and uniformity means assuming the position of the originator of the Kantian categorical imperative, denying the plurality of values, and reducing everyone, irrespective of race, sex, gender, or class, into one supposedly neutral and universal entity. Far from being ethical, this search prevents us from appreciating the other in his/her own terms: the other, as Levinas argued, is singular, unique, and cannot be reduced to our own picture of her nor can we expect her to subscribe to our rules. Acting ethically therefore does not mean acting in accordance with a universal principle but responding to the needs and demands of the other in her own uniqueness and singularity. Ethics for Levinas starts from an acceptance not of symmetry, reciprocity, or commonality but of irreducible otherness: 'Intersubjective relation is a non-symmetrical relation. In this sense I am responsible for the other without waiting for reciprocity, were I to die for it. Reciprocity is *his* affair . . . I am responsible for a total responsibility.'[12]

---

[9] Zigmunt Bauman, *Intimations of Postmodernity* (London: Routledge, 1992), at ix.

[10] See, for example, Anthony Carty, (ed.), *Postmodern Law* (Edinburgh: Edinburgh University Press, 1990).

[11] Costas Douzinas and Ronnie Warrington, *Justice Miscarried: Ethics, Aesthetics and the Law* (Hemel Hempstead: Harvester Wheatsheaf, 1994).

[12] Emmanuel Levinas, *Ethics and Infinity: Conversations with Philippe Nemo* (Pittsburgh, Pa.: Duquesne University Press, 1985), trans. Richard Cohen, at 98–9.

Levinas's ethics of alterity starts with the other 'prior to any act'[13] and refuses to reduce the other to the same. Against the claims of moral philosophy, this demand does not depend on universal reason or general law but on the concrete empirical encounter with the other in all his or her nudity. The other, as Douzinas and Warrington argue, comes first in any ethical system and is the condition of existence of language, self, and law; the demand that we consider her precedes not only legal rules but also consideration of our own self-preservation. Our desire for justice, they suggest, also arises from our own lack and desire for the other: justice is 'the fantasiacal screen that philosophers, poets and lawyers have erected to shield themselves from the question of the desire of the other'.[14] Conversely our tragedy is that we can never know fully the other: we can never put ourselves in her place, experience her experiences, understand her in her concrete particularity, in those unique, unrepeatable situations. We may touch but we cannot enter her without violence. The challenge is to try to touch her without compromising her, without inflicting on her the violence and pain of our desire. Our inability to be the other person and our essential separateness from the other, need not mean despair. Instead it can be a source of delight at the other's otherness and an opportunity for negotiating our own sense of self: for the attempt to touch the other may expose and explode our own secure sense of identity.

Justice, as Douzinas and Warrington conclude, will always remain an aporia: contingent, unpredictable, and therefore unlegislatable. One way of negotiating this impasse of justice and our desire for the other is to acknowledge that being just involves an incessant movement between the general rule and the specific case. Justice is not a set of universal and unchanging principles but a variety of criteria which are local, practical, momentary, infinitely open, and contingent. At the same time, by respecting the other as a full person and the unique historical situation in which she is heard, the same criteria are more concrete and less anonymous than modernist rules and give justice a face, a body, a gender, and a place. For Douzinas and Warrington this challenge and this ethical duty can be negotiated by keeping 'the tales in motion and circulation, keep interchanging narrators, narratees and narrated, keep making the judge defendant and the defendant judge'.[15] One way, therefore, of bearing witness, as Lyotard calls it, to the différend of uttering the unutterable is to listen to the other's stories, in her own words, rather than assuming the power of telling her stories and of legislating on her behalf. Lyotard rejects the idea of justice as sameness and consensus and gives prominence to micro-narratives in which one listens to, rather than judges, the other. The task is not easy: it involves finding new genres, new languages, and new idioms that express, rather than absorb and co-opt the other's difference: 'A lot of searching must be done to find new rules

---

[13] Sean Hand, (ed.), *The Levinas Reader* (Oxford: Basil Blackwell, 1989), at 290.

[14] *Justice Miscarried, supra*, at 80.

[15] Costas Douzinas and Ronnie Warrington with Shaun McVeigh, *Postmodern Jurisprudence: The Law of Text in the Texts of Law* (London and New York: Routledge, 1991), at 110.

for forming and linking phrases that are able to express the différend disclosed by the feeling, unless one wants this différend to be smothered right away in a litigation and for the alarm sounded by the feeling to have been useless. What is at stake in a literature, in a philosophy, in a politics perhaps is to bear witness to différends by finding idioms for them.'[16] This task, he suggests, may be performed by the artist who does not feel herself bound by pre-established rules, criteria of judgement, and familiar categories.[17]

Literature and the imagination in general may be one way out of the difficulty of reaching out towards the other without invading or appropriating her. Morrison certainly shares this hope: 'Imagining', she says, 'is not merely looking or looking at; nor is it taking oneself intact into the other. It is, for the purposes of the work, becoming. . . . The ability of writers to imagine what is not the self, to familiarize the strange and mystify the familiar is the test of their power.'[18] The hope is that literature and the imagination in general may redeem us from our self-enclosures by enabling us to see and listen to the other. Although literature cannot pretend to remedy injustices to the other on the everyday, material level, its capacity to help us appreciate, understand, and empathize with what is not ourselves is a starting point to other forms of legislation.

The ethical task of communicating, conveying, or reaching towards the other through literature is shared by both writer and reader: as Cixous puts it, 'reading is a limitless journey'[19] and the reader's imagination and willingness to project and empathize with the other is integral to this process. Rather than affirming one's stability or autonomy, the experience of reading can ideally lead to the dissolution of the self into what is new and different from the self.

3   APPROPRIATING LANGUAGE

The fashioning of the self in relation to the other and our embrace of multiplicity can only ever take place in language. The search for a new language is therefore inseparable from the search for new principles of justice in which there is no context-free standard of truth. As identity is constituted in language, language and its unmaking can make, unmake, and remake identities. Although the end of colonialism and the institution of slavery meant, in legal terms, a change of sovereignty, this did not mean the end of exploitation or effective self-determination. For that, the myth of white superiority and the pervasive influence of European languages, literature, and culture

---

[16] Jean-Francois Lyotard, *The Différend: Phrases in Dispute*, trans. G. Van Den Abbeele (Manchester: Manchester University Press, 1983), at 13.

[17] Jean-Francois Lyotard, *The Postmodern Condition: A Report on Knowledge*, trans. Geoffrey Bennington and Brian Massoumi, (Minneapolis, Minn.: University of Minnesota Press, 1984), at 81.

[18] *Playing in the Dark: Whiteness and the Literary Imagination* (London: Picador 1993), at 4, 15.

[19] Susan Sellers (ed.), *The Hélène Cixous Reader* (London and New York: Routledge, 1994), at 172.

had to be negotiated and contested. It is supremacy over the latter that has been more difficult to dislodge and to which post-colonial writers and critics have turned their attention in recent years. On the one hand colonial writing assumed a universalist mantle, purporting to talk for an undifferentiated humanity and time; on the other colonial critics followed this cue, presenting the texts and the values they found therein as unchanging and universal.

A major task for post-colonial writers and critics has therefore been to challenge the view of liberal humanist critics that literature reflects and celebrates timeless values irrespective of time, place, colour, or culture. Only once such claims were exposed as serving the interests of a white middle class rather than humanity as a whole could the colonized begin to find their own voice and start reclaiming their past.[20] Not only did western writers often assume the authority to speak on behalf of all of us, they also bestowed on the other the qualities they did not choose to acknowledge or repressed in themselves.[21] So, where the white European was intelligent, the other was emotional, where the European was civilized, the other was savage, where the European was good and saved, the other was evil and lost. In Camus's *The Outsider*, as we have seen, the Arab is featured as sensual, lazy, exotic, and, unlike the European characters, homogeneous and lacking in differentiation. The European assumption of the right to speak for, name, and define the other meant again that knowledge was a major means of exercising domination. One major consequence of post-colonial writing and criticism has been to put the notion of 'race' into quotation marks, that is, as Barbara Johnson argues, to extract it from the confines of essentialist and biologistic determinism, and display its status as a construct of historical, political, and social conditions.[22] To achieve that they had to wrestle with a language that had been used to repress rather than express difference.

For black writers, as for feminists, language, in law or in literature, is a site of struggle since slavery and the colonial process began and was instituted in language. The emblem of the English book, says Homi Bhabba, was one of the most important of the 'signs taken for wonders' by which the colonizer controlled the imagination of the colonized.[23] While military, economic, and legal power enabled the colonizer to exercise control and write on the body of the colonized, the control and reification of language enhanced that control by writing the values of the colonizer on the soul of the colonized.[24] Or, as the black slaves find out in *Beloved*, not only their labour and

---

[20] See especially Frantz Fanon, *The Wretched of the Earth* (London: Penguin, 1967) [1961], trans. Constance Farrington.

[21] See especially Edward W. Said, *Orientalism: Western Conceptions of the Orient* (London: Routledge, 1978) and *Culture and Imperialism* (London: Vintage, 1993).

[22] *The Feminist Difference: Literature, Psychoanalysis, Race and Gender* (London, UK and Cambridge, USA: Harvard University Press, 1998), at 11.

[23] 'Signs Taken for Wonders: Questions of Ambivalence and Authority Under a Tree Outside Delhi, May 1817', *Critical Inquiry* 12(1), (1985), 144–65.

[24] Nguigi Wa Thiongo, *Decolonizing the Mind: The Politics of Language in African Literature* (London: James Currey, 1981).

their bodies but also the meaning, the 'definitions' of what and who they are 'belong to the definers, not the defined' (190).

Since these values are inscribed and constituted in language, in order to express new values and new subjectivities, we need not only new laws but a new language, or as Morrison puts it, we must 'break the back of words': 'The most valuable point of entry into the question of cultural (or racial) distinction, the one most fraught, is its language—its unpoliced, seditious, confrontational, manipulative, inventive, disruptive, masked and unmasking language'.[25] Many black writers, especially women writers are cautious about using the master's language to bring down the master's house. For Audrey Lord, 'the master's tools will never bring down the master's house. They may allow us temporarily to beat him at his own game but they will never enable us to bring about genuine change'.[26] And Jamaica Kincaid worries 'that the only language I have in which to speak of this crime is the language of the criminal who committed the crime. And what can that really mean? For the language of the criminal can contain only the goodness of the criminal's deed.'[27]

Homi Bhabba, however, disputes the view that power and discourse are possessed entirely by the colonizer. Hegemonic discourse, as he argues, is also ambivalent, contradictory, and polysemic, and therefore outsiders can invade it, reopen its gaps, exploit its ambiguities and thereby challenge, unsettle, and subvert their authority.[28] The dilemma of using an inherited language, the double sense of belonging and estrangement or 'hybridity', as Bhabba calls it, need not be debilitating but instead an occasion for growth: it is in the very dynamics of that 'wrestling contradiction of being white in mind and black in body',[29] in the dichotomy between the colonized's simultaneous rejection of and reliance on the colonizer's culture for her identity and definition, as well as on the native's attraction to and fear of white culture, that new genres may be developed and new voices can be heard. The most beautiful of such voices, as my discussion of Toni Morrison below argues, rather than purporting to represent a universal set of values and beliefs, are at home with change, diversity, and difference. And rather than rely on imaginary resolutions that efface conflicts and contradictions, they aim to deal with the concrete particularity of the other in her unique and unrepeatable situation.

---

[25] 'Unspeakable Things Unspoken: The Afro-American Presence in American Literature', in Harold Bloom (ed.), *Modern Critical Views: Toni Morrison* (New York: Chelsea House, 1990), at 210.

[26] 'The Master's Tools Will Never Dismantle the Master's House' in Cherrie Moraga and Gloria Anzaldua (eds.), *This Bridge Called My Back: Writings by Radical Women of Color* (Latham, New York: Kitchen Table Press, 1983), at 99.

[27] *A Small Place* (London: Virago, 1988), at 13.

[28] 'The Commitment to Theory', *New Formations*, 5 (1988), 5–23.

[29] Derek Walcott, 'What the Twilight Says: An Overture' in *Dream on Monkey Mountain and Other Plays* (London, 1972), at 12. See also Abdul Jan Mohammed, *Manichean Aesthetics: The Politics of Literature in Colonial Africa* (Amherst, Mass.: University of Massachusetts Press, 1983).

4 SETHE'S, MARGARET'S, OR TONI'S STORY

Terms such as narrative, story, history, fiction, reality have been frequently used in this story/history/fiction/narrative of law and literature. These terms, as pointed out in other parts of this book, are ambiguous, open-ended, and often tautologous. Thus the *Concise Oxford Dictionary* defines *story* as 'an account of imaginary or past events; a narrative'; *narrative* as 'a spoken or written account of connected events in order of happening' and *fiction* as 'an invented idea or statement or narrative'. It is part of the argument of this chapter and indeed of this book, that the distinctions between 'fiction', 'story', 'narrative', and 'reality' are contingent rather than fixed. Morrison's *Beloved* like Márquez' *Chronicle of a Death Chronicle*, illustrates this blurring of definitional boundaries by narrating a story and creating a fiction inspired by real past events. The effect is that it is no longer possible to disentangle 'real' from 'fictitious' events not only because of Morrison's intervention but because the so-called real events surrounding Margaret Garner's story were already mediated by fiction: the law's and white journalists' attempt to write the story could only be couched in terms that the law and the papers' readership could understand and explain. The story was also far from complete: in newspaper accounts it 'ends' when the law pronounced its guilty verdict, beyond which there is more conjecture and rumours. In these circumstances Morrison attempts to retell the story and glimpse a truth that would otherwise remain hidden and lost. Her ambition is that literature and the imagination may help redeem us from at least some narrative gaps, silent or silenced witnesses, and inappropriate or inadequate reports.

In discussing *Beloved* I focus on themes that are central to my Law and Literature project: Morrison's deconstruction of received notions of truth, knowledge, history, the self, motherhood, and the family; how her deconstruction of received knowledges is used to bear witness to the other, in this case the mother who kills her children. Above all, how Morrison breaks language, using 'a combination of contempt and respect'[30] for it, in order to voice the unutterable. As the language at her disposal is the language of the master, of the criminal who committed the crime, Morrison searches for a new language, 'the right combination, the key, the code, the sound that broke the back of words. Building voice upon voice until [she finds] it, and when [she does] it is a wave of sound wide enough to sound deep water and knock the pods off chestnut trees' (261).

Beloved tells the story of a young woman, Sethe, who escaped slavery and has, for the last eighteen years, been living with her daughter Denver and the ghost of Sethe's dead daughter Beloved, at a house referred to as 124. Sethe's life is absorbed in the serious work of 'beating back the past' (73): 'Her brain was not interested in the future. Loaded with the past and hungry for more, it left her no room to imagine, let

---

[30] Danille Taylor-Guthrie (ed.), *Conversations with Toni Morrison* (Jackson, Miss.: University of Mississippi Press, 1994), at 187; hereafter referred to as *Conversations*.

alone plan for, the next day' (70). 'The one set of plans she had made—getting away from Sweet Home—went awry so completely she never dared life by making more' (38). Instead 'the future is a matter of keeping the past at bay' (43) of 'dis-remember[ing] everything' (118), or of 'remember[ing] as close to nothing as was safe' (6) while '[rinsing] the rest out of her mind' (119). The past is revealed only gradually, and in fragments, with the arrival of Paul D, another former slave at Sweet Home.

Like all patients suffering from traumatic neurosis, Sethe and Paul D are pre-occupied not with the traumatic events themselves but with *not* remembering, an effort that attests to their inability to forget.[31] Morrison portrays the characters' con-stant oscillation between wanting to forget and needing to remember; Sethe's mother-in-law Baby Suggs urges her to leave the past behind: 'Lay em down Sethe. Sword and shield . . . Don't study war no more. Lay all that mess down' (86). But the past will not go away; like anything repressed, it is a part of them, at first through the presence of the baby ghost which is spiteful, venomous, shattering mirrors, and 'raising hell from the other side' (5). The arrival of Paul D drives the spirit away only to be supplanted by a young woman called Beloved who appears to be a reincarnation of Sethe's dead daughter. The presence of the past in the form of Beloved, whether as a ghost or embodied spirit throughout the narrative is a reminder that 'nothing ever dies' (36), and that time, rather than conveniently compartmentalized into past, present, and future, is unrelentingly one: not linear and progressive but obstinately and always present. Neither remembering nor forgetting is therefore ever complete. They vie for repetition, expansion, contraction, and any seeming relaxation of the process is temporary and illusory.

Sethe finds rememorying painful since '[a]nything dead coming back to life hurts' (35). Paul D's presence, however, makes it bearable because the past 'was his as well—to tell, to refine and tell again' (99). Though both Sethe and Paul D prefer not to remember, Paul D keeping his memories in 'a tobacco tin buried in his chest where a red heart used to be' (72–3), when they start remembering, above all when they start *sharing* their memories, the healing process begins. Through their 'rememorying', we learn of Sethe's and the other slaves' treatment at Sweet Home (which 'wasn't sweet and it sure wasn't home' (14)), the white boys' theft of her milk, her attempt to escape while pregnant and brutally beaten, and her discovery a few weeks later by the 'men without skin' (210). We learn of Sethe's mother 'throwing away' her children who were the product of rapes by her white masters, we learn how 'they buttered Halle's face; gave Paul D iron to eat; crisped Sixo; hanged her own mother' (188). We learn how those slaves 'who hadn't run off or been hanged, got rented out, loaned out, brought back, stored up, mortgaged, won, stolen or seized' (23). The most horrific revelation, however, the one around which the narrative circles and repeats in

---

[31] 'Beyond the Pleasure Principle', in *The Major Works of Sigmund Freud* (Chicago, Ill.: Chicago University Press, 1952), at 641: 'I am not aware that the patients suffering from traumatic neuroses are much occupied in waking life with the recollection of what happened to them. They, perhaps, strive rather not to think of it'.

fits and starts but can never fully tell, is Sethe's murder of her two-year-old 'crawling already?' baby Beloved in a desperate attempt to prevent her children's return to slavery.

Important as remembering is for Sethe's negotiation with her past, this collective remembering, Morrison suggests, is also a responsibility owed not only to the self but to one's disremembered ancestors and to one's community, past, present, and future. The novel is based on the true story of Margaret Garner who in 1851 killed her child and attempted to kill herself rather than return to slavery. As with Sethe, the price of young women slaves was often greater than the men's because they were 'Property that reproduced itself without cost' (228). Margaret Garner, as Morrison tells it, became a cause célèbre for the abolitionists who argued that she should be tried for murder. That would have assumed that she was responsible for her own actions as well as for her children as legally a slave woman and her children were the property of her slaveowner. But in the subsequent trial the abolitionists were unsuccessful and she was tried for her 'real' crime, running away, and was convicted, imprisoned, and subsequently returned to the slaveowner.[32]

Consulting the law report on the case is one method of seeking knowledge on slavery in general and the circumstances of Margaret Garner in particular. That this knowledge, however, can only be partial, as we saw in *Chronicle of a Death Foretold* is underlined further by the fact that African Americans took no part in the writing of so-called 'official' historical and legal records. Indeed under the terms of the Fugitive Slave Law 1850 fugitives could not testify in their own defence.[33] The narratives written by slaves from which Morrison draws for the work, were also ridden with gaps and silences, deliberately excluding experiences that were too terrible to relate or would have been unpalatable to the white readers those narratives aimed to reach. Above all, those narratives cannot give access to the 'interior life' of the slaves; if our interest, like Morrison's, is not only in the institution of slavery but 'about those *anonymous* people called slaves'[34] the story has to be told or supplemented, by other means. The means favoured by Morrison, as by this book, is the imagination.

---

[32] This is the account given by Morrison in an interview in 1989; *Conversations, supra* at 251. In an earlier interview (1985) Morrison says 'They put her in jail for a little while and I'm not even sure what the denouement is of her story'. *Conversations, supra*, at 207.

[33] Newspaper accounts of the trial are investigated by Cynthia Griffin Wolff who points out that Margaret Garner was allowed a limited right to speak briefly on behalf of her children but again not in her own defence. Cynthia Griffin Wolff follows the trial until Margaret Garner's conviction and the court's order that the fugitives be returned to their owner. Although a requisition was made in Ohio for Margaret Garner her master refused to sell her into freedom and it is not known what happened to her after being returned to slavery: '"Margaret Garner": A Cincinatti Story', *Massachusetts Review*, 32 (1991), 417–40.

[34] *Conversations*, at 257.

5 OTHER KNOWLEDGES, OTHER HISTORIES

Morrison takes the story of Margaret Garner as her starting point and wrote *Beloved* to bear witness to a history that is unrecorded, untaught, and artistically to bury those 'unburied or, at least unceremoniously buried'.[35] This is doubly crucial for black women whose stories had not been told either by the colonizers, or by the slave narratives whose focus was often the journey from slavehood to manhood as much as the journey from slavehood to freedom.[36] Since historical records cannot give Morrison access to the internal life of the slaves, their memory can only be evoked through the imagination and just as importantly by employing a different language.

As the outsider within American culture, Morrison inhabits what Bhabba calls a hybrid space which gives her the freedom to appropriate and repudiate the master's tongue, use it and subvert it at the same time. Among the first things to be deconstructed are the notions of truth and knowledge as understood by the west since the Enlightenment. Following Foucault, Gayatri Spivak describes how imperialism created a 'whole set of knowledges that have been disqualified as inadequate to their task or insufficiently elaborated: naive knowledges, located low down on the hierarchy, beneath the required level of cognition or scientificity'.[37] Morrison aims to recover these subjugated knowledges by redefining what counts as history and interrogating totalized narratives that silence all but the master voices. The problem for Morrison as for other post-colonial writers, is that the same masters sought to deny the validity of their perceptions of the world: as García Márquez put it, 'The interpretation of our reality through patterns not our own serves only to make us ever more unknown, ever less free, ever more solitary'.[38] The challenge is to reclaim those structures and alternative ways of knowing things, knowledges that were 'discredited only because Black people were discredited'.[39]

The use of dreams, superstition, myth, and the supernatural in general have attracted the label 'magic realism', a term that itself relies on distinctions already drawn by western philosophy between knowledges that are common sense or 'natural' (read obvious, true, and thereby superior) and others as 'supernatural' (read fictitious, false, and thereby inferior). More than a stylistic technique, the strategy is political in that it questions these distinctions and explores and explodes the interests involved in

---

[35] *Ibid.*, at 209.

[36] See Valerie Smith, *Self-Discovery and Authority in Afro-American Narrative* (Cambridge, Mass.: Harvard University Press, 1987), at 34; also Carole Boyce Davies, *Black Women, Writing and Identity: Migrations of the Subject* (London: Routledge, 1994).

[37] Gayatri Chakravorti Spivak, 'Can the Subaltern Speak? Speculations on Widow Sacrificing', *Wedge* 7/8 (Winter/Spring), 120–30, quoting Michel Foucault, *Power/Knowledge: Selected Interviews and Other Writings 1972–77* (New York: Pantheon, 1980), at 82.

[38] 'The Solitude of Latin America: Nobel Lecture, 1982' in Julio Ortego (ed.), *Gabriel García Márquez and the Powers of Fiction*, (Austin, Tex.: University of Texas Press, 1988), at 89.

[39] 'Rootedness: the Ancestor as Foundation' in Mari Evans (ed), *Black Women Writers (1950–1980): A Critical Evaluation* (Garden City, NY: Doubleday, 1984), at 342.

maintaining the separation. In the hands of feminist and post-colonial writers in particular, magic realism can authorize a place for the invisible that was excluded by 'white male authors who decided that whatever cannot be controlled does not exist'.[40]

For Sethe and other characters in the book the existence of the ghost needs no explanation or justification: Sethe 'took it for granted—like a sudden change in the weather' (37) and Paul D feels its presence the instant he steps through the door. Baby Suggs rejects the suggestion of moving because 'What'd be the point? . . . Not a house in the country ain't packed to its rafters with some dead negro's grief' (5). In this context, the appearance of Sethe's dead daughter Beloved at her doorstep challenges our perceptions of what is real and what denigrated as the product of the imagination. Critics, though in agreement as to Beloved's symbolic status, (in particular of the 60 million 'disremembered and unaccounted for' (274) who died in the Middle Passage and whom Morrison dedicates the book to), are unsure about *how* she symbolizes. If she is a ghost, she is, unlike Cathy's ghost in *Wuthering Heights* 'an embodied spirit', a trait which aligns her more to African traditional belief than to motifs derived from Euro-American gothic.[41]

For me Beloved is less a ghost than a dream: the description of Beloved's appearance is strongly reminiscent of Borges' 'The Circular Ruins' where a man arrives at a ruined temple with the specific aim of 'dreaming' another man.[42] Just as 'No one saw him disembark in the unanimous night, no one saw the bamboo canoe sinking into the sacred mud', in Morrison's text 'A fully dressed woman walked out of the water . . . Nobody saw her emerge or came accidentally by [or go] past a giant temple of boxwood' (50). In Borges' tale the old man discovers, to his astonishment and horror, that his dream of dreaming a man had already been dreamed by someone who dreamed him. Is Beloved, I wonder, the creation of Sethe's dream, of the same Sethe who hopes that 'if she'd only come, I could make it clear to her' (4)? Is Sethe's dream of explaining herself to the daughter she killed also a delusion, a way of depriving herself 'having any dreams of her own at all'(20)?

Just as in my reading of Borges dreams have the capacity to invade, permeate, and influence reality, Sethe's 'dream' alerts us to other truths and other laws that the insistence on unitary explanations based on reason would have neglected. As well as redefining what counts as truth and knowledge, *Beloved* demonstrates how any narrative has the potential to conceal other narratives and how authoritative discourses (legal, historical, religious, and political accounts), silence other voices. Margaret Garner's case, and Sethe's in the book, were accompanied with a law report and the case was used by abolitionists to illustrate the brutality of slavery: the lawyer who represented Sethe 'managed to turn infanticide and the cry of savagery around, and built a further case for abolishing slavery' (260). But none of these accounts did justice

---

[40] Isabelle Allende in Peter Lewis, 'Making Magic', The *Independent*, 3 April 1993, 24–6; quoted in Linden Peach, *Toni Morrison* (London: Macmillan Press, 1995), at 12.

[41] Barbara Christian, 'Fixing Methodologies: *Beloved*', *Cultural Critique*, Vol. 24 (Spring 1993), 5–15.

[42] I discuss this story in chapter 10.

to the story of Margaret Garner or her baby, or the sixty million who perished in the Middle Passage. In trying to enter the silence of the voiceless Morrison suggests that existing accounts of the events are incomplete and unrepresentative. Slavery laws defined slaves as property while deliberately masking the voice of the slaves who were objects but not subjects of a law they could not apply to themselves.[43] Sethe also dismisses the newspaper report of her case, 'Sethe could recognize only seventy-five printed words (half of which appeared in the newspaper clipping) but she knew that the words she did not understand hadn't any more power than she had to explain' (161). And Stamp Paid, another character in the book who escaped slavery only to become a witness to the Kentucky lynchings, is unimpressed with the accounts he sees of the atrocities, 'Detailed in documents and petitions full of *whereas* and presented to any legal body who'd read it, it stank' (180).

The reader who wants to listen to these alternative accounts must be prepared to participate as co-author of the text. The text does not have a beginning, a middle, and an end, as favoured by the classic realist tradition, or an omniscient narrator responsible for giving us the whole truth: instead, Sethe's story is accompanied, as well as broken, by the stories of Denver, Paul D, the community, and Beloved herself. The reader is thereby alerted to competing perspectives, experiences, and subjectivities. This strategy is a continuation of black oral tradition where everyone participated in story-telling and story-listening and there was no separation between teller and text.[44]

Morrison's subversion of authoritative knowledges is accompanied with a deconstruction of western understandings of time; while the ethical dimension of similar interrogations of time is not explicit in Borges' fiction, in Morrison such interrogations have a clear political message: the interrogation of time alerts us to Levinas's time of the 'other', of the black slave but also of woman who is at home with the notion of non-linear time. Sethe herself says it is hard for her to 'believe' in time (35), a disbelief strengthened by the text's rendition of time as arbitrary, circular, repetitive, contradictory, and ambiguous. Sethe and her two daughters belong to a different temporality to the sequential time of law and institutions, operating in what Kristeva calls 'women's time',[45] a cyclical arrangement linked to repetition, reproduction, and eternity rather than to progression, finality, and arrival.

Beloved's return, ghostly or in the real, thus achieves not only the collapse of distinctions between life and death but also of western understandings of history as linear, progressive, and teleological. Past, present, and future co-exist and collapse into an eternal present, 'Today is always here . . . Tomorrow, never' (60). In this timeless present, space also does not follow the rules of geography; as events from the past go on happening in the so-called present, not only memories, but characters themselves

    [43] J. Noonan, Jr, *Persons and Masks of the Law* (1976), 42; quoted in Betsy B. Baker, 'Constructing Justice: Theories of the Subject in Law and Literature', 75, *Minnesota Law Review* (1991), 581 at 582.
    [44] See Suzan Willis, *Specifying: Black Women Writing the American Experience* (London: Routledge, 1987), at 14–16.
    [45] Julia Kristeva, 'Women's Time' in Toril Moi (ed.), *The Kristeva Reader* (Oxford: Blackwell, 1986). I discuss this theme further in chapter 10; 'women's time' is also the time of Ariadne in my closing chapter.

reside, simultaneously, in Africa, Kentucky, Cincinnatti, and most painfully of all in journeys they were forced or tried to take in-between. Whether Beloved therefore is a symbol, a 'real' person, a dream, or a ghost is beside the point; to deny her ambiguity, to seek, in other words, to dissolve the mystery in accordance with pre-existing epistemological schemas, is to rob the book and ourselves of not just entertaining puzzles but of the ethical questions it challenges us to confront. When this timelessness is invaded by Paul D and the wider community, the challenge becomes one of envisaging an arrangement where men's and women's time, cyclical and linear time, the time of the dead and the time of the living, the time of law and the time of love can co-exist and cohabit. This challenge cannot be met unless we can also imagine new ways of perceiving ourselves and others; in particular, by being prepared to acknowledge that we are not separate, secure, and autonomous, and thus in competition with each other, but are always and forever related to the other, indeed that we are extensions of the other, starting, always and inevitably, with our mother.

6 MAPPING NEW SELVES

A constant worry in our efforts to project and understand the other, is the temptation to perceive her as whole, changeless, and uncomplicated. Morrison alerts us instead to identities that are anything but static, stable, or unified: starting with Sethe, characters are portrayed in all their tensions and contradictions. Rather than pre-given, knowable, and centred, Sethe and her surroundings, animate or inanimate (including the houses filled with the angry or benign breaths and longings of their alive as well as dead inhabitants) are multiple, fluid, dynamic, and socially contingent. Further, she communicates the anguish of identities that are not chosen, formed, or developed by the inhabitants of those bodies but are inscribed on by others. As in *Measure for Measure*, the woman's body is written on by white male ink, significantly the ink that Sethe herself makes for the schoolteacher and which he uses to record his slaves' 'animal' versus 'human' characteristics in his notebook. Sethe, like her mother whom she knew only by a circled cross on her breast, is also literally inscribed on by the nephews who, having held her down and stolen her milk, beat her so brutally that they leave a mark on her back resembling a 'chokeberry tree'. The pain causes Sethe to bite her tongue, literally depriving herself of the instrument of speech and metaphorically causing her to lose her voice (202). This violation kills the nerves on Sethe's back and crushes her husband who witnesses it and is powerless to intervene. Sethe prefers not to talk about it, and to Paul D's question as to how things are 'inside' replies 'I don't go inside' (45). The mark on her back however is a constant reminder of the 'homelessness' of her mind (205) and serves in its turn as an incentive to articulate her story and to share its pain. As Deleuze and Guattari put it, 'if one wants to call this inscription in naked flesh "writing", then it must be said that speech in fact presupposes writing, and that it is this cruel system of inscribed signs that renders man capable of language, and gives him a memory of the spoken word'.[46] However, there is one story Sethe is unable to put into words: the story surrounding the murder of her daughter Beloved: 'Sethe knew that the circle she was making around the room, him, the subject, would remain one. That she could never close in, pin it down for anybody who had to ask. If they didn't get it right off—she could never explain' (163).

Sethe's mother-in-law, 'after sixty years of losing children to the people who chewed up her life and spit it out like a fish bone' (177), is puzzled when asked what she calls herself: 'I don't call myself nothing' (142). Instead, sadness becomes the 'desolated center where the self that was no self made its home. Sad as it was that she did not know where her children were buried or what they looked like if alive, the fact was she knew more about them than about herself, never having had the map to discover what she was like' (140). This 'map', sought for in the confirming gaze of another person or persons, is not, however, 'one': both subject and object of the gaze inhabit varying positions affected by, amongst other factors, class, race, sex, and gender, their identity and self-understanding changes with each encounter. Morrison's insistence on multiple narrators, discontinuous time sequences, and fragmentary narration compounds this sense of the fragility of identity. The threat that one is not whole, stable, and thus knowable, infects not only the characters in the book but also the reader, as Morrison herself appears to have hoped, 'The reader is snatched, yanked, thrown into an environment completely foreign . . . Snatched just as the slaves were from one place to another, from any place to another, without preparation and without defense'.[47]

In a Lacanian reading of *Beloved* Evelyn Jaffe Schreiber describes how the black characters in the book alternate between perceiving themselves as the objects of the white look (which is, more often than not, also male) to gradually and painfully coming to perceive themselves as subjects. Paul D recognizes that it is the perception of others, whether allegedly well-meaning others like Garner, or the fierce schoolteacher, that defines his identity, 'It troubled him that, concerning his own manhood, he could not satisfy himself on that point. Oh, he did manly things, but was that Garner's gift, or his own will? . . . Did a whiteman saying it make it so? Suppose Garner woke up one morning and changed his mind?' (220). Objectification takes its extreme form with schoolteacher dividing the slaves' characteristics into animal and human while subjectification starts with connection with and love for, and by, another person. In contrast to 'the parasitic nature of slavery [which usurps] the Other's subjectivity in one's own service', the loving gaze of another person helps them attain self-knowledge and a belief in their own worth.[48]

Such conceptions of the self belie the reliance of western legal systems on the

---

[46] Gilles Deleuze and Felix Guattari, *Anti-Oedipus: Capitalism and Schizophrenia* (New York: Viking Press, 1983) trans. Robert Hurley, Mark Seem, and Helen R. Lane, at 145.

[47] 'Unspeakable Things Unspoken: The Afro-American Presence in American Literature' in Harold Bloom (ed.), *Toni Morrison, supra*, at 228.

[48] Evelyn Jaffe Schreiber, 'Reader, Text and Subjectivity: Toni Morrison's *Beloved* as Lacan's Gaze *Qua* Object', *Style*, Vol. 30, No. 3, (Fall 1996), 445–61, at 457.

notion of a stable, coherent, self-centred, and unified individual. Baby Suggs' sermons instead see the self as relational to the community and demand collective rather than individual political action.[49] 'Claiming ownership of the freed self' involves further learning to understand and experience one's own body and one's own desires which were forbidden articulation under slavery and subjugated to the desires of the masters. Baby Suggs' sermons invert the traditional hierarchy between mind and body which served to justify and maintain slavery and imperialism by a duality that put the white mind in control of the black body. Her sermons instead urge her audience to start with loving their bodies, 'their life-giving private parts', their 'flesh; flesh that weeps, laughs; flesh that dances on bare feet in grass. Love it. Love it hard' (88).[50]

The concept of rememory enhances the impression of identity as relational since memory, rather than being the property of one individual, is portrayed as having a spatial dimension with past events living 'out there, in the world', for anyone to 'bump into'.[51] Sethe is able to remember and retell her past by laying her story 'next' to Paul D's (273). The 'meaning' of these shared experiences, unlike the meaning found in the law report of her case, does not aim to be final, unitary, or monologic, but is the (open) sum of an on-going dialogue between several voices. The employment of multiple as well as competing voices reminds us that self-recognition can only take place in dialogue with others, a dialogue that leaves us conscious that we are 'always one and the other, at the same time'.[52]

7 IMAGINED FOUNDATIONS

The decision to present the black other as malleable and indeterminate is not without its contradictions: Morrison insists that the 'best art is political and the writer must be able to make it unquestionably political and irrevocably beautiful at the same time'.[53] She describes her own political agenda as reclaiming the past for African Americans and reconnecting the African community to what she calls the Ancestor as Foundation. This means that she cannot avoid engaging in identity construction, falling prey, in other words, to the perils of essentialism. For the post-colonial writer in general, the desire for a lost identity comes into conflict with post-modernism's denial of

---

[49] See April Lidinski, 'Prophesying Bodies: Calling for a Politics of Collectivity in Toni Morrison's *Beloved*' in Carl Plasa and Betty J. Ring (eds.), *The Discourse of Slavery: Aphra Behn to Toni Morrison* (London and New York: Routledge, 1994).

[50] This theme is the focus of David Lawrence, 'Fleshly Ghosts and Ghostly Flesh: the Word and the Body in *Beloved*' *Studies in American Fiction*, Vol. 19, (1991), 189–201.

[51] 'If a house burns down it's gone, but the place—the picture of it—stays; and just in my rememory, but out there, in the world . . . it's when you bump into the rememory of someone else' (36).

[52] Luce Irigaray, *This Sex Which is Not One*, trans. Catherine Porter (Ithaca, New York: Cornell University Press, 1985), at 217.

[53] Toni Morrison, 'Rootedness: the Ancestor as Foundation' in Mari Evans (ed.), *Black Women Writers: 1950–1980* (New York: Doubleday, 1984), 344–5.

stable identities, past *or* present. Gayatri Spivak questions the idea of recovering a subaltern voice as an essentialist fiction; there is no subaltern that can know and speak itself, she argues, because the colonized subaltern *subject* is irretrievably heterogenous and its identity is its difference.[54]

In *Beloved* the black community at first denounces Sethe because she appeared proud and self-sufficient and refused to condemn her act as evil. In claiming the child as her exclusive property, Sethe was challenging not only the system of slavery that denied her the right to her children but offended against the community by denying the child's connections with it. Sethe's excessive mothering ('dangerous' for a used-to-be-slave-woman as Paul D says, as the fate of her children, like her own, was always in the hands of the slave-owners) involved a denial of other loves, in particular community ties. The community, accustomed to a regime of poverty and self-denial also read Baby Suggs' excessive generosity as 'reckless' and proud. They have still to learn that an ex-slave had the right to desire, enjoy, or share such riches. Sethe is therefore judged and punished not only by the white man's legal system but by the black community whose own version of imprisonment is social ostracism. The community refuses to enter Sethe's house or share her food and she will not enter or share theirs: 'Nobody speaks to us. Nobody comes by,' says Denver (14). Even for those, like Ella, who sympathize with Sethe, Sethe's refusal to accept the help of the community, to acknowledge, in other words, the need for other people in the constitution of her own identity, is a mark of pride.

At the end, however, it is the community of women who come to rescue Sethe and bring her back to the symbolic order. The instrument for this negotiation is Sethe's daughter Denver who resolves to leave the confines of her family and enter the public realm by seeking employment and help in the outside world. The text suggests the importance of the community in the making of identity and for resolving the conflict between self and other, implying that we are both individuals and members of the social group and that we are only truly free in relation to other people. Morrison's politics are reminiscent of Hannah Arendt's view of freedom as citizenship and participation rather than separation and lack of interference.[55] Arendt significantly appeals to the Greek polis as a model for the individual's involvement in the public arena; Morrison too has commented on the influence of Greek tragedy on her writing, especially the participation of the community in the action as well as the telling of the story.[56] In *Beloved* the community acts throughout like the chorus in Greek tragedies, initially condemning Sethe but gradually coming to understand, accept, and support her.

The book's epigraph, 'I will call them my people, which were not my people; and her beloved, which was not beloved' suggests that deliverance from the law of male

[54] 'Can the Subaltern Speak?' *supra.*

[55] Hannah Arendt, 'What is Freedom' in *Between Past and Future: Six Exercises in Political Thought* (Cleveland, Ohio: Meridian Press), 1961.

[56] *Conversations*, at 132 and 176.

white fathers can be achieved through the redemptive qualities of a loving community.[57] The role of the community, however, is not univocal. Of course slavery and its proponents represent utter evil in the novel. The community however, who saw Schoolteacher approaching and failed to warn Sethe, shares part of the responsibility. Beloved's return serves therefore as a reminder of the repressed past not only to the mother that slit her throat but to the community that, in its jealousy and 'meanness' failed to protect her from the act. If Morrison's texts, Barbara Johnson suggests, hold out the promise of 'home', this promise is in the context of a home that is 'always already lost'.[58] Moreover, it is Sethe as the outsider, who lets the community know and define itself by marking the boundary between what is inside and what is outside. Morrison therefore problematizes the community that she celebrates and this celebration is matched with a celebration of the outsider.[59] The community evoked at the end of the book is therefore in part an 'imagined community', to use Benedict Anderson's phrase, but nevertheless, Morrison suggests, one that is a necessary foundation for individuals and groups.

The role of the community in the realization of freedom is further complicated by the fact that 'Freeing yourself was one thing; claiming ownership of that freed self was another' (95). The end of slavery by itself is not sufficient, Morrison suggests, for the realization of freedom. Baby Suggs, having lost seven children to the horrors of slavery, is the first slave in the book to experience freedom and it scares her: her remaining son gives up his Sundays for five years to buy her out of slavery and 'gave her freedom when it didn't mean a thing' (23). Freedom, Paul D says, means 'to get a place where you could love anything you chose—not to need permission for desire— well now, *that* was freedom' [162]. Though Baby Suggs experiences briefly this state of 'grace', the community's rejection of her and her family after Sethe's act, leaves her uninterested in 'leaving life or living it' (4). Sethe's legal freedom also does not deliver her from the desires of her body, the demands of her two daughters, or the hauntings of an unspeakable past. The community comes to help her in negotiating the conflicting demands of these desires but only once she is ready to confront and negotiate them: community, Morrison suggests, cannot be coerced but must be freely chosen before it can be endowed with the redeptive power of helping the self realize freedom.

In so far as the community serves as foundation, or conclusion, therefore, this is not reached by essentializing a black community, a black self, or a black history: the identity of the black community, like the identity of the other, is not fixed and knowable; it is fluid, in process, morally ambivalent, and thankfully for us, the readers, inexhaustible.

---

[57] See Mae G. Henderson, 'Toni Morrison's *Beloved*: Remembering the Body as Historical Text' in Hortense Spillers (ed.), *Comparative American Identities* (New York: Routledge, 1991).

[58] *The Feminist Difference, supra,* at 75.

[59] See Cynthia Davis, 'Self, Society and Myth in Toni Morrison's Fiction' in Bloom (ed.), *supra* at 14.

8 RETHINKING THE MATERNAL ARCHETYPE

In the gallery of western literature there are few figures more powerful and terrifying than that of the mother who kills her children. Adrienne Rich suggests that the stereotype was created to counter men's fear of the mother's powers, 'the power to give or withold nourishment and warmth, to give or withold survival itself'.[60] This is of course what Sethe and other mothers in *Beloved* and in Morrison's other fiction actually do. Sethe's sons leave 124 as soon as they are old enough to run. 'I guess they'd rather be around killing men than killing women' (205) is their sister's explanation. Sethe's murder of 'her own best thing' evokes the horror with which western culture has endowed killing mothers since Euripides' *Medea*. Unlike Medea, however, Sethe does not kill her children 'because of some guy' but acts out of an excess of love and responsibility for those she loves. In her work on the portrayal of infanticide in eighteenth and nineteenth English literature Josephine McDonagh explores how the killing mother is used to bear the burden of her society's own unresolved and unresolvable longings at times of rapid change. The murderous mother is portrayed alternatively as the ultimate other, the barbaric and uncivilized woman who, in rejecting motherhood threatens to undermine society's fundamental structures, and on the other hand as the ultimate mother, the heroic martyr whose sacrifice of her most precious possession, points out the failures and oppressiveness of those structures.[61]

These tensions and contradictions are explored again in Morrison's text; far from the text dissipating or resolving the ambivalence and desperation of her act, it maintains it throughout. By doing the unmentionable, the unthinkable, Sethe bears witness to the despair of a black woman slave faced with the threat of having 'the best part of her . . . sullied'.[62] More than an exceptional act of resignation, infanticide can therefore be seen as an act of resistance, one of the *few* acts of resistance available to the powerless.[63] Although Sethe herself is in no doubt that she had no other choice, the black community, including the man who loves her, refuse to condone her act. Like Baby Suggs, the reader who witnesses Sethe's act can neither 'approve or condemn' her 'rough choice' (180).

For Morrison herself *Beloved* is as much about motherhood and the mother-daughter bond as about slavery; it is about 'murdering as part of mothering,

---

[60] Adrienne Rich, *Of Woman Born: Motherhood as Experience and Institution*, (London: Virago Press, 1977), at 67.

[61] Josephine McDonagh, 'Infanticide and the Boundaries of Culture from Hume to Arnold' in Susan C. Greenfield and Carol Barash, *Inventing Maternity; Politics, Science, and Literature, 1650–1865* (Ky: University Press of Kentucky, 1999).

[62] *Conversations, supra*, at 207.

[63] See Elizabeth Fox-Genovese's argument that infanticide under slavery was a form of challenging the master's property right to one's child and reclaiming it as their own: *Within the Plantation Household* (Chapel Hill, NC:: University of North Carolina Press, 1988), 324. Also Jon-Christian Suggs, Letter to the Editor, *Forum* 116.

the perversions of nurturing and the violence of love', 'the tension between being yourself, one's own beloved, and being a mother'.[64] The split between being a mother and existing as an autonomous self, and the experience of pregnancy as an extreme challenge to identity[65] are described by Sethe to Beloved: 'You asleep on my back. Denver sleep in my stomach. Felt like I was split in two' (202). After birth, this split is followed by a dissolution of the boundaries between self and other as motherhood is experienced as totality and completeness: 'I am Beloved and she is mine . . . I am not separate from her there is no place where I stop her face is my own . . . she is the laugh I am the laughter I see her face which is mine . . . she smiles at me and it is my own face smiling' (210–13).

The danger of Sethe's 'thick love', as Paul D calls it, is her complete dissolution into her children; rather than conceiving her identity as separate and autonomous, Sethe clings to her role as a mother as the only secure element of an otherwise fragile identity. As a black woman slave who has been further ostracized by her own community, Sethe makes up in excessive love and mothering what she cannot provide to her children in social, legal, or financial terms. This conception of the mother-child bond as fusion is dangerous not only for the mother but also for the child: as Irigaray says, 'if the woman is uniquely mother, the child has no image of woman and thus of sexual difference'.[66]

The bond between Sethe and Beloved is increasingly described in terms that evoke the relationship between a vampire and his victim.[67] In a manner not dissimilar to the white boys' drinking Sethe's milk and the white men's chewing Baby Suggs' life and spitting it out 'like a fish bone' (177), Beloved literally and metaphorically starts consuming Sethe's life with her own 'bottomless longing'. Her desire, 'barely in control' (59), is to dissolve into her mother, while her mother dissolves into her: 'I am not separate from her . . . her face is my own and I want to be there in the place where her face is and to be looking at it too' (210). Beloved's appetite, particularly for sweet things, is insatiable, with Sethe being 'licked, tasted, eaten' (57) not only by Beloved's eyes but by her desperate efforts to keep Beloved's desire for food constantly gratified. 'The bigger Beloved got, the smaller Sethe became . . . Beloved ate up her life, took it, swelled up with it, grew taller on it' (250).

The correspondence in their growing/shrinking weights parallels but is also an inversion of pregnancy, in that it is the daughter who grows 'plumper by the day' (239) while Sethe shrinks, as if Sethe is trying to enter the security of *Beloved's* womb. Such an extreme identification between one self and an other poses again the challenge faced by Angela Carter's beauties and beasts, that is to find a means whereby one's appetite for the other need not be the other's extinction. The vision of a

---

[64] *Conversations*, at 5, 241, 286, 254.

[65] See Julia Kristeva, 'Stabat Mater' in Toril Moi (ed.), *The Kristeva Reader, supra*, where the 'splitting' experienced in pregnancy is described as the ultimate form of challenge to the subject's identity.

[66] Luce Irigaray, 'Etablis une généalogie de femmes' *Maintenant*, 12, 28 mai 1979, at 44; quoted in Elizabeth Grosz, *Sexual Subversions: Three French Feminists* (St Leonard's, Aus.: Allen & Unwin, 1989), at 120.

[67] See Pamela E. Barnett, 'Figurations of Rape and the Supernatural in *Beloved*', *Proceedings of the Modern Language Association*, Vol. 112, (1997), 418–27.

community sharing food and love evoked in Baby Suggs' sermons is one part of the solution Morrison proposes to the problem of 'eating well'.[68] When the mother-daughter relationship is extracted from the narrow confines of two all-too-close individuals and redefined in the context of a community, its potential destructiveness to both mother and daughter can be checked. This is the lesson Sethe slowly acquiesces to through the intervention of her other daughter Denver who seeks out community in the present as a means of planning for the future that Sethe has been at pains to ignore.

The text therefore problematizes rather than romanticizes the meaning of motherhood, reminding us that, as Patricia Clough argues, its boundaries are not fixed by nature, nor by culture but are a site of struggle. It makes clear the difficulty of recovering women's experience of mothering and suggests that it is only with the imagination that there can be remembering.[69] Paul D accuses Sethe of loving her children too thickly but Sethe resists his condemnation, as she has rejected the law's, the slaveowners', and the black community's condemnation of her act: 'Too rough for him to listen to. Too thick, he said. My love was too thick. What he know about it? . . . when I tell you mine, I also mean I'm yours. I wouldn't draw breath without my children' (203). Sethe herself is aware that 'unless carefree, motherlove was a killer' (132) but throughout the book, any identity she ascribes to herself, is overwhelmingly around being a mother: 'the best she was was her children' (251), she insists and even at the end, when Paul D urges her to believe that 'you your own best thing, Sethe. You are', she does not seem convinced and her last words in the novel are a questioning 'Me? Me?' (273).

What Paul D cannot understand is that for Sethe, as for other mothers, the experience of motherhood is not just a splitting but a 'spreading . . . an embrace of multiplicity'.[70] As Kristeva describes it, the arrival of the child extracts the mother out of her oneness, affording her the possibility of reaching out towards the other and forgetting oneself.[71] As Marie Ashe and Elizabeth Tobin have argued in greater detail, *Beloved* represents the repressed discourse of motherhood and reminds us of aspects of motherhood that legal definitions miss or ignore because they cannot be pinned down: in particular, the law's insistence on the separability and self-sufficiency of the subject cannot satisfactorily account for the mother-child bond.[72] It further reminds

---

[68] Jacques Derrida, 'Eating Well or the Calculation of the Subject', in *Points . . . Interviews, 1974–1994*, ed. Elizabeth Weber, (Stanford, Ca.: Stanford University Press, 1993), trans. Peggy Kamuf and others; I discuss this point further in chapter 6.

[69] *Feminist Thought*, (Oxford: Blackwell, 1994), at 58. These themes are addressed in greater detail by Barbara Hill Rigney, *The Voices of Toni Morrison* (Colombus, Ohio: Ohio State University, 1991).

[70] Barbara Hill Rigney, *The Voices of Toni Morrison, ibid.* 46.

[71] 'The heterogeneity that cannot be subsumed in the signifier nevertheless explodes violently with pregnancy (the threshold of culture and nature) and the child's arrival (which extracts the woman out of her oneness and gives her the possibility—but not the certainty—of reaching out to the other—the ethical.' 'Stabat Mater' in Toril Moi (ed.), *The Kristeva Reader, supra* at 182.

[72] Marie Ashe, 'The Bad Mother in Law and Literature: A Problem of Representation', 43, *Hastings Law Journal* (1992), 1017, and Elizabeth Tobin, 'Imagining the Mother's Text: Toni Morrison's *Beloved* and Contemporary Law', 16, *Harvard Women's Law Journal* (1993), 233.

us of the need to racialize and historicize our definitions of motherhood and of the family by creating families that do not conform to the western nuclear unit. The discourse of motherhood may crucially provide the beginnings of a new ethics, an ethics that, by starting from a mother's love for the strangest and most intimate of others, undermines the notion of the individual as separate, self-interested, and uniquely self-sufficient.

9 MURMURING THE UNUTTERABLE

Beloved itself dramatizes such an ethics of alterity by mediating the conflict between self and other and enabling us to recognize ourselves in, as well as our nearness to, another. In that sense, the text achieves what Levinas refers to as proximity.[73] As Maria Ashe, Elizabeth Tobin, and Robin West have argued, where the slave mother had been a silent and silenced victim, an object rather than a subject of her own narrative, Morrison gives her a voice that attests to Lyotard's différend and speaks the unspeakable.[74] For this unutterable to be heard, however, Morrison must break the back of words. As a black writer, the language at her disposal is one that expresses as it conceals unconscious preferences for white superiority. She therefore has to manoeuvre herself through language, forever alert to its traps and pitfalls in order to free it from its racial undertones.[75] 'Sixo, the wild man' (11) appreciates this danger and refuses to speak English, but in *Beloved*, as in Morrison's other fiction, it is the women who offer the possibility of subverting existing forms and creating a new language. This task, 'word-work' as Morrison calls it, is 'sublime'[76]: it not only undoes old meanings but generates new meanings that can secure women's difference, new subjectivities and new ways of reading, writing, and living.

Sethe is aware that her Ma'am had a different language that she thinks she did not understand or has forgotten. This language, however, has retained its power, not so much as words but as music, rhythms, and images. These return to Sethe gradually and in pieces: for words are not important, the message was, and 'the message—that was and had been there all along' (62). 'The thoughts of the women of 124, unspeakable thoughts, unspoken' (199) occupy what Kristeva calls the semiotic chora, a maternal language that is anterior to masculine language and the law of the father. After Sethe's boys and Paul D are driven away by Beloved, the house falls prey to the dictates of the semiotic, a language that men like Paul D and Stamp Paid

[73] 'The relation of proximity cannot be reduced to any modality of distance or geometrical contiguity nor to the simple "representation" of a neighbour; it is already an assignment—an obligation, anachronistically prior to any commitment': Emmanuel Levinas, *Otherwise than Being, or Beyond Essence* (Kluwer: The Hague 1981), trans. Alphonso Lingis, at 100–1.

[74] *Supra*; Robin West, 'Communities, Texts, and Law: Reflection on the Law and Literature Movement', *Yale Journal of Law and the Humanities*, Vol. 1 (1988), 129–56.

[75] *Playing in the Dark*, *supra* at xii–xiii.

[76] The *Guardian*, 'The Looting of Language', December 9, 1993.

cannot understand. The semiotic, making itself felt in the pulses, tones, rhythms, contradictions, and silences of masculine language threatens to disrupt, unsettle, and undermine the symbolic order.[77]

Kristeva wonders at the subversive power of this language but warns also of the dangers of endorsing it too fully. 'A woman', she warns, 'has nothing to laugh about when the symbolic order collapses . . . She can take pleasure in it, by identifying with the mother, the vaginal body, she imagines she is the sublime, repressed forces which return through the fissures of the order . . . But she can just as easily die from the upheaval'.[78] For Kristeva the point is to change, not to destroy the symbolic order, to express oneself within the law and to find one's own way within it by challenging and redefining it rather than obliterating it. In *Beloved* it is Denver who realizes that the semiotic cycle must be broken and calls the other women to help rescue her mother. The women come and pray but then 'they stopped praying and took a step back to the beginning. In the beginning there were no words. In the beginning was the sound, and they all knew what that sound sounded like . . . For Sethe it was as though the Clearing had come to her with all its heat and simmering leaves, where the voices of women searched for the right combination, the key, the code, the sound that broke the back of words. Building voice upon voice until they found it, and when they did it was a wave of sound wide enough to sound deep water and knock the pods off chestnut trees' (261).

It is also the language, as I describe in my closing chapter, of Ariadne, a language that starts not with a word, but an emotion, and that emotion was love. The lawyer in his labyrinth, I argue, frightened of this language, seeks to deny its veracity and declares it invalid in his legal system. Sensuous, plural, and fluid, it exceeds and explodes the language of the law which insists on singular, fixed, and precise meanings. Law's insistence on reducing events to manageable categories has the effect of collapsing their complexity and plurality. In contrast to legal classifications, Morrison portrays the reciprocal nature between good and evil and guilt and innocence. Sethe's murder of Beloved takes place out of a love that is not guided by rationality but is singular, unique, and unrepeatable. By desiring the other unto death Sethe challenges the symbolic order's insistence on denying the link between desire and death, a link and a repression that we saw in *Measure for Measure* and *Wuthering Heights*. Morrison, however, does not exonerate Sethe from responsibility, nor the black community who failed to warn her of the slaveowners' approach. At the same time she warns us against judging Sethe and refuses to judge her herself. In a subsequent interview she said that 'although it was the right thing to do Sethe had no right to do it'.[79] This moral ambiguity and the 'paradox of infanticide as ethical responsibility'[80] persists through-

---

[77] Julia Kristeva, *Revolution in Poetic Language* (New York: Columbia University Press, 1984), trans. Margaret Waller, at 50: 'in "artistic" practices the semiotic—the precondition of the symbolic—is revealed as that which also destroys the symbolic.'

[78] *The Kristeva Reader, supra*, at 150.

[79] *Conversations, supra*, at 272.

[80] The phrase is Elaine Jordan's, '"Not My People": Toni Morrison and Identity' in Gina Wisker (ed.), *Black Women's Writing* (London: Macmillan Press, 1993), at 123.

out the novel. The result, as Maria Ashe and Elizabeth Tobin have shown, is that the moral absolutism claimed by legal categorizations are avoided and the validity of both sides is maintained.

More generally the text challenges assumptions embedded in our law and legal theory that we are rational, self-interested, unified, stable, and coherent; it reminds us that legal definitions of guilt and innocence do not exhaust what we understand by those concepts; that legal language is often used to exclude and oppress rather than include and liberate and that law is often based on repression and fear rather than rationality and consent; it reminds us that law's notions of free will and responsibility are not neutral or self-evident; that for those outside such categorizations legal language excludes and oppresses rather than includes and liberates; and lastly, that law's insistence on the absolute legitimacy of its own classifications distorts individual experience and suppresses otherness.

10 THE PERSISTENCE OF DESIRE

Telling stories, in law, literature, or law and literature is a means of seeking knowledge, truth, and fullness, expecting the response of the other to signify the self, and the self to recognize the other. Such a communication must necessarily take place in language, ensuring that no reading or writing in law, literature, or law and literature is politically neutral. 'Everything is already interpretation'[81] and all of us readers participate in a form of hermeneutical violence, bringing our own assumptions and concerns on the objects of our reading. Like analysis, such interpretations are interminable, offering not a cure but, at most, temporary treatment. The danger is that new narratives foreclose questions, resolve contradictions, in other words that we attribute to literature all the truths, presence, and meanings we found lacking in law. If literature and the imagination are the repressed unconsious of law, the danger is making literature the new mistress that fulfils our yearning for completion and wholeness. If legal texts and rules attempt to control, write, and even replace our unfulfillable desire for the other, literary texts hold out not only the same hopes but also the same consolations. In reading we transfer our unfulfillable desires to the text and the gaps in language as well as the lack of agreement on the meaning, or law, of the text means that interpretation of texts, like analysis, is never finished. For Lacan, the obligation to retain the otherness of the text is an ethical one: ideally the reading experience should lead to the reader, not the text, being transformed.[82] The challenge is that our interpretive interventions and our violence, should not become totalitarian, should not claim the last word.

[81] 'A Conversation with Michel Foucault', 38, *Partisan Review* 192 (1971), 200.

[82] See Elizabeth Wright, *Psychoanalytic Criticism: A Reappraisal* (Cambridge: Polity Press, 1998), at 99–119.

It may be that this demand and this challenge can be met only through a practice of reading and writing that blurs the distinction between art and politics, ethics and aesthetics, fiction and reality. Such a practice does not lay claim to a single, universal, or objective truth but abdicates the temptation of legislation for the more humble task of interpretation: keeping the stories open, forking forward into the future and backward into the past. The effect is to challenge, from within the institution, the limits of academic professionalism and its claims on what counts as knowledge. By tolerating explanatory gaps and refusing to legislate this approach may achieve not a fusion but a widening of our horizons whilst remaining faithful to the law and literature project's distrust of totalizing or synthesizing explanations of contingent and plural phenomena. There is both an assumption and a hope behind this practice: the assumption is that we are more likely to achieve communication and empathy with the other through reciprocal dialogue and interpretation than unilateral legislation. The hope is that an aesthetics that refuses to adjudicate, satisfy, and close can help us in the ethical task of discovering the other in what is not the self and the self in what is other than ourselves.

For the attempt to write self and other is illusory: the stories we tell are constructions rather than facts, provisional rather than final, partial rather than total. Furthermore, the language at our disposal is not neutral but arises from the same culture that it addresses; it is always already borrowed, always already second-hand. The same language that promises closure, fullness, and resolution is the vehicle through which new stories, new interpretations, and new resolutions will be negotiated and contested.

Our craving for justice is itself one way of negotiating our desire for the other: like Beloved's, however, this desire is bottomless, unappeased, and unappeasable. While acknowledging that we will never attain it, we can agree, with Douzinas and Warrington, that we must not begin by pronouncing universal laws which, by purporting to apply to all, reduce the other to the self and the different to the same. In Morrison's *Beloved* justice can only be satisfied by understanding Sethe in her own unique, unrepeatable situation. Our desire for Sethe, however, is matched by our inability to know what Sethe wants; this ignorance means justice always remains an aporia: 'the radical dissymmetry, the abyss of the other's desire will always leave behind a remainder for which neither law nor fantasy can fully account'.[83]

If the desire for the other impels our reading and writing, the same desire ensures that the stories we read and write never entirely satisfy. Morrison knows that any closure, any neat answers or resolutions, would be the satisfaction and hence the end of desire. She therefore resists closures, leaving her books open-ended, using language with 'holes and spaces' for the reader to come in. 'It's not over just because it stops. It lingers and it's passed on. It's passed on and somebody else can alter it later'.[84]

---

[83] Costas Douzinas and Ronnie Warrington, *Justice Miscarried, supra*, at 80.

[84] Marsha Darling, 'In the Realm of Responsibility: A Conversation with Toni Morrison', *Women's Review of Books*, 5, March 1988, 6.

Morrison has often compared her writing with trying to do something that has only been expressed by black music: jazz, she says, unlike classical music which satisfies and closes, 'always keeps you on the edge. There is no final chord. There may be a long chord, but no final chord. It agitates you. It has the ability to make you want it and remember the want. It never fully satisfies. Never fully. It makes you hungry for more. It never gives you the whole number. It slaps and it embraces, it slaps and it embraces'.[85]

Reading and writing persist because our desire for the other, and the other's desire, can never be fully satisfied. On the one hand desire depends on lack and its fulfilment would be a cause of loss. On the other, it is absurd to expect that our own lack can be filled by the lack of another. The other is also inconsistent, confused, misunderstands us as much as we misunderstand her, and cannot respond to our desire either unconditionally or forever. Such paradoxes, however, are not as strong as the promises of love and justice, hence our persistence with telling stories. Amidst this dilemma and this impasse, Morrison's aesthetics holds out a promise of an ethics of writing and reading which may speak the silence of the other and the aporia of justice, of writing the other and through the other, ourselves. Weaving its way inside, beyond and against language, it may offer, lastly, one way of writing law, literature, and, law and literature.

[85] *Conversations, supra*, at 155.

10

'DREAM HARDER':[1] DREAM OF A GODDESS IN BORGES' FICTION[2]

Why do we journey, muttering
Like rumors among the stars?
Is a dimension lost?
Is love?

Maya Angelou

1 TWIN DESIRES: THE WRITER AND THE READER

Reading and writing take place in a state of desire, our desire for the other's desire, our wish to negotiate, postpone, or cope with our inability to be alone. Both law and literature offer brief respites from this inescapable loneliness. The law, armed with the material weapons of state institutions, writes on the body magisterially and allegedly conclusively, the 'right answer'. Equally ambitiously, literature aims to write on the soul, with writer and reader looking in their interaction for the ultimate epiphany, the moment when our bewilderment and agony is finally dissipated.[3] Writing and reading, in law or in literature, temporarily provide the illusion of anchors in a world devoid of foundations. However, the limitations and fears that create this desire and generate the search, function simultaneously as the obstacles that forbid and prevent its realization and fulfilment. If the experience of reading offers a feeling of plenitude, the end of reading also brings with it a little death: the pleasure of the text is

---

[1] The Waterboys, *Dream Harder* (Getten Records Inc., 1993).

[2] References in the text are to Jorge Luis Borges, *Labyrinths*, (ed.) Donald A. Yates and James E. Irby (London: Penguin, 1970) hereafter referred to as '*Lab.*'; Jorge Luis Borges, *Collected Fictions*, trans. Andrew Hurley (London: Penguin, 1998) hereafter referred to as '*CF*;' Jorge Luis Borges, *Selected Poems 1923–1967*, (ed.) Norman Thomas di Giovanni, (London: Penguin, 1985); hereafter referred to as *Poems*.

[3] Although it has been well argued that the law writes on the soul of the subject, as I suggest in my next chapter, the female imaginary is not so captured. See Peter Goodrich (ed.), *Law and the Unconscious: A Pierre Legendre Reader*, trans. Peter Goodrich with Alain Pottage and Anton Schütz (London: Macmillan, 1997).

accompanied by the experience of loss at its apparent ending, giving rise to more reading and writing in a proliferating exchange between ever more writers and readers. The search is endless and there is no possibility of arrival, hence the continual telling and retelling, reading and rereading, writing and rewriting of stories, old and new, in law as much as in literature.

That we read and write at all is testament to our unwillingness to despair, our reluctance to abandon reading and writing, in law or literature. Though our ability to understand fully, or even in part, is forever frustrated, though the search itself consoles, displaces, and postpones our confrontation with our isolation, fear, and absurdity, our ability to create and recreate new stories and new laws shows that despair is itself inexhaustible. Kafka's hero, having been denied access to the law, dies allegedly humiliated, 'like a dog'. His phantasm, however, persists, not only in Kafka's later fiction but in the minds and imaginations of countless readers who experience their own, again transient, 'deliverance' in their readerly encounter with Josef K. There is always more to be said, more to be done, a remainder, something which always 'slips away, or lies beyond',[4] as Blanchot puts it, that prevents us from reaching the goal, and urges us to search, say, read, and write more while alive. For the hope of *always*, of conclusions, finality, and permanence, can be fulfilled only with death.

In this chapter I wish to untie once more some of the threads unwound by this narrative lest the printed page appears to bestow on them a finality that they, and their writer, forever lack. And in the obligatory homage that has become commonplace on many a comment on Borges' work, I begin by saying that 'I owe the discovery of this [chapter] to the conjunction of, insomnia and a question in some formal space of interview.

'[N]arrative', writes Barthes, 'is determined not by a desire to narrate but by a desire to exchange: it is a *medium of exchange*, an agent, a currency, a gold standard'.[5] If this is the ambition of the writer, the hopes of the reader are no less modest: we read to lose ourselves in a book, and the pleasure of applying ourselves to a text derives not only from recognizing ourselves in its pages but from imagining ourselves differently and in becoming other than ourselves.[6] There is an understanding or 'sympathy', as Poe called it, between the writer and the reader who opens a book, a sympathy that the writer intensifies by magnanimously implying that the events and ideas in the text somehow occurred to writer and reader together.[7] Borges allows the reader the

---

[4] Maurice Blanchot, 'The Disappearance of Literature' in Michael Holland (ed.), *The Blanchot Reader* (Oxford: Blackwell, 1995), at 142.

[5] Roland Barthes, *S/Z*, trans. Richard Miller (Oxford: Blackwell, 1974), at 90.

[6] See Paul Ricoeur, in Mario J. Valdés, (ed.), *A Ricoeur Reader: Reflection and Imagination* (Hemel Hempstead: Harvester Wheatsheaf, 1991), at 492–3: 'When a reader applies a text to himself, as in the case of literature, he recognizes himself in certain possibilities of existence ... but at the same time, he is transformed; the becoming other in the act of reading is as important as the recognition of self', at 492–3. Also Jacques Derrida, *Positions*, trans. Alan Bass: 'Reading is transformational' (Illinois: University of Chicago Press, 1981), at 63.

[7] Letter to Thomas H. Chivers, quoted in Terence Whalen, 'Edgar Alan Poe and the Horrid Laws of Political Economy', *American Quarterly*, Vol. 44(3), Sept. 1992, 381 at 410.

pleasure of thinking that she dreamed of the ending, or of the world, or of the man herself; like any magnanimous creator, he allows the objects of his creation as well as his readers to believe that they are autonomous, that they thought the thoughts and directed the actions themselves.[8] Like the lover teasing the beloved, the author also can prolong, defer, and expand the relationship and the pleasure, by misleading, confusing, and puzzling the reader, by suggesting, omitting, and hinting rather than declaring, stating, or asserting.

Recognizing this readerly desire, Borges provides us with an extreme example of a reader who not only loses himself in the text but begins to imitate, identify with, and merge with the words until he becomes one with the author and is writing the words himself. In 'Pierre Menard, Author of *Don Quihote*' the author is killed and replaced not by the critic but by the reader who literally re-creates and re-authors the original text. This is Menard's 'invisible' work, 'the subterranean, the interminably heroic, the peerless. And—such are the capacities of man!—the unfinished' (*Lab.*, 65). To rewrite the *Quihote*, Menard, a resident of turn of the twentieth-century Paris, could have learned old Spanish, fought against the Moors, and forgotten the history of Europe in the intervening years; this route is rejected as too easy and uninteresting: 'To compose the *Quihote* at the beginning of the seventeenth century was a reasonable undertaking, necessary and perhaps even unavoidable'(*Lab.*, 68). Instead, Menard rewrites the *Quihote* through his own experiences: the end-product is a text that is verbally identical to Cervantes' text but, according to his friend and critic, more subtle and 'almost infinitely richer. (More ambiguous, his detractors will say, but ambiguity is richness)' (*Lab.*, 69). For any set of words, though they may be identical to those uttered by another person, have a different sense when uttered by someone else and in a different context. The experience of writing and of reading, changes from writer to writer and from reader to reader each time the text is rewritten or reread.

2 DREAMS OF ORIGINS AND TOTALITY

Menard 'decided to anticipate the vanity awaiting all man's efforts; he set himself to an undertaking which was exceedingly complex and, from the very beginning, futile' (*Lab.*, 70). The same vanity motivates, and the same futility awaits, Borges implies, all men's efforts, especially intellectual ones: 'There is no exercise of the intellect which is not, in the final analysis, useless' (*Lab.*, 69). As I discuss in my opening chapter, of all such efforts none seems to be more persistent as the desire to find a point of origin, a transcendental signifier that will confer meaning to the universe and its creatures. Many of Borges' characters are engaged, consciously or unconsciously, in this quest.

---

[8] To his readers Borges was fond of saying 'the story is more yours than it is mine' in Richard Burgin (ed.), *Jorge Luis Borges: Conversations*, (Jackson, Miss.: University of Mississippi Press, 1998), at 231; hereafter referred to as *Conversations*.

In the manner of a detective seeking clues to the circumstances, motive, and identity of the murderer, Borges' 'detectives' seek the cause behind all causes, the origin of origins, the arch-designer behind all designs. The answers, however, in another inversion of the genre, are anti-answers, leading the searcher back to where he started, to himself, or to death. Reliving their adventures, the reader in turn marvels at the futility of the quest, but also at the heroism, vanity, and often arrogance of the seekers.

The desire inspiring these quests is that a single letter, or a single object could contain the entire universe, and provide the key to its secret plan. It is the hope, entertained by Tennyson, 'that if we could understand a single flower, we should know what we are and what the world is' (*Lab.*, 197). The 'aleph' is the first letter of the Hebrew alphabet and symbolizes all the other letters; in Cabbalistic thought, to decipher the letters is to discover God and the secret of the universe. In the title story, the narrator is fortunate enough to witness the aleph, bizarrely from a point on the stairs of the basement of a house in Buenos Aires which is about to be demolished. It is 'a small, iridescent sphere of unbearable brightness . . . two or three centimeters in diameter, but universal space was contained inside it, with no diminution in size' (*CF*, 283). Its 'center is everywhere and circumference nowhere'(*CF*, 282) and in it one can see all the possible aspects of the universe at the same time: 'The place where, without admixture or confusion, all the places of the world, seen from every angle, coexist' (*CF*, 281). The aleph endows the narrator with the experience of infinity and eternity, though of course not the ability to express it: 'the central problem—the enumeration, even partial enumeration, of infinity—is irresolvable. In that moment, I . . . saw the earth in the Aleph, and the Aleph once more in the earth and the earth in the Aleph, saw my face and my viscera, saw your face, and I felt dizzy, and I wept, because my eyes had seen that secret, hypothetical object whose name has been usurped by men but which no man has ever truly looked upon: the inconceivable universe'(*CF*, 283–4).

A similar experience befalls the narrator in 'The Zahir' when he is given an unforgettable coin as change in a bar in Buenos Aires. Like Tennyson's flower, the coin may contain 'universal history and the infinite concatenation of cause and effect' and the narrator hopes that perhaps 'behind the coin I shall find God' (*Lab.*, 197). In a similar fashion, the condemned man in 'The Secret Miracle' stumbles upon the magic letter that allows him to hear the voice of God on a map of India and is able to hear God and have his last prayer answered (*Lab.*, 122). In these stories the narrator has an, albeit brief, glimpse of eternity, of all experience united simultaneously in a single point, moment, object, or place. He is blessed with the miracle of seeing 'the union with the divinity, with the universe . . . all things that are, were and shall be . . . the causes and the effects . . . the universe and the intimate designs of the universe . . . the origins . . . the faceless god . . . infinite processes that formed one single felicity' (*Lab.*, 206–7).

The experience, however, is only transitory and not always positive or enlightening: man, (and the noun 'man' is used here deliberately, as no women are fortunate or unfortunate enough to witness this totality, a theme that I return to later) Borges suggests, is forever condemned to experience 'the imminence of a revelation that never comes'.[9] The narrator of 'The Zahir' is unable to forget the coin whose image becomes 'intolerable' to him: 'When all the men on earth think, day and night, of the Zahir, which will be dream and which a reality—the earth or the Zahir?' (*Lab.*, 197). The quest that is couched as a search for God or the mysteries of creation, leads not to revelation but back to oneself or, as Lonnrot finds in 'Death and the Compass', his search for the unutterable name of God leads indeed to the creator, that is his death. The face they are searching for, the face of God, is no more than the trace of one's own face: 'A man sets out to draw the world. As the years go by, he peoples a space with images of provinces, kingdoms, mountains, bays, ships, islands, fishes, rooms, instruments, stars, horses, and individuals. A short time before he dies, he discovers that that patient labyrinth of lines traces the lineaments of his own face.' (*CF*, 327). At other times it is suggested that the God they are searching for is Himself in search of another God, and 'so on to the End—or better yet, the Endlessness—of Time. Or perhaps cyclically.'(*CF*, 85). The narrator in these stories is therefore describing 'the process of failure, the process of defeat'(*CF*, 241), a process and a quest that leads to, and ceases only, with death.

3 DREAMS OF STRUCTURES

The search for the secret of the cosmos, for the aleph or the zahir that contains the key to the universe, is couched in other terms as the search to understand the secret plan of the universe, of finding not *a* but *the* way of classifying and categorizing its disparate data into a comprehensive and enduring structure.

Foucault claims that the inspiration for *The Order of Things* is owed to Borges' account of a certain Chinese Encyclopaedia in which animals are classified as '(a) belonging to the Emperor, (b) embalmed, (c) tame, (d) sucking pigs, (e) sirens, (f) fabulous, (g) stray dogs, (h) included in the present classification, (i) frenzied, (j) innumerable, (k) drawn with a very fine camel brush, (l) etcetera, (m) having just broken the water-pitcher, (n) that from a long way off look like flies'.[10] Identifying with Borges the author, the reader Foucault extrapolates from the bizarre classification of animals in that encyclopaedia that any attempt at classification, representation, or systematization of the 'order of things' involves arbitrary selection and thereby falsification: 'This book first arose out of a passage in Borges, out of the laughter that shattered, as I read the passage, all the familiar landmarks of my thought—*our* thought, the thought that bears the stamp of our age and our geography—breaking up all the ordered surfaces and all the planes with which we are accustomed to tame

---

[9] Jorge Luis Borges, *Other Inquisitions 1937–1952*, trans. L. C. Simms (Austin, Tex.: Texas University Press, 1964), at 5.

[10] 'The Analytical Language of John Wilkins' in *Other Inquisitions, supra*

the wild profusion of existing things . . . [including] our age-old distinction between The Same and the Other'.[11]

For Borges, 'There is no classification of the universe that is not arbitrary and conjectural. The reason is very simple: we do not know what the universe is'.[12] It is not only encyclopaedias, dictionaries, and libraries that create the illusion of a semblance of order from a mass of chaotic and random materials. Any attempt to order the world, by means of symbols and language, in law or in literature, aims to capture and tame what is beyond our knowledge. While Borges and his successors admit, however, and draw attention to the contingency and artificiality of their constructions, legal language aims to conceal its artificial origins. For the yearning to believe in a point of origin, in a universe with a beginning, middle, and end, which functions in accordance with clear rules and predictable outcomes is as strong as the impossibility of its discovery.

The nations of planet Tlon resist the temptation to simplify and categorize and remain 'congenitally idealist' (Lab., 32): for them the universe has no material existence outside the mind and 'Every mental state is irreducible: the mere fact of naming it—i.e., of classifying it—implies a falsification' (Lab., 34). The universe for them 'is not a concourse of objects in space; it is a heterogeneous series of independent acts. It is successive and temporal, not spatial' (Lab., 32). Since language is our chief instrument for ordering our experiences, the language of Tlon seeks to avoid its pitfalls: language conveys the impression that there are objects independent of our mental perceptions of them. But linguistic terms are inevitably selective and arbitrary and give only a partial and often tyrannical impression of the varied ways different people experience the world in different places and at different times. Threading words together in sentences also imposes a semblance of order which implies linearity, succession, and progression. This impression is alien to the way we experience the world and each other, which is simultaneous.[13] Resisting these facile impressions, Tlon language contains no nouns, only an accumulation of adjectives and impersonal verbs. 'For example: there is no word corresponding to the word "moon", but there is a verb which in English would be "to moon" or "to moonate". "The moon rose above the river" is . . . "upward behind the onstreaming it mooned" ' (Lab., 32–3).

Since for Tlon there are no objects outside our perceptions of them, the notion that objects exist over time is also alien. Doctrines that presume to connect facts to each other, or imply causation between separate events, like materialism, are rejected as 'verbal fallac[ies]' (Lab., 35). The concept of 'identity' is also a metaphor: one cannot claim that something 'lost' on Tuesday is the same object as the one 'found' on Wednesday or that a cloud of smoke on the horizon, a burning field, and a half-extinguished cigarette are causally connected. Though sciences, including philosophy,

---

[11] The Order of Things: An Archaeology of the Human Sciences, trans. Alan Sheridan (New York: Vintage, 1970), at xv.

[12] 'The Analytical Language of John Wilkins' in Other Inquisitions, supra, at 104.

[13] The narrator in 'The Aleph' has the same problem: 'What my eyes saw was simultaneous; what I shall write is successive, because language is successive' (CF, 283).

do exist in Tlon, they are no more than 'dialectical games', seeking not 'the truth, or even verisimilitude, but rather for the astounding. They judge that metaphysics is a branch of fantastic literature' (*Lab.*, 34).

The Postscript (dated seven years after the story's publication) explains the origins of Tlon: in early seventeenth century London 'a secret and benevolent society' arose to invent a country. Two centuries later this persecuted fraternity sprang up again in America where the ascetic millionaire Ezra Buckley scoffed at the plan's modest scope: 'He told the agent that in America it was absurd to invent a country and proposed the invention of a planet' (*Lab.*, 40). The idea is as vain and arrogant as it is admirable, indeed glorious: 'Buckley did not believe in God, but he wanted to demonstrate to this non-existent God that mortal man was capable of conceiving a world' (*Lab.*, 40).

This idealism, or conceit, proves irresistible even to those who cling to reality for security. 'Centuries and centuries of idealism have not failed to influence reality' (*Lab.*, 37). A pivotal instrument for this influence is the appearance of *hronin*. These are objects produced by mental activity in Tlon; at first they are 'the accidental products of distraction and forgetfulness' (*Lab.*, 38) but once their power to modify our perception of the world is recognized, they start being produced deliberately and methodically. Their fabrication 'has performed prodigious services for archaeologists. It has made possible the interrogation and even the modification of the past, which is now no less plastic and docile than the future' (*Lab.*, 38). *Hronin* soon start appearing in the narrator's world: more volumes of the Tlon encyclopaedia are discovered, a princess in Buenos Aires finds amongst her silver from Poitiers a vibrating compass, and a youth dies on finding in his pocket a cone of intolerable and oppressive weight which is an image of the divinity in certain regions of Tlon: 'Such [were] the first intrusion[s] of this fantastic world into the world of reality' (*Lab.*, 41).

Before long, fantasy not only intrudes into reality but becomes the only reality. Faced by a world whose design is incomprehensible and unpredictable, people are seduced by the vision of an alternative planet devised by men; 'The truth is that it longed to yield. Ten years ago any symmetry with a semblance of order—dialectical materialism, anti-Semitism, Nazism—was sufficient to entrance the minds of men. How could one do other than submit to Tlon, to the minute and vast evidence of an orderly planet?' (*Lab.*, 42). Unable to comprehend the laws governing its own laby-rinth, a labyrinth governed by non-human, even inhuman, laws that it cannot grasp, the world longs to yield to a labyrinth like Tlon which, having been devised by men, is 'destined to be deciphered by men' (*Lab.*, 42). Enchanted by the orderly world of Tlon, people start learning Tlon language and Tlon history and forget their own languages and histories. The narrator has given up hope of reminding them that Tlon's order is man-made, 'a rigour of chess masters, not of angels' (*Lab.*, 42). His own resistance to the seduction that is Tlon condemns him to loneliness and futility which he accepts with resignation as he buries himself amongst ancient books: 'A hundred years from now', he predicts, 'someone will discover the hundred volumes of the Second Encyclopaedia of Tlon. Then English and French and mere Spanish will disappear from the globe. The world will be Tlon' (*Lab.*, 43).

The volume of a Tlon encyclopaedia discovered by Borges describes this world 'with no visible doctrinal intent or tone of parody' (*Lab.*, 31). In the same tone, Borges blends real and fictitious people, searching in real and fictitious encyclopaedias, real and fictitious atlases for a fictitious country that started making its presence felt in the real Buenos Aires. While these authorial intrusions remind us of the story's status as a fiction, Borges alerts us more gravely to the possibility that our own ways of ordering the world, through philosophy, law, or literature are equally fictitious, metaphysical games. The more pleasing or sensational their design, the greater their capacity to astound and absorb us, and the lesser our capacity to resist being seduced and submitting to them. Who can tell whether the archives we studiously search, the architecture and histories of our courts and legal system, the law reports and textbooks we use to fathom the legal universe, are not so many *hronin*, deliberately fabricated by a powerful and laughing intellect for its own amusement and to which we submit in our desperate yearning for reassurance and consolation in the face of the unknown?

4 'PARADISE IS A LIBRARY'? (*POEMS*, 129)

'The universe (which others call the Library) is composed of an indefinite and perhaps infinite number of hexagonal galleries . . . The distribution of the galleries is invariable. Twenty shelves, five long shelves per side, cover all sides except two . . . One of the free sides leads to a narrow hallway which opens on to another gallery, identical to the first and to all the rest' (*Lab.*, 78). Seduced by the order and symmetry of its architecture, the narrator, like all men of the Library, searches for the book, 'the catalogue of catalogues' that will reveal the origin of the Library, the origin of time, indeed the origin behind all origins. One thinker has concluded, from the fact that all the books, however diverse, are made up of a limited number of symbols (the letters of the alphabet and the period, comma, and space) and that no two books are identical, that 'the Library is total', and that it includes absolutely everything in every language. This discovery is greeted with universal jubilation: 'There was no personal or world problem whose eloquent solution did not exist in some hexagon. The universe was justified, the universe suddenly usurped the unlimited dimensions of hope' (*Lab.*, 82). The triumph, however, is short-lived: hope turns to depression as the certainty that the Library contains the answer only increases the despair that comes with the impossibility of ever finding the book that contains it. Jubilation turns to violence and librarians strangle each other on the divine staircases, go mad, or commit suicide.

As in 'Tlon', a brief hope that an idea or a theory contains the answers, whether materialism, idealism, communism, or nazism, deludes the questers into the search for more knowledge, more answers, more books but instead exacerbates the feelings of frustration, loneliness, and futility. The Library may contain everything but with no system of classifying or finding its holdings, any order it contains remains secret and indecipherable. The truth, if there is one, remains hidden from the searchers. The narrator is resigned to the fact that the task of understanding the design or finding the designer is futile. The library, which exists *ab aeterno*, is unlimited, unending, 'illuminated, solitary, infinite, perfectly motionless, equipped with precious volumes, useless, incorruptible, secret' (*Lab.*, 85). He consoles himself with the thought that the Library is cyclical, that 'the same volumes were repeated in the same disorder (which, thus repeated, would be an order: the Order)' (*Lab.*, 86). A cyclical pattern, however, only reinforces the impression that the search is both futile and endless: 'Obviously no one expects to discover anything' (*Lab.*, 83). As in Kafka's fiction, salvation comes not with ultimate knowledge or enlightenment but only with death: the narrator looks forward to that day when other pious librarians will throw him over the railing 'into the fathomless air; my body will sink endlessly and decay and dissolve in the wind generated by the fall, which is infinite' (*Lab.*, 79).

In a less Kafka-esque fashion, 'Funes the Memorious' evokes not the agony but the sadness of our inability to categorize information in such a way as to suggest an overall order and purpose. 'Chronometric' Funes, who can tell the time without consulting a clock or the sky, is endowed with the gift of total and infallible memory. Before the accident that left him physically paralysed, Funes 'had been what all humans are: blind, deaf, addle-brained, absent-minded', living as in a dream, 'he looked without seeing, listened without hearing, forgetting everything, almost everything.' (*Lab.*, 91). After the accident however, he wakes up from the sleep that the rest of us are condemned to: he perceives the world in all its richness and sharpness. Indeed the story, Borges suggested, is a metaphor for insomnia.[14] Where the rest of us, in our sleep and forgetfulness, may perceive three glasses of wine on a table, 'Funes can see all the leaves and tendrils and fruit that make up a grape vine.' Where the rest of us see a circle drawn on a blackboard, Funes can do the same 'with the stormy mane of a pony, with a herd of cattle on a hill, with the changing fire and its innumerable ashes, with the many faces of a dead man throughout a long wake' (*Lab.*, 91–2). He can recall, without hesitation, all the events of a day but each reconstruction requires a whole day . . . Funes gives up any attempt to classify his memories, because the task would be both interminable and useless. Moreover, his inability to forget renders him incapable of thinking: 'To think is to forget differences, generalize, make abstractions. In the teeming world of Funes, there were only details, almost immediate in their presence.' (*Lab.*, 94). His total knowledge does not bring enlightenment but more frustration, more obtuseness, ever more loneliness; he becomes a 'perpetual prisoner' of his own memories.

The suggestion that amassing information without the tools with which to select and organize them deadens rather than brings enlightenment seems an accurate prediction of the nightmare of proliferating data in western capitalist technologies. It evokes also the sense of uselessness, anguish, and futility faced by the law student whose hopes of grasping an overall design and plan to the legal system are dashed by

---

[14] *Conversations, supra*, at 29.

the bombardment of confusing and often contradictory information from sources equally unable to understand or communicate that plan. At times a case, a theory (communism, liberalism, postmodernism), a new approach (Law and Philosophy, Law and Economics, Law and Literature) may bring the illusion of an overall design, even of unquestionable truth. More searches however, reveal these brief moments of ecstasy to be also based on arbitrary, partial, and inconsistent information. If a god designed the Law, then, like the god who designed the Library, he is no longer present, has abandoned his design, or if present, will not reveal himself. Though the search does not end, like the narrator in this story she may have to resign herself to the view that the only design behind the chaos is a recurring circle.

Or, even more alarmingly, as I suggest further in the next chapter, the answer may be that there is no design, that there is no Minotaur inside the labyrinth, and that the search has been in vain because 'nothing is all there is' inside. The law that seduced us with its semblance of order and design is an emptiness that confuses not only those who try to enter its empire but also itself.

5 ORDER BY CHANCE

It is a truth universally acknowledged, at least by legal doctrine, that in theory, if not always in practice, it is possible to distinguish between acts that take place voluntarily and acts that take place without the agent's control. Offences as much as defences, in civil as much as in criminal law, assume that the legal subject acted consciously and willingly and could have acted otherwise, could have agreed to different terms, could have prevented an accident, could have refrained from a crime. The concept of causation assumes further that future events can be predicted from preceding events, with the degree of 'reasonable foreseeability' determining the nature of the crime or liability, and the gravity of the punishment or damages. Borges' short story 'The Lottery at Babylon' shakes some of these convictions by inviting us to imagine 'what the Greeks do not know, incertitude' (*Lab.*, 55).

Babylon is 'a dizzy land where the lottery is the basis of reality' (*Lab.*, 55). The lottery system had started out in an 'elementary' fashion, and involved selling tickets and holding the draw 'in broad daylight' when the winners would win silver coins. This system, directing itself at only one of men's faculties, hope, soon led to indifference. But when unlucky tickets were added to lucky ones, conferring not only prizes for the winners but also fines for the losers, 'the Babylonians threw themselves into the game' (*Lab.*, 56). The poor, protesting at their exclusion from the 'delicious rhythm' of terror and hope, persuaded the Company to make the lottery 'secret, free and general' (*Lab.*, 57). The rewards and punishments also ceased to be exclusively monetary and become more varied: 'A fortunate play could bring about [one's] promotion to the council of wise men or the imprisonment of an enemy (public and private) or finding, in the peaceful darkness of his room, the woman who begins to excite him and whom he never expected to see again. A bad play: mutilation, different kinds of infamy, death'(*Lab.*, 58).

The operations of the Company soon start to pervade every aspect of life in Babylon; everyone takes part and every detail of their existence is subject to its operations so that it becomes impossible to distinguish between chance events and designed ones: 'incertitude' is not just one of, but life's *only* condition. 'The drunkard who improvises an absurd order, the dreamer who awakens suddenly and strangles the woman who sleeps at his side, do they not execute, perhaps, a secret decision of the Company?'(*Lab.*, 60). Although some suggest that the Company never existed and 'that the sacred disorder of our lives is purely hereditary, traditional' the Babylonians reject this view as abominable (*Lab.*, 61). They prefer to believe that behind the disorder they encounter daily, there is an all-pervasive plan directing their lives, albeit that plan is indistinguishable from a world abandoned to the vagaries of chance. Their inability to understand the methods by which the Company regulates chance, indeed the tautology of the concept of 'regulated chance', only intensifies their fervent belief in the Company's existence.

Could we not, perhaps, be suffering from the same delusion, refusing to believe that our lives and structures, laws and loves, are not the result of an overarching design but 'nothing else than an infinite game of chance'? (*Lab.*, 61) If we resist this unsettling suspicion, it is not because we have not been warned: the lottery, we are told on the first page, is 'an institution which other republics do not know or which operates in them in an imperfect and secret manner' (*Lab.*, 55). Chance may be the basis of reality in all republics, not only in Babylon, but other republics are reluctant to countenance this possibility. The anecdote of the slave who stole a lottery ticket that ordained the burning of the tongue suggests that it is impossible to distinguish between the law, that is, order imposed by design and the lottery, that is, order imposed by chance: for the legal code fixed an identical penalty for someone stealing a ticket. If the operations of the legal code and the lottery lead to the same outcome, on what basis do we distinguish between the law and the lottery? In another Borges story the workings of chance and destiny are again difficult to distinguish from the workings of the law: when Monk Eastman, 'Purveyor of Iniquities' is caught for the umpteenth time, the police are relieved and amused by his arrest; and 'the judge prophesied for him, quite accurately, ten years in prison' (*CF*, 29).

The forces preventing us from accepting this possibility are powerful. Like the man from the country in Kafka's parable 'Before the Law', we prefer to believe that there is something inside the law, however secret and indecipherable it may be to us. We refuse to despair, desperately hoping instead that there is a secret origin, a secret design that will be revealed to us on arrival, although the journey may be arduous and the waiting long. We prefer to believe that the Company operates in accordance with rules and proficient officers, even though we may never see them and even though we find it hard to understand them when they speak to us. 'The individuals of the Company were (and are) omnipotent and astute. . . . Their steps, their manoeuvrings, were secret.' It is no coincidence that one of their sacred latrines is called 'Qafka'

(*Lab.*, 58), evoking again the sense of a universe that is both complex and ultimately indecipherable.

When the officials' decisions are challenged, the Company, 'with its usual discretion', does not answer directly. When the frightening possibility of mistakes is raised, the Company replies that 'the lottery is an interpolation of chance in the order of the world and that to accept errors is not to contradict chance: it is to corroborate it' (*Lab.*, 58). Though tautologous, such replies appease the public and acquire the status of sacred scriptures. For tautologies, as Barthes says, are 'a faint at the right moment, a saving aphasia', rescuing the speaker from his inability to explain and enabling him to take 'refuge behind the language of authority'. The cost exacted by tautologies is correspondingly high: 'a refusal of language, a death, a motionless world'.[15] In effect, mistakes become the law which is another way of suggesting that the law may be a mistake.

The law, like the Company, is loath to admit that it makes mistakes. Through the system of appeals and further legislation, mistakes are not admitted but incorporated as intrinsic parts of the law's miraculous workings and re-workings towards an inexorable progress. But is law also not only an attempt to regulate chance, but itself a game of chance, its officers and institutions working hard to present it as planned, organized, and infallible? One can go further and suggest that chance is not the exception to knowledge but the *other* of knowledge, perhaps the only knowledge, the only truth.[16] 'After all, what is chance', as one character exclaims, 'if not the effect of a cause that escapes us?'[17] Reason, unable to integrate chance within its system, tries to exclude, ignore, or repress its workings.

It is also no accident that in western thought, the concept of chance or tyche, has been associated, as in *Oedipus Lex*, with woman. Man-made attempts to order the world through law and reason can only succeed by banishing what they do not understand and cannot control: chance and woman. The excision, however, is never entirely successful; as I suggest in my closing chapter, the repressed figure of Jocasta and chance returns not only with Nietzsche's *amor fati* but with the return of women as both law-makers and truth-bearers.

6   ONE MAN IS ALL MEN IS ONE LITERATURE

Pierre Menard's ability to rewrite, word for word, and without direct transcription, the *Quihote* is an extreme form of the identification between writer and reader. Since our language is constitutive of our personalities, the repetition of another's language

---

[15] Roland Barthes, *Mythologies*, trans. Annette Lavers (London: Vintage, 1993) [1953], at 152–3.

[16] See Georges Bataille, *On Nietzsche*, trans. Bruce Boone (New York: Paragon Press, 1992).

[17] Erchmann-Chatrian, 'L'Esquisse Mystérieuse', quoted by Tzvetan Todorov, *The Fantastic: A Structural Approach to a Literary Genre*, trans. Richard Howard (Ithaca, New York: Cornell University Press, 1975 [1970]), at 110.

implies 'an interpenetration of personalities',[18] challenging our faith in the absolute autonomy of the self. In Borges' stories identity is not singular or unique but indistinct, incomplete, and fragile; fluid, indefinite, and ambiguous, it often dissolves altogether as characters blur into one another, repeat each other's deeds, write each other's words, even die each other's deaths. Indeed any semblance of stability is derived from the presence of the other, the 'double', against whom the individual compares and contrasts himself. In these stories, murderer and victim, traitor and hero, spy and target, Jesus and Judas, father and son, dreamer and dreamed, hero and coward, the believer and the heretic, not only share similar characteristics, but *are* each other.[19]

The concept of universal oneness, Schopenhauer's doctrine that 'I am all other men; any man is all men' (*Lab.*, 99) is epitomized in 'The Immortal', the man who encompasses all men's identities, present, past, and future. His endless existence means that he is, has been, and will be all men. 'No one is anyone, one single immortal is all men ... I am god, I am hero, I am philosopher, I am demon and I am world, which is a tedious way of saying that I do not exist' (*Lab.*, 145). Menard also understands that this is the gist of his ambitious task. 'My undertaking is not difficult, essentially,' he says, 'I should only have to be immortal to carry it out' (*Lab.*, 66). Funes the Memorious shares the same view: 'we all know deep down that we are immortal and that sooner or later all men will do and know all things' (*Lab.*, 92).

The theme that with infinite time someone will rewrite Homer means that characters, events, images, identity itself, are unimportant. Since individual experiences are bound to be repeated, the concepts of uniqueness and originality are irrelevant: everything has been said before, written before, read before, and will be so again in the future. The prospect of eternity, however, does not render all our efforts meaningless and futile: although 'there no longer remain any remembered images', words, 'displaced and mutilated words, words of others' remain (*Lab.*, 148). The endless space that is eternity is also the endless space of literature: literature, words, may be a 'poor pittance' but they are also life's only revenge on death and forgetting.

For Borges this does not refer to individual or consecutive literature, marked by the name of single authors and the dates of composition, but a literature that, as in Hebrew thought, is collective and cumulative: 'the circumstances of the writing do not matter, individuals do not matter, history does not matter, nor chronological order. All is attributed to one author, the Spirit'.[20] Menard himself suffers from arriving 'at the end of a very long literary period and he comes to the moment when he doesn't want to encumber the world with any more books'.[21] Menard has taken

---

[18] Shilomith Rimmon-Kenan, 'Doubles and Counterparts: The Garden of Forking Paths' in Harold Bloom, (ed.), *Jorge Luis Borges, supra*, at 191.

[19] The theme of the 'double' recurs in many stories, including 'Theme of the Traitor and the Hero'; 'Three Versions of Judas'; 'The Circular Ruins'; 'The Life of Isidoro Cruz'; 'The Shape of the Sword'; 'The Theologian'; 'Death and the Compass'.

[20] *Conversations, supra*, at 246.

[21] *Conversations, supra*, at 15.

seriously, and decades before it was made, John Barth's suggestion of 'the difficulty, perhaps the unnecessity, of writing original works of literature'. Borges' favoured concept of infinite regression is another image of the 'exhaustion of possibilities' due to the 'used-upness' of literary forms and conventions.[22]

Long before Barthes and Foucault, Borges questioned the modernist notion of art as property and the author as proprietor whose rights the law would recognize and enforce. No work of art can be original since it is composed in the context of previous works of art so 'each writer's contribution is infinitesmal' (*Lab.*, 32). In Tlon books are not signed and the concept of plagiarism does not exist because 'knowledge is one and eternal' and 'all works are the creation of one author, who is atemporal and anonymous' (*Lab.*, 37). The romantic notion of the talented artist of genius who creates through sheer individual effort a unique work of art is, in an age of mass production and consumption, replaced with one who resembles more the 'uncertain, anonymous and immortal author' of the Book of Job.[23] 'What is good', insists Borges, 'belongs to no one . . . but rather to the language and to tradition.' (*Lab.*, 282).

In the face of the seeming exhaustion of literary themes and conventions, one device the writer can exploit, as Barth suggests and as writers in Tlon do, is to repeat the same plot 'with all its imaginable possible permutations' (*Lab.*, 37). Borges was fond of saying 'that universal history is the history of the different intonations given a handful of metaphors' (*Lab.*, 227), and 'Of course, I'm not saying anything new';[24] or, of *Ficciones*, 'I wonder if there is a single original line in the book'.[25] His repetitions, nevertheless, do more than duplicate the original in the manner of a Pierre Menard but employ parody, irony, and exaggeration that recontextualizes and alters the meanings of the original. As Borges himself admits, this is an important strategy for colonized groups: treating the European canon 'without superstition, with an irreverence . . . can have, and already does have, fortunate consequences.' (*Lab.*, 218).

In 'Three Versions of Judas' Judas rather than Jesus is postulated as the son of God, and in 'The Sect of the Thirty' the money Judas cast away after betraying Christ is described as 'the price of our souls' salvation' (*CF*, 445). The cliches of the detective genre are similarly deployed in 'Death and the Compass' only to be subverted when the detective cast in the mould of Poe's Auguste Dupin leads himself not only to the mystery of the murders but also to his own murder. The seemingly simplistic explanations given by the policeman, on the other hand, turn out to have been accurate. Borges' fondness for heretics also gives a voice to those outside the dominant culture, those contesting and undermining authority, in law or in literature. While paying lip-service to the European literary canon, Borges ransacks his sources and carves out a

---

[22] John Barth, 'The Literature of Exhaustion' in Raymond Federman (ed.), *Surfiction* (Ohio: Swallow Press, 1975) [1967].

[23] Jorge Luis Borges, 'The Book of Job', in Edna Aizenberg (ed.), *Borges and His Successors: The Borgesian Impact on Literature and the Arts* (Columbia and London: University of Missouri Press, 1990), at 267

[24] *Conversations, supra*, at 235.

[25] *Conversations, supra*, at 91.

new language, and thereby a new geography and identity, and not only for the Latin American continent.[26]

7 OTHER TIMES, OTHER PLACES

The notion of stable and continuous identities is one foundation we choose to anchor our experience of ourselves and others. By blurring identities, genres, living, and dreaming, real and fictitious places, actual and imaginary characters, Borges suggests that the notions we rely on as commonsensical and irrefutable may be no more than consolatory illusions. Stories of identities dissolving or repeating themselves shatter this illusion, leaving us with a sense of vertigo, the feeling that we experienced it all before and will do so again. The correlative dismantling of the concept of time exacerbates this sense of irreality. In 'A New Refutation of Time' Borges wonders why, 'Once matter and spirit, which are continuities, are negated, once space too has been negated, I do not know what right we have to that continuity which is time' (*Lab.*, 256–7).

Borges reminds us that the view of time as absolute, uniform, linear, and progressive, is only one of many, equally arbitrary, ways of understanding time. Time in his fiction can regress backwards into the past, as in Herbert Quain's novel, *April March* in which 'death precedes birth, the scar precedes the wound, and the wound precedes the blow' (*CF*, 108). Or branch forwards into diverse and innumerable futures which themselves proliferate and fork, as in Ts'ui Pen's novel (*Lab.*, 52). It can be circular, as in Hladik's drama *The Enemies* which begins and ends as the clock strikes seven, and with the first actor repeating the lines he had spoken in the first scene of the first act (*Lab.*, 121). Time can be immobile, as in 'The Secret Miracle' where a whole year passes in the instant between the firing squad standing to attention and firing the shots that kill the condemned man.[27] Time can be lengthened, shortened, or brought to a standstill. Some events, particularly painful ones like the death of a loved one, are outside time and 'go on happening endlessly . . .

---

[26] See, for example, Carlos Fuentes: 'This dazzling prose of his, so cold it burns one's lips . . . attests basically to the fact that Latin America is in want of language, and that therefore it must be constituted. To do so, Borges blurs all genres, rescues all traditions, kills all bad habits, creates a new order, rigorous and demanding, on which irony, humor and play can be built . . . and . . . constitutes a new Latin American language which, by sheer dint of contrast, reveals the lie, the submission, and the falseness of what traditionally passed for "language" amongst us.' Quoted in Gene Bell-Villada, *Borges and His Fiction: A Guide to His Mind and Art* (Chapel Hill, NC: University of Carolina Press, 1981). Also Vargas Llosa: Borges shaped 'our personal geography out of an intense involvement with European literature'; quoted in Suzanne Jill Levine, 'Notes to Borges's Notes on Joyce: Infinite Affinities' *Comparative Literature*, Vol. 49, (1997), 344–59, (1997) at 345.

[27] This 'unassuming miracle' as Borges called it (*Conversations, supra,* at 25) enables Hladik to finish his play and seal his life's work, thereby justifying his existence to both himself and to God, the only two people who are aware of the miracle.

either because the immediate past is as if disconnected from the future, or because the parts which form these events do not seem to be consecutive'(*Lab.*, 164–6). Time may be infinitely divisible, as in Zeno's paradox of Achilles and the tortoise where Achilles never overtakes the tortoise (*Lab.*, 237). Or, as the pre-Socratics taught, time, movement, and change may be an illusion conceived from within an eternal present: the events of the past may be no more than dreams of the present, even though we insist on calling these dreams 'memories'. As Bertrand Russell hypothesized, it is possible that the past never existed at all and that we all sprung into being a few minutes ago, furnished with remembrances of an illusory past (*Lab.*, 34). Time may be malleable so that the past may be open to revision and rewriting as in 'The South' for 'reality is partial to symmetries and partial anachronisms' (*CF*, 174). Events may recur eternally as in 'The Circular Ruins', or there may be 'an infinite series of times, in a growing, dizzying net of divergent, convergent and parallel times' (*Lab.*, 53), though we, blinkered mortals, perceive only a limited number of such possibilities.

The narrator of 'The Garden of Forking Paths' reproduces (with the first two pages missing) a statement dictated by Dr Yu Tsun which suggests why an attack by British troops during the First World War had to be postponed for a few days. Yu Tsun is a spy for the German army and, by his own confession, 'a cowardly man'. On realizing that he is about to be caught and killed, with limited time and limited resources— some coins and a revolver with only one bullet—he conceives of a plan whereby he can communicate to his chief in Germany the location of the new British artillery park and 'prove to him that a yellow man could save his armies' (*Lab.*, 46). The plan takes him to the house of a Stephen Albert, an eminent British sinologist. Albert's 'garden of forking paths' evokes in Yu memories of his ancestor Ts'ui Pen who was once governor of Yunnan but had 'renounced worldly power' and 'the pleasures of both tyranny and justice' to dedicate himself to two tasks: 'to write a novel that might be even more populous than the *Hung Lu Meng* and to construct a labyrinth in which all men would become lost' (*Lab.*, 48). In the garden, beneath English trees, Yu meditates on that lost maze: 'I imagined it infinite . . . a labyrinth of labyrinths, of one sinuous spreading labyrinth that would encompass the past and the future and in some way involve the stars' (*Lab.*, 48).

Ts'ui Pen's labyrinth, however, was never found and Yu and Ts'ui Pen's other descendants deplore the publication of his book which he judges as 'an indeterminate heap of contradictory drafts . . . in the third chapter the hero dies, in the fourth he is alive' (*Lab.*, 50). This is in contrast to other fictional works, where, 'each time a man is confronted with several alternatives, he chooses one and eliminates the others; in the fictions of Ts'ui Pen, he chooses—simultaneously—all of them . . . all possible outcomes occur; each one is the point of departure for other forkings' (*Lab.*, 51). Albert's explanation is that the book and the labyrinth were not two heterogeneous projects but one and the same: the labyrinth Ts'ui Pen built, he suggests, is 'a labyrinth of symbols . . . Ts'ui Pen must have said once: *I am withdrawing to write a book*. And another time: *I am withdrawing to construct a labyrinth*. Everyone imagined two works; to no one did it occur that the book and the maze were one and the same thing' (*Lab.*, 50).

Albert interprets Ts'ui Pen's novel as a 'riddle, or parable, whose theme is time.... In contrast to Newton or Schopenhauer, [Ts'ui Pen] did not believe in an uniform, absolute time. He believed in an infinite series of times, in a growing, dizzying net of divergent, convergent, and parallel times. This network of times which approached one another, forked, broke off, or were unaware of one another for centuries, embraces *all* possibilities of time' (*Lab.*, 53). Yu's reflections before meeting Albert also refute the compartmentalization of time into past, present, and future: 'everything happens to a man precisely, precisely *now*. Centuries of centuries, and only in the present do things happen' (*Lab.*, 45). Not only the past but also the future blend into one eternal present so the future is as irrevocable as the past: 'The future already exists' (*Lab.*, 54). Time is not linear but simultaneous, with past, present, and future existing in one single moment.

Like other concepts we use to order reality like identity, law, literature, the concept of time is also a creation of the mind, and 'if time is a mental process, how can thousands of men—or even two different men—share it?' (*Lab.*, 258). Echoing Borges, Derrida reminds us that 'The real presence of Time in the World is called *Man*. Time *is* Man, and Man *is* Time'.[28] The interrogation of time in literature is not only entertaining and puzzling but can provoke ethical questioning: in Levinas' thought, irreversible time, infinite time, or time as duration rather than linear progression, is also the time of the other and opens the way towards our experience of alterity.[29] And it is no accident that our understanding of time, as the quote from Derrida suggests, is *man*-made: the concept of time is not only cultural and contingent, it is also male. The time of Ariadne, as I suggest in my last chapter is, unlike the time of the law, not unified, linear and progressive but discontinuous, circular, and unpredictable; it is the time of eternity rather than finality and of continuity rather than arrival.

8 TO DREAM A WORLD, OR A MAN

If the idealists of Tlon created a fictional planet that slowly penetrates and infects the reality of Earth, the ambition of the protagonist in 'The Circular Ruins' is no smaller:

---

[28] *Speech and Phenomena and Other Essays on Husserl's Theory of Signs*, trans. D. B. Allison (Evanston: Northwestern University Press, 1973), at 85. Quoted and discussed in Paolo Bartolini, 'Spatialised Time and Circular Time: A Note on Time in the Work of Gerald Murnane and Jorge Luis Borges', *Australian Literary Studies*, Vol. 18(2), (1997), 185–90.

[29] Emmanuel Levinas, *Time and the Other*, trans. Richard Cohen (Pittsburgh, Pa.: Duquesne University Press, 1990) [1948] and *Ethics and Infinity*, trans. Richard Cohen (Pittsburgh, Pa.: Duquesne University Press, 1985) [1982]. See especially discussion in Costas Douzinas and Ronnie Warrington *Justice Miscarried: Ethics, Aesthetics and the Law* (Hemel Hempstead: Harvester Wheatsheaf, 1994) who suggest that this is the time of Antigone and of ethics.

'The purpose which guided him was not impossible though it was supernatural. He wanted to dream a man: he wanted to dream him with minute integrity and insert him into reality' (*Lab.*, 73). His method is so obvious that we forget we all do it, all the time: dissatisfied with the structures, rules, and characters we encounter in our every-day world, we create alternative, autonomous worlds and characters in our imagin-ations. Our tools are the same as those of the 'obscure man' who disembarks in the 'unanimous night' with no one seeing him, and 'without pushing aside (probably without feeling) the brambles which dilacerated his flesh' (*Lab.*, 72). Like the reincar-nation of Beloved in Morrison's text, he arrives silently and unnoticed and sets out to perform his single, sacred task, 'sleeping and dreaming' (*Lab.*, 73).

At first he dreams of a circular amphitheatre where he is lecturing to a crowd of students and seeks, out of their number, to 'redeem one of them from his status of pure appearance and interpolate him into the world of reality' (*Lab.*, 73). Students who passively accept his doctrines, though worthy of his love and affection, are rejected as unable to rise to the status of individuals. He selects instead a student who, like himself, is 'sallow, sometimes obstinate, with sharp features which reproduced those of the dreamer' (*Lab.*, 74). The effort to maintain his dream with such consist-ency as to make it a reality is enormous, 'much more arduous than weaving a rope of sand or coining the faceless wind' (*Lab.*, 74). Unlike the rest of us, however, who despair of trying to 'mould the incoherent and vertiginous matter' of dreams, the obscure man perseveres, until one night he is rewarded by dreaming of 'a beating heart' (*Lab.*, 74). More hours of sleeping and dreaming are spent to satisfy himself of the quality of the heart, before he sets out to dream the other organs. It is another year before he reaches 'the skeleton, the eyelids. The innumerable hair was perhaps the most difficult task' (*Lab.*, 75). Having dreamed of a complete man, however, night after night the dreamer dreams his creation asleep. The God of Fire responds to his supplications and gives life to the sleeping phantom, in such a way that all creatures except Fire and the dreamer would believe him to be a man of flesh and blood. At that point, 'In the dreamer's dream, the dreamed one awoke' (*Lab.*, 76).

As the father and teacher of the boy, the dreamer finds the prospect of separation painful and finds excuses to postpone it. (Un)like the Biblical God, he redoes 'the right shoulder, which was perhaps deficient'. He continues sleeping, thinking when closing his eyes, '*Now I shall be with my son*. Or, less often: *The child I have engendered awaits me and will not exist if I do not go to him*' (*Lab.*, 76). When he can no longer postpone his son's 'birth', he kisses him for the first time, instils in him '(so that he would never know he was a phantom, so that he would be thought a man like others) . . . a complete oblivion of all his years of apprenticeship' (*Lab.*, 76) and directs him to another temple. Some years later the dreamer hears of a magic man who walks through fire without being burned. Remembering the words of the God of Fire, the old man fears that his son would 'meditate on his abnormal privilege' and realize that he was a mere image. This thought fills him with dread, 'Not to be a man, to be the projection of another man's dream, what a feeling of humiliation, of vertigo!' (*Lab.*, 77). His worries are interrupted when fire also engulfs his own temple and, submitting to the prospect of death, he walks into the fire. Only to discover that the flames caress rather than hurt him: 'With relief, with humiliation, with terror, he understood that he too was a mere appearance, dreamt by another' (*Lab.*, 77).

A second reading alerts us to this ending: the dreamer, we have been told, was at times 'troubled by the impression that all this had happened before' (76). The epigraph to the story from Lewis Carroll's *Through the Looking Glass* 'And if he let off dreaming about you . . .' underlines the suspicion that, if Alice has no independent existence other than as an object in the King's dream, perhaps we are all being dreamed by another who is dreamed by another and so on ad infinitum. The dream of creation has already been dreamed by the infinite line of dreamers who dreamed other dreamers including dreaming the dreamer who dreamed us. Though the idealist Berkeley postulated God as the ultimate dreamer anchoring our perceptions, for Borges there is no such point of origin, only more infinite regression. We are confronted with the terrifying thought that we may be no more real than the images in someone else's dream, no less fictitious than the characters in a book written by another, no more autonomous than the unsuspicious pawns in a game of chess who

> do not realize the dominant
> hand of the player rules their destiny.
> They do not know an adamantine fate
> Controls their will and pays the battle plan . . .
> God moves the player, he in turn the piece.
> But what god beyond God begins the round
> of dust and time and sleep and agonies?
> (*Poems*, 133–5)

Why is this thought disquieting? 'Why does it disturb us that the map is included in the map and the thousand and one nights in the book of the *Thousand and One Nights*? Why does it disturb us that Don Quihote be a reader of the *Quixote* and Hamlet a spectator of *Hamlet*? I believe', says Borges, 'I have found the reason: these inversions suggest that if the characters of a fictional work can be readers or spectators, we, its readers or spectators, can be fictitious' (*Lab.*, 231).

As in Tlon, an idea, the product of the mind and imagination, attains an independent existence only for us to be reminded that this independence is also a dream, a delusion, since our dreams are also dictated by the dreams of the one who dreams us. The circular temples where these events unfold suggest that there will be more dreamers, more repetitions of the same dream, in the same way that the dreamed man resembles his father in both his intellectual and physical characteristics. History does not signal change, much less progression, but cyclical repetition of the same characters and events. Like the artist who creates characters who have no independent existence outside his words, the dreamer tries to create, to imitate, and indeed to become God. By 'fathering' or creating ideas, we may attain the ecstasy the old man experiences on completing 'his life's purpose' (*Lab.*, 76). This ecstasy, however, is short-lived; someone else has dreamed it before and will do so again. Which does not prevent us from fashioning and 'fathering' new words, new worlds, new characters and places and so on till death.

9 THE ABSENT SEX: ONE WOMAN IS ALL MEN

I say 'fathering' because mothers, natural births, and indeed sex itself are present only in the gaps and silences of Borges' *ficciones*. In 'The Sect of the Phoenix' Borges describes a pagan cult who are united by an unnamed rite and whose secret assures immortality: the Secret 'is transmitted from generation to generation, but good usage prefers that mothers should not teach it to their children, nor that priests should; initiation into the mystery is the task of the lowest individuals . . . The act in itself is trivial, momentary, and requires no description . . . The Secret is sacred, but is always somewhat ridiculous; its performance is furtive and even clandestine, and the adept do not speak of it. There are no decent words to name it, but it is understood that all words name it, or rather, inevitably allude to it . . . A kind of sacred horror prevents some faithful believers from performing this very simple rite; the others despise them, but they despise themselves even more' (*Lab.*, 133). As in 'The Garden of Forking Paths', the answer to the riddle will not be found on the surface of the words but in what is hidden between the lines. Like the members of this cult, Borges goes to elaborate lengths to avoid naming an act that is celebrated as much as denounced and broadcast as much as hidden: the basic fact of sex.

One of his few female protagonists, Emma Zunz, is a young woman for whom sex is loathful and in whom men inspire 'an almost pathological fear' (*Lab.*, 165); she has sex with an unknown sailor in order to avenge her father who committed suicide after his name was sullied by her unscrupulous employer. She perceives the act as a 'sacrifice' to her cause of avenging her father and it leaves her pained and disgusted. When she kills her employer it is less in the name of her father than in the name of 'the outrage she had suffered. She was unable not to kill him after that thorough dishonour' (*Lab.*, 168). Thinly veiled behind Emma's scheme is the theme of incest: the narrator suggests that she thought of her father during the act 'and in that moment she endangered her desperate undertaking. She thought (she was unable not to think) that her father had done to her mother the hideous thing that was being done to her now' (*Lab.*, 167).

The writer whose hope is to engender, through his unlimited power and sheer force of his will, a tiger,[30] who emulates the divine act of creation with words and creates idealized realms of the mind that compete with, and at times invade, the material world, is notoriously reluctant to describe or even name the human activity that leads to biological procreation, continuity, and eternity. Borges the writer and librarian

---

[30] 'Dreamtigers': '*This is a dream, a pure diversion of my will, and since I have unlimited power, I am going to bring forth a tiger*' (*CF*, 294).

retains a fascination for a life of action like that of his ancestors and bemoaned having lived a life of words, amongst books: at the age of thirty-four he apparently remarked that 'life and death have been lacking in my life'.[31] As Suzanne Hill Levine points out, Borges also harboured a secret envy for James Joyce who, unlike him, did not die 'without sighting / the twofold beast'.[32] Borges' dream of mental dominance, as John Irwin argues, is mind's revenge on the physical world, 'a defence mechanism against the frustrations of the physical world, on the one hand, against the dangerous and humiliating demands of the body on the other'.[33] Borges' characters dream of returning to a point of origin from where one can create a world that conforms to our dreams and is more orderly than the one we inhabit. It is also, as I suggested in my reading of *Oedipus Rex*, and discuss further in the next chapter, the dream of *man* rather than of *woman* and the journey leads either back to oneself or to death.

Women are not conspicuous in Borges' fiction; their brief appearances are in roles that consign them to either virgins like Emma Zunz, or inconstant creatures like Beatriz in 'The Aleph'. In a male economy of desire, such as René Girard's, desire is triangular, the object of desire deriving value for the desiring subject by virtue of the fact that she is the object of desire of a third person.[34] Women's presence in Girard's, as in Borges' homosocial world, in life as much as in death, causes rivalry and destruction between men and the danger they pose must be eliminated by killing the object of desire, woman.[35]

In 'The Interloper' woman is a 'servant', a 'mere thing', that does not matter 'beyond desire and ownership' and who obeys the two brothers who share her with 'beastly submissiveness'. She is also an 'intruder', causing rivalry between the brothers and as such must be sacrificed in the cause of restoring the fraternal bond: when one brother announces to the other that he has killed her, 'Almost weeping, they embraced. Now they were linked by yet another bond: the woman grievously sacrificed, and the obligation to forget her'(*CF*, 351). If we follow Girard's analysis of sacrifice, woman here is the scapegoat needed to restore stability to the (male) community whose order was threatened by her presence. As Irigaray suggests, it is because women are conceived as objects of exchange and do not enter relations as autonomous subjects, that sacrifice is perceived as necessary in a male economy. If Borges' characters valued the process of fertility and continuity women bring, violence would

---

[31] Quoted in Gene Bell-Villada, *Borges and His Fiction, supra*, at 263.

[32] Suzanne Jill Levine, 'Notes to Borges's Notes on Joyce: Infinite Affinities', *Comparative Literature*, Vol. 49, (1997), 344–59, at 357.

[33] *The Mystery to a Solution: Poe, Borges, and the Analytic Detective Story* (Baltimore and London: Johns Hopkins University Press, 1994), at xiv.

[34] 'In the birth of desire, the third person is always present': René Girard, *Deceit, Desire and the Novel: Self and Other in Literary Structure*, trans. Yvonne Freccero (Baltimore and London: Johns Hopkins University Press, 1965), [1961], at 21.

[35] This theme is discussed further by Sharon Magnarelli, 'Literature and Desire: Women in the Fiction of Jorge Luis Borges', *Review Interamericana*, Vol. 113(14), (1983), 138; Magnarelli also argues that women in Borges' fiction are linked with literature and that they are often associated with the colour red and are 'linked to the exotic, passion, hot temper, blood and death'.

not be the only solution, it would not be necessary to 'cut up and eat'.[36] When, unlike Juliana, who is given no voice in Borges' text and unlike Iphigeneia who is gagged by her father, woman, like Ariadne in my next chapter, starts to speak and write, she can shutter the male economy that conceives of her as an object of exchange between men. This is the case whether those exchanges act to cement men's bonds (as in Lévi-Strauss's scheme of marriage), or to shutter it (as in Girard's scheme of desire). Furthermore, just as man thinks he is in control of language but language precedes and frustrates him, man may think he can exchange women, but when women, like Ariadne in my next chapter, express and act out their independent desires, they can exceed and escape the male attempt to exchange and thereby to contain them.

The absence of women in Borges' homosocial universe, where men love, hate, and indeed become each other, is accompanied with an equal repression of 'effeminate' men whose homosexuality is only thinly veiled in 'The Shape of the Sword'.[37] The usually gentlemanly Borges allowed himself to express anger and disgust at a film adaptation of 'The Interloper': 'It's madness. And it's not my story . . . But there it is with the title of my story, and with my name. And with incest, homosexuality and sodomy. Charming'.[38] One can go further and suggest that this refusal to acknowledge and represent homosexual desire is another form of the writer's repression of the feminine within. Where women do appear in Borges' fiction, they are not mothers, and children are entirely absent. The analogy between the artist's act of creation and the act of giving birth hints at not only a confusion but a 'rivalry between *genius* and *gynein*', between women's ability to procreate naturally and the artist's attempt at artificial creation.[39] Borges' mother, ubiquitous in his own life, is nevertheless absent from his fiction. The absence of mothers in his work hints at an unconscious desire to be the mother, to create and engender a world in writing. The desire for a genesis that takes place without sex and without reference to the body reaches its apotheosis, in 'The Circular Ruins' where an *ascetic man fathers himself a son*: by a sheer act of will, by willing himself to dream him.

Borges' characters search in these stories for the origin of origins, the designer behind the design, the name of God, the letter, the book, the moment, the place, that will reveal as well as justify to them, their life, their meaning, their existence. Perhaps the fact that women do not undertake these journeys suggests that they are already in possession of a knowledge that the male characters are in search of. The absence of

---

[36] Luce Irigaray, 'Women, the Sacred, and Money', *Paragraph*, 8, October 1986, 6–18.

[37] Herbert Brant, 'The Mark of the Phallus: Homoerotic Desire in Borges' 'La Forma de la Espada' *Chasqui-Revista de Literatura Latinoamericana*, Vol. 25(1), (1996), 25–38. Brant argues that in 'The Shape of the Sword' Moon is the effeminate man frightened of combat. Society perceives gay men as dangerous for, having betrayed their gender, they might betray their nation. In Moon's version of the story his desire for the young hero is transformed into identity. 'The final words of the story summarize the lesson society has been pounding into homosexuals' heads for centuries: "now you know who I am, despise me!"'.

[38] *Conversations, supra*, at 226.

[39] Elizabeth Bronfen, *Over Her Dead Body: Death, Femininity and the Aesthetic* (Manchester: Manchester University Press, 1992), at 111.

women in Borges' stories hints further at the possibility of another journey, not a narcissistic journey that leads back to oneself and to death, but a journey towards others. This hides not only a secret envy of, but also a fear of woman: despite the intrepid exploring that Borges' characters undertake, the one journey they do not undertake is the journey towards woman; woman is the destination they distance themselves from, and create obstacles from reaching. If, as Adam Phillips suggests, love is a problem of knowledge and 'lovers are detectives',[40] the one mystery Borges' detectives do not try to explore, let alone resolve, is woman.

Both fearful of and envious of woman's ability to procreate, Borges on paper and his characters in their dreams, dream dreams of creation. They dream, and thereby create, another man. They dream, and thereby create, a whole country. They dream, and thereby create, an entire planet (and wake up to find that planet earth has been invaded by their dream planet). They dream of God: a God who answers their dreams, makes time stand still and justifies their short life to eternity. In short, as I argued in my opening chapter, Borges and his characters take on the task of inventing reality. One dream they dare not dream of, however, is woman; in their dreams they evade the real of their desire. Indeed they dream in order to *avoid* the real of their desire.

What is, after all, Borges' refutation of time other than an attempt to incorporate, without naming it, what Kristeva has called 'women's time' a time which is not linear but cyclical, repetitive, and eternal? And if, as Borges suggests, the book might be our only universe, our only promise of immortality, does not the association of women with literature in many of these stories suggest that both the desire and frustration at the unattainability of these goals arises from man's desire for and inability to understand and thereby possess woman? Malcolm Bowie suggests that the remedy Lacan finds to the impossibility of desire is literature; further, that it is women, whose 'existence' Lacan allegedly erases, that guide him back to the pleasures of the text: 'women, freed from the servitude of the phallus have already got what men will always crave'.[41] Borges' characters can similarly be said to envy women their desire that they cannot understand and do not dare explore. Like the male lawyer, like Angelo in *Measure for Measure*, like the Minotaur in my closing chapter, to protect themselves from the indecipherable labyrinth of female desire and its insistent demands, they create their own labyrinth. In the process, however, they succeed only in imprisoning themselves; woman is the remainder, the excess that escapes from both the labyrinth and the text. She is also, like Angela in *Chronicle of a Death Foretold*, the guardian of a truth that promises the totality, immortality, and eternity that eludes the male questers.

---

[40] Adam Phillips, *On Flirtation*, (London and Boston, Mass.: Faber and Faber, 1994), at 40.
[41] Malcolm Bowie, *Lacan* (London: Fontana Press, 1991), at 148, 156.

10 'PERPLEXITIES RATHER THAN CERTAINTIES'[42]

Borges has been accused of engaging in writing that is escapist, consolatory if not also reactionary: he himself admitted that his aim was not to offer political or ethical opinions, but to be true to the plot, or more accurately to the dream: 'I don't think I have any moral purpose when I write', he says.[43] Even some of his staunch admirers comment on the lack of political messages in his work: 'There is nothing in them' John Sturrock writes, 'for those whose tastes are moralistic or sociological; everything in them for those whose tastes are literary'.[44] And Carter Wheelock concludes that 'These stories, suggestive of highbrow detective fiction and of Symbolist poetic theory applied to prose, are utterly lacking in social consciousness or moral implication: unemotional, sexless, and uncontemporary, they wave no banners and press no points. They allude to everything and recommend nothing'.[45]

This assessment, however, assumes a distinction between theory and practice, between reality and fiction, living and dreaming, philosophy and literature, politics and philosophy. If Borges' work, and indeed this book, has any message, it is that these distinctions are themselves arbitrary, problematic, and contingent. For Borges a fantastic tale is as real if not more real than newspaper accounts: 'I always get rather angry at those who speak of reality on one side and of literature on the other as though literature were not part of reality. If you read a book it's as much of an experience as if you had travelled, or if you were jilted'.[46] Indeed, while so-called realistic accounts report on accidents and mere circumstances, literature can claim to be more 'real' by enabling us to transcend the here and now and 'to get away from time and to write about everlasting things. I mean we do our best to be in eternity'.[47] Borges' work like Marquez' *Chronicle of a Death Foretold*, thus interrogates and problematizes the distinctions between literature and reality, intimates new ways of knowing 'reality' and in the process stimulates thinking that may one day turn to action. If his dreaming postpones or distracts us from living, it also enables us to return to so-called reality with new insights that inform the way we perceive the world we live in.

Echoing the people of Tlon, Borges does not expect philosophy or science to tell us the 'truth'; long before Derrida, Borges suggested that poetry is no different from philosophy as they both aim to express puzzlement, 'I've looked at metaphysics rather more as a branch of fantastic literature'.[48] For man to find *the* truth would be anathema, because 'doubt', the investigation of the truth, is more exciting, more fun: other

---

[42] *Conversations, supra*, at 74.
[43] *Conversations, supra*, at 121.
[44] John Sturrock, *Paper Tigers: The Ideal Fictions of Jorge Luis Borges* (Oxford: Clarendon Press, 1977), at 4.
[45] 'Borges's New Prose' in Bloom (ed.), *Jorge Luis Borges, supra*, at 106.
[46] *Conversations, supra*, at 10.
[47] *ibid.*, at 78.
[48] *ibid.*, at 57, 177.

than love and friendship, he says in a late interview, the most precious gift is *doubt*.[49] The longed-for dissolution of differences, between self and other, night and day, past and future, real and imaginary, can come, as my reading of *Wuthering Heights* suggested, only with death. Only death puts an end to searching and to doubt: while alive, human beings continue searching. To believe that one has found 'truth', the 'definitive text' is to succumb to consolatory illusions, 'to religion or fatigue'.[50]

In the legal labyrinth the view, or hope, that behind the mass of diverse and contradictory cases, doctrines, rules, and principles, may lie a theory or theories capable of presenting a coherent view of law as a whole, explaining, if not justifying, the same, represents the apotheosis of theory, the hope that it will synthesize, integrate, express, and anchor our disparate and incoherent experiences. To pursue Borges' scheme, we can argue that theory is historically contingent just as language, man, woman, culture, and reason are. This acknowledgment does not mean the abandonment of ethical thinking and practice, or being apolitical, amoral, nihilistic, or pragmatic. 'Doing' or 'teaching' theory does not mean giving answers but enabling questions to be constantly raised; it does not mean changing the world but creating the space in which it can be changed. This is theory not in the sense of grand ideas but theory which unravels our own assumptions and enables us to become children again,[51] when we did not take the world, let alone the western world, its law, or its legal system for granted. By tolerating explanatory gaps we may remain faithful to the distrust of totalizing or synthesizing explanations of disparate phenomena and enable them to become acceptable for academic knowledge, that is to keep rethinking and keep redefining what counts as legal knowledge.

Borges, and after him, Foucault reminded us that there are incommensurable ways of ordering things and posed the question, how do we, modern westerners, order things or, what are the limits of our own way of thinking. In the same way that there is nothing natural about Borges' classification of animals in his encyclopaedia, there is nothing natural about legal classifications on the nature of truth, reason, guilt, or innocence. To be constantly re-examining the latter means to be better informed about the contingency of our own classifications. As Shoshana Felman puts it, the value of this approach in education is to teach people 'to think beyond their means';[52] we can, and should, in other words, learn from the limitations of theory and from our own ignorance.

Above all, we must remember that ways of reading, teaching, and writing are not politically neutral but are ways of living and being in the world. As academics, far

---

[49] *ibid*, at 241 and 245.

[50] Jorge Luis Borges, 'Las versiones homericas' Discusion (Buenos Aires: Emecé, 1966), quoted in Alfred Macadam, 'Translation as Metaphor: Three Versions of Borges' *Modern Language Notes*, Vol. 90, (1975), 747–54, at 749.

[51] Terry Eagleton, *The Significance of Theory* (Oxford: Blackwell, 1990), at 34.

[52] Shoshana Felman, 'Psychoanalysis and Education: Teaching Terminable and Interminable', in *Jacques Lacan and the Adventure of Insight: Psychoanalysis in Contemporary Culture* (Cambridge, Mass.: Harvard University Press, 1987), at 15.

from assuming the role of prophets or legislators bent on legislating on how to change the world, we must see ourselves as 'interpreters' aiming to decode our traditions, recognizing, all the time, their and our own contingency. In Foucault's words, the role of the intellectual is not to express the truth, not 'to place himself 'somewhat ahead and to the side' in order to express the stifled truth of the collectivity; rather it is to struggle against the forms of power that transform him into its object and instrument in the sphere of 'knowledge', 'truth', 'consciousness', and 'discourse".[53] By refusing to adjudicate, this approach achieves not a fusion but a widening of our horizons, exposing their plurality and contingency. If this means that instead of 'universal intellectuals' we become 'specific intellectuals',[54] then this is an ethical demand and a role that we must accept. The fact that our bewilderment may not be dissipated is not a reason for settling for answers that are constructions rather than facts, fictions rather than truths, provisional rather than final. Perhaps, as in psychoanalysis, there is no cure, only treatment, or as Freud himself suggested 'we must be content . . . with having clearly recognized the obscurity'.[55]

The political importance of this demand and this role cannot be overestimated if we agree, that, as Peter Goodrich puts it, 'To remove the space of interpretation is to abolish all possibility of dialogue and to bleed dry the idea of a lived law while leaving only its form in place. . . . The problem that faces critical legal studies is that of reappropriating the space of interpretation, the space of the sublime, and so of recreating the distance necessary to communication, the overflow of communication'.[56] Abandoning legislation for interpretation is not therefore to abandon practice for theory; theory in this sense 'does not express, translate, or serve to apply practice: it is practice'.[57]

11 WOMAN, FORTUNATELY, IS DREAMING

In this search for more perplexities rather than certainties, Borges blurs the edges between essay and fiction, literary criticism and literature, reality and fantasy, living and dreaming. His night-time self dreams of immortality, infinite times, totality in a single object, eternity in an instant, perfect memory, a complete library. The

---

[53] 'Intellectuals and Power: a conversation between Michel Foucault and Gilles Deleuze' in *Language, Counter-Memory, Practice: Selected Essays and Interviews by Michel Foucault*, D. F. Bouchard, (ed.), (New York: Cornell University Press, 1977), at 206.

[54] Michel Foucault, 'Politics and the Study of Discourse' in *Ideology and Consciousness*, 3 (1978), 7–26, at 24.

[55] 'From the History of an Infantile Neurosis', in *The Standard Edition of the Complete Psychological Works of Sigmund Freud*, James Stratchey (ed.), (London: Hogarth Press, 1955), Vol. 17, at 105.

[56] Peter Goodrich, *Languages of Law: From Logics of Memory to Nomadic Masks* (London: Weidenfeld & Nicolson, 1990), at 296.

[57] 'Intellectuals and Power: a Conversation Between Michel Foucault and Gilles Deleuze', *supra*, at 206.

consequences of these quixotic ideas are then pursued as if they were real.[58] Literature allows a space for our night-time selves, where the imagination is not restricted by day-time laws, where another law rules, and Morpheus, not Athena, is the law-maker. 'I have glimpsed or foreseen a refutation of time, in which I myself do not believe, but which regularly visits me at night and in the weary twilight with the illusory force of an axiom' (*Lab.*, 253). During the day, however, the symbolic order reasserts itself and the other Borges relents to its intransigent demands: 'The world, unfortunately, is real; I, unfortunately, am Borges' (*Lab.*, 269).

The dream, however, continues to consume the dreamer when awake: like the fictitious planet Tlon whose teachings invade earth, like the German theologian who, 'in the early seventeenth century, described the imaginary community of Rosae Crucis—a community that others founded later, in imitation of what he had pre-figured' (*Lab.*, 29). Borges' admirers have envisioned a time when there will be 'a Borges encyclopaedia . . . the work of a group of people devoted to the annihilation of the external universe and its replacement with a universe made by a human being, with its own inevitable logic and order. The human being will in time recede as a physical being and achieve the status of an idea. Then those future generations of scholars will forget the existence of English or Argentine or Latin literatures. The world will be Borges'.[59]

Borges' dreams and fantasies interrogate existing categories and our understanding of the world; his writing influenced, as Borges himself wrote of Kafka, the writings not only of his successors, but also of our readings of his predecessors, including Kafka. Like the inhabitants of Tlon, he fabricates a new world, characters, and events which invade and infect our existing universe. Like Ts'ui Pen's novel, they influence not only the future but also the past. It is because fantasy and dreaming are not external to, or opposed to, reality but a part of reality, that we 'long' to give in to them. Reality is not only always already open to penetration by the imagination, the imagination is part of reality, its repressed unconscious that keeps returning and keeps disrupting so-called reality. As I discussed in my opening chapter, reality and imagination, law and litera-ture, living and dreaming co-exist and overlap, constantly and mutually interfering with and penetrating each other.

Of course, even the dreams we dream are constrained by the language available to us: Funes the Memorious finds it difficult to accept that 'the generic symbol 'dog' embraces so many unlike individuals of diverse size and form; it bothered him that the dog at three fourteen (seen from the side) should have the same name as the dog at three fifteen (seen from the front). His own face in the mirror, his own hands, surprised him every time he saw them' (*Lab.*, 93–4). Funes recognizes that language is not a tool with which to represent the world and reality but constitutes that world and

---

[58]   For the view that literature is an 'as if', an 'illusion', 'a work of bad faith' on the part of both writers and readers see Maurice Blanchot, 'How is Literature Possible' and 'The Novel is a Work of Bad Faith' in, *The Blanchot Reader*, Michael Holland (ed.), *supra*.

[59]   D. Balderston, *The Literary Universe of Jorge Luis Borges*; quoted in Evelyn Fishburn and Psiche Hughes, *A Dictionary of Borges*, (London: Duckworth, 1996), at 1.

reality, reducing its inconsistencies, perplexities, and absurdities into convenient and manageable categories. Borges expresses the same disquiet about the limits of language: 'The world of appearances is most complex and our language has realised only a very small number of combinations which it allows. Why not create a word, a single word, for our simultaneous perception of cattle bells ringing in the afternoon and the sunset in the distance?'.[60] Funes' tragedy, all our tragedy, is that without reducing the general to the particular, without language, communication is impossible. As Borges muses, only angels can converse directly without language. For us, 'the never angels, the verbal ones', our destiny is 'to adapt ourselves to syntax, to the traitorous concatenations, to imprecision, to uncertainty, to overemphasis, to the reservations, to the hemisphere of deceit and shadows in our speech.'[61]

Can Ariadne's language, in my next chapter, perhaps mediate the impasse between dreaming and reality? Can poetry and music mediate between the language of humans and the language of angels, between law and literature? Can it suggest a third way, an 'orbis tertius', that may allow us a brief glimpse of the indefinable beyond? In contrast to scientific observation, which aims to be direct and immediate, Poe contrasts the oblique approach of poetry and music.[62] In its attention to the surface of the words and the appearances of things, poetry may enable us to see 'truths' that scientific reasoning in its urge to understand and categorize can miss. As I discuss in the next chapter, Poe also suggests that in order to understand a mystery, we need to be not only mathematicians but also poets; we need the faculties not only of reason but of imagination, not only the language of law but also the language of poetry. Borges' fiction suggests further that we need to think in images as well as abstractions[63] and to allude rather than to express: 'At the worst, things can be expressed; but by allusion we bring out a memory in the reader, and thus a great many things can be done.'[64] Poetry and music can reopen the gap between signifier and signified to go back to a time before signification, and reveal the arbitrariness of the signs we choose to rely on and keep mistaking as laws. As Peter Goodrich speculates, perhaps 'every time the unconscious is reduced to prose, there is a minor victory of the juridical over the poetics of an interior law'.[65] In that sense writing and living in poetry and music is not an evasion of reality or of the law, but a reaching out towards a deeper truth, an anterior or greater law.

As Kristeva argues, the language of the symbolic order, the language of the father is

[60] Quoted in James E. Irby, 'Borges and the Idea of Utopia' in Harold Bloom, (ed.), *Jorge Luis Borges, supra*, at 98.

[61] Quoted in Thomas R. Hart Jr, 'Borges' Literary Criticism' in Harold Bloom, (ed.), *Jorge Luis Borges, supra*, at 16–17.

[62] See discussion in Maurice J. Bennett, 'The Detective Fiction of Poe and Borges', *Comparative Literature*, Vol. 35(3), (1993) 262–75.

[63] This is a distinction Borges makes in his essay on 'Nathaniel Hawthorne' in *Other Inquisitions, supra*.

[64] In interview with Keith Botsford, 'About Borges and Not About Borges', *Kenyon Review*, Vol. 26 (1964), 723, at 732.

[65] Peter Goodrich, 'Courting Death', in *Courting Death: The Law of Mortality*, Desmond Manderson (ed.) (London: Pluto Press, 1999), at 220.

not monolithic and impervious but its gaps and contradictions leave open spaces for incursions from the anterior, semiotic language of the mother. In the same way the language of the law is permeable to the language of the imagination and the language of dreams; indeed law would not be able to succeed in convincing and seducing its subjects, were it not successful in appealing to the senses and to their dreams.[66] Poetic language, though contained by the symbolic, can also unsettle and renew the symbolic order. Fortunately, Ariadne has dreams of her own that are not dictated or delimited by, nor do they coincide with, those of the law. As I argue in the next chapter, this poetry, music, mystery, and rhythm is closer to Ariadne's language than to that of the lawyer in his labyrinth. It is closer to Nietzsche's 'universal language'[67] of music than tied to specific laws, and may be one way of negotiating the distance between reason and madness, between self and other, between humans and angels, between temporality and eternity. Its apotheosis is not law but love, not the word but the flesh, not the love letter but the love song.

If we long to yield to Tlön, to the dream, it is because it arouses more senses than reason. 'Reason', Borges suggests, 'will never give up its dream' (*Poems*, 219). *But reason is dreaming too*: the dream of reason and dreams and nightmares have the power to unsettle our reality. Though 'the world, alas, is real', Borges provides us with an intimation of other possibilities, other times, when the dream conquered reality. And the intimation is enough. Our night-time writing, when our thoughts are ambiguous and indeterminate, insinuates itself in our day-time experiences. Dreaming is not the underside of thinking, or the irrational, but an integral part of our thinking processes and of ourselves, alluding to truths that cannot be ignored. Indeed, in Lacan's words, when awake '*After all, I am the consciousness of this dream*'.[68] Our refusal to acknowledge the dream is a refusal to accept the Real of our desire, which we may find more terrifying than so-called reality. As Žižek puts it, 'Reality is a fantasy construction which enables us to mask the Real of our desire'.[69] The only way, therefore, we have of approaching the real of our desire, is through the dream. Dreaming is not an alternative to, not an escape from, or different from living, but part of living and more importantly part of our identities. The stuff that dreams are made of is also the stuff that maps our making as human subjects. Literature, art, poetry, music, can provide us with more images, more maps, more signs, more words with which to fashion and express our dreams, and thereby ourselves. In dreams we can become goddesses recreating the world, unsettling and remaking its laws. Reason's inability to understand, let alone tame and control the realm of dreams, suggests that dreams may be the sublime form of intelligence, an oneiric logic or law whose murmurs we ignore at our peril. As Gianni Vattimo puts it, the point is 'to know that one is dreaming and

---

[66] See especially Peter Goodrich (ed.), *Law and the Unconscious: A Legendre Reader*, *supra*.

[67] *The Birth of Tragedy*, trans. Francis Golffing (New York: Doubleday, 1956), at 98.

[68] Jacques Lacan, *The Four Fundamental Concepts of Psychoanalysis*, trans. Alan Sheridan (London: Penguin, 1979) [1973], at 76.

[69] Slavoj Žižek, *The Sublime Object of Ideology* (London and New York: Verso, 1989), at 45.

yet to continue dreaming'.[70]And fortunately, there is always more to dream: it may not be law yet, 'it doesn't matter if it's true or not now, because it will be, with time'.[71]

If Borges' characters are frustrated in their quest for a god who is forever absent, always elsewhere, if their journeys lead them back to themselves, and to death, could the god they are looking for not be a god after all, but a goddess? A goddess who is not fixed, disembodied, fleshless, and unknowable, but fluid, multiple, and corporeal? 'A feminine god' that, as Irigaray observes, 'is yet to come'.[72] Future Pierres and Petras Menards must dream harder: dream of a gay God, dream of a goddess.

And is the dream, the unknowable, frightening, untameable, and inexhaustible, the Real of man's desire, and which neither reason nor law can tame, also the dream of Ariadne in my next chapter? For to extend Borges,[73] in the beginning there was not space, or time, or the word, or law, or literature, but an emotion within a dream, dreamed by a goddess. The dream alluded rather than expressed, with images rather than text, in music rather than words: the song, a lullaby, 'is love?'.

---

[70] 'Myth and the Fate of Secularization', *Res*, Vol. 9, (Spring 1985), at 34. Quoted in Richard Kearney, *Poetics of Imagining: From Husserl to Lyotard* (London and New York: Routledge, 1991), at 183.

[71] Gabriel García Márquez, *The Autumn of the Patriarch*, trans. Gregory Rabassa (London: Penguin, 1996) [1975], at 143.

[72] Luce Irigaray, *Divine Women*, trans. Stephen Muecke (Sydney: Local Consumption, 1986), at 8.

[73] 'In the beginning there was an emotion', *Conversations*, at 243.

11

A REBEGINNING: THE LAWYER IN HIS LABYRINTH AND 'FROM HER TO ETERNITY'[1]

In the history of Western reason, births are the object of all sorts of care, anticipation, precaution, preventive measures, and so on. Prenatal therapy is institutional. When a new science is born, the family circle is always already prepared for astonishment, jubilation and baptism. For a long time now every child, even a foundling, is reputed to be the son of a father, and when he is a prodigy, fathers would be fighting each other off at the ticket window were it not for the mother and the respect owed her. In our replete world a space is anticipated for birth; a space is anticipated even for the anticipation of birth: 'prospective'.

Louis Althusser

1 A BIRTH

The ingredients are there, the equation simple, the formula well-tested:

> Man = Reason; Man + Reason = Birth; Birth + Father = Science;
> Science + Naming = Baptism; Baptism + Family = Institution.

Result (in bold capitals, since we have no access here to neon signs or loudspeakers):

CHILD = SON OF THE FATHER

And, repeat: Man, using his reason, gives birth to science, becomes a father, the family, always already prepared for the birth, astonished and jubilant, capture the child as it emerges from 'the ticket window', the baptism immerses it into the

---

[1] 'From Her to Eternity' in *The Best of Nick Cave and the Bad Seeds* (London: Music Records, 1998); for a performance, watch Wim Wenders, *Wings of Desire* (Connoisseur Videos, 1987).

institution and names *him*. For it goes without saying that 'every child, even a found-ling, is reputed to be the son of a father'.[2]

And repeat: the son accepts his father's name, his language and his law, guided all the time by the radiant light of his father's reason, and when fully grown he in turn gives birth to a son, that is, a new science. The new science, Althusser and other tellers of such tales would have us believe, kills and replaces the old science, the son allegedly commits parricide and takes the father's place. But old habits are hard to change: the new science is a continuation, not a repudiation of the old one. The old pattern remains intact and open to repetition: more children, more sons of fathers come along, kill and replace their father, give birth to a new son, who in turn kills and replaces them.

And repeat.

And repeat.

And repeat?

'Were it not for the respect due to the mother'; a slip? a remainder? a reluctant acknowledgment? '*Were it not for the respect due to the mother*': in italics; for mother needs no capitals, nor neon signs, nor loudspeakers to broadcast her contribution to the birth. WERE IT NOT THAT MAN, and the sound gets louder, prefers to hide her between the lines, mention her in passing, before, supposedly, surpassing her. (For the preference of the father over the mother, as father Freud, whom Althusser chooses to go on to discuss, at length, constitutes a victory of intellectuality over sensuality, of the abstract over the bodily, of the word over the flesh: a triumph, in Freud's terms, of civilization over savagery.[3])

One wonders whether this man, this father, was present at the birth: did he see the mother's body, the blood and the tears, the laughter and the delirium, the anguish and the ecstasy? If he did, he shuns any allusions to them. What about the time of concep-tion? Was he present then? (crucial once, but alas? no more). If he was, did he think, if only once, if only briefly, that the act he was engaged in was perhaps not driven by logic but by instinct, not by science but by nature, not necessarily by sanity but maybe madness, not by reason but intuition, not by words but by music, not by competition but connection, not by law but an emotion—an emotion called love?

Half way through my first year of teaching 'Law and Literature' back in 1994, (the first such course in Britain, I believe) I was alarmed to detect in myself signs of the classic Almodovar heroine, never quite certain of her own distance from *What Have I Done to Deserve This?* or *Women on the Verge of a Nervous Breakdown*.[4] My students spurred me on by reciprocating my enthusiasm, thoughtfully pleading, at the same time, that I should wait for the end of the course before becoming one. It is not at all

---

[2] Louis Althusser, *Writings on Psychoanalysis: Freud and Lacan*, trans. Jeffrey Mehlman (New York: Colum-bia University Press, 1996), at 15.

[3] '*Moses and Monotheism*' in *Complete Psychological Works of Sigmund Freud*, (ed.), James Strachey, (London: Hogarth Press, 1953–74), Vol. 23, at 113–14.

[4] Pedro Almodovar, *Women on the Verge of a Nervous Breakdown* (Universal Videos, 1985); Pedro Almodovar, *What Have I Done to Deserve This?* (Tartan Videos, 1984).

clear that I obliged: trying to remember what got into me to launch this strange course in a strange place like Bristol, England, I am not reassured that the beginnings were any sounder: the inspiration came from the philosopher of madness (worse, a French man), himself inspired by a writer of dreams (bad again, an Argentinian).

It goes like this: the Argentinian writes, without a trace of irony or flippancy, of a certain Chinese encyclopaedia in which animals are classified as '(a) belonging to the Emperor, (b) embalmed, (c) tame, (d) sucking pigs, (e) sirens, (f) fabulous, (g) stray dogs, (h) included in the present classification, (i) frenzied, (j) innumerable, (k) drawn with a very fine camel brush, (l) etcetera, (m) having just broken the water-pitcher, (n) that from a long way off look like flies'.[5]

'Normal' people might shake their heads in sympathy, offer Borges some help, suggest perhaps that he gets out more. The Frenchman, however, knew better: this proves, he announces, that there is nothing 'natural', about our ways of thinking; nor between the divisions we make between different ways of reading, writing, or learning; or between different disciplines like law, literature, history, mythology, philosophy, alchemy, psychoanalysis, witchcraft. All these distinctions are not only cultural rather than natural, contingent rather than given, they are also hierarchical, made by those with an interest in portraying their version of 'the truth', as superior to that of other people. Philosophers, including of course, legal philosophers, assume their methods and sources are more likely to find the truth about the world, and about law, than the views of poets, painters, tarot card readers, soap operas, pop musicians, cartoonists! To suggest, however, that these old-fashioned distinctions are 'normal' ways of distinguishing 'reason' from 'madness' would just prove Foucault's point.[6]

The rest is geography: if the distinctions we make between law and literature, reason and feelings, ethics and aesthetics, are not natural or god-given but cultural and contingent then the claim that we can only find out 'the truth' about law from statutes and law reports, by learning more rules and principles, by using our reason and not our emotions, can also be abandoned. Not that the Law and Literature critic, versed and delighting in her postmodern condition, claims that she will find the 'truth' about law from literature. Abandoning herself to reading as widely as possible, she is content to suggest that there are many ways of learning, seeing, thinking, and understanding and the scientific mode is not necessarily the only, or the best, one. She will argue that judgements do not have to stem from logistic syllogisms or dialect-ical reasoning to be valid or valuable and that aesthetic judgements, judgements based on feeling, or aroused and explored in myths and stories can be just as valid and

---

[5] Jorge Luis Borges, 'The Analytical Language of John Wilkins' in *Other Inquisitions, 1937–1952*, trans. L. C. Simms (Austin, Tex.: Texas University Press, 1964).

[6] 'This book first arose out of a passage in Borges, out of the laughter that shattered, as I read the passage, all the familiar landmarks of my thought—*our* thought, the thought that bears the stamp of our age and our geography—breaking up all the ordered surfaces and all the planes with which we are accustomed to tame the wild profusion of existing things ... [the bizarre taxonomy of animals in Borges' Chinese Encyclopaedia threatened to] collapse our age-old distinction between The Same and the Other', *The Order of Things: An Archaeology of the Human Sciences*, trans. Alan Sheridan (New York: Vintage, 1970), at xv.

valuable as intellectual calculations if not less deceptive, and less oppressive, than the latter.

Of course, as with all projects, what she finds from literature will be influenced by what she is looking for. At first, those engaged in the project confidently asserted that they would make a better man of the lawyer and a better lawyer of the man (perhaps woman needed no, or was beyond hope of, improvement). But then 'who's going to teach other lawyers to be human?', as a Chicago attorney protested recently to a Wyoming law firm's project 'to turn lawyers into human beings': 'other lawyers? Big mistake'. Rather than embarking on a grand humanistic project, she is content to try and broaden her understanding of law as part of her culture, a culture that it shares with literature, claiming, at most, that literature is often quicker and more likely than law to challenge and question that culture.

The idea, for example, that we are rational and self-interested rather than self-destructive and masochistic; that our relationships with other people are based on antagonism and competition rather than connection and relatedness; that human instinct is to resist rather than embrace authority; that legal definitions of guilt and innocence exhaust what we understand by those concepts; that, as those definitions are linguistic constructs, a new language may express and redefine our understanding of those concepts; that legal language includes, encompasses, and liberates rather than excludes, restricts, and oppresses; the assumption that we act and talk freely and responsibly rather than unconsciously and unknowingly; the view that law is based on rationality and consent rather than repression and fear; the view that events are causally connected rather than isolated and discontinuous; the view that the distinctions we make between copy and original, sign and referent, mind and body, reason and madness are arbitrary prejudices rather than natural and self-evident; the view that the world of dreams and the imagination is not only the repressed or unconscious of the so-called real world, but more real than the latter; the view that the legal system and legal language are not monolithic or secure enough to resist incursions from the world of dreams and fantasy; the view that law is deliberately designed rather than the result of chance; the view that law is a seamless web of right answers rather than an accumulation of mistakes (or, to put it another way, that an accumulation of mistakes has become the law); the view that the legal system is the place for teaching moral values; the view that the marriage bed is the place where conflicts and contradictions can be silenced, if not necessarily resolved; the view, finally, that finality, unity, and oneness can come only with dissolution, only with death.

Whilst exploring these themes, the Law and Literature student does not assume that the emotions, imagination, dreams, the supernatural, are beyond her scope of inquiry. She will point out that lawyers and legislators, in debates about criminalizing or decriminalizing conduct, assume there is a stigma attached to criminality; but in many portrayals of criminals in novels and popular culture the criminal is depicted as a hero, a fascinating human being. To banish an understanding of culture and the self from legal education, she will argue, is not likely to lead to meaningful changes. Nor will she claim that we understand things 'better' through literature; simply that we may understand different things, and in a different way. And who is rational (or mad) enough today to say that one form of learning, one form of knowledge is more valid or better than another?

As far as I know none of my students (men or women) showed signs of the Almodovar affliction; it is even tempting to say that they enjoyed it, a lot, or at least so they kept saying. Of course neither their views nor mine can decide whether the Law and Literature approach will suit you, the choice, and the responsibility, for that decision being yours. The furthest I would go is to suggest that if you are amused rather than irritated by Borges, if you think his story is ludicrous or drug-induced but not necessarily 'wrong', if, in other words, you are happy exploring and exploding your own assumptions, pushing your thinking to the limits and then teasing it you may well enjoy Law and Literature. You might even, like me, and like many of my loved and loving guinea pigs, go as far as to love it. And then of course you'll be more likely to learn and benefit from it than if you were doing it from any other motive.

2 A JOURNEY

The archetypal image in western literature is the journey of a man like Ulysses whose long trials and tribulations lead to arriving home older, braver, and wiser. Though the homecoming appears to be a bit of an anti-climax, (the hero, after all, has nothing to do once he arrives other than to rest and die), as another Greek poet says, what matters is not reaching one's destination, nor even what that destination is, but the incidents, loves, fears, beauties, and horrors we encounter on the way: 'And if you find Ithaca poor, Ithaca has not cheated you: Ithaca gave you the beautiful journey. Without her, you wouldn't have gone on the road'.[7]

My own minor odyssey started with a paradox, a contradiction: it followed Sophocles' Oedipus' journey and that of future Oedipuses from Freud, Lévi-Strauss, to Lacan and wondered why this myth has been held out as informing the origins of the human psyche, of law, and of civilization itself. A father, fearing the overthrow of his authority, and of his person, attempts to destroy his son. The son is fortunate enough to escape and after long wandering returns home where he unwittingly kills his father and marries his mother. He thereby replaces his father both in the private realm of the marriage bed and the public realm of law and kingship. Oedipus' anagnorisis at the end, finding out his name and thereby that he committed par-rincest, is accompanied with an acknowledgement and acceptance of his guilt. This recognition, however, does not prevent him from pronouncing a similar curse on his sons, thus setting off a pattern for future antagonisms between future fathers and their sons. The chapter analysed interpretations of Oedipus from humanistic responses to

---

[7] Κ.Π.Καβάφη, *Τα Ποιήματα 1897–1918*, trans. Aristodemov (Ικαρος, 1963), at 28.

the story as a manifestation of Apollo's edict 'man know thyself', to structuralist readings that propose the incest taboo as the lynchpin of civilization, to psycho-analytic readings that instal the phallus or the name of the father as the arch-signifier anchoring the self, law, and civilization as a whole. The analysis pointed out the gendered nature of these interpretations and suggested that these journeys reproduce the journey taken by the father, leading to the birth of a son who attempts, in turn, to overthrow his father, just as every son born of the science of psychoanalysis that Althusser discusses, returns to kill the father who gave birth to him.

My reading explored the possibility of journeys that are not couched around the doctrine of knowing oneself and of returning to oneself, but of reaching out beyond the self, that is, reaching out towards knowing not oneself but another; of journeys that do not lead to competition and death, but journeys where one wanders, even aimlessly. Why start with the first recorded incident of road rage, an incident which turns on the boyish game of who got where first and open the way for endless antagonisms and substitutions between future fathers and sons? Why not start with the mother?

If depictions of the Oedipus myth ignore the journey away from oneself towards others, this is, I suggested in my reading of the *Oresteia* because they ignore, or attempt to ignore, the journey that starts with the mother. The effacement of the mother, indeed her murder and the legal system's acquittal of that murder, is used to found not only the legal system but civilization itself. For this 'progress' to take place, the law requires not only the murder of an adulterous woman who dared to reflect back to her husband not his fullness and greatness, but her own independent desires, but also of a virtuous (in Greek, as in so many cultures, virtuous = virgin) daughter whose beauty and innocence were equally threatening: having arrived at Aulis as an object to be offered in marriage by her father to another man, Iphigeneia is sacrificed by a group of men led by her father who choose the 'masculine' game of war over the 'feminine' game of love. My reading suggested ways in which the debt owed to the mother and to Iphigeneia is restored in readings and performances of the play, in particular with characters who return the male gaze, and with audiences who refuse the role of passive recipients of the performance. Since words and other signs, as I argue in my opening chapter, not only reflect but create reality, it is possible to reopen the gap between representation and reality and go back to a time *before* the word was born, *before* what began as myths and plays became law and started to demand to be taken seriously.

In *Measure for Measure* the law attempts not only to regulate the subject's desire, but also to replace, fill and fulfil it. Its attempt to order human behaviour starts, as always, with words: the law aims to name human relationships and thereby bring them within its ambit. Characters or relationships that refuse to be named, to be pinned down, that wander outside the name of the law, threaten law's claim to be the arch-namer, and the law has no choice but to restrict and, if necessary, eliminate them. Such a destruction appears successful in *Measure for Measure*, but my reading sug-gested that not all characters in the play, nor every member of the audience need be convinced. For the concepts of justice and mercy that the law claims to embody, pertain not only to male definitions of power, kingship, and politics, but also to sexuality, desire, and the family. By exploiting the rhetorical excess and ambiguities in the text, I questioned interpretations of the play as teaching that 'law must be tempered with mercy' or that marriage represents a just distribution to the multiple exchanges of bodies that take place in the course of the play. I focused in particular on law's perception of unregulated desire as threatening social instability and law's attempt to police desire through surveillance. In the process, however, the law betrays its own dependence on desire for its definition, existence, and perpetuation. Conversely, desiring subjects need law against which to measure the strength and breadth of their desire, whether positively, through obedience, or negatively, through transgression. Although women are depicted as objects of exchange in these circulating desires—as blank pages to be written on by desiring men—I pointed out signs of female resistance to these exchanges. The play ends with multiple weddings but marriage is not unambiguously presented as securing either self-fulfilment or justice. Whether the marriages are imposed by the duke or freely entered into, the suspicion lingers that marriage may be another form of social control silencing men and women and guaranteeing hierarchical divisions. The frequent equation of marriage with death hints at the only end of desire and undermines any conviction that justice has been achieved: these textual remainders hint that some differences and desires are uncontainable, and persist obstinately outside the allegedly happy resolution at the play's close.

***

When Maria Cardenal is not playing the part of a highly successful lawyer, she is the expert seductress of men whom she kills at the climactic moment. Her own desire, however, remains unfulfilled: until she meets another being like herself, retired master bull-fighter Diego Montez. For these avid lovers, the art of loving is indistinguishable from the art of killing: to stop killing is to stop living. The culmination of their relationship can only be one: the ultimate consummation is not only the climax of the sexual act but the closure afforded only by the climax of death. The law that attempted to deny the identification between eroticism and death, arrives at the scene seconds too late. And its officers have no choice but to acknowledge that the faces of the corpses look sublimely content.

***

Almodovar's *Matador*[8] is the apotheosis of Bataille's view that eroticism 'is assenting to life up to the point of death.'[9] The identification between death and desire in *Measure for Measure* is pronounced again in *Wuthering Heights*. Emily Brontë for Bataille 'had the sort of knowledge which links love not only with clarity, but also with violence and death—because death seems to be the truth of love, just as love is the

---

[8] Pedro Almodovar, *Matador* (Iberoamericana de TV, SA, 1986).

[9] Georges Bataille, *Eroticism*, trans. Mary Dalwood (London and New York: Marion Boyars, 1962), [1957], at 11.

truth of death'.[10] Catherine and Heathcliff's relationship in *Wuthering Heights* also resists being named and contained by the law; although Catherine and Heathcliff's victory over the law requires their own dissolution, their protest in favour of a higher law that sanctions this love and demands this death, remains both in the consciousness of other characters in the book and in that of generations of readers. Emily Brontë suffuses us with a vision of a world without differences, of a world of undifferentiated unity and oneness where love and death are the only truths and the only laws. Her unorthodox (illegal?) fusion of realistic representation with gothic and supernatural motifs forces us to wonder whether it is the outside world that is irrational, absurd, unreal, and unjust. Catherine's alleged ravings in front of the mirror, where she can no longer recognize herself, lead us to question whether it is the so-called 'real' world of 'reasonable' Nelly and Lockwood that has lost its sense. Catherine and Heathcliff's relationship can not be named either in law, or in literature, because it subsists in the imaginary, the atemporal, that is, the eternal.

In *The Outsider* we caught the writer of the absurd making meaning out of the experience of meaninglessness, of expressing the experience of not being able to express, of trying to understand our inability to understand. Having rejected God, law, bourgeois morality, and romantic love as transcendental signifiers that could confer order on our disorder, Camus' answer to the impasse of the absurd, was a Nietzschean will to express meaninglessness not through reason—law's preferred arch-narrative—but through the body and the senses in particular and through art, literature, and the aesthetic in general. Camus' text reveals law's fear of the body, of beauty, and of the senses and its attempt to expulse them in favour of a disembodied ethics and arbitrary signifiers like reason, the nation, or God. My reading suggested that there is another fear the text dare not speak openly about, but that can nevertheless be glimpsed between the lines: the fear, as well as envy, of woman, the fear of engulfment by, as well as inability to get away from, the mother. Meursault envies women and, I argued, Arabs, because they are the 'others' whom he perceives can realize their desire better than he: what Meursault is at pains to achieve, (live through the senses, ignore the strictures of bourgeois morality, stay silent), women or Arabs do effortlessly. I suggested that while according precedence to art, beauty, and the senses, Camus' neglect of woman also robs him of the possibility of making Meursault's anagnorisis on the eve of his execution, not transitory, not adhering only to the present moment, but lasting: woman as the neglected signifier in the text can introduce the dimension of time, continuity, and eternity. Woman is the repressed unconscious of Camus' text, and she returns to haunt his hero's reluctance to acknowledge, express, or discuss his emotions. Meursault seeks to deny the feminine in him, to reject the mother who died and whom he claims not to have mourned and to whom his thoughts keep reverting time and again in the text. One could go as far as to argue, that had Camus, metaphorically, been willing to listen to woman, had Meursault, literally, not returned to

---

[10] Georges Bataille, *Literature and Evil*, trans. Alastair Hamilton (London and New York: Marion Boyars, 1973) [1957], at 16.

the beach as a way of escaping the sound of women's tears, none of this would have happened! Meursault's acknowledgement of the feminine in him has to wait until the eve of his execution when his thoughts wander not to the law of the father, that both priest and magistrate tried to captivate him with, but to the love, language, and law of his absent mother.

In the opening chapter I argued that cultural representations are not only unavoidably, and always already political, they also have far-reaching, if not more, far-reaching effects than the law that assigned them to a lower ranking in the hierarchy of discourses. This is the case in particular with tales that are widely known and disseminated from the legal and cultural subject's so-called formative years. Fairy tales are not only entertaining but normative, alluringly legislating sexual roles and laws for young children and their growing parents. Such tales not only describe but prescribe, suggesting appropriate patterns of behaviour for men and women in the symbolic order. By focusing on Angela Carter's retellings of traditional tales such as Beauty and the Beast, Little Red Riding Hood, and Bluebeard, I examined intertextuality as a strategy for telling alternative stories or retelling old stories differently. Carter re-reads the Marquis de Sade as a moral pornographer, follows him in his demystification of motherhood and shatters the notion of the virtuous victim as a goal for women. At the same time she rejects the models offered by Sade's heroines Justine and Juliette (both of whom are defined in accordance with rules laid down by men), in favour of a model of the relationship between self and other that does not reduce the self to the other or the other to the self. Like Irigaray, Carter uses the strategy of mimesis to challenge patriarchy by playing its own game; she flirts with male philosophers, writers, and pornographers in order to write new stories for women and shows art's potential to unravel old laws, disrupt traditional structures and imagine new orders and new identities. Such retellings define sexual identity outside masculinist paradigms and write women not only in myths and fairy tales but also in history. The successful heroine in these tales becomes the authoress and authority of her own story and her own sexuality, independently of male desires and patriarchal norms and expectations. Such reinventions or 'performances' expose the constructed nature of gender and break away from essentialist definitions of gender roles.

If the relationship between fathers and sons in patriarchal society revolves around competition and leads to death, the relationship between mothers and daughters also does not escape the effects of patriarchy. In *Wuthering Heights* and in *Chronicle of a Death Foretold* we witness real and surrogate mothers who have internalized the values of patriarchy and become its enthusiastic and sometimes brutal upholders. It is the mother, the most frequent chief carer, who has the opportunity to teach her children the ways of adulthood, an opportunity that she too often misses by following the strictures of patriarchy and teaching her boys to be like *men* and not like *women* and her daughters to be like *women* and not like *men*. It is the mother rather than the father who teaches her daughter the father's law, the obligation to abide by it and at times also urges her to become a lawyer. It is the mother who suppresses in her daughter the opportunity to discover her own law, and to become her own law-maker.

When the mother or surrogate mother belongs to a lower social class, like Nelly in *Wuthering Heights* or is a subaltern mother, like Pura Vicario in *Chronicle of a Death Foretold*, her insistence that her daughter enter the father's law is all the stronger: the mother sees the law as her daughter's opportunity to enter not only the kingdom of men, which she perceives to be superior to that of the kingdom of women, but also the kingdom of middle-class western men, that her own status as a servant or her own childhood under the colonizer taught her to perceive as superior to that of her own class or native law. On entering into a relationship with the law, however, the young daughter discovers that 'every kiss leaves a bruise', every conception is a violence, every birth a frustration.[11]

Can the daughter escape, as James go on to sing, 'the spell of the mother'? Only when the daughter understands and empathizes with the mother, when she accepts that the mother's complicity with patriarchal, and often western patriarchal law and expectations, is not malicious but unknowing. Angela in *Chronicle of a Death Foretold* comes to understand that her mother is herself a prisoner of patriarchal ideology and has learned to side with the forces she perceived to be victorious. Angela rises above these expectations by not colluding with her girlfriends' insistence that she hide her 'dishonour' and by discovering her own secret strength: writing. Patriarchy of course imprisons not only women but also men; Angela's brothers, though brought up to be *men*, are markedly reluctant to fulfil the duty that falls on them: to kill the man who allegedly 'deflowered' their sister and brought 'dishonour' to the family name.

Decades later, the murder is still experienced as an 'open wound' by the survivors in the town and competing discourses fight for the right to derive, and write, the 'truth' and 'origin' of the tragedy. The narrator, in the manner of a detective, juxtaposes their competing stories and memories, oral and written, only to leave us feeling that the truth not only eludes him but that if it exists at all, it is made rather than found, textually invented rather than discovered, constructed rather than detected. Underlying the narrator's frustration and glimpsed between the lines of the text, is, I suggested, another enigma, not the enigma of the murder but the enigma of female sexuality. Angela and the town prostitute are the guardians of this different truth, this different law, and significantly, unlike other women in the story, escape masculinist constructions of femininity and succeed in avoiding collusion with patriarchal values. Maria Alejandrina Cervantes' name aligns her with the truth not only of woman but of literature and enunciates a different law from the law that the men in the story are at pains to enforce. The affirmation of male law, a law which is based on the contractual exchange of women and which demands retribution when the goods are perceived to be 'damaged', leads not to reconciliation, order, and catharsis, but to continuing pain for everyone in the community. While this law is being enforced (by butchering Santiago in the town square with the entire community standing by), Maria Alejandrina enunciates a different law, the law of love, a law that dictates not

---

[11] 'Lullaby' in James, *LAID* (London: Blue Mountain Music, 1993) and 'Born of Frustration' in *Seven* (London: Phonogram, 1992).

competition with and annihilation of the other, but of giving without accounting, without judgment, and without an eye to investment or future returns. Rather than leading to death and tragedy, this law embodies—not only metaphorically but also literally—connection with, rather than engulfment of the other: in Maria's 'apostolic lap' lovers and beloveds lose themselves in the 'quicksand of her tenderness'. Angela similarly inserts herself on the side of literature and of love, by rising above her mother's efforts to 'bury her alive' after her supposed disgrace, and starting to write: this writing, significantly taking place at night, away from the watchful eyes of patriarchy and its staunch defender (her mother), enunciates a different law and a different truth: it talks not of law but of love, not of death but of eternity, not of duty but of beauty and is uttered not by a god but a goddess: not male-born Athena but Venus. Through writing, Angela inserts herself both in law and in history: she is writing a story that the narrator, despite his repeated efforts to gather as much evidence as possible, has entirely missed: the story contained in her love letters. Herstory, hidden between the lines of the text, persists beyond the climactic moment of death which leaves the rest of the cast (Santiago, his murderers, the spectators, the narrator) and their creator raw and wordless.

As in *Oedipus*, in Borges we encounter characters who set out to find the origin of origins, the designer behind the design, the name of God, the letter, the book, the moment, the place, that will reveal as well as justify to them, their life, their meaning, their existence. The search however leads back to oneself as the elusive contours of the face of God turn out to be no more than a trace of their own face; their destination leads nowhere but to death. My reading asks why not venture somewhere other than back to oneself, why not travel towards others? The absence of women in Borges' stories, I suggested, hints at the possibility of another journey, not a narcissistic journey that leads back to oneself, and to death, but a journey towards others. I suggested that this hides a secret envy, as well as a fear, of woman: despite the intrepid exploring Borges' characters undertake, the one journey they do not undertake is the journey towards woman; woman is the destination they distance themselves from, and create obstacles from reaching.

Envious of woman's ability to procreate, Borges on paper and his characters in their dreams, dream dreams of creation. Borges' homosocial universe is filled with dreamers: his characters dream a lot. They dream, and thereby, create, another man. They dream, and thereby create, a whole country. They dream, and thereby create, an entire planet (and wake up to find their own planet earth invaded by their dream planet). They dream of God: a God who answers their dreams, makes time stand still, and justifies their short life to eternity. In short, as I argue in my opening chapter, Borges and his characters take on the task of inventing reality. One dream they dare not dream of, however, is woman; in their dreams they evade the real of their desire. They dream in order to *avoid* the real of their desire. In my reading I urged future Pierre Menards to dream harder: to dream of a gay God, to dream of a Goddess.

Man in these texts, fearful of woman, projected onto her his fears, convinced her that she is dirty, guileful, unstable, deceitful. Her crime: to love. While man was running away, or hiding in his own, self-created prisons, in labyrinths variously called law, reason, science, or God, woman, without fear, guilt, or shame, has travelled the world. From the prison he imposed on her called home she has been on a journey that does not return back to oneself, or lead to death, but reaches out towards the other: 'to bring you my love'.[12]

3 THE LAWYER IN HIS LABYRINTH

A story; less than three pages long; suggesting, as always with Borges, and any Pierre Menard (and why not a Petra Menard) who joins him, infinity in a small coin, eternity in one instant.

The narrator of 'The House of Asterion'[13] describes a house, his own, that is so immense, that it 'is the same size as the world; or rather, it is the world' (171). The number of rooms, courtyards, pools, mangers, is infinite. Though he knows 'they accuse me of arrogance', he has no illusions about his own greatness: 'Not for nothing was my mother a queen; I cannot be confused with the populace, though my modesty might so desire' (170). He muses that 'Perhaps I have created the stars and this enormous house'. He compares himself to 'the intricate sun' (171). 'Every nine years', he tells us, 'men enter the house so that I may deliver them from all evil. I hear their steps or their voices in the depths of the stone galleries and I run joyfully to find them. The ceremony lasts a few minutes. They fall one after another without my having to bloody my hands.' (172).

Outside this short ceremony, Asterion has no one to share his life or house with, though he longs to show it, or perhaps to show it off. Beautiful, arrogant, proud, he moves us with his desperate soliloquy, a soliloquy filled with longing: longing for companionship, for another being like himself that he can talk to, play games, share jokes, and laugh heartily with, 'for the nights and days are long' (171). Asterion craves to be delivered from his loneliness and looks forward to the fulfilment of a prophesy that 'some day my redeemer would come'.

When Theseus arrives to kill him, Asterion offers no resistance: ' "Would you believe it, Ariadne?" said Theseus "The Minotaur scarcely defended himself" ' (172).

***

'[W]hat I fantasize in the system,' Barthes' lover pleads, 'is quite modest: I want, I desire, quite simply, a structure'.[14] However bizarre it might appear to us, Borges'

---

[12] P. J. Harvey, *To Bring You My Love* (Hothead Music/EMI Music Publishing, 1994). For an acknowledgement of the different journeys taken by men and women by a male artist, listen to 'The Whole of the Moon' in The Waterboys, *This is The Sea* (Ensign Records, 1985): 'I pictured a rainbow, you held it in your hands / I had flashes, but you saw the plan / I wandered out in the world for years / While you just stayed in your room / I saw the crescent / You saw the whole of the moon.'

[13] Jorge Luis Borges, *Labyrinths: Selected Stories and Other Writings* (London: Penguin, 1970), at 170–2; page references in the text are to this edition.

[14] Roland Barthes, *A Lover's Discourse, Fragments*, trans. Richard Howard (London: Penguin, 1990) [1977], at 46.

fictitious Chinese encyclopaedia suggests *a* structure with which to classify the world's innumerable animals. Its unfamiliarity and outlandishness, however, remind us that any categories we choose with which to classify the world are bound to be arbitrary, selective, and incomplete. Borges suggests that the universe is a labyrinth, too complex and infinite for human beings to unravel. In attempting to understand its mysteries, in trying to reach the Minotaur, human beings create frameworks with which to order their experiences; literature, religion, philosophy, psychoanalysis, games are all attempts to impose order on chaos, of taming and imprisoning the irrational, the frightening, the ungraspable Minotaur. In the process, I suggest, these attempts become their own labyrinths.

Law is one such labyrinth, a concept or abstraction like time, space, or identity, devised to create order out of chaos. Unlike literature, law is also able not only to create but impose that order on the bodies, if not the souls, of its subjects through its penal machinery. As a man-made labyrinth, law retains the appearance of having a deliberate design, seducing us into believing that it can, in principle, and with enough perseverance, be deciphered. However, after centuries of building, law's design is difficult to discern; its attempt to impose order on chaos has become its own labyrinth, confusing as much as enlightening those who try to enter.

Like Asterion's house, the doors of the law 'are open day and night to man and to animals as well' (170). There is an infinite number of doors however, so it is difficult if not impossible to reach the centre. Perhaps in the beginning there was a creator, an origin, or a centre, but that centre is now impossible to find. Those who embark on the journey find themselves disoriented, confused, frustrated. They may conclude that there never was an origin, that if a God created the labyrinth, God abandoned it, or he was a mad, bad, merciless, ignorant, or uncaring God. Or that perhaps there never was a God, that the workings of the law, like those of the Company in 'The Lottery at Babylon', are none other than the workings of chance. If there was an order, an arch-design behind the chaos, that order is now lost or hidden and we are left only with the enigma. Like Kafka's Joseph K they may find that the end of the search leads not to God but to a humiliating death. Like the old man from the country, they may wait a lifetime to see the door shut in their face. Even more alarmingly, the labyrinth may contain no Minotaur, inviting endless and futile wandering in search of a centre, origin, or meaning that does not exist.[15] Like the little boy in Blanchot's sequel to 'Before the Law', they may see the 'absence . . . that nothing is all there is, and first of all nothing beyond'.[16]

---

[15] Of one of his sonnets Borges said, 'I was thinking of the labyrinth without a Minotaur. I mean, if anything is terrible, it is terrible because it is meaningless . . . Because the Minotaur justifies the labyrinth' in, *Jorge Luis Borges: Conversations*, Richard Burgin (ed.) (Jackson, Miss.: University of Mississippi Press, 1998), at 86.

[16] Maurice Blanchot, *The Writing of the Disaster*, trans. Ann Smock (Lincoln and London: University of Nebraska Press, 1986), at 72. Of Ts'ui Pen's labyrinth in 'The Garden of Forking Paths' Borges said, 'I amused myself with the idea, not of losing oneself in a labyrinth, but in a labyrinth which also loses itself.' Georges Charbonnier, *Entretiens avec Jorge Luis Borges* (Paris: Gallimard, 1969), quoted by D. L. Shaw, *Ficciones* (London: Grant & Cutler, 1993), at 39.

The legal labyrinth, I suggest further, confuses not only those who try to enter it but also itself: 'all has since always and forevermore been lost therein'.[17] Asterion confesses that he gets lost in his own house: 'sometimes I make a mistake' (171) he says, and hopes that his 'redeemer will take [him] to a place with fewer galleries and fewer doors' (172). Although those who try to enter the law, or a legal battle, are faced with one of two answers (winning or losing), the builders of the legal labyrinth are faced with a multitude of alternatives, each of which will influence not only the way future decisions will be decided, but also how past ones will be read as well. The makers of the labyrinth are forever having to choose and may lose themselves in the labyrinth as much, and perhaps more, than those who are lured inside. The labyrinth they create to protect the mystery of the law disorients not only outsiders and alleged intruders but imprisons and confuses the monster inside: the law misunderstands itself as much as it is misunderstood by others.[18]

Law also, like the Minotaur, kills without knowing its powers, oblivious to the fact that it inspires awe and fear: Asterion cannot understand why the sight of him in the streets causes people to 'pray, flee, prostrate themselves' (170). For the Minotaur is not evil: lonely, dark, insecure, he murders without malice and without distinction. From the point of view of the Minotaur, as from that of the law, 'human faces are as discolored and flat as the palm of one's hands' (170); although Asterion kills everyone who enters, he concedes that 'I do not know who they are' (172). The unique features of each distinct face, so crucial to our understanding and empathizing with the suffering of the other in Levinas' thought,[19] are completely lost on Asterion, on the law: 'Bothersome details have no place in my spirit, which is prepared for all that is vast and grand' (171). Its role is to ignore details, ignore differences, to make no distinctions.

Above all, Asterion is proud of the fact that in his house, one will find 'no female pomp' (170).

4 SLEEPING WITH THE MINOTAUR

Ariadne, we all know, gave Theseus a ball of string to enable him to find his way out of the Cretan labyrinth. A generous woman enabled the future Athenian legislator to emerge victorious from his encounter with the Minotaur but Ariadne's love, we also remember, is rejected by Theseus: on his return journey he abandons Ariadne asleep

---

[17] *ibid.*

[18] Asterion, of course, dismisses this possibility: 'Another ridiculous falsehood is that I, Asterion, am a prisoner. Shall I repeat that there are no locked doors, shall I add that there are no locks?' (170)

[19] 'The face "signifies" beyond, neither as an index nor as symbol, but precisely and irreducibly as a face that *summons me*': Emmanuel Levinas, 'Beyond Intentionality' in *Philosophy in France Today*, Alan Montefiore (ed.), (Cambridge: Cambridge University Press, 1983), at 112.

in Naxos, or in another version of the story, pregnant in Cyprus.[20] Significantly, like Oedipus' (like *all* men's?) journey, Theseus is on his way to another (accidental?) parricide. He 'forgets' to change the colour of his ship's sails from black to white, thus wrongly signalling to his father Aegeus that he has been killed by the Minotaur. Aegeus, in grief and despair at the loss of his son, throws himself in the (thereafter) Aegean sea. The way is open for Theseus to replace his father as the new King and law-maker of Athens. Plutarch (and Freud), would suggest that this was no mere oversight on Theseus' part,[21] a theme that I explored in the chapter on *Oedipus*.

Can abandoned Ariadne enter the labyrinth and find the Minotaur for herself? It took thousands of years and countless more abandoned Ariadnes, before women were offered (or did they seize?) the promise of entering the legal labyrinth. Seduced by the promise of a centre, the hope of encountering the Minotaur, they have gone as far as to promise not to kill him (as Theseus did) but to understand, love and accept him. They realize that the Minotaur, the law, is not evil, just too wrapped up in his own image as unique, omnipresent, and omnipotent. Like Orwell in his role as the British Empire's policeman in Burma, the Minotaur has to kill those who approach, Orwell has to shoot the elephant, because *others are watching*.[22] His name, his power, his authority, would all come under ridicule if he showed a sign of weakness, a sign of hesitation, a sign of reluctance. Like Pedro and Pablo Vicario in *Chronicle of a Death Foretold*, the Minotaur is just as trapped by the system as those he traps. He would rather go to war, destroy others, and risk destroying himself too, rather than allow his 'feminine' side to show through; he would rather fight than court, kill rather than love.

When Ariadne approaches the law, the Minotaur offers, albeit slowly and miserly, the promise of admission, the promise of inclusion. He proffers some string, though he is in control of how much he will give, when, and where. On paper, he has granted her equal rights, equal opportunities, equal pay. In practice she discovers that her male colleagues have long been paid way in excess of her; when she challenges his rulings, she is told she was not aggressive enough when negotiating status and pay, paradox of paradoxes, deceitful woman is told she is not as deceitful as man when it comes to such things. Probably because she is interested in games that matter, that matter more to her, games of love.

When at his most lonely, during the long nights of craving for companionship, Asterion unwittingly gives Ariadne more than he intends, more than he planned to give. She draws closer but her approach frightens him: he has been dreaming of her in

---

[20] In Plutarch's account of the second version, Theseus tries, but fails rejoin Ariadne in Cyprus: Plutarch, *The Rise and Fall of Athens: Nine Greek Lives*, trans. Ian Scott-Kilvert (London: Penguin, 1960) at 26–7.

[21] 'His forgetfulness and neglect of the command about the sail, can hardly, I think, escape the charge of parricide': *Plutarch's Lives*, trans. Bernadotte Perrin (Cambridge, Massachusetts: Harvard University Press, 1982), Vol. 1, at 197.

[22] George Orwell, 'Shooting an Elephant', in *Inside the Whale and Other Essays* (Harmondsworth: Penguin, 1962).

his sleep, but he hesitates to greet her when she arrives, does not offer a welcome, will not make room for her in his house, or in his bed. The law offers excuses: she is wearing the wrong clothes, she is speaking the wrong language: 'no female pomp' can enter the legal palace. Her untamed sexuality, her unknowable desires, her inexpressible emotions, frighten and drive him further away. Like Bayardo in *Chronicle of a Death Foretold*, the Minotaur, unwilling to betray his feminine side, pretends to be 'oblivious to her delirium'.

Asterion has also been playing the game far longer than she has: he knows how to guard every piece, pause over every move, allow a pawn to be taken here and there, but jealously guarding his King, the source of his authority. He tenders the woman lawyer some string, reforms pieces of the law, leads her to believe that the game can be redesigned to include her, that Law's Empire is open to her. In the words of one song, he 'leaves a trail that's always changed, to keep her hopes alive'; meanwhile, his beliefs, his ideals (justice, equality, impartiality), keep leading her on. At times, she even comes to feel that 'the way *she* is is wrong'.[23]

At other times, the law's silence to her pleas for change appears to be as final as that of a statue: perhaps he is only an image, an illusion, one she created herself, no more substantial than the sound of her dreams. It was, after all, she who built his statue, who 'cast him in her mind, made his face from clay and straw, precious stone for his eyes'.[24] At other times the law's silence, its deafness to her difference, means that the image she created of him starts to fade. When she challenges him he admonishes her for going too far, for crossing the limits, for not respecting boundaries. She has dared to talk about emotions, about the body, sinnest of sins, once she appeared to be on the verge of tears. No tears can be allowed to break the silence of the labyrinthine walls: witness the lawyers' impatience with Marie's lachrymose signs during Meursault's trial. Worse still, woman, the untameable, the insatiable, has neglected to hide her body; perhaps she even chose to display it. How much worse if it was a pregnant body, a body that transgressed the boundary between nature and culture, that threatened to bring to the labyrinth, not the pain and death Asterion secretly longs for, but promised to bring to the law life and eternity.[25]

The law nods an acceptance to her 'difference', allows modest maternity rights, at least at the work place. Even there, however, she discovers that these 'rights' are begrudged her: she returns to work to echoes along the corridors that her maternity leave was really a holiday, 'time off' from *real*, that is, *men's* work. Ariadne and her girlfriends ignore the echoes: Ariadne comes back in different clothes, reforms her language, tries to imitate his. She tries to talk in the abstract, avoid allusions to the body (let alone her body), refrain from expressing her desires (let alone her desires).

---

[23] 'Dream Thrum' in James, *LAID, supra*; emphasis mine.

[24] *ibid.*

[25] As Julia Kristeva argues, woman's pregnant body, even as it guarantees the continuance of the symbolic order, disrupts the law of the father and his word: 'Stabat Mater' in Toril Moi (ed.), *The Kristeva Reader* (Oxford: Blackwell, 1986).

Only to find that her renewed efforts are treated with renewed suspicion: the more successful she is at his game, the more he distrusts her. The Minotaur intimates that she is showing off; upsetting though this accusation is, Ariadne is not disheartened. She realized, some time ago, that the contract that created the legal system, that built the labyrinth, did not include her, but she does not care for contracts, for exchanges and does not calculate the costs. Not suffering from castration anxiety, Ariadne gives without thought of savings, investment, or returns. But any Greek, especially a Greek woman, bearing gifts is treated with suspicion in a male economy of the 'proper' where gifts mean power and inequality.[26]

In the academic labyrinth, 'radical' new approaches seduce her into believing that at last a door may have opened for her: critical legal scholars promise to demystify legal dogma, unravel the politics hidden behind the 'neutrality' of law, and expose the injustices of the legal system's hierarchical divisions. Including, she hopes, injustices based on race, sex, and gender. She draws closer, hoping this promise will not prove, once more, to be illusory, 'less critical than hypocritical'.[27] For she has watched critical scholars before, both at home and abroad, returning to the same horse race they once appeared to have bolted from, succumbing to the lure of higher status and salaries, 'this tumbrel', as Nick Cave put it in another context, 'this bloody cart of severed heads and glittering prizes'.[28]

She ventures to ask for a map to the centre, but the Minotaur does not understand her request: the doors of my house, says Asterion, the doors of the law, says Kafka's chaplain, are always open. Woman goes back to trying to find the map by herself; with little to go on, she perseveres, with her books during the day, in her dreams at night. She learns to accommodate to the law's demands, learns to ask for little, less and less, offers to wait, for ever! She comes, at the end, seeking nothing, only that the law be good, fair, just. Not inclusion but acknowledgement that she has not been knocking on the wrong door. But he mistakes her last wish; her despair turns him ever more cold, ever more distant, ever more strange. The string that had been tendered is pulled back viciously; so-called landmark changes to the law are reopened and redefined against her.[29] The law becomes increasingly defensive, meaner. If she waits any longer he will turn violent. She must, in Nick Cave's words, 'go, go'.[30]

---

[26] For the male economy of the 'proper' see Hélène Cixous and Catherine Clément, 'Sorties: Out and Out: Attacks/Ways Out/Forays', trans. Betsy Wing *The Newly-Born Woman* (London: I. B. Tauris, 1996).

[27] Costas Douzinas, Peter Goodrich, Yifat Hachamovitch (eds.), *Politics, Postmodernity and Critical Legal Studies: The Legality of the Contingent* (London and New York: Routledge, 1994), at 14. For an update on this theme, see Peter Goodrich, 'The Critic's Love of the Law: Intimate Observations on an Insular Jurisdiction' *Law and Critique*, Vol. 10(3), (2000), 343–60.

[28] 'The New Romantic', *The Times Magazine*, 27 March 1999, at 18.

[29] See, for example, Susan Faludi, *Backlash: The Undeclared War Against Women* (London: Vintage, 1992).

[30] Nick Cave and the Bad Seeds, 'From Her to Eternity', *supra*.

5 HERSTORY: WOMAN ON THE VERGE

Why the impasse? Why the dead-end? Why the stale-mate, misunderstanding, lack of communication? Could it be that she was always speaking a different language? A language of the body, of the senses, that he did not understand, that he was frightened of? The law's language, seductive though it was, started, and ended with words: with disembodied writing, words without touch, without sound, without taste. Always cautious, measured, slooooooow. The law writes solipsistically, talking only to and for himself, so as to perpetuate his own image, his self-definition, his existence. Law would admit her only if she also became a text, a disembodied body of words. She, on the other hand wanted to go beyond and outside words. When forced to use words, she would abandon herself to them, they slipped through her fingers, sometimes they escaped when she was not looking, when she resolved she had tried enough, when she had resolved to try less. Unlike the Minotaur, whose 'generous impatience' leads him to suspect communication ('like the philosopher', Asterion says, 'I think that nothing is communicable by the act of writing' (171)), she did not have to go *looking* for words: words would find *her*. She said, too often, more than the law could understand, more than the law could hear, more than the law could bear to hear. She transgressed boundaries, pushed the limits, seemingly out of control. At times she forgot to appeal to precedent, ignored footnotes, wrote in an unauthorized fashion: she did not write *like a man*. She took the risk of talking nonsensically, of meaninglessness, craving communication, to reach, to touch, to move him. As women are prone to do, she told the law her life-story, her fears, her hopes, her desires. Law accused her of blabbing, of saying too much, of writing too much, and, as generations of Sophocleses taught us 'Women should be seen, not heard'.[31] 'You mean there are people who can stop themselves writing and don't?' she retorts (echoing Gide, but she has forgotten the source, the origin, the authority). But what he meant is that she did not write like *he* did, she was not talking *his* language.

Her words were maps, her dreams were countries, her songs celebrations, showing the way in, inviting, welcoming, summoning: to her country. *His* words were cold, abstract, logical: erecting barriers, setting limits, detaching, distancing, exiling the body, exiling her. *History* was linear, progressive, causally connected; for him to admit her would have been to deny the progress he had made over thousands of years, the progress of civilization over savagery, of the abstract over the corporeal, the triumph he celebrated in the *Oresteia*. She can point out that *that* story, *that* progress, began in blood, fear, tears, and leads to repeated antagonisms, repeated parricides, repeated wars: it leads to death. *Herstory* is cyclical, stumbling at times, with accidents, twists and turns, moves backwards and forwards, at times both at once, stands still, lasts an eternity.

---

[31] *Ajax*, 292, in Sophocles, *Electra and Other Plays*, trans. E. F. Watling (Harmondsworth: Penguin, 1953).

Legal language appeared, at times, to allow for her different language. But only, she discovers, on condition that she did not go too far, did not say too much; when she breaches the limits, her words upset, disturb, exhaust him. The Minotaur intimates that she is mad: her language is not abstract, cooked, threaded together in neat categories and hierarchies. Highly self-conscious, excitement for the Minotaur was a 'kind of ecstasy of self-control'; against his ideal of 'high prosperity, propriety, and the aristocratic life', Ariadne's excesses appeared 'base, vulgar, ignoble'.[32] It is not the language of law, it is the language of poetry, hisgod forbid, it may be the language of music. And such 'female pomp' cannot enter the legal labyrinth: it is far too chaotic, far too perilous, far too on the verge of a nervous breakdown. When she retorts that madness, the ravings of a Dionysian maenad, may hide another truth, even a higher truth, the Minotaur resorts to the only defence left to him: deceitful woman, he accuses, your words are not true. Worse, you have been using the same words to enter other kingdoms, other labyrinths, other laws. You have been courting too many Mino- taurs, not just law but literature, not just philosophy but music, not just reason but madness: Ariadne, you are a whore, a whore who has 'whored with many before me'.[33]

When the law pronounces this judgment, Ariadne might well wonder whether they ever communicated. Though, unlike Theseus, she came as a friend, not a killer, the Minotaur never trusted her intentions; accustomed to perceiving relationships in terms of competition, overcoming, and devouring the other, he could only envisage admitting her at the cost of his own self-preservation. Meanwhile Ariadne's fling with the law has ended in tears: her dream of admission has turned into a nightmare, her love song into a weeping song, her love story into a horror story.

For a person who has lost everything, writes Cixous, 'language becomes the coun- try'.[34] Though Ariadne could speak several languages, the law had insisted that she restrict herself to one: the language of words. When the law cast suspicion on those words, accommodation is no longer possible: to deny her words is to deny *her*.

6 A REBEGINNING

Marina is a porn-movie star and a junkie. Ricky is a 23-year-old who has spent most of his life in a mental institution and whom the judge has just pronounced fit and free to enter society. Like the Minotaur, Ricky is 'all alone in the world' but dreams of finding a job, getting married, raising a family: 'the judge said I'm normal', he reminds the director of the institution when she points out to him that being free also

---

[32] In another 'illegitimate' mixing of authorities, these terms are borrowed from Henry James's descrip- tion of Gilbert Osmond in *The Portrait of a Lady* (London: Penguin, 1984) [1881], at 401, 480–1.

[33] This is an extension of Harold Bloom's description of the male writer's fickle muse: *The Anxiety of Influence* (Oxford: Oxford University Press, 1973), at 61.

[34] *The Hélène Cixous Reader*, Susan Sellers (ed.), (New York and London: Routledge, 1994), at xxvii.

means being alone. Ricky is also convinced he can realize this dream with Marina. Though Marina does not appear to know him, he has a fool-proof strategy for getting her to fall in love with him: first he performs a handstand, and when she is singularly unimpressed, he breaks into her house, threatens her with a knife, gags her and kidnaps her. Marina at first resists her captor, tries to escape, but in time she starts wondering whether she wants to be rescued at all: at the end of Almodovar's film, Marina pleads Ricky 'Tie Me Up! Tie Me Down!'[35]

***

Has Ariadne fallen in love with Asterion? Was she, like Catherine in *Wuthering Heights*, seduced by the ideal of a world without difference, approximated in an incestuous relationship with her step-brother? Did she, like her mother Pasiphae, fall in love with a bull? Has she started enjoying his constant vacillation between love and brutality? Has she become, as Legendre would have us believe every legal subject becomes, erotically attached to the law?[36]

There are differences: like Eve (like *every* woman?), Ariadne was curious to see what was inside the labyrinth; like another outsider called Meursault, she watched, intrigued, amused, and fascinated by its Byzantine politics, but remained throughout a spectator of the stage-production called law. Like other outsiders, like Heathcliff, and unlike Kafka's man from the country, her desire did not 'already belong to the law'.[37] Ariadne always had a suspicion that the Minotaur did not want her to look inside because he was nervous she would discover that *nothing* was all there *was* inside. Furthermore, the law, unlike Ricki, was never in love with Ariadne; true he captured her, true he seduced her with his words, true she marvelled at his power, true she admired his beauty. But that seduction, well meaning and sincere though it was, was at best that of a benevolent father taking care of his daughter. It was not that of a lover. Ariadne's fling with the law reflected to the Minotaur his own sense of greatness, but his ambiguous love started to choke her, to threaten her own self-esteem, her own royalty. For it was Ariadne who, in the words of another song, 'came from Greece and had a thirst for knowledge', it was she whose dad, King Minos, 'was loaded', but she had bravely disobeyed his royal commands because, young and inquisitive as she was, she 'wanted to see how common people live, wanted to do what common people do, wanted to sleep with common people: *like him*'.[38]

While Ricky at the end of the film draws Marina a 'map of his life', the Minotaur

---

[35] Pedro Almodovar, *Tie Me Up! Tie Me Down!* (Enterprise Pictures, Eldeseo, 1990).

[36] *Law and the Unconscious: A Legendre Reader*, trans. Peter Goodrich with Alain Pottage and Anton Schütz, Peter Goodrich (ed.), (London and New York: Macmillan, 1997). For an introduction to Legendre's work see 'Law's Emotional Body' in Peter Goodrich, *Languages of Law: From Logics of Memory to Nomadic Masks* (London: Weidenfeld and Nicolson, 1990). For a critique from the point of view of the feminine, see Alain Pottage, 'The Paternity of Law' in Douzinas, Goodrich and Hachamovitch, (eds.), *Politics, Postmodernity and Critical Legal Studies, supra.*

[37] This is a distinction drawn by Hélène Cixous in her reading of Lispector's and Kafka's approach to being 'before the law'; in Hélène Cixous, *Readings: The Poetics of Blanchot, Joyce, Kafka, Kleist, Lispector and Tsvetayeva* (Hemel Hempstead: Harvester Wheatsheaf, 1992), at 15.

[38] 'Common People' in Pulp, *Different Class* (Island Records, 1995).

always kept the secrets of his galleries well hidden. And while Ricky risked his life trying to find drugs to feed Marina's addiction, the Minotaur kept Ariadne starving. Even if the Minotaur did love her, his conception of relationships in terms of eating the other would have led him to devour her: without malice of course. When her words started to disturb him, when she appeared to pull and stretch the string he had given her to dance to her own tunes, he ended the relationship the way Ricky started: by stifling her voice. Both untamed and innocent at the same time, Ariadne, like Iphigeneia, like the wild rose, is too unsettling for the Minotaur, for father Agamemnon, for her lover. She has to be silenced, gagged, sacrificed: 'and I bid her goodbye, said all beauty must die and knelt down and planted a rose between her teeth'.[39]

Ariadne, like Euripides' Iphigeneia, fantasized at times about this death, but this time, taking a lesson from Aeschylus' Iphigeneia, she protests not only mutely but by walking away from the sacrificial altar. She has learned that her attempt to enter into a relationship with the law, stimulating and exciting though it was, was always an attempt to decipher the indecipherable, to reorient the disorienting, to touch the untouchable. Though nocturnally she allowed herself to imagine it, the barely imaginable turns in the cold English daylight to be also the impossible: the Minotaur will never let her in. She knows it is time she stopped trying to bring him out of his labyrinth, time she stopped trying to decipher him. She teetered on the edge of the labyrinth for too long, at times she appeared to be on the verge of disintegration, on the brink of madness. Her language, however, the same language that was threatening to official society, to the law, also held her together. A combination of words, images, sounds, this language, amidst 'bewildering deserts of confusion' was held together 'by taut threads, semi-formed, evolving, unrepeatable collisions and exotic collusions'.[40] The Minotaur denied the veracity of that language because it was not *his* language, it did not speak *his* truth, it did not follow *his* law.

Conversely, the Minotaur, while intimating that she was unstable, betrayed his own confusion and inconsistency: it was the law that would beckon her to his labyrinth, and to his bed, but every time her desire, that bottomless desire which is not one, came closer, he would retreat in fear and panic. Like Lockwood in *Wuthering Heights*, he locks out Catherine's ghost in a vain attempt to repress what lies beyond his comprehension. And like Lockwood, who admits to having been fascinated by 'a real goddess—as long as she took no notice of me', when the woman returns his gaze, he hides back in his labyrinth, 'shrinks icily in his shell, like a snail'.

Ariadne must now start rediscovering and founding her own law, in her own language, in her own country. Though her attempt to enter the law did not lead to admission, her journey was not wasted: to rephrase another song, though she gave the law 'more than she thought she should, the law also gave her more than he thought he would'.[41] Though to the Minotaur she appeared to be on fire, 'like a heifer to the

---

[39] Nick Cave and the Bad Seeds, 'Where the Wild Roses Grow', *supra*.

[40] Introduction to James/Eno, *WAH WAH* (New York: Blue Mountain Music, 1994).

[41] '(Song for my) Sugar Spun Sister' in *The Stone Roses* (Silverstone Records, 1989).

slaughter', as the song goes, ' that type of experience was necessary for her learning'.[42]

Ariadne can now speak two languages: good mimic that she is, she quickly learned his, but she can also remember another language, the language of the mother. Like any good student, she learned his law, but she also remembers another law, the law of the mother. She understands the law of reason but she knows also the law of love: her patterns, her laws, are not limited by such arbitrary binary oppositions. She can live simultaneously in two laws, two jurisdictions, two countries, speak two languages, speak sense and nonsense, day and night, be mother and lover, wife and daughter, young and old, passive and active, inside and outside, pained and happy, obedient and rebellious, transgressive and conformist, all at once. Some call this schizophrenic, others duplicitous; she knows that she has found her own version of the aleph or zahir. She already possesses what Borges' male questers spend a lifetime searching; and while, in the rare instances when those few men witness it, they find its image 'intolerable', she opens her arms and welcomes it. If pan-signification is the world of drugs and madness, she never wants to leave. Because for her this is not disorder but a higher order, not chaos but creativity, not a weakness but a strength. If it is the female condition, she delights in it.

Ariadne does not have to abandon the law, she does not have to ignore, destroy, or kill the Minotaur: true, in her approach she came close to courting her own dissolution. True, the Minotaur will not apologize for the pain he caused, for having threatened to engulf her: indeed he is oblivious to it. In its inexorable drive towards progress (towards death), the law drives off without checking on the pedestrian he ran over and very nearly killed.[43] Asterion leaves his victims 'where they fell', their dead bodies helping him to distinguish between one gallery and another (172). And as we saw in the *Oresteia*, the first corpses to grace the legal labyrinth are those of women: a murdered mother, Clytemnestra and a sacrificed daughter, Iphigeneia.

But Ariadne is generous and offers to make friends with the law; she knows she can deliver the Minotaur from his loneliness, appease his hunger, ensure that he does not have to eat alone. She knows also that the labyrinth is a dark place to live in: that the labyrinth he created to protect himself from her, also imprisoned him. The Minotaur is lost in it, lonely, and, by now, old and tame; not a liminoid being but someone confused, inconsistent, dedicated to the worship of his laws and his traditions. Like Angelo in *Measure for Measure*, he has surrendered his desire to the illusion that is law in a vain effort to avoid admitting that he is prey to desires of the flesh: he 'scarce confesses that his blood flows'. He clings to all that is 'old, consecrated and

<hr>

[42] 'Baby's on Fire' in Brian Eno, *Here Come the Jets* (Virgin EG Records, 1973). See also Roberto Calasso's *The Marriage of Cadmus and Harmony*, trans. Tim Parks (London: Vintage, 1994), where Ariadne is described as one of a line of 'mad heifers' who fall in love with a bull, including Io and Ariadne's own mother Pasiphae; at 10–11.

[43] The metaphor of man driving off without looking at the road victim is made in the pilot episode, of *Ally McBeal*, 'Fools' Night Out'. Though Ally is talking about men in general and Billy in particular, I stretch it to refer to the law; the series starts, after all, with the line: 'Law and love are the same: romantic in concept but the practice can give you a yeast infection'.

transmitted', in a desperate effort to hold together his fragile identity. For it goes without saying that the law, the Minotaur, is not just conventional, he is convention incarnate, 'convention itself'.[44]

These conventions, however, were created not only without consulting Ariadne, but more importantly for the purpose of keeping her out of the labyrinth. Ariadne's exclusion from their benefits means that she also escapes their costs: she does not feel the need to love, live with, or respect them in order to confirm her own identity; much less so when they threaten to choke her. She can, moreover, use her youth, her enthusiasm, her freshness, (the same energy that frightened the well-seasoned and aging Minotaur), not only to create, and keep recreating her own laws, but also to show to the Minotaur that *his* laws, *his* conventions, *his* traditions are old, sterile, tedious; that, as I argue later, *his* law, *his* reason, *his* language, are a bad, boring, deadening, joke.

Ariadne also knows that these conventions, and the labyrinth he built to preserve them, are artificial things, and since made by men, they are in principle decipherable and replaceable by men. But as men have increasingly found it hard to decipher and rebuild their own labyrinth, as Kafka's old man from the country dies at the doorstep without being admitted, as Joseph K dies humiliated, 'like a dog',[45] woman can help man find and indeed build new entrances. For, unlike Asterion's home, the legal labyrinth is a *moving*, a *living* labyrinth: 'it's tangled and it entangles us but it's growing'.[46]

Woman, having written herself and herstory, can hold a mirror up to the Minotaur to reflect back to him, not only his fullness, beauty, and dignity (which she is more than happy to acknowledge), but also his absurdity, his artificiality, his irreality. Woman, who for so long served to reflect man's greatness, who acquiesced in the role of being the repository of his fears, insecurities, and loneliness—to all the 'feminine' characteristics the Minotaur did not dare acknowledge in himself—can draw Asterion out of his self-created labyrinth and show him that he is imprisoned by it just as much as he tried, but failed, to imprison her. Rather than continuing to feed the Minotaur with his own reflection (at twice its natural size, as Virginia Woolf put it), woman can reflect back to him his own confusion and unreality. By seeing himself in woman's mirror, the Minotaur may also awake to reflect on himself.

Rather than giving the string to Theseus, this time Ariadne takes the string herself and enters the labyrinth by and *for* herself. She always had her own pen ('a metaphorical penis?'),[47] she also always had paper, a limitless blank space. And, as one

[44] Again these are terms with which Gilbert Osmond describes himself to Isabel Archer: 'You say you don't know me but when you do you'll discover what a worship I have for propriety . . . No, I'm not conventional, I'm convention itself'; also, 'He was fond of the old, the consecrated, the transmitted . . . He had an immense esteem for tradition': *The Portrait of a Lady, supra*, at 362 and 480.

[45] Kafka, *The Trial* (Harmondsworth: Penguin, 1953), at 251.

[46] Borges here is describing the labyrinth that is literature: Richard Burgin (ed.), *Conversations, supra*, at 16.

[47] Sandra M. Gilbert and Susan Gubar, *The Madwoman in the Attic: The Woman Writer and the Nineteenth Century Literary Imagination* (New Haven and London: Yale University Press, 1979), at 3.

nursery song goes, 'with tuppence for paper and string, you can have your own set of wings'.[48]

Ariadne starts to write: in her writing she does not respect the law of genres, she breaks old rules, creates new forms, invents new genres. She does not write law, she does not write literature, she writes law *and* literature. She mixes comedy with romance, philosophy with pornography, fact with fiction, law with music, words with images, night-time dreams with daytime 'realities'; she is expressing a different truth, a different law, a different reality, a reality that starts to invade and infect the Minotaur's version of reality. She sings her own songs, paints her own images, writes her own poems. Intoxicated with the sound of her own voice, she swims in fountains of ink, drinks thirstily, sits back 'quiet and satisfied' for a while before wading in the inkpot again.[49] Her near-fatal encounter with the Minotaur has led not to death, but to a new genesis; like Angela in *Chronicle of a Death Foretold*, she is 'reborn'. Like another story-teller called Scheherazade, Angela and Ariadne, by writing themselves and their stories, escape death and enter herstory. The origin Ariadne was searching for did not lie, after all, at the centre of the labyrinth; the Minotaur did not give her what she wanted, less because he did not want to, but because he had nothing to offer. What she wanted was not inside the labyrinth, where 'nothing was all there was', but in herself.

Ariadne starts dreaming her own dreams: dreams that the Minotaur did not know how to dream, dreams that he did not dare to dream. Dreams also that are not dictated by the Minotaur's dreams of her, rules that are not limited by his strictures, games that are not dictated by his prizes, laws that are not delimited by his limits. Ariadne starts reflecting to the Minotaur her own laws, her own games, her own desires: dreams in which she is both dreamer and dreamed, desired and desiring, desiring *because* she is desired: herself.

Ariadne, unlike Almodovar's Marina, did not fall in love with her captor; she does not suffer from the erotic attachment to the law Legendre would have us believe is a universal human condition. Ariadne did not ask to be protected by the Minotaur, indeed it is the Minotaur who, like the disabled director of Marina's film, needed Marina to fight off his fear of death and kept resisting drawing the film to a close. It was the disabled director, the Minotaur, the law, who wanted to seduce her, not the other way round. When that seduction, however, threatened to annihilate her, she can walk away. Much better than sleeping with the Minotaur, she discovers what she knew before she entered the law, before the legal labyrinth tried to imprison her: she can *fly*.

---

[48] 'Lets Go Fly a Kite' in *Mary Poppins* (Walt Disney, 1964).

[49] This image was aroused in Jorge Luis Borges, 'The Monkey and the Inkpot', *The Book of Imaginary Beings* (London: Penguin, 1974), at 101.

7 FEAR OF MIRRORS, FEAR OF WOMAN

In Hoffman's 'Tale of the Lost Reflection' a woman begs her departing lover to leave behind with her his image reflected in the mirror. Her lover agrees because he considers that leaving her his image 'would not be a great loss because any reflection is only an illusion, because the contemplation of oneself leads to vanity, and finally because such an image divides the self into two parts: truth and dream'.[50] Man here, guided by reason, renounces the mirror for blurring the distinction between appearance and reality, between truth and representation, between original and copy. Western philosophers' distrust of mirrors and reflections is itself a reflection: of the fear of seeing oneself and the world upside down, of being led to question the 'wisdom, dignity and security' provided by the belief that one's identity is separate from one's image: 'many philosophers strictly forbid looking into the mirror of the waters, for in seeing the world upside down, one may be stricken with vertigo'.[51]

Art, writes Borges, should be like a mirror 'which reveals to us our own face'.[52] Borges' fiction is perhaps because of this reason, replete with distrust of mirrors: 'As a child', one narrator tells us, 'I knew that horror of the spectral duplication or multiplication of reality' mirrors cause and 'their cosmic pantomime would seem eerie to me'.[53] For mirrors may show us more than we want to see, more than we can bear to see. Rather than reflecting reality and thereby securing the subject's identity and stability, mirrors repeat, multiply, and disperse reality, disorienting the looking subject and decentring its sense of self. Like dreams, they also alert us to the frightening thought that we also may be no more than mere reflections of another more real self elsewhere.[54]

The saddest part of Disney's *Toy Story* is for many the moment when Buzz awakens to the realization that he is not the real Buzz Lightyear after all, 'Space Ranger of the Universe Protection Unit in charge of protecting the galaxy from the threat of invasion from Evil Emperor Zurg' but a mere replica, a child's plaything, a toy. His anagnorisis occurs when he sees his image reflected on the television screen, when thousands of other Buzzes, each one identical to him, are being offered for sale in an

---

[50] 'The Tale of the Lost Reflection', discussed in Tzvetan Todorov, *The Fantastic: A Structural Approach to a Literary Genre* (Ithaca, New York: Cornell University Press, 1975), [1970], at 69–70.

[51] See E. T. A. Hoffman, 'Princess Brambilla' in *The Golden Pot*, (Oxford: Oxford University Press, 1992), trans. and ed. by Ritchie Robertson: 'Many spectators who saw the whole natural world and their own images in this mirror, uttered cries of rage and pain as they stood up. They said it was contrary to reason, to the dignity of the human race, to the wisdom acquired by long and painful experience, to see the world and oneself thus reversed'. Discussed in Tzvetan Todorov, *The Fantastic*, at 120–3.

[52] 'Ars Poetica' in Jorge Luis Borges, *Selected Poems*, (ed.) Norman Thomas di Giovanni, (London: Penguin, 1985), at 157.

[53] 'Covered Mirrors' in Jorge Luis Borges, *Collected Fictions*, trans. Andrew Hurley, (London: Penguin, Allen Lane, 1999) at 297.

[54] Paul de Man, 'A Modern Master' in Harold Bloom (ed.), *Jorge Luis Borges* (New York: Chelsea House Publishers, 1986).

aggressive advertising campaign.[55] As Emir-Rodríguez Monegal points out, mirrors, by showing an inverted image of what is not in them but outside them, are not only deceptive but may lead to 'reflection', to contemplation. Like the riddle of the Sphinx, the mirror may awaken the subject to self-consciousness and reveal what is hidden from one's own being.[56] As in Oedipus' example, as in Buzz's example, the revelation is painful, leads to tragedy, to disintegration, to mental breakdown. While Oedipus, however, escapes with a mere self-blinding, worse is still to come for poor Buzz: see shortly.

That mirrors have 'something monstrous about them' and are not to be trusted is I suggest linked to western philosophers' fear of woman. Woman, like the mirror, has the ability to multiply, and rather than finding the mirror's ambiguity and confusion 'abominable', searches for the mirror, embraces its multiplicity, of herself and of the world around her. Woman's embrace of the mirror is labelled by men as vanity, duplicity, inconstancy; she knows this stems from their fear of the mirror, their envy of her ability to multiply and disperse. Her promise to bring eternity is for men not a promise, but a threat. As one of the heseriarchs of Uqbar opined: 'mirrors and copulation are abominable, because they increase the number of men'.[57]

In contrast, as Todorov suggests, it may be through the mirror, and I add, through woman, that we may see not the ordinary but the extraordinary, not the simple but the mysterious.[58] The mystery that man and reason are trying to evade and dare not glimpse is none other than woman. Woman's wish for her lover's image and the association of woman with dissimulation, suggest that philosophy's distrust of mirrors is also a fear of woman. The legal Minotaur is frightened of the mirror, frightened of woman, especially the woman who does not reflect back to him his alleged fullness and greatness but reflects instead his insecurity, his irreality, his hunger, his loneliness: all the 'feminine' characteristics he fought hard to excise and project onto woman, all things he could not bear to admit in himself. The Minotaur was happy, for a time, to see his image reflected in Ariadne because he had found in her 'a quick and fanciful mind which saved [him] repetition and reflected his thought on a polished, elegant surface . . . he hated to see his thought reproduced literally—that made it look stale and stupid; he preferred it to be freshened in the reproduction even as 'words' by music . . . He found the silver quality in this perfection in [Ariadne; the Minotaur] could tap her imagination and make it ring'.[59]

When Ariadne, however, starts playing, stretching, and distorting the Minotaur's image of himself, when she not only reproduces but undermines it, the Minotaur starts worrying that to look at the mirror, to look at himself through woman, he

---

[55] *TOY STORY I*, (Los Angeles: Disney, 1995). In *TOY STORY II* (Los Angeles: Disney, 1999), Buzz's awakening to self-consciousness becomes crucial to distinguishing between the 'real' Buzz and other, 'unreal' Buzzes.

[56] Emir-Rodríguez Monegal, 'Symbols in Borges' Work' in Harold Bloom (ed), *Jorge Luis Borges, supra*.

[57] 'Tlon, Uqbar, Orbis Tertius' in *Labyrinths, supra*, at 27.

[58] 'Vision pure and simple reveals an ordinary world, without mysteries. Indirect vision is the only road to the marvellous,' Tzvetan Todorov, *The Fantastic, supra*, at 122.

[59] *The Portrait of a Lady, supra*, at 401.

might, like Oedipus, like Angelo, like Lockwood, like Buzz, see more than he wants to see, he might disintegrate. When Clytemnestra reflects to Agamemnon not his greatness but her own desires, when Angela reveals to Bayardo herstory that started without and before him, the entire community comes to the rescue of the injured party: the aggrieved man.

How much worse when Ariadne uses her imagination to reflect back to him not only his artificiality but her own desires and strengths. Seeing himself in the mirror held by Ariadne, man would be forced to acknowledge that we do not know that western philosophy's insistence on the separation between mind and body, subject and object, perceiver and perceived, reality and representation, original and copy are any more than prejudices, arbitrary superstitions, mistakes even. He would have to admit that we cannot be sure that these states are any less normal than the ones advocated by reason: 'Science', as Edgar Allan Poe said, 'has not yet told us whether madness may not be the sublime form of reason'.[60] The position inhabited by so-called mad people, children, drug addicts, women too, threatens to dissolve these separations and reveal their fragility. The law cannot tolerate this prospect and sets out to police, 'cure', restrict their incidences. It demands that the madman, the child, the drug-addict, the woman, accede to its language and to its rules; the alternative is punishment, suppression, imprisonment. For woman this possibility does not hold such terror: because it was always *man's* reason.

Fearful of play, fearful of theatre, fearful of poetry, Plato, I argued in my opening chapter and in my reading of the *Oresteia*, tried to banish actors, poets, image-makers of all kinds from his ideal state. His concern was to guard an essential and unchanging identity from the perils of impersonation: this essential and unchanging identity is, however, only *masculine* identity. The worst scenario for Plato was men imitating women; his distrust of theatre and art in general is the male philosopher's, and legislator's, fear of woman. Irigaray points out Plato's own dependence on images, mimicry, and above all on woman for pronouncing these 'truths'. Following Irigaray, I suggested that woman can take advantage of her ability to mimic to exceed the original and to create new representations in the imaginary that may in turn enter the symbolic order and become law. She can appropriate mimesis from a device used to reflect male fullness, truth, and sameness, into a tool with which to express difference, including gender difference. By inverting the hierarchy between presence and representation, reality and fictionality, mirrors, theatre, and woman can reveal law's dependence on plays and on woman to create its own foundations. Woman can reveal the production and contingency of societal constructs that deny their own artificiality and reopen the gap between representation and reality to a time *before* existing practices, began as myths and plays, became law and started to take themselves (extremely) seriously. Woman can take us back to a time *before* the word was born. For in the beginning, there was not reason but an emotion, not the word but music, not a love letter but a love song: a lullaby.

---

[60] Quoted in Tzvetan Todorov, *The Fantastic, supra*, at 39.

Mimetic creature that she is, woman can use signs, and herself as sign, to express her desires and make them known to others. Though male laws and male language get in the way, there is always room for more signs, more mimeseis, more plays; in the process she can reveal to male laws and institutions the mimetic nature of their own so-called reality, their own theatricality, their own dependence on poetry and their suppression of, as well as desire for, her. This journey does not lead to death but to poetry, a poetry that she creates as much as it creates her.

Although Ariadne's journey took thousands of years, she is now 'younger than she used to be': in the teeming world of words, poetry, and music, outsider Ariadne finds a home. A home, moreover, that she does not guard proprietorially like the Minotaur, but 'which everybody owns'.[61] Like anonymous literature, like all literature, this home belongs not to the author/proprietor/copyright owner, but to everyone.

By seizing the power of representation and law-making from Theseus, Ariadne has gazed at the Gorgon and the encounter has not blinded her, it has 'opened her eyes and dried up the tears: she will never live in blessed darkness again'.[62] The Gorgon, moreover, is not only beautiful and laughing; she has moved beyond the Minotaur's 'age of innocence' and like Ariadne, has grown up with the times. Unlike the Minotaur who suspects communication and insists on the authority of the written word, she carries a mobile phone and can be contacted at any time by mad heifers in distress.

If 'the creation of beauty', as Paul de Man says, 'begins as an act of duplicity',[63] if writing is always dissimulation, an act of plagiarism, then the labels of deceitfulness, duplicity, and inconstancy levelled at woman also hide a secret envy for her ability to mimic, to play, to take risks. In 'The Immortal', Borges suggests that the promise of immortality and eternity lies in what remains of the 'words of others'.[64] That endless space that is eternity is also the endless space of literature. The association of women with literature in many of these stories suggests that both the desire and frustration at the unattainability of these goals, arises from man's desire for, and inability to understand and thereby possess, woman. While for Lacan death is the only way of regaining the fullness the subject experienced before the intrusion of language,[65] for woman death does not hold such terror, nor is it 'the end': woman and woman as literature are life's revenge on death and forgetting.

---

[61] 'Sly' in Massive Attack, *Protection* (Circa Records, 1994).

[62] This is a paraphrase of Countess Olenska's description of her encounter with the Gorgon in Edith Wharton, *The Age of Innocence* (Harmondsworth: Penguin, 1996) [1920], at 237–9. And, more recently, Hélène Cixous 'The Laugh of the Medusa' in Elaine Marks and Isabelle de Courtivron, (eds.), *New French Feminisms* (Brighton: Harvester Wheatsheaf, 1980).

[63] Paul de Man, 'A Modern Master' in Harold Bloom (ed.), *Jorge Luis Borges, supra*, at 23.

[64] Jorge Luis Borges, *Labyrinths, supra*, at 149: ' "When the end draws near . . . there no longer remain any remembered images; only words remain." Words, displaced, mutilated words, words of others, were the poor pittance left him by the hours and the centuries.'

[65] 'When we wish to attain in the subject what was before the serial articulations of speech, and what is primordial to the birth of symbols, we find it in death': Jacques Lacan, *Écrits: A Selection*, trans. Alan Sheridan, (London: Routledge, 1977) [1966], at 105.

Malcolm Bowie suggests that the remedy Lacan finds to the impossibility of desire is literature; further, that it is women, whose 'ex-istence' Lacan allegedly erases, that guide him back to the pleasures of the text: 'women, freed from the servitude of the phallus have already got what men will always crave'.[66] The lawyer in his labyrinth envies women their ecstasy, their desire that he cannot understand and does not dare explore. Well might he search 'the holy books, read the poets and the analysts, study the books on human behaviour: the answer refuses to be found'.[67] Though Nick Cave is baffled, though Freud admitted to the same impasse in his enquiries, the reason 'she's nobody's baby now', is that, like Angela in *Chronicle of a Death Foretold*, she is now her own baby, mistress of her own free will and recognizes no other authority than her own. 'This desire to possess her', meanwhile becomes for her potential lover 'a wound, nagging at him like a shrew; that little girl will just have to go'.[68] To protect himself from the indecipherable labyrinth of female sexuality, man has created his own labyrinth, to distance himself from its insistent demands; in the process of excluding her, however, he has succeeded only at imprisoning himself.

As if realizing that he is a mere toy was not tragedy enough for Buzz Lightyear, as if discovering that he cannot fly is not devastating enough, a greater catastrophe befalls him: sadistic Sid's sweet little sister rescues him from his fall, dresses him up in women's clothes and serves him darjeeling tea! The law cannot tolerate this, far greater, calamity: Sheriff Woody rushes to the scene, reasserts Buzz's reason, and his masculinity, and reimmerses him in boys' games: fighting. Fighting back, that is, against the threat of becoming a woman.

8 'THE RESPECT OWED TO THE MOTHER'

In Poe's story 'The Purloined Letter' the arch-detective Auguste Dupin marvels at a little boy's ability consistently to win at games of chance. The boy explains that when he wants to find out what someone is thinking, or whether they are good, wicked, or stupid, he tries to fashion the expression of his face in accordance with the other person's. This *mimicry* or *identification* enables him to imagine the thoughts and feelings of the other person. Dupin goes on to suggest that to solve a mystery one needs to be not only a mathematician, to have not only what has 'long been regarded as *the* reason *par excellence*',[69] but also a poet. The ability to amass disparate data is useless without the imagination with which to interpret them, project new solutions to old problems, and go beyond the here and now. Here the ability to mimic suggests an ethical dimension: through acting, through imitation, we can try to understand,

---

66 Malcolm Bowie, *Lacan* (London: Fontana, 1991), at 148, 156.
67 'Nobody's Baby', in *The Best of Nick Cave and the Bad Seeds, supra.*
68 'From Her to Eternity' in *The Best of Nick Cave and the Bad Seeds, supra.*
69 Edgar Allan Poe, *Selected Writings* (Harmondsworth: Penguin, 1967), at 342.

empathize with, and as far as possible identify with the other, her desires, and her sufferings. When the other is a text, especially a canonical text whose 'truth' has been verified and repeated by generations of critics and readers, woman may start rewriting, à la Pierre Menard, those texts. In doing so she can find out the fears, hopes, and emotions hidden between the lines of the text. She can then begin to rewrite them, with a twist, with humour, with irreverence, with blasphemy even.

In my opening chapter and again in the chapter on Toni Morrison's *Beloved* I explored the relationship between ethics and literature and in particular the celebration of the imagination as enabling us to envisage new possibilities of existence that transcend existing laws and categories. The suggestion is that literature allows us a space that law, in its refusal of differences and in its drive towards uniformity and oneness, denies. This is the space before representation, before the word, before law, before identity, even before time. In *Beloved* this space enables us to imagine and empathize with the figure of a mother who kills her children. In her search for this space, Morrison deconstructs not only received discourses on the nature of history, knowledge, and the self, but language itself. As existing discourses are inscribed in language, our ability to imagine new narratives, new laws, and new selves depends on our ability and willingness to imagine new languages or, as Morrison puts it, to 'break the back of words'. Morrison finds such a language in the pre-Oedipal articulations of a mother and her two daughters, a language that other characters in the book, especially the men, do not understand and perceive as madness: madness because it threatens the stability of the symbolic order.

In the space left by Hobbes' isolated man in the state of nature, by Locke's proprietary and antagonistic self, by Descartes' doubting mind, and by John Stuart Mill's sovereign individual, the mother offers an ethics of undifferentiated relatedness between oneself and others. The mother-child relationship reminds us that, rather than arriving in the world isolated and independent, we arrive always already related to others. The journey to the other that so many male characters run away from (in an alleged search for 'God', 'self-knowledge', or 'Law'), starts with the mother. Although in our craving for the other we run the risk, like Sethe and Beloved, of dissolving into the other and losing our sense of self, an ethics that refuses to acknowledge this relatedness also robs both the self and the other.

The experience of motherhood in particular undermines the notion of the legal subject as self-contained, autonomous, and self-interested by hurling the self out of its imagined oneness into the perils and thrills of connectedness and relatedness. The relationship that starts from 'this first body, this first home, this first love'[70] demands, with a pain that is also a pleasure, a closer identification with the other's experiences and provides one model of a relationship with another which spreads towards the other rather than returning to oneself and without annihilating or eating the other. The ability to translate and project the other is also the privilege, as well as the

---

[70] Luce Irigaray, 'The bodily encounter with the mother' in Margaret Whitford (ed.), *The Irigaray Reader* (Oxford: Blackwell, 1991), at 39.

predicament, of those who have experienced discrimination; the anguish of enforced marginality affords also a freedom to criticize the dominant hegemony and create a counter-hegemony.[71]

It is because woman, and especially subaltern woman, has occupied for so long the space of the other in western culture, that her experiences, dreams, and fears, alternatively represented or silenced in these texts, can serve as a springboard for a better understanding of the ethics of the other. These experiences are sometimes condemned or ridiculed as madness, the ravings of a Dionysian maenad that was the derivation for the word. In various degrees, Mariana in *Measure for Measure*, Catherine in *Wuthering Heights*, Angela in *Chronicle of a Death Foretold*, in articulating their desires in music, in front of a mirror, or on paper, appear to lend credence to the depiction of madness as an extension of the female condition, in particular of the condition of a woman in love.[72] It is not a coincidence that the speaker of the truth, of the Oracle in *Oedipus Rex* is also a frenzied woman, Pythia, whose words are at best ambiguous, at worst indecipherable. Where the language of the law, however, would seek to contain, punish, or silence this madness, the language of the imagination and of poetry can seek to understand, express, and convey it. The mad-woman in the attic, as Gilbert and Gubar argued, may, through her ravings, disrupt and subvert the rationality of male texts and is therefore one means of deconstructing patriarchy and its laws.

In its drive towards oneness, law and reason seek to expulse difference, the unconscious, the supernatural, the nocturnal, mirrors, dissimulation, wandering, abandon, laughter, madness, dreams, excess. Woman, by holding a mirror up to law, can remind him that what he strives to achieve through language and through metaphors, she can achieve literally and materially through the body. Woman's capacity to give birth, as Nancy Huston argues, has led men to try and find a similar trait for themselves that is as spectacular in its consequences. When that desire is not appeased by making laws, men are not reluctant to assert their masculinity by making war.[73] That this masculinity is fragile and in need of constant ratification is shown further by their insistence on excluding homosexuals from the military. In contrast, woman's potential to reproduce links her with life and eternity rather than war and death and with the other rather than with the self.

When Iphigeneia does not acquiesce in her own death, when she does not offer herself on the sacrificial altar, above all, when she starts speaking and writing herself, she can exceed and shutter the male economy of war. For *that* economy, as Ariadne discovered, is both inconsistent and fragile: on the one hand it treats her as an object

---

[71] bell hooks, *Feminist Theory: From Margin to Center* (Boston: South End Press, 1984), at 15. See also Toni Morrison who argues for a special ability in black people to perceive and accept differences because 'Our interests have always been on how unlike things are rather than how alike things are': Danille Taylor-Guthrie (ed.), *Conversations with Toni Morrison*, (Jackson, Miss.: University Press of Mississippi, 1994), at 162.

[72] See Helen Small, *Love's Madness: Medicine, the Novel and Female Insanity, 1800–1865* (Oxford: Clarendon Press, 1996).

[73] Nancy Huston, 'The Matrix of War: Mothers and Heroes' in Susan Rubin Suleiman, (ed.), *The Female Body in Western Culture: Contemporary Perspectives* (Cambridge, Mass.: Harvard University Press, 1986).

of exchange to cement homosocial bonds, as in Lévi-Strauss's scheme of kinship, on the other hand it perceives her as a threat to the maintenance of the same bonds, as in Girard's triangular scheme of desire. In both cases that obscure object of exchange and desire eludes and frustrates male searchers: the fact that for generations of male philosophers, psychoanalysts, musicians, lawyers, she is always unknown, always elsewhere, always absent, is also, they must admit, 'the secret of her strength'.[74] Santiago, as I argued, is a prime candidate for a scapegoat, and his sacrifice is necessary to restore order in the community, not because he 'deflowered' Angela but because, by encouraging plays and disguises amongst the mulatto girls, by blurring the distinction between mother and lover and between client and prostitute, he compounds the mystery that is woman rather than dissolving it, *like a man.*

The association of woman with theatre (*Oresteia*), chance (*Oedipus*), madness (*Measure for Measure, Wuthering Heights*), literature (*Ficciones, Chronicle of a Death Foretold*), the senses (*The Outsider*), laughter and play (*The Bloody Chamber*), and another language (*Beloved*) may afford the opportunity that the new child, the child born of the marriage between Ariadne and the Minotaur, between literature and law, need not *necessarily* be a boy. Or, if a boy, that it is 'Venus as a Boy', a boy who, unlike generations of male lawyers down to Disney's Woody, is not horrified by the idea of dressing up in women's clothes: a child, boy or girl, who is happy with performing and reperforming gender; happy, in short, 'messing around gender roles'.[75] That the new child need not be a new 'science', as Althusser insists on calling it in the opening quote but also music. Furthermore, that the child will not forget this other language, the language of the mother and that it will learn the mother's name as well as the mother's law.

***

The journey that started for me with *Women on the Verge of a Nervous Breakdown* has led not only to tragedies but also to comedies and celebrations: for women these genres need not be distinct. Almodovar's latest film, *All About My Mother* affirmed my irregular journey: the film is dedicated not only to mothers but to women and men who act. For to be a mother is to play a part, just as to play a part is to become another. In reverse order, the dedication goes: 'to my mother, to all people, men or women, who want to be mothers, to all men who act and become women, to all women who act, to all actresses who have played actresses'.[76] Here, acting, dissimulation, the ability to be other than oneself, to be a man or a woman, to produce new selves, on the stage or in the maternity ward, are celebrated, not expelled, ignored, or, as in Althusser's quote at the start of this chapter, hidden between the lines.

---

[74] Jean Baudrillard, *Seduction*, trans. Brian Singer (New York: St Martin's Press, 1990) [1979], at 6.

[75] Listen to 'Venus as a Boy' in Bjork, *Debut* (London: Basi / One Little Indian, 1993) and 'Laid' in James, *Laid, supra.*

[76] Pedro Almodovar, *All About My Mother* (Renn Productions: Spain and France, 1999).

9 THE LAUGHING DETECTIVE

Talking to other women, starting with her mother, Ariadne can remind herself, and Asterion, that the labyrinth is an artificial thing, deliberately constructed to lure and confuse those who try to enter. Though she might have been foolish trying to enter the legal fortress, though she never found the centre to the labyrinth, though she never encountered the Minotaur (perhaps because the labyrinth contained neither a centre, nor a Minotaur), the search has not been in vain. She has not only learned something about herself, she has shown something to the Minotaur. Ariadne is not frightened of Asterion because she discovered that he is a prisoner, not a god. Though he thought of himself as 'unique', and compared himself to the 'intricate sun', though he fancied that 'his sun blazed upon her head', and, like all creatures who think of themselves as gods, claimed to be 'the resurrection and the light', he was the one craving to be admired, worshipped, and adored.[77] Ariadne knows now that he is no Minotaur but a mouse, a mouse that dared not look at woman: a mouse, moreover, that having exiled the body, the aesthetic, music, humour, play, and the emotions, has left himself with only one hole (reason), only one language (abstraction), only one faculty (the mind): and 'a mouse with only one hole cannot last long'.[78]

In turn, Ariadne, whom he imagined as a little girl, whom he compared to a little mouse, is not only entering his labyrinth, she is a 'waterfall', 'drilling holes in [his] walls', 'burning down his house'; in her attempt to reach the unreachable, Ariadne found that the law's game is not *her* 'idea of a good time'.[79] Perhaps, like Marina in *Tie Me Up! Tie Me Down!*, like the girl in 'Laid', Ariadne 'only comes when she's on top': but comes not *against*, or *instead* of, but *with*, *for*, and above all, *to* the other. Ariadne can now teach Asterion more games, games with different rules, different pieces, and different prizes. *His* methods, *his* techniques, were no fun: reason is a bad joke: overworked, told and retold, it bores; more than it bores, it deadens.

The law insisted that Ariadne could not enter a relationship with him without knowledge; it turns out that the knowledge he meant was *his* knowledge, that is, knowing *him*. The law insists that the woman lawyer must learn, often by heart, everything about him; the law, however, made no attempt to get to know her. Generations of (male) philosophers, from Plato to Nietzsche, the law claimed, insisted on knowledge as a prerequisite to truth, to understanding, to loving. Did not Nietzsche also say, that since no one is at home in the world, one might as well be at home in the only place in the world one would *wish* to be at home, that is Greece? Rather than trying to enter his labyrinth, Ariadne invites the Minotaur to *her* home, to *her*

---

[77] These terms are borrowed from '*Do You Love Me?*' in *The Best of Nick Cave and the Bad Seeds, supra*, and 'Resurrection' and 'I wanna be adored' in *The Stone Roses, supra*.

[78] Quoted by Peter Goodrich, 'Courting Death' in Maderson (ed.), *Courting Death: The Law of Mortality* (London: Pluto Press, 1999), at 222.

[79] These terms are borrowed after listening, in that order, to: 'She's Waterfall' in *Stone Roses, supra*; 'Laid' in James, *LAID, supra*; 'Not My Idea', in Garbage, *G* (London and Los Angeles: Mushroom Records, 1995).

country: the Greece not only of Plato and Aristotle, not only of reason and knowledge, not the Greece that exiled Helen for her beauty, condemned Jocasta for courting chance, sacrificed Iphigeneia for her innocence, and murdered Clytemnestra for daring to reflect to her royal husband not his greatness but her own desires. Not the imagined Greece that exiled the body and the emotions but the Greece of the golden mean between mind and body, the Greece also of Dionysus, of Maenads, of beauty, of play, of theatre, of the senses, of madness, of excess.

Truth is not, or not only, the prerogative of the mind, of reason, and of knowledge but also of chance, of humour, and of madness. Feeling, not just knowing, is believing. There are two ways of looking at interpretation, writes Derrida: 'The one seeks to decipher, dreams of deciphering a truth or an origin which escapes play and the order of the sign and which lives the necessity of interpretation as an exile.' There is, however, a second way, 'the Nietzschean *affirmation*, that is the joyous affirmation of the play of the world and of the innocence of becoming, the affirmation of a world of signs without fault, without truth and without origin, which is offered to an active interpretation. *This affirmation then determines the noncenter otherwise than as loss of the center*. And it plays without security'.[80]

Ariadne's style is not characterized by the 'high seriousness' Matthew Arnold perceived to be the hallmark of great literature. She talks tongue in cheek, makes jokes, absurd ones, unsettling even; she exaggerates, outrageously: she pushes the limits of what is sayable, pushes the limits of language, and with them, the limits of law. This irreverence is not an escape from, or a denial of, reality but an *expansion* of reality. It subverts and undermines conventional ways of perceiving the world: *his* ways of perceiving the world. What Foucault confesses shattered his thoughts on encountering Borges' encyclopaedia and led him to question the age-old distinctions in the existing order of things, was 'laughter'. If the universe is a frustrating labyrinth whose centre we may never find, Ariadne appreciates that 'laughing at the universe, can liberate us from its enormous weight'.[81] Knowledge is not the only precondition to truth, to freedom, to authenticity: 'he who wants to kill most thoroughly—*laughs*'.[82]

The Minotaur, it appears, had no sense of humour. Ariadne's humour unsettled him because it undermined his assumptions and the security of his reason: it dared to explore and explode the law's limitations and failures. Like Angela Carter's Little Red Riding Hood, Ariadne looked back at the Minotaur, with interest, and laughed 'full in his face'. This is *her* way, not only because '*the* way does not exist',[83] but because *his* way was no fun, because it led to death.

If the hall-mark of the classical detective is someone who collects clues and signs and succeeds in disclosing the hidden pattern of events, then he is not dissimilar to the academic who sees himself as engaging in the task of explaining the world to a mass of

---

[80] Jacques Derrida, 'Structure, Sign, and Play' in *Writing and Difference*, trans. Alan Bass (London: Routledge, 1978), at 292.

[81] Michael Richardson (ed.), *Georges Bataille: Essential Writings* (London: Sage, 1998), at 115.

[82] Friedrich Nietzsche, *Thus Spoke Zarathustra*, trans. R. J. Hollingdale (London: Penguin, 1961), at 324.

[83] *ibid*, at 213.

less talented and less well-informed lay people.[84] In that sense, the woman who engages in law and literature is not a good detective but an anti-detective. Lonnrot, the 'pure logician', in Borges' 'Death and the Compass' assumes that by gathering all the evidence, all the available clues, by using his intellect and powers of reason, he will reach the definitive answer. Indeed he derives the only definitive answer open to man: death. Ariadne, however, always knew what Greek fathers sometimes forgot: 'incertitude'.[85] Like the Greek mother Jocasta, she is at ease with the possibility that chance might be the only order we have. Since we are unable to penetrate the design of the labyrinth or our position in it, all explanations are possible but none can be advocated as final or certain. There is not one, but many truths and the approach offered by Ariadne, and by law and literature, is one of many ways of living with and understanding, without killing the Minotaur.

The search for knowledge and in particular self-knowledge that started in my journey with Oedipus, is not only illusory, it is also a conceit, perhaps also a male conceit. Indeed this conceit is used as the excuse for fighting, the search for absolute knowledge being adduced as the main cause of wars, just as wars are a clear and tragic example of the limits of that knowledge.[86] Wars are fought in the name of asserting fragile identities and creating 'imagined communities' that last only as long as other interested parties, for political and economic reasons, exploit their fluidity and reopen them for more negotiation and often more fighting.[87] Adduced as necessary in the interests of national or international security, they stem from *in*security, the need to find an enemy outside to avoid confronting the enemy within. If war and death are the outcome of the search for knowledge, then we might learn, as Jacqueline Rose argues, from 'the ethics of failure',[88] from an acceptance of uncertainty, doubt, even defeat, as another type of knowledge, another type of truth.

The woman law and literature 'detective' is not expecting to find the solution or even to amass and categorize all the disparate information. Rather than looking for the 'final' solution that will dissipate the mystery and arrive at what Derrida calls a 'monument', she maintains the mystery, opens more paths, keeps the story going for future Pierre and Petra Menards. Like Ts'ui Pen's novel in 'The Garden of Forking Paths', her journey, herstory, does not end, but proliferates and forks, opening the way for new stories, new beginnings, and more rebeginnings. Unlike Lonnrot who suggests

---

[84] This theme is developed by Dennis Porter, *The Pursuit of Crime: Art and Ideology in Detective Fiction* (London and New Haven: Yale University Press, 1981); especially chapter entitled 'The Professor and the Detective'.

[85] Jorge Luis Borges, 'The Lottery at Babylon', in *Labyrinths, supra*, at 55.

[86] Jacqueline Rose, *Why War? Psychoanalysis, Politics, and the Return to Melanie Klein* (Oxford UK and Cambridge USA: Blackwell, 1993), at 16.

[87] See especially Benedict Anderson *Imagined Communities: Reflections on the Origin and Spread of Nationalism* (London and New York: Verso, 1991); Thomas Hylland Eriksen, *Ethnicity and Nationalism: Anthropological Perspectives* (London and Chicago: Pluto Press, 1993).

[88] 'Virginia Woolf proposes ridicule, poverty, censure and contempt as antidotes to vanity, egotism and megalomania . . . Hang on to failure, hang on to derision . . . if you want to avoid going to war—failure and derision that would not invite triumphalism but pre-empt it.' Jacqueline Rose, *Why War? Supra*, at 37.

to his murderer that in another encounter the labyrinth should be reduced to a straight line leading to his own, and every writer's/reader's death, she prefers to maintain the multiplicity of its infinite twists and turns. No closures, just more paths, more unending stories. In this proliferation of words, readings are not final but aim to arouse rather than convince, or indeed, in law's case, to convict, by an aesthetics that precedes and informs, that *is*, an ethics.

With play, games, chance, risk, humour, fun: not as the opposites of truth and reality but as another type of truth, another type of reality long banished by philosophers and particularly lawyers. If they are also attributes associated with woman, then she embraces them and laughs at law's and male lawyers' inability to laugh at themselves. With words that do not dispel but conserve the mystery, that linger rather than die, embrace rather than choke, multiply rather than annihilate. Words that allude to other mysteries, to other pasts, other futures, that touch, penetrate, couple, unite, grow, and spread: from her to eternity.

10 THE DEBT OWED TO THE OTHER

A young man hovers awkwardly in front of a bed; a disembodied voice asks him to take off his clothes and approach a mirror. In front of the mirror he is told to kiss his own lips, touch his own image reflected in the mirror and then return to the bed. Having began shyly, the young man appears to abandon himself to the auto-erotic act asked of him; the climax reached, the voice stops talking. It becomes a face, then a body who comes forward and leaves a pile of banknotes on the bedside table. The actor has played his part, the director has switched off the camera. They are both pleased with the 'performance'. In Almodovar's *Law of Desire*[89] desire begins, desire always was, desire always is, 'mimetic before it is anything else'.[90]

***

So with the desires in this book: desires that were always already there, just as desiring subjects sing of their beloved before they meet her, just as they know before they meet her that they will lose her.[91] No writing ever takes place outside the mirroring love of, and for, others and I was fortunate to have plentiful mirrors that reflected, and enabled me to reflect on this love, though without granting me the ability to express it, even in part. Fresh, clear, old, new, disorienting, blurred, these mirrors reflected both more and less than I knew, more and less than those others wanted me to know. A desire mediated by and composed of multiple labyrinths and mirrors, diverse dreams

---

[89] Pedro Almodovar, *Law of Desire* (Metro Pictures, 1993).

[90] Mikkel Borch-Jacobsen, *The Freudian Subject*, trans. Catherine Porter (Stanford, California: Stanford University Press, 1988) [1982], at 26.

[91] For an example of the first, listen to 'Something Changed' in Pulp, *Different Class, supra*, and of the second, to Nick Cave and the Bad Seeds, '*Do You Love Me?*' *supra*.

and worlds: family, friends, books, places, laws, songs, films, images real and imaginary. I often got lost in them, lingered in some parts longer than I should have done, criminally neglected others. For desire, even when it begins and ends with words, or especially when it begins and ends with words, is a crime.

My infinite thanks, in eternity, to: Harry McVea for putting up with endless moaning over endless cups of cafe latte; if there is one thing I will miss most about Bristol, it is Harry's infinite patience, good will, and blind trust in my failings. Panu Minkkinen for urging me throughout to 'stop apologizing' for what I was trying to do and for who was I to be doing it. (It is no coincidence that when I met Panu, at my first Critical Law Conference in Stoke-on-Trent in 1992, he was wearing a 'Bad Seeds' baseball cap—the first lawyer I ever met who had heard of them; such a momentous occasion had to be marked by calling not only the future, but eternity to witness.) Peter Goodrich whose work, words, and friendship were a fountain of inspiration throughout. My colleagues at Birkbeck for their warmest welcome, both socially and intellectually. Peter Goodrich, Panu Minkkinen, Costas Douzinas, Richard Weisberg, Adam Gearey, and Iain Grant were periodically my challenging readers. Tómas, for keeping his infinite doors wide open, and whose library became, at the loneliest stage of this project, my whole universe and a paradise. My intrepid explorer Ben Capps for surfing the net while I was plodding pathetically along. Rachel Nee and Mike Drew for being amused rather than exasperated with my technological incompetences. For inconsequential gossip and utilitarian information, for chats about law and love, ethics and aesthetics, the mind and the body, my colleagues at Bristol: Aileen, Andrew, Brenda, Laura, Paul, Rod, Ruth, and many others; they unfailingly came to the rescue along, and beyond, the Will Building's labyrinthine corridors when the latter threatened to drown the second part of these conversations. The beautiful mothers of my reading group, for tolerating my monologues about books for far longer than the extraordinary surroundings should have allowed. Michaela Coulthard and Matthew Cotton at Oxford University Press whose virtual 'cheer ups!' (in the plural) would time and again jump off my screen and lighten up more than my desk; uncannily, they always arrived at times when I could not even make out if the song goes 'she knows where to hide in the dark' or 'she's nowhere to hide in the dark'.[92] Karin Littau and Iain Grant for their challenging, even at times intimidating, enthusiasm for both books and friendship. Philli for reminding me, with her *Absolutely Fabulous* and untamed energy, that reading and writing can at times be anti-social. Carolyn, Sarah, Rosa, Sally, for intimating to a late-comer and a slow learner, an aesthetics that preceded and informed ethics. Beth and Ella for combining both: effortlessly. Chris, Michael, Mark, James, Panos, Mike for, without ever knowing what I was trying to do, claiming to be impressed by my efforts, even when (or perhaps because), no tangible benefits appeared to be forthcoming. Simon for never pretending to be impressed. Charlotte, Caroline, Jane, and Ada for letting me into the extreme joys and the single most intense pain motherhood can bring; I hope my celebration of motherhood in

---

[92] 'She's a Star' in *The Best of James, supra.*

this book is also an occasion to remember a loss that took place eight years ago but will go on happening forever. Dia, Elsa, and Aristi (as I will always call her).

Above and beyond all, Mark μου, for frequently, as he typically put it, 'bringing trivia to my door', trivia that unfailingly exceeded and exploded the pretensions of my so-called serious texts. And for always and forever picking up the, at times, barely human remains of love, and of the day, and for delivering them back to me, in music and in colours, without ever dissipating their madness: 'heroin chic', 'anorexic protest' or, my favourite, 'the prettiest mess I've ever seen'.[93] And gorgeous Charis μου for articulating, in the semiotic, in the symbolic, in Greek, in English, the advice, 'be careful mummy', followed by *the* three words we all long to hear: in *any* language. To rewrite, à la Pierre Menard, Almodovar's latest dedication, these words would go out to my untold charises and charites, my poets, my image-makers, my melody-weavers; to the one who entered eternity with me, to my son.

This, theirs and mine, invisible work, the nocturnal, the unrepresented and unrepresentable: the unfinished. For the crime that is desire, in law, literature, or law and literature, does not begin or end with words: it precedes and goes beyond words, beyond and outside knowledge, beyond and outside law. It is its own law and demands its own penalties; unappeased, unappeasable, forever before or ahead of the subject, always elsewhere. In the closing scene of *Law of Desire*, Pablo, the object and subject of some of the most intense passions Almodovar has depicted, hurls his typewriter over his lover's corpse, out of the window and into the abyss: the traffic of more awaiting, circulating, and burning desires.

---

[93] P. J. Harvey, *Is This Desire?* (London: EMI Music Publishing, 1998).

INDEX